# BRAZIL

# BRAZIL

## THE FORTUNES OF WAR

World War II and the Making of Modern Brazil

# NEILL LOCHERY

BASIC BOOKS

A MEMBER OF THE PERSEUS BOOKS GROUP

NEW YORK

Designed by Pauline Brown

Library of Congress Cataloging-in-Publication Data

Lochery, Neill.

 Brazil : the fortunes of war : World War II and the making of modern Brazil / Neill Lochery.

    pages cm

 Includes bibliographical references and index.

 ISBN 978-0-465-03998-2 (hardback)—ISBN 978-0-465-08070-0 (e-book)  1. World War, 1939–1945—Brazil. 2. World War, 1939–1945—Participation, Brazilian. 3. Brazil—Strategic aspects. 4. Brazil—Politics and government—1930–1945. 5. Brazil—Foreign relations—1930–1945. 6. Vargas, Getúlio, 1883–1954. I. Title.

 D768.3.L64 2014

 940.53'81—dc23

                         2013050354


10 9 8 7 6 5 4 3 2 1

*For Emma, Benjamin, and Hélèna*

# CONTENTS

# INTRODUCTION

NESTLED IN THE FOOTHILLS of the Serra do Mar mountains and fronted by the brilliant strip of Copacabana Beach and the glassy expanse of Guanabara Bay sits Rio de Janeiro, known to its inhabitants as *Cidade Maravilhosa*, or "Marvelous City." Founded in the sixteenth century in a dimple in Brazil's southeastern Atlantic coastline, Rio de Janeiro today has more than earned its nickname. The city's waterfront districts bristle with skyscrapers, museums, monasteries, and luxury apartment buildings interlaced with parks, shopping centers, and pedestrian malls. Rio's famed Carnaval annually draws millions of Brazilians and tourists to comingle in the city's streets. During the rest of the year, tourists and locals dance to the rhythms of samba in Rio's ample array of bars and nightclubs, soak up the sun on its magnificent beaches, inspect its colonial architecture, or rotate through its historic neighborhoods on its many subway, bus, and rail lines.

In Rio, the vibrant economic energy that has come to characterize Brazil thrums loudest. At the dawn of the twenty-first century, Rio is the second largest city in Brazil, and the sixth largest in the Americas. And while Rio's domestic political importance may no longer match its economic might, for much of the eighteenth, nineteenth, and twentieth centuries Rio was the federal capital of Brazil and thus the locus of Brazilian power, fully defined: first during the country's colonial period, then during its brief elevation as a kingdom within Portugal's transcontinental monarchy, and finally in the first one hundred and forty-odd years of Brazil's existence as an independent state.

By the time Brasília—the newly minted federal capital—supplanted Rio in 1960, the Marvelous City had left an indelible mark on the rest of the country. In the decades before that switch, the federal leaders who reigned from Rio presided over Brazil's transition from a lush but neglected tropical backwater to one of the most dynamic nations in South America, and indeed in the entire world. Brazil today ranks among the top ten countries in the world by gross domestic product (GDP), and with its growth rate remaining reliably high, the nation is poised to rise even further in the decades ahead. The story of how this economic miracle occurred, however, has never been fully told.

At the outbreak of World War II, Brazil was a completely different place than it is today. In 1938, the year before the war began, Brazil was the fourth largest nation on the planet and covered nearly half of the total area of South America.[1] At 3,275,510 square miles it was larger than the continental United States, but its population at the start of the 1940s was roughly forty-three million people—about a third of the US population at the time, and less than a quarter of Brazil's current size of two hundred million.[2] The country was largely divided between its developed areas, which included the cities of Rio de Janeiro and São Paulo, and the hugely underdeveloped interior of the country. Good-quality infrastructure was almost totally absent, with substandard road and rail links between even the most populated parts of the country.[3]

Links to the outside world were equally inadequate. Air service to the United States took days, and connections to Europe were not fully developed. Rio de Janeiro was a frequent port of call for ocean liners, but only very rich Brazilians could afford to travel abroad. Most Brazilians only read about cities such as London, Paris, and New York in the local newspapers; they never saw them. Partly as a result of its geographic isolation and also due to its language (Brazil was the only Portuguese-speaking country in South America), Brazil remained largely cut off from the outside world.

During the course of World War II, this was all to change. Thanks in large part to an alliance with the United States, in the 1940s Brazil's industry, transportation infrastructure, and political position in South America and the world underwent a radical transformation. The war led to the birth of modern Brazil and its emergence as one of the economic powerhouses of the world. And Rio de Janeiro was, and indeed still is, the linchpin of the Brazilian dynamo.

Astute observers may have detected in prewar Rio something of the restless energy that would give the city such a pathbreaking role in Brazil's future. Prior to the outbreak of World War II, Rio de Janeiro was a beautiful, exotic, and slightly chaotic off-the-beaten-track location for wealthy locals and superrich international playboys seeking fun and adventure. The lack of top-quality port facilities and a decent international airport made it more difficult for international businessmen and all but the hardiest tourists to reach Rio. Once they arrived, however, these intrepid men and women found themselves in a city that clearly aspired to a level of cosmopolitanism all but unknown in South America.

Rio in the late 1930s was a hub for sophisticates, powerbrokers, and intellectuals who, whether by birth, choice, or necessity, found themselves in the southern hemisphere of the Americas. Central to the city's vibrant social scene were the five-star Copacabana Palace Hotel, located in front of Rio's most famous beach, and the Jockey Club, built on land reclaimed from the city's large lagoon. The Copacabana Palace, which opened in 1923, was one of the best examples of art deco buildings in the city, and was the place to been seen for international revelers and members of Rio's high society. Fred Astaire and Ginger Rogers danced in its magnificent ballroom. The Jewish writer Stefan Zweig, who fled Nazi persecution in Europe, stayed at the hotel before he and his wife committed suicide in 1942 in the city of Petrópolis, some forty-five miles from central Rio. During World War II the likes of Clark Gable, Douglas Fairbanks Jr., and Walt Disney were in residence in the Copacabana Palace Hotel, all on special wartime missions for the American government.

Across the city, the Jockey Club was where the elite of Brazilian society met and did business during the long horse racing season. The racing took place on balmy evenings from spring through autumn as the sunset cast its shadows over the skyscrapers in the city. Chairs next to the racetrack were arranged in strict social order, with society ladies—decked out in fur coats and designer dresses from the top fashion houses in Europe—taking their place in the front row. Male members of the Jockey Club were carefully turned out with slicked-back hair and wore loosely cut white linen and cotton suits, white shirts, and colorful kipper ties, all rounded off with shiny two-tone correspondent shoes.

A frequent patron of the Jockey Club was Brazil's charismatic president, Getúlio Dornelles Vargas. Physically, he was not a memorable man; short and portly, he had a waistline that ballooned during his later years. While sensitive to the allegations of vanity leveled at him by political opponents, Vargas did nothing to dispel them. He was known to color his hair and was always well dressed; in winter, he often wore his favorite blue-gray suit, and in summer, he was seen in white cotton suits and club striped ties. Despite his lack of physical presence, however, there was an aura around Vargas. He projected an air of calmness and contentment, and his legal background—Vargas had been trained as a lawyer before entering politics—gave him a deliberative and circumspect quality. He was often found gently puffing on a Brazilian cigar or hosting intimate card games; poker was his personal favorite.

Vargas's arrival in power at the start of the 1930s had represented a major power shift in Brazilian politics, and initially led to a great deal of political instability within the country. In the years prior to 1930, Brazil had been dominated by a powerful group of Paulistas—politicians, industrialists, and coffee producers from the São Paulo area. The Paulistas ran Brazil in alliance with the leaders of Minas Geraes, a landlocked state immediately inland from the much smaller coastal state of Rio de Janeiro. Together the two groups took turns controlling the presidency and the parliament.

In the 1930 presidential election, however, a political group known as the Gaúchos challenged the Paulista-Minas Geraes junta. The new contenders hailed from Rio Grande do Sul, known in Brazil as "gaúcho country" because of its large ranches, many of which stretched for hundreds of miles. Vargas was a native of this region and its governor at the time and, thus, one of the most prominent members of the opposition. Chosen as the Gaúcho party candidate, he ran a highly impressive campaign but ultimately lost the presidential election to Júlio Prestes, governor of the state of São Paulo. Claiming electoral fraud, Vargas refused to concede, and with the support of a wide range of Brazilian military officers and middle-class urbanites, launched a bloodless coup that succeeded in toppling the Paulistas and installing the Gaúchos in Rio de Janeiro with Vargas at their head. In July 1932, São Paulo tried to take its revenge by mounting a counterrevolution, but after three months of fighting, Vargas and his supporters succeeded in putting down the plot.

Having seized control of Brazil through a combination of political subterfuge and sheer force, Vargas rushed to consolidate his power in the face of new threats. In 1934, he introduced a new constitution that created a constituent assembly and enabled his formal election as president. In the following year, there was another serious challenge to Vargas's rule, this time from the communists. The government took swift action against the revolt, arresting and imprisoning thousands of communists. Several leaders of the revolt were given lengthy prison sentences by the courts. The communists did not disappear from the political map of Brazil after this failed putsch, but Vargas's government had greatly weakened them.

Like 1930, the year 1937 also witnessed great political drama in Brazil. A presidential election was held that year, under the terms of the 1934 constitution; the winning candidate was to serve a four-year term beginning in 1938. The constitution prohibited President Vargas from running for reelection, yet he found a way around this problem by refusing to support any of the declared candidates and working in secret with members of his regime to draw up a new constitution. In November 1937, Vargas made his move, declaring martial law, canceling the elections, and dissolving parliament, where, on arrival, deputies found its doors locked shut. It was a bloodless coup. President Vargas remained in power, but he was now effectively a dictator empowered by a new authoritarian constitution known as the Estado Novo, or "New State." Crucially, for Vargas, the United States continued to develop ties with Brazil as if nothing had happened.

President Vargas understood that Brazil was a weak economic and military power and that, as its leader, he had not been dealt an especially strong hand. Yet his ambitions for Brazil—and for his own political career—remained undimmed. Central to his policies were the goals of entrenching his own regime and consolidating new power structures in Brazil, so as to develop the country into a major player in regional economics and politics. Even before the war, Vargas was keenly aware of the economic tools that he might use to achieve both goals. And the issue of trade and its potential to enhance Brazil's economy dominated the cables and papers that reached his desk in Rio during the war itself.

At the outbreak of World War II, Brazil enjoyed a reasonably strong—and immensely profitable—relationship with Germany. Trade was organized in a manner that suited the Brazilians, with Berlin agreeing to special terms of payment for the Brazilians. Central to this trade was the desire of the Brazilian military to buy German arms, and the willingness of Berlin to sell weapons to Brazil. Indeed, even during the German invasion of Poland at the start of the war in the autumn of 1939, and its rapid advances into Western Europe in the spring and summer of 1940, Berlin possessed enough additional weapons to sell arms to Brazil.

Meanwhile, the United States edged toward war with Germany, and plotted to win Brazil over to the Allied camp. The United States believed

Brazil was the most reliable local partner in their mission to check growing Nazi influence in the region—particularly in Argentina, which had a pro-Nazi government that made the country an attractive outpost for Hitler's agents. US intelligence warned President Roosevelt that the Germans wanted to establish a strong permanent political and military presence in Latin America. This was unacceptable to the Americans, who were willing to invest heavily—granting trade concessions—in order to prevent the Germans from gaining a foothold so close to the United States.

President Vargas understood the US position very clearly, and carefully tried to maximize Brazil's gains from the war. Indeed, this aim was at the heart of every Brazilian negotiation with the Americans. President Vargas also understood that in order to gain significantly from World War II, Brazil had to alter its initial position of neutrality. In short, Brazil needed to first formally end its extensive and extremely lucrative trade ties with the Germans, and then, eventually, formally join the war against the Axis powers.

Vargas did eventually pivot toward the Allies, going so far as to send Brazilian troops to the European theater to participate in Germany's defeat in the final months of the war. As he had anticipated, his relationship with Washington ultimately improved the economic situation in Brazil, but it was at the expense of his own power. His coziness with the United States deepened internal tensions and jeopardized both his leadership and the continuation of the Estado Novo when the war ended. Yet Brazil itself thrived. Following World War II, Brazil joined the very small list of countries that benefited hugely from the conflict; the European neutral powers make up the rest of this select club.

A famous list of Brazilian war aims prepared by the country's pro-American foreign minister Osvaldo Aranha (who later became the first president of the General Assembly of the United Nations) underscores its tremendous gains during World War II. Aranha prepared this wonderfully ambitious list for President Vargas's secret meeting with President Roosevelt, which took place in Brazil in January 1943, and the document can be used as something of a scorecard for evaluating what Brazil achieved during the war.

According to Aranha, the eleven objectives that Brazil should pursue were:

1. A better position in world politics.
2. A consolidation of its superiority in South America.
3. More secure and closer relations with the United States.
4. Developing greater influence over Portugal and the Portuguese colonies.
5. Development of Brazilian maritime power (Navy).
6. Development of air power (Air Force).
7. Development of Brazilian heavy industries.
8. Creation of a Brazilian military industrial complex.
9. Creation of industries—such as agricultural, extractive, and mineral enterprises—to complement those in the United States, which were essential for postwar world reconstruction.
10. Expansion of Brazil's railways and roads for economic and strategic purposes.
11. Exploration for essential combustible fuels.[4]

Taken together, the items on Aranha's list constituted a bold assertion of Brazil's rightful place in the international order. They represented a concerted attempt to transform the nation and move it into the twentieth century. These aims were all the more ambitious given that at the outset of World War II Brazil was still a tremendously underdeveloped country. In 1940, two-thirds of Brazilians were illiterate, nearly 70 percent of the population lived in rural areas, and the nation's exceedingly basic communications and transport systems left large parts of the country hugely isolated. Furthermore, unlike the majority of developed nations, whose main economic engines were manufacturing industries, Brazil's major industry was agriculture, with coffee still the dominant export.

Vargas changed all of this and led Brazil firmly onto the world stage. Under his leadership Brazil was modernized—a new national steel mill was built, new roads and railways were constructed, and improvements were made in its agriculture sector. Most of all, however, its military forces were transformed into the most powerful in the region. Brazil became a regional military, political, and economic superpower.

# PROLOGUE
## THE GOOD NEIGHBOR

IT WAS SATURDAY, MARCH 4, 1933, a cloudy late-winter day in Washington, DC, when Franklin D. Roosevelt took the oath of office from Chief Justice Charles Evans Hughes. Following his swearing-in ceremony, the newly minted president of the United States delivered a twenty-minute inaugural address that was broadcast to a radio audience of tens of millions across the United States. The speech, best known today for Roosevelt's assertion "the only thing we have to fear is . . . fear itself," concentrated almost entirely on the new president's domestic policy objectives, which had dominated the campaign and had helped Roosevelt to his landslide victory over the Republican incumbent, Herbert Hoover. And for good reason: with the United States in the depths of the worst economic depression in the nation's history, Roosevelt's domestic agenda could not have been more pressing.

Only one short paragraph of the new president's speech was devoted to foreign affairs. Yet this aside—and the powerful analogy it contained—would launch one of the most important programs in the history of American foreign policy. "In the field of world policy," Roosevelt told his fellow Americans, "I would dedicate this nation to the policy of the good neighbor—the neighbor who resolutely respects himself and, because he does so, respects the rights of others—the neighbor who respects his obligations and respects the sanctity of his agreements in and with a world of neighbors."[1]

Roosevelt's brief but pointed comment reflected the same domestic concerns he had highlighted in the rest of his address, but from a different angle. At its heart—and at the center of the resulting Good Neighbor Program—was the principle of nonintervention and noninterference in the domestic affairs of Latin American countries. Yet Roosevelt's aims were not purely altruistic. Under the Good Neighbor Program, the United States developed mutually beneficial, reciprocal exchanges with Latin American countries in the hope of also creating new opportunities for trade between the United States and its southern neighbors, thereby deepening the influence of the United States in the region.

The US secretary of state, Cordell Hull, was assigned the job of making the US president's declaration a reality by developing more cooperative relationships between the twenty-one republics of North, South, and Central America. From the outset this proved to be no easy task. In most Central and South American countries there was deep suspicion about the aims and intentions of the United States, which up until 1933 could be characterized as mainly exploitative and interested primarily in dividing and ruling whatever regions it could. Hull bemoaned America's "inheritance of ill will," reflecting that "it was probated under the name of intervention. . . . Piled high on political antagonism was economic resentment. The high tariffs of the previous administration, coupled with the panic of 1929, had brought grave economic distress to the Latin American countries."[2] America's problems had rippled down to its southern neighbors and compounded already simmering resentments toward policies that were perceived as paternalistic and self-interested.

The United States faced not only deep suspicion from the countries of Latin America, but also divisions among them. Many Latin American countries felt deep mutual suspicion toward one another. Hull, as a result, intended to foster the development of confidence, friendliness, and cooperation between the Latin American nations.[3] This was a lofty aim.

Perhaps no Latin American rivalry was as intense as that between Brazil and its neighbor Argentina, both of which vied for military, economic, and political domination of the continent. Their rivalry was based on historical conflicts over territories; the states had achieved independence from Portugal and Spain, respectively, and the colonial tensions that had dominated relations between those two European countries tainted Argentine-Brazilian relations, as well. Brazil, for instance, did not settle its long-running disputes over the shared border between the two states until the start of the twentieth century. Both countries remained competitive during the 1930s, their defense policies reflecting their traditional suspicion of one another. This suspicion also colored both nations' foreign policy, and circumscribed America's diplomacy toward them. Any move by the United States to help Argentina was viewed with deep suspicion by the government in Brazil, which assumed that American aid to the Argentines was detrimental to Brazilian interests. Needless to say, the Argentine government harbored the same assumptions.

A key American intelligence report succinctly explained Brazil's problems with Argentina in the 1930s. It argued:

> In the last few years Brazilians have expressed concern regarding Argentine designs on their territory . . . Argentina was considered the most powerful of Latin American nations. Brazil's vast and underdeveloped hinterland and its heterogeneous population were regarded as a source of weakness rather than strength. Argentina was more wealthy; its centers of population and production were more compact and closely knit together; and its inhabitants, overwhelmingly white, enjoyed a higher standard of living than did most Brazilians. Many observers considered Argentina's armed forces, particularly the Navy, to be by far the best in South America.[4]

The major fear in Brazil during the pre–World War II years was that Argentina would use the growing Nazi influence in the country as a pretext to strengthen its military and mount a military campaign against Brazil. There were good grounds for Brazil's fears; Argentine political culture during this period was strongly nationalistic, and the country's armed forces were extremely pro-German and looking to expand Argentine influence in the region. Faced with the very real possibility of Argentine military aggression, ranging from military skirmishes along the Argentine-Brazilian border to a full-scale invasion of Brazil by Argentine forces, Brazil's leaders sought practical ways to counter the Argentine threat. Naturally, this included talking up the Argentine threat with outside powers, particularly Great Britain and—increasingly—the United States.

President Roosevelt was receptive to news of the strong and potentially destabilizing internal rivalries between the American republics, as well as to the perceived pro-German sympathies of some of them. The day after President Roosevelt's inauguration speech, Adolf Hitler and the Nazi party were elected across the ocean in Germany, winning 52 percent of the vote in the German parliamentary elections. The electoral victory helped entrench Hitler in power and led to a more openly expansionist German foreign policy.[5] The impact of Hitler's consolidation of power, however, was not confined to the European continent. It was well known that Argentina was pro-German; the British and the Americans were worried that Brazil was, too. The central aim of the Good Neighbor Program was therefore to enhance US security by safeguarding the region from hostile foreign influence. The Good Neighbor Program, as a result, was characterized primarily by efforts in Washington to check the advances made in the region by Germany and Italy. Yet in the years prior to World War II, Cordell Hull and, following his appointment in 1937, the undersecretary of state, Sumner Welles, failed to achieve the lofty goals of the program. Much of this failure came down to factors that the United States could not control.

Germany was keen to develop ties with Latin American nations, especially Brazil, where it saw major possibilities for trade. Using a complex scheme of compensation marks, Brazil developed strong commercial ties with Berlin that it would not otherwise have been able to afford.[6] All of this proved to be extremely frustrating to the United States and Great Britain, which hitherto had been the major trading partners with Brazil.[7] Germany appeared to be willing to go much further than the United States or Great Britain in using trade links to help further its political influence in Brazil.

Germany's massive program of rearmament, which was intended primarily to develop the German armed forces into the most powerful on continental Europe, raised the possibility of arms sales from Berlin to Brazil. This was an extremely enticing prospect for the leaders of the Brazilian military, who were keen to develop their nation's armed forces in order to counter any aggression from Argentina. Germany appeared willing to supply Brazil with high-quality weapons. Great Britain remained steadfastly opposed to allowing German weapons to reach Brazil, primarily due to fears that arms shipments would help entrench the alleged pro-Nazi sentiments held by the officer ranks in the Brazilian armed forces. Yet Great Britain could not offer its own weapons to the Brazilians. In London, a policy of appeasing the Germans was still in force. Individuals who were calling for rearmament, such as Winston Churchill, were in the minority. Even if Great Britain wished to supply Brazil with arms (and

given concerns over Brazil's political leanings, that was unlikely), it had
no spare weapons to sell.

The United States, while not as worried about the arms question as
the British, became extremely concerned about the attempts of both Germany and Italy to foster ties with the large German and Italian immigrant
communities in Brazil. As the situation in Europe grew ever more tense
in the late 1930s, the American embassy in Rio de Janeiro fretted: "The
Italian and German governments have made in recent years a determined
attempt to organize the Italian and German colonies in Brazil and to
inspire the most ardent loyalty among their nationals, not only to the fa-
therland but to the present political regimes now functioning in Italy and
Germany."[8] The possibility of a second, overtly pro-Axis power in South
America was beginning to look frighteningly real.

In Washington the State Department noted that, in many ways, Brazil's Italian and German immigrant communities represented all that was
wrong with the country. The immigrants lived in closed communities
in the south of the country and their children were educated in foreign
schools in German or Italian.[9] Both immigrant groups, however, were influential in local business, particularly in aviation and in commerce. Daily
German- and Italian-language newspapers brought local and international
news to these immigrant groups.[10]

President Roosevelt set out in 1933 to foster closer ties between the
nations of Latin America and the United States. The trouble with Brazil was that the country's internal divisions were so strong that it made
Roosevelt's goal nearly impossible to achieve. As Getúlio Vargas's recent
election illustrated, power in Brazil rested in its states; the federal government was rather weak. Political instability was rife, and more often than
not power changed hands at the end of a gun rather than at the ballot box.
Fragmented and lurching from one direction to another, Brazil needed a
leader who could command widespread support and would therefore have
the time and opportunity to order and transform the country.

In an effort to illustrate the change in American policy toward Brazil
since 1933, President Roosevelt visited the country in November 1936.
Huge crowds greeted him on his arrival in Rio de Janeiro, where President Vargas received him with full honors. Brazilian warships, along with
ancient-looking planes from the air force, guided the US president's ship
into harbor.

At the conclusion of his visit, President Roosevelt was full of praise for Vargas and "the great republic of Brazil." In a speech following a banquet held in his honor, he invited the diners to join him in toasting the Brazilian president, saying, "I am leaving you tonight with great regret. There is one thing, however, that I shall remember, and that is that it was two people who invented the New Deal—the president of Brazil and the president of the United States."[11]

Roosevelt's connection of Vargas to his famed US economic program was a nice touch, and one that Vargas greatly appreciated. In addition to highlighting Vargas's work transforming Brazil since he came to power in 1930, Roosevelt meant to flatter Vargas and to inspire him to do more to industrialize Brazil. Despite his own ambitions—and due, in part, to deep internal divisions in Brazil—Vargas had achieved only modest transformations of the state by 1936.

President Roosevelt's visit was portrayed in Brazil and the United States as a huge success, and was credited with generating mutual goodwill between the countries. In truth, however, the visit changed little. While it was clear that the Brazilian people held a deep affection for Roosevelt, Brazilians continued to harbor deep suspicions about America's intentions in Latin America.

A more somber analysis of Brazil and Latin America came from Cordell Hull, who traveled with President Roosevelt to Brazil and subsequently to Argentina for the Conference of the American Republics, which involved all the countries of the American continent. Hull would later write:

> The Latin America I now visited differed from the Latin America I saw just three years before, because Axis penetration had made rapid, alarming headway under various guises. For many months we had received reports from our representatives in the countries to the south of us, which added together, created a picture of threatening colors. Nazi Germany, in particular, was making intensive efforts to gain the ascendency among our neighbors, but Italy and Japan were working feverishly as well.[12]

To an American visitor such as Hull, it seemed painfully clear that fascists, Nazis, and other Axis sympathizers would soon be on the US doorstep if nothing was done to stop them.

Confirmation of Hull's fears appeared to come the following year in Brazil when President Vargas cancelled scheduled elections, banned political parties, suspended the constitution, and declared the Estado Novo. In a speech to the nation on November 10, 1937, Vargas explained the reasoning behind his actions. He argued that the political situation in Brazil had become unmanageable and that, after consulting key members of the Brazilian state (a clear reference to the military leadership), he had no choice but to take action.[13] Vargas acknowledged it was "an exceptional decision . . . over and above ordinary government decisions," but insisted that it was his duty as the Brazilian head of state.[14]

On the surface, it looked like the establishment of the Estado Novo would push Brazil further into the orbit of the Germans. There were, however, marked ideological differences between the Brazilian and German systems. The Estado Novo of Brazil and its resulting government resembled the Estado Novo of Portugal, the old colonial ruler of Brazil, and both systems lacked the strong militaristic trappings of the Nazis. Still, the United States was increasingly concerned over the Vargas regime's attitude toward Jewish immigrants in the south of the country. Reports of anti-Semitic attacks on Jews and Jewish property in Brazil were growing. And while perhaps not directly involved, it was clear that the Brazilian authorities were doing very little to prevent such assaults.[15]

The Roosevelt administration chose to ignore the plight of the Jews in Brazil and focus on geostrategic issues alone. The Good Neighbor Program, after all, called for the United States not to intervene in the internal politics of a Latin American state, and Roosevelt had no intention of reneging on that promise. The United States was much more interested in the external political orientation of Brazil. Following the establishment of the Estado Novo, key figures in the Vargas administration reassured Washington that Brazil would not shift toward the Axis powers and away from the United States. On the contrary, Brazil wished to continue to develop trading ties with the United States, as well as with the Axis powers. Believing it had a firm handle on the new regime in Brazil, the US State Department brushed aside concerns over the pro-Nazi orientation of the key leaders of the Brazilian military.

While he worked to soothe the Americans, Vargas also moved quickly to consolidate his own power. In his speech to the nation on November 10, most of his rationale for the establishment of the Estado Novo centered on the threat of a communist takeover in Brazil. Known as the Cohen Plan (its name a testament to the latent anti-Semitism in the country's power structure), the threat was exaggerated by the military, which forged several documents to support its assessment. In reality, after the failed communist plot of 1935 and the arrest of the main plotters, the communists were not in any position to mount a second putsch. Rather, Vargas's new authoritarian constitution was a response to a different and more troubling threat—not from the far left, but rather from the far right.

Though in the past conservatives had been strong supporters of President Vargas and his regime, they were now proving to be its most dangerous opponents. Vargas had to act quickly if he was to avert the same sort of coup that had brought him to power. Less than a month after the establishment of the Estado Novo, he signed a decree disbanding all political parties. Included in this list was the fascist party, the Ação Integralista Brasileira (AIB), better known locally as the Integralistas. Vargas had turned to this group for support in his previous campaigns, but with the banning of all political parties under the Estado Novo, he turned against them.

Unsurprisingly, the leadership of the Integralistas felt betrayed, and carefully plotted revenge against their onetime ally. Supporters of the Integralistas included several leading members of the armed forces— especially the Brazilian navy, where they were particularly strong. They also had links to fascist Italy and Nazi Germany, and their leaders were directly in touch with the Nazis—seeking help to remove Vargas from power.

On a balmy evening in Rio de Janeiro in May 1938, the Integralistas made their move against the president and his family. The subsequent drama, which unfolded within the beautiful grounds of the presidential palace in Rio de Janeiro, would prove important not only for Brazil as a nation but also for Brazilian relations with the United States and Brazil's attitude toward the onrushing world war itself. Indeed, given the links that the leadership of the Integralistas enjoyed with Germany and Italy, the events that evolved in the presidential palace that evening could not possibly have been confined to Brazil's internal politics. The stakes could not have been higher.

# PART ONE:

## PRELUDE TO WAR

# 1

# THE KEY

ALZIRA VARGAS DO AMARAL PEIXOTO POSSESSED such natural beauty and strong vitality that she was sexually alluring to almost every man she met. Like her father, she was not tall, but her fine chiseled cheekbones, elegant widow's peak, full sensual mouth, and piercing dark eyes more than made up for her lack of height. It was Alzira's smile, however, that disarmed most men. It was a smile that came from both the eyes and the mouth, lighting up rooms and raising the spirits of even the most hardened military and political men—both those in Brazil itself, and those who hailed from beyond its sunny shores. When he was in a gay mood, Getúlio Vargas, president of Brazil, beamed backed at her with the look of absolute joy that parents reserve for their favorite child.

Alzira was a homebody by nature, and thus the perfect political hostess. She added her own distinctive personal touch to official receptions held at the presidential palaces and retreats. Her father's friends and foes alike noted that she was cool, possessed a good legal mind (she was at the top of her class at law school), and was politically calculating. When Vargas held personal meetings, particularly one-on-ones, Alzira sat quietly at the table, watching the guest with both eyes. Her goal was to become aware of the general trends and direction of the conversation and to gauge its outcome and implications for her *papai*. At the end of each meeting she escorted the guest from the room, "polishing the rough parts" of their impressions of her father, and returned to him with a detailed report.[1]

Unofficially, Alzira served as her father's antenna, advisor, critic, social secretary, hostess, bodyguard, and nurse. She was also good with a revolver.[2] Years of practice on the family ranch in Brazil's southern province of Rio Grande do Sul meant that she wasn't afraid to pick up a weapon and put it to good use. On the night of May 10, 1938, Alzira's skills would be tested to the full.

The evening started as usual for Alzira and her father. They were together, as they often were, at Brazil's presidential office, the Guanabara Palace in Rio de Janeiro. The stifling heat of the hottest summer months—January and February—had long passed, but at 10 P.M. it was still pleasant enough for the upstairs windows of the palace to be left slightly ajar. President Vargas was working alone in his small office on the first floor. It was meant to be a quiet night for the president as he planned out Brazil's economic and political future using different colored pencils for different subjects related to his many ambitious projects for the development of Brazil.[3]

One of the main goals of Vargas's strategy was to carefully position Brazil within the international system in order to maximize its economic and military gains. Brazil primarily derived these gains from trade: on the one hand, with the United States and Great Britain; and on the other hand, with Nazi Germany. Vargas wanted to use trade with these countries to help transform key sectors of the economy—to decrease Brazil's reliance on imports and grow its ability to export its own goods and resources.

Vargas was no visionary, but he believed hard work and political discipline would allow Brazil to transform itself. Moreover, if the European war that President Roosevelt had told him was inevitable did materialize, Vargas was ready to take full advantage of it to maximize Brazilian gains. In this, he perfectly mirrored the assessment of the British foreign office. Long admirers of Vargas, the office's staff described him as "brave, a persuasive orator and a genius in the art of political maneuver," an "astonishing little man" who "has guided Brazil's policy with extreme prudence."[4] Vargas's American biographer, John Dulles, put it another way: "He is a calm man in a land of hotheads," Dulles wrote, "a disciplined person in a land of undisciplined people, a prudent person in the land of imprudent people, a temperate person in the land of squanderers, a silent person in the land of parrots."[5]

On this night, Vargas had chosen to sit back and reflect on Brazil's progress while others in his administration celebrated it. The new Brazilian constitution, the Estado Novo, was six months old, and across the city cabinet ministers and local VIPs were marking the event by listening to Francisco Campos, the framer of the constitution, address the nation from the city's old Senate building. The central theme of the address was the political peace and quiet the country could expect now that plans for presidential elections had been put on hold. Vargas had become an authoritarian leader with an agenda of unifying Brazil and strengthening the central government at the expense of the local regional governments that had dominated Brazil for decades. It was a huge gamble, but Vargas enjoyed the tacit support of the United States, which was keen to see a strong leader in Brazil who would take action against German and Italian interests in the country.

After the broadcast, several of the key figures in the Estado Novo joined together and moved to Campos's residence, where they sipped champagne and caught up on local and diplomatic gossip. President Vargas had been invited to attend the soiree, but as was usual, he chose to avoid this type of gathering, preferring instead the company of his family and closest friends. To Vargas, the hours following dinner were his most productive, giving him the opportunity to go through his paperwork, light up a large cigar, and ponder national and international news. It was also quite common for him to host an intimate poker game in his study. On the evening of May 10, exhausted from a full day of meetings, he retired early to his bedroom.[6] "Goodnight—until tomorrow," he muttered to Alzira before giving her a kiss on the cheek. The final task for Vargas before sleep was to make his daily entry into his diary. He wasn't a great diarist—his entries were written in a flat factual style—but he took the task seriously, faithfully recording his basic thoughts of the day and details of whatever important meetings had taken place.

All was quiet in the palace, which despite its central location in Rio was set back off the road with woodland to the side and rear. Vargas liked to work in the little upstairs study, where his papers were carefully arranged on his desk, and where there was little in the way of outside noise or distraction.[7] It was for this reason that he liked to spend as much time as possible in the Guanabara Palace rather than in the official presidential office, the Catete Palace, which had served as Brazil's presidential palace since 1894. Although relatively modest in size, the Guanabara Palace's rooms contained some of the finest art in the city, and the large, secluded, and well-designed gardens provided the perfect place for Vargas to walk and mull over important arguments. Many of the most significant decisions in Brazilian history, such as the resolution to participate in World

War I (Brazil ultimately joined in opposition to the Central Powers), had been made in the long majestic ballroom of the palace, which also served as the cabinet room. President Vargas regarded the Catete Palace as his office and the Guanabara Palace as his residence. He preferred to use the Catete Palace in the morning and the Guanabara Palace in the evening.

On the evening of May 10, there was little activity outside the gates of the Guanabara Palace, and only a handful of guards, secretaries, and domestic staff were inside the palace. It was a typically placid night. Vargas was preparing to retire when, suddenly, a noise broke the silence.

Alzira cried out, "What was that?" Her first instinct was that one of the guards' guns had gone off by mistake.[8] After a few moments there was a second noise, this time accompanied by the sound of a ricochet and falling plaster. Alzira realized that the palace was under attack, but she wasn't sure by whom. "Where's Daddy?" she screamed at Vargas's private secretary. Before long, the president was in the room with Alzira, dressed in his pajamas and waving around a revolver. No sooner had he appeared than the power was cut, plunging both the palace and its gardens into darkness.

The attackers had achieved complete surprise. The shots grew in frequency and accuracy as those inside the palace scrambled around searching for weapons.[9] Alzira calculated that the attackers were at the front gates of the palace, but had not yet entered the grounds. She spoke quickly and nervously to her father. "Daddy," she implored, "we have to get you out of here and get help." Vargas replied, "I'm going nowhere, but see if the phones are working and call everyone and tell them that the president of the republic is a prisoner in the palace."[10]

Alzira tried the phone in the president's study. Much to her surprise, it was still functioning. She yelled at her father, "The phones are not cut. Whom should I call?" Vargas replied, "Everybody we know."[11]

Alzira made a mental list of names. As she made her first call, the shooting grew more frequent. "At least sit down and don't act as a target by walking in front of the window," she instructed her father.[12] As bullets continued to fly into the palace, Alzira reached the chief of police and the chief of staff of the army. Both promised to help, but first they had to gather their forces.

It soon became clear to Alzira and her father that the attack at the Guanabara Palace was not an isolated incident. The conspirators had surrounded the homes of the top figures in the Vargas regime.[13] They had attacked the residences of the chief of police and the army chief of staff, along with two senior generals. Other groups of rebels had seized two radio stations and had gained control of the naval ministry.[14]

Miraculously, the palace's phone line remained open, and Alzira continued to call for help. When she got through to her brother, Lutero, she yelled at him to "get help and come soon or we'll all be dead."[15] The attackers, she could tell, were preparing for the final assault on the palace. Alzira heard the sounds of pistol fire coming from inside the palace: the president and his staff were returning fire in the general direction of the main gate.[16]

A presidential car screeched up to the palace's entrance; it was carrying the president's younger brother, Benjamin, who was quickly dispatched to get reinforcements. As his car sped out of the palace grounds, the attackers fired on it, but it got away and headed at speed in the direction of downtown.

Outside the palace, the rebel leaders were having problems of their own. Most of the volunteers they had counted on to join them that night had not shown up at the collection point in downtown Rio. It later transpired that most of the men who did not show up to fight had stayed home, believing that, as one of the plotters later testified, "The coup had already failed before it was born."[17] The forty-five men who did make good on their promise gathered at the headquarters of the coup at 550 Niemeyer Avenue, where some nine of them were judged too old for combat and sent home.[18] The remainder had little combat experience or firearms training, and the last-minute rifle training they received did little to inspire confidence. To make matters worse, the rebels donned navy uniforms, but due to a lack of boots continued to wear their own civilian shoes and socks. A white neckerchief emblazoned in green letters with the motto *Avante* (Forward) topped off the uniform.

When they arrived outside the palace gates, the rebels' uniforms immediately gave them away.[19] They exchanged fire with the palace guards, but the element of surprise—and a traitor in the guards' ranks—allowed the rebels to initially overpower the defenders, killing one of them and locking up the rest.[20] Many of the rebels then hid out in the palace gardens. Instead of following their motto, *avante,* however, they were content to let off the occasional shot and adopt a wait-and-see attitude.[21] Most of the rebels were, in truth, terrified by the evening's events and hoping to slip away to their homes in the city when the time was right. To make matters worse, the untrained assailants found themselves woefully under-equipped. The two trucks that brought them to the palace swiftly departed after dropping them off. In their rush to flee the scene, the drivers drove off without unloading the rebels' heavy machine guns and homemade bombs, so the men were faced with the prospect of mounting an assault on the palace with only light weapons and a single light machine gun. Most of the rebels, moreover, appeared none too keen to use their lone machine gun, so it was left to their leader on the ground, Lieutenant Severo Fournier, to personally take charge of it. Fournier told his rebels, "Shoot at the upstairs study where Vargas is no doubt holed up. Don't hold anything back." He fired a quick burst from the machine gun, as much to inspire his own men as to shake up the people inside the palace.

Just as Alzira Vargas was frantically calling for help and reinforcements, Fournier dispatched a man to do the same on behalf of the assailants, and to check on the coup's progress in Rio and in the rest of the country. "Find out who controls the radio and the police and check where the force is to kidnap the president," Fournier instructed his messenger. For good measure, he added, "Return only when you have the reinforcements and guns." In his heart Fournier knew that he would never see the messenger again: the man simply slipped away and returned home.[22]

The assault on the palace devolved into a standoff, as both sides awaited news and the arrival of reinforcements. Inside the palace, Alzira was getting desperate. She suspected that the rebels wanted to kill her father, and she couldn't reach most of the senior figures in the Estado Novo, who were having their own troubles and intrigues.[23] It seemed increasingly likely that the promised reinforcements would not arrive in time.

Suddenly, Alzira had an idea. "*Papai*," she said, "why don't we check the tunnel that links the palace with the grounds of Fluminense Soccer Club." The secret tunnel ran directly under the palace gardens and came out at the stadium, where Alzira hoped that the expected reinforcements might be waiting; perhaps they had even entered the tunnel and were making their way to the palace.

Vargas approved the plan, but they soon discovered that the door to the tunnel was locked. The president ordered a search for the key, and tried to calm everyone down. "Let's sit tight and wait," the president instructed before returning to his study. "Alzira, tell the chief of police to get his men to try to enter the tunnel from the soccer stadium end."

Vargas paced his study with his revolver in his hand, becoming increasingly agitated. His life was in danger, a rescue force had yet to arrive, and he had a packed morning of official engagements and meetings to attend; he wanted to get to sleep.[24] As happens in most coups, reliable information was also proving difficult to come by, and it was even harder to know who was personally involved in the plot. With the power cut to the palace, neither Alzira nor her father heard the broadcast by the rebels from a radio station that they had successfully seized, providing news of the uprising.[25] Still, Vargas knew which political group was behind the coup.

Vargas was perhaps most astute at gauging the strength of his political enemies, and there were many. On the left of the political spectrum were the communists, on the right, the fascist Green Shirts—the Integralistas—who were members of the Ação Integralista Brasileira. He also had a great deal of opposition from within the ranks of his own administration. Ministers and local governors all needed to be watched carefully, and Vargas often had to bring his full political skills to bear to dampen down mutinies, personality clashes, and ideological disputes that might otherwise tear his government apart. Now trapped in his office, with his administration and life in peril, Vargas was cool enough to understand just who was behind the attack. "The Integralistas will pay for this," he informed his daughter in a monotone.

Given the events of the past few months, it hadn't been difficult for the president to come to this conclusion. Ever since the Estado Novo had banned all political parties some six months earlier, Vargas's former fascist allies had been craving retribution. This Vargas could have anticipated—yet he didn't understand how successful the rebels had been in securing support among Brazil's armed forces, especially the navy. Sympathizers in the military had been essential in helping to organize and outfit the rebels now surrounding the Guanabara Palace and threating to topple the young Estado Novo.

Alzira paid little attention to her father; she was more concerned with organizing his potential escape through the tunnel to the soccer stadium. With the key still not found, the people trapped inside the palace considered trying to break down the door, but this would have been no easy task; it was made of thick wood with strong, old-fashioned hinges. The group briefly considered shooting the lock off, but just as quickly dismissed the idea. None of the guns inside the palace were of a high enough caliber, and the sound of the shooting might have alerted the rebels outside of the existence of the tunnel. For the time being, the standoff continued.

The lack of information on the situation in the rest of Rio continued to be a major source of concern to Alzira. There were rumors inside the palace that the rebels had taken over key radio stations across the country and were broadcasting anti-Estado Novo messages. Word also reached Alzira that there had been a traitor in the presidential guard, and that at least one of the loyal guards had been killed. This news heightened tensions inside the palace.

Suddenly, a sustained outbreak of shooting erupted from the direction of the front gates. This time, however, the gunfire had not been directed at the palace. Finally, reinforcements had arrived—though not of the sort that Alzira and her father had been expecting.

Eurico Gaspar Dutra, the minister of war, had been lucky. At the last minute, the rebels assigned to detain him and move him to a safe location in the center of Rio had lost their nerve, failing to surround his downtown home and sparing him the fate that had befallen other leaders of the Estado Novo. Following an urgent call from the palace to his home at 1 A.M., Dutra had left on foot to rally reinforcements, passing a bar inside of which were a dozen leaderless rebels sitting around drinking. Finally arriving at Leme Fort, Dutra had found some twelve soldiers, and he brought them to the palace in a single truck.[26] The men were greeted at the gates by a burst of gunfire from the rebels camped outside. During the initial exchange of fire, two of Dutra's men were wounded and a bullet nicked the minister's ear. Instead of engaging the rebels in a prolonged firefight, Dutra appeared to lose his nerve and sought instructions as to what to do from Alzira.[27] When no advice was forthcoming, Dutra sped off in a motorcycle sidecar in order to fetch more reinforcements.

Although not quite the salvation Vargas and Alzira had been hoping for, Dutra's intervention had a salutary effect. The presence of his small contingent of soldiers caused most of the rebels to abandon their positions at the front gate and flee into the woods surrounding the palace. Dutra himself, meanwhile, arrived at police headquarters to find other members of the Estado Novo trying to organize a group of special police to go to the palace. It was proving difficult, as most of the force had been given the night off by their commanders in order to celebrate the six-month anniversary of the Estado Novo. Finally, at Dutra's urging, the head of the special police dispatched a single truckload of special police dressed in civilian attire to join the fight at the palace.

Back at the palace, the danger was still acute. While they had driven many of the rebels into the woods, the first group of soldiers had not managed to capture or kill any of them, much less free the people trapped inside the palace. The situation was still deemed to be too dangerous for Vargas to try to exit through the front gates, so the tunnel and locked door became the sole focus of attention for those trying to get the president out. The special police arrived at the soccer stadium, following Dutra's orders, and now entered the tunnel, making their way to the other side of the locked door under the Guanabara Palace. They were close enough to communicate with people on the palace side of the door, and together both parties hatched a plan to blow the door open. Fortunately, perhaps, for those on both sides of the door, this desperate plan was abandoned at the last moment.

Just as the clock inside the president's study was about to chime 5 A.M., the president's secretary located a porter who had a key. They opened the door, and special police and other officials poured into the building, ending the siege. Alzira informed her father, "The police are here and it is over, but there is still much to be done to secure the palace gardens and the city." In truth, however, the arrival of the police led most of the rebels at the front gate and in the woodlands of the palace gardens to abandon their positions. Most merely stripped off their uniforms, which they had worn on top of their civilian clothes, and tried to sneak back to downtown Rio. The majority were rapidly apprehended as they left the palace grounds or traversed the road back to the downtown. At the Guanabara Palace, the police removed the bodies of the seven rebels killed in the exchange of fire. As word spread of the failed assault on the palace, the rebels who had attacked the radio stations and the homes of leading Estado Novo members simply melted into the crowds.[28] By 7 A.M. the uprising was over, save for the sounds of sporadic gunfire as the police continued to come across individual rebels or small groups of fighters who had not yet heard news of the uprising's total failure.[29]

Following the liberation of the palace, the tense atmosphere of the siege gave way to a festive mood as the leading figures of the Estado Novo swapped stories of what had happened that night outside their offices and homes. Alzira noted, however, that while everyone else was in high spirits, her father "spoke little and seemed withdrawn." He was already planning his response to the coup and the plotters.

Responses to the night's drama were swift and varied. The coup had been so amateurish that some of Vargas's critics maintained that it had been staged by the president and his supporters as an attempt to justify the establishment of the authoritarian Estado Novo.[30] Subsequent events, however, came to reveal the extent of the plot and those involved in its planning and execution. As for Vargas's typical modus operandi, a friend and advisor remarked to the British ambassador in Rio: "Senhor Vargas dislikes recourse to bloodshed in disposing of his enemies. He prefers to win them over by persuasion—or so skillfully to place the banana skin that they break their own necks. This calls for much patience."[31]

Later that same morning, while the police continued to round up rebels still hiding in the palace gardens, President Vargas took his usual walk to the presidential office at the Catete Palace, accompanied—as was normally the case—by only one aide.[32] He was prepared to take whatever draconian measures were needed to see that the plotters were tracked down and brought to justice. The nascent investigation into the uprising was carried out surgically and rapidly, two words not usually associated with Brazilian authorities of the day.

As Vargas prepared to strike back against his would-be assassins, Alzira and Benjamin worked to overhaul the security provision for the president. Members of the Vargas family, especially Alzira, found it hard to understand how it could have taken so long for reinforcements to arrive at the palace. They speculated that many security officers had been waiting to see which side prevailed, and that this ambivalence had left the president isolated and vulnerable. Furthermore, while Dutra eventually carried out his duty, Alzira noted his initial hesitancy to fully engage the rebels during the attempted coup. Later, Alzira suggested that Dutra had hesitated because he, too, had been considering joining the Integralistas.[33] Her father was less critical, writing in his diary that "the minister of war [was] the only senior member of the state that risked his own life to save me during the attack. The rest fled to first protect themselves."[34]

Following the attempted coup, Benjamin decided that the president needed a personal bodyguard who would report directly to him. The guards were to be drawn from the gaúchos from the São Borja district, men with whom Benjamin had previously served in the military and whose loyalty he could vouch for. "They will be loyal to you," he assured his brother, "and guard the palace while you sleep or work, and accompany you wherever you go."[35] The men were to be heavily armed, and—Alzira avowed—"would trust no one," as was the custom from their region. These Brazilian cowboys were rough, with little time for the niceties of city life let alone presidential protocol, but they were given some training and dressed in suits. Their appointment as the presidential bodyguard proved a catastrophe for the president some sixteen years later, but in the aftermath of the uprising they surely brought comfort to him and the rest of the shaken presidential family.

His stiffened security detail would not, however, protect Vargas from any future political challenges—especially not those that, like this uprising, had partially originated within his regime. As he now turned his attention to making sure that there would be no repeat of the uprising, his daughter kept a close watch over any ministers she believed posed an internal threat to her father. Her attentiveness would, in due time, earn Alzira the nickname of "the right eye of Vargas."[36]

## 2

# THE LEFT EYE OF VARGAS

PRESIDENT VARGAS WAS KEEN TO RETURN TO BUSINESS as usual following the uprising. He especially wanted to avoid any appearance of weakness or instability, either domestically or internationally, and he took care to project an image of calmness and strength despite his recent ordeal. "The country is absolutely tranquil and the president of the republic continues to be supported by all the organized forces of the nation," the Brazilian ministry of foreign affairs proclaimed the day after the attempted coup.[1] A statement sent out to the foreign diplomatic corps based in Rio boasted of "hundreds of arrests" and claimed that the culprits would be dealt with swiftly and fairly.

On May 16, 1938, Vargas and his cabinet introduced two amendments to the Brazilian constitution as a direct result of the uprising.[2] The first imposed the death penalty on anyone convicted of attacking the president's life or liberty. "The new law is not to be used retroactively against the plotters of May 11," Vargas informed the meeting.[3] In truth, there wasn't any appetite for use of the death penalty, but the president hoped it might serve "as a deterrent against future plots." The second amendment, Article 177, allowed the government to dismiss civilian or military personnel for reasons that were in the public interest—as defined by the regime—for an indefinite period.[4]

In Rio, senior police officers keen to make up for their poor showing on May 11 moved quickly against those they suspected of having any involvement in the plot. Before the police had finished rounding up the usual suspects, their investigation got a big break when officers in Rio located a car used by Severo Fournier, the hapless leader of the rebellion at the Guanabara Palace. Inside the car, the police found detailed plans for the rebellion, including many of the names of the rebels involved. The plans confirmed Alzira's gut instincts about the uprising; the rebels had planned to kidnap, or kill, her father and several other members of the regime. While the plans found in Fournier's car proved that the Integralistas were behind the plot, they also revealed that a number of disaffected military non-Integralistas, such as Fournier, had taken part in the attempted coup. The plans also revealed the extent of the Brazilian navy's role in the plot. Within days the police had arrested some 1,167 civilians and 437 military personnel, the majority of whom were from the navy.[5]

At the end of the siege at the Guanabara Palace on May 11, Fournier had slipped quietly away and avoided capture. He took refuge with friends in Rio, but his photograph had been published in all the newspapers, and a sizable reward had been offered for information that led to his arrest.[6] His friends grew more anxious with each day they hid him. Eventually, they hatched a plan. "We can get you to the Italian embassy, and then you're on your own," one of the men informed him. "There you can ask for political asylum," another added. Because the Italian government had tacitly supported the Integralistas before the putsch, there was a chance—however slim—that it would now give sanctuary to one of the rebel leaders.

It was a desperate gamble, but Fournier was feeling the same pressure as his friends. He had heard reports that the police were torturing people who had been detained in raids following May 11, and the prospect of sharing their fate—combined with the lack of any other viable alternative—led Fournier to go along with the plan.[7]

On June 25, 1938, an old car crept slowly around the streets of central Rio, occasionally misfiring and doing its best not to attract the attention of the police. Both the driver and his passenger were wearing military uniforms, their shoulder lapels indicating they each held the rank of captain. The officers were trying not to show the anxiety they were feeling, either to one another or to the pedestrians who walked past when they stopped at traffic junctions. "The police are everywhere," the driver informed his passenger, who could see perfectly well for himself.

In truth, the police presence in central Rio was no greater than usual. The major police operation to capture the members of the uprising of May 11 had long since been scaled back, and most of those arrested had already been charged and sentenced. Vargas had sped up Brazil's normally snail-like judicial process; under new emergency powers, the accused of May 11 were given just five minutes to mount their defense, and verdicts and sentences were issued within thirty minutes by increasingly grumpy, overworked judges.[8] By June 25, the police in downtown Rio were more interested in looking for traffic violations and suppressing the city's increasing crime rate than looking for any rebels who might have remained at large. Nonetheless, the driver of the car was sweating profusely and took Rio's side roads wherever possible, avoiding the city's long tree-lined avenues, which were awash with traffic policemen.

In the trunk of the car, lying in the darkness, was Severo Fournier. As the car approached the Italian embassy, the driver refused to stop, plunging straight past the police guards and into the embassy grounds.[9] There the men unloaded Fournier from the boot of the car and drove back past the guards, saluting as they left. It had taken them no more than twenty minutes to dispose of their explosive human cargo.

Ambassador Lojacono experienced something approaching a panic attack when his secretary quietly interrupted his meeting by whispering in his ear, "Severo Fournier is inside the embassy grounds and wishes to seek political asylum."[10] After the ambassador had calmed down, he cabled Rome, and waited anxiously for instructions. As news spread quickly through Rio of Fournier's arrival at the embassy, Eurico Dutra, the Brazilian minister of war, dispatched two senior military officers to negotiate with the Italian ambassador. The officers reported back to Dutra: "Lojacono was uncooperative, arrogant, and reluctant to hand over Fournier and therefore violate the very principle of political asylum." Dutra was barely able to contain his anger.

After much diplomatic maneuvering, pressure, and threats from the Brazilian government—as well as the personal intervention of Fournier's own father and the Italian foreign minister, Galeazzo Ciano—Fournier was eventually persuaded to leave the embassy on July 7. He was given a choice of being arrested by the military or by civilian police; he chose the military option in the hope that they would treat him better.[11] Fournier was convicted and given a lengthy jail sentence, but spared the death penalty.[12] His arrest and conviction officially ended the rebellion, which became known in Brazilian history as the "revolution of the cowards."[13]

Fournier's gradual ouster from the embassy was meant to signal a renewal of Brazilian-Italian friendship, which had been strained even prior to the events of June 25 when Brazil had frozen Italian funds in the country. While the Fournier dilemma was a potential cause for a further decline in relations between the two nations, it ultimately served as something of an olive branch. Fournier was encouraged to write a letter in which he thanked Lojacono for his hospitality and stated clearly that he would leave the embassy of his own accord. For his part, Lojacono was asked to write a personal letter to Dutra expressing his most sincere gratitude for the minister's understanding of the moral dilemma the ambassador had found himself in over Fournier's request for asylum. Subsequently, Lojacono was recalled to Rome for his pains.

All of this internal political drama had important implications for the future of Brazilian foreign policy. One of the people who helped smuggle Fournier into the embassy was, it was soon discovered, a certain Captain Manuel Aranha, the brother of Osvaldo Aranha, the Brazilian minister of foreign affairs. The minister of war, Dutra, wanted to quickly dismiss Manuel Aranha, as well as his coconspirators in the embassy incident, from the army without a hearing. "Use the new powers invested in you by Article 177 of the constitution to fire the officers immediately," Dutra urged the president.

Vargas hesitated, however, as he always did in disputes involving Aranha, his oldest and closest political ally. A miffed Dutra subsequently resigned over the issue, and only withdrew his resignation when the president gave in to his demand and dismissed Manuel and the other guilty officers. This decision, in turn, caused Osvaldo Aranha to resign, and it looked for a while as if Vargas would be unable to keep both Osvaldo Aranha and Eurico Dutra in the cabinet. Osvaldo argued to Vargas that he had acted too hastily in dismissing Manuel, did not understand all the facts of the case, and should at the very least, as a courtesy to Osvaldo, grant Manuel a personal hearing.[14]

The president, Alzira noted, was "caught between something of a rock and a hard place." Vargas remarked on the affair in his diary on June 26, 1938, the day after the embassy incident. "I was called urgently to deal with a crisis. . . . The most serious part is that the minister of war, my best helper [at the Guanabara Palace uprising], wants to resign. I slept with the feeling that this could be the beginning of the collapse of the new regime."[15]

The Aranha family dug in its heels, and Vargas grew increasingly frustrated at the impasse throughout the first week of July, at the same time he was facing a crisis in his relations with Italy. The Aranha problem became even more complex and dangerous for Vargas when the powerful head of the Brazilian armed forces, General Góes Monteiro, threatened to resign as well.[16] Vargas refused to accept Góes Monteiro's resignation, telling the general in no uncertain terms "to get on with his job." On July 6, Vargas added that the crisis "is complicated . . . the minister of war is tired and nervous."[17] The president was working hard for a resolution, but was growing more pessimistic about the prospect of keeping these two key men in his administration.

At this point, the president decided to talk with some of Aranha's extended family. The men were old friends and brothers in arms, and the two "old families" from Rio Grande do Sul shared a common history; approaching the elders of the Aranha family was a sensible tactic. Alzira also suggested that her mother, the president's wife Darci, "talk with Osvaldo's mother, and get her to broker a compromise with him." She added, "Osvaldo will listen to her." Alzira knew full well that Aranha's mother had a great deal of influence over her son, and was the de facto head of the powerful extended Aranha family.[18]

The plea that Darci conveyed to Osvaldo's mother came directly from the president. "The two Gaúchos," she said, "should stick together." Osvaldo responded favorably to the message, and eventually he and Vargas reached a compromise of sorts, allowing the two ministers to remain in their respective positions in the cabinet, at least for the time being. The episode—and its solution—was indicative of the close-knit, traditional nature of Brazilian politics. Old family ties remained a strong feature of the politics and economics of the Estado Novo era, and both Alzira and the president's younger brother Benjamin were dab hands at knowing when and how to use interfamily politics to win support for the president—or, as in this case, to resolve a major political crisis.

But family ties did not bind every politician together, nor could they help to resolve the biggest questions facing Brazil. The conflict between Dutra and Aranha was much more than a simple power spat or personality clash. The two ministers held fundamentally opposed visions of Brazil's place in the increasingly polarized international world order. Osvaldo Aranha was, at heart, a strong supporter of democracy. He believed that in any coming war between fascism and democracy, democracy would emerge victorious, although the victory might not be absolute. For Aranha, Brazil's natural partner and ally was the United States, and he wished to move toward much closer relations with Washington.

Eurico Dutra, on the other hand, was a well-known admirer of Nazi Germany. He was especially impressed with its military prowess, and was keen to develop closer military and economic ties between the two nations. Needless to say, Dutra found a willing partner in Berlin. Dutra was a powerful man, and he enjoyed strong support within the Brazilian military. His actions in helping to rescue the president on May 11 had made him all the stronger politically within the Estado Novo regime. The bad blood between him and Aranha would become a thorn in the side of the Vargas regime, especially when it came to geopolitics.

The Jewish American intellectual Waldo Frank, who had dubbed Alzira "the right eye of the president," called Osvaldo Aranha "the left eye of Vargas." Getúlio Vargas and Osvaldo Aranha were a political double act, and seemed to complement one another perfectly. Their similarities started and ended with being Gaúchos, hailing from Rio Grande do Sul.

Vargas was cautious and a good listener, and he liked to weigh both sides of an argument before deciding which side to support. His oratory skills were sufficient, but he relied on the depth and detail of the content of his speeches, rather than the range of his vocal chords, to carry the audience. More often than not, he left the wining and dining of foreign dignitaries to Aranha, preferring instead to work late in the Catete Palace or the Guanabara Palace.[19] But there was one important social aspect of Vargas's character: he liked golf. Indeed, he used the golf course as a mobile office. Even in times of national or international crisis, he was able to get in a round of golf each week. Although Vargas was not by any stretch of the imagination an accomplished golfer, he recorded almost every round in his diary and enjoyed the peace and quiet of the course.[20]

Aranha, on the other hand, was outgoing, charismatic, and slightly crazy-looking, the kind of man who assumed the spotlight the moment he walked into any room. Physically, he could not have been more different than the president. Aranha was tall and handsome, with a full head of gray hair and passionate eyes that burned brightly. He loved being the center of attention, and he enjoyed the trappings of the formal dinners and banquets that the foreign ministry put on at the Itamaraty Palace for diplomats and other foreign guests. By 1938, Aranha had already shown himself to be equally at home with a range of political leaders, leading intellectuals, and cultural icons—from President Franklin D. Roosevelt to Walt Disney. In truth, Aranha regarded himself as an intellectual, or

at the very least the equal of men like Waldo Frank. Following a meeting
with Aranha, Frank summed him up: "Within the brilliant volubility of
his speech are intuitive perceptions that disarm you. He is a gay man,
a lover of high living, of horses and, I suspect (like all Brazilians), of
women. He gives the impression of well ordered madness: of a mad energy on a rail."[21]

Frank, like many other intellectuals, was seduced by Aranha's energy
and gusto, though he understood all too well that Aranha was something of a rascal and an operator. Aranha knew how to make people feel
important. When Frank visited Rio in 1942, Aranha arranged for his
plane to be met at Rio's Santos Dumont Airport by a large delegation of
journalists, photographers, intellectuals, and representatives of the foreign ministry. The head of the international office of the foreign ministry
informed Frank on the tarmac he was "the guest of honor of Brazil."[22]
Lots of American VIPs received the same red carpet treatment when
they arrived in Rio during World War II, and each reception was carefully choreographed by the Brazilian foreign ministry. The American film
producer and actor Orson Welles, whom Aranha befriended while Welles
was shooting a film in Brazil during the war, wrote a typically verbose and
edgy tribute to the foreign minister as part of his introduction for a joint
Thanksgiving national radio broadcast to America:

> Here's a passionately honest statesman, an eloquently indiscreet diplo-
> matist who looks you in the eye and talks straight from the shoulder . . .
> a great American—who wears easily and with style the authentic mag-
> nificence of the history maker. You know what he looks like, then—those
> twinkly shrewd eyes have taken yours from the pages of magazines and
> newspapers, honest eyes that appraise and appreciate.
>
> Dr. Aranha is that rarest of public figures, a handsome man who looks
> like you could trust him. They certainly trust him in Washington and
> you've probably heard all about his popularity there when he was his
> country's ambassador . . .
>
> Osvaldo Aranha is many things plus. First off, he's a hero, a real one
> straight out of Brazil's modern revolution. Crowds have been known to
> carry him through the streets of Rio. He understands how to shoot a gun
> and he's also realized what it is like to be shot at.[23]

Orson Welles, a man who liked the sound of his own voice, then quickened his pace, putting on a thick cowboy accent. Reaching a crescendo, Welles recommended that the United States listen to this patriotic, clever, and down-to-earth leader. For many Americans who listened to the radio show, this was the first time they had heard the name Osvaldo Aranha. Welles, for all his theatrical language and silly voices, had done Aranha, and Brazil, a great service.

Welles's wartime radio introduction was spot-on regarding one point: in Washington, where Aranha had previously served as the Brazilian ambassador, he was regarded as the Americans' "main man" in South America, and he could rely on the direct support of the White House. The British understood this point very clearly. Yet the British, due in part to competition with the United States over trade links with Brazil, were less complimentary about Aranha's character than American celebrities such as Frank and Welles. As the British embassy in Rio put it:

> Senhor Aranha has charm and a very quick intelligence, but his desire to please and a native optimism lead him often into assurances which are not to be taken too literally. He has kept many valuable contacts in the United States of America, remains steadily devoted to the development of close relations with that country, and may be counted the most important agent of United States influence in South America.[24]

Whatever shortcomings the British may have thought he had, Aranha possessed a rare gift at the time in Brazil, and in South America more broadly: he had a world vision. Not just a vague idea, but also a set of goals for his country and a road map for how best to get there. He saw where Brazil currently fit into South America and the wider world, and he wanted to change its position in both spheres. In this, Aranha was markedly different from his old friend Vargas. The president was a national leader, and he spent his working days trying to dismantle Brazil's powerful old elites and manage the country's shifting coalitions. It would be an exaggeration to suggest that the nation was ungovernable, for it was not. Ruling it was, however, a full-time job, and one to which Vargas was completely dedicated. He, like Aranha, had a sense of how Brazil could fit into the regional and international systems. Aranha, however, had a clear plan of how best to achieve this vision, while Vargas, bogged down in balancing Brazil's shifting domestic coalitions, did not. Vargas, in a sense, was blind to everything but the immediate political imperatives of running the country; for everything beyond that, he relied heavily on Aranha and Alzira, who helped him see distant threats, challenges, and possibilities of which he might otherwise not have been aware.

The Vargas-Aranha alliance had problems even before the events of June and July 1938. "There were numerous times that these two friends fought and made up," Alzira admitted.[25] There was a sense, too, among many of Vargas's loyalists that one day Aranha, whose pro-democracy views were to the left of Vargas's, would try to assume power for himself. Indeed, during the Dutra-Aranha crisis of 1938 there were suspicions among some Vargas supporters that Aranha was trying to become a focal point for Brazilian pro-democracy groups that were dissatisfied with the authoritarian Estado Novo. There was a palpable sense of relief at the Guanabara Palace when Aranha agreed to return to the fold and continue to lead Brazil's foreign policy.

The feeling of relief at Aranha's return to the foreign ministry was shared across town at the American embassy. The US ambassador, Jefferson Caffery, had arrived in Rio in 1937 from his previous appointment as ambassador to Cuba. In May 1938, Caffery was feeling pretty pleased with his life in Rio, gloating that, after much searching, he had managed to find himself an excellent house—not quite as nice as the Argentine ambassador's residence, he acknowledged, but a place whose owner had at least "refused to rent it to the British ambassador."[26] The ambassador's comments said much about the diplomatic pecking order in Rio. Brazil's historic rival, Argentina, occupied the pole position, while the American delegation was looking to put one over on their British rivals in the city.

Caffery was a southern gentleman, a trained lawyer, and a career diplomat who was well trusted and liked inside the State Department.[27] Tall, well-dressed, and polished, he was nevertheless something of a whiner, consistently complaining in official dispatches to the State Department about poor conditions in Rio.[28] Despite his complaints, however, Caffery regarded his posting as the most important one in South America and did not take kindly to anyone who tried to undermine his authority.

The British were quite naturally suspicious and hostile to Caffery. "He could do no wrong as far as the State Department was concerned,"[29] complained Sir Noel Charles, the British ambassador to Rio, who also took issue with Caffery's Irish extraction and Roman Catholic faith. The foreign office was equally down on Caffery, and sent a calming note to Charles. It had been carefully worded; earlier drafts were marked up with much stronger anti-Caffery sentiments written, in pencil, by officials who had dealt directly with him during his time in Cuba. "You have my sympathy in having as your colleague a person with such a character, which can only complicate the relations, already somewhat delicate, between our own and the American representatives in Latin America," the note to Charles said. "A consoling thought is that his predecessor was still more exasperating by all accounts."[30]

While Caffery was seemingly disinterested in smoothing over Anglo-American relations during his tenure in Brazil, he moved swiftly to show US support for both Vargas and Aranha. The events of May 11 had caught the Americans somewhat unawares, but President Roosevelt was quick to send to Vargas what the embassy files describe as "a telegram of felicitation upon his escape from the attempt on his life."[31] The subsequent arrests of the Integralistas and the crisis between Dutra and Aranha had all been closely monitored by the Americans, as had the Germans' reactions to these events. Caffery may have been quick to dismiss the British as serious rivals to US interests in Brazil, but he most certainly did not underestimate the Germans or Adolf Hitler's desire to develop closer ties with the Brazilian regime. The increase in Brazilian trade links with Germany and Berlin's massive rearmament program, along with its willingness to provide Brazil with arms, made the Germans a serious threat to US efforts in Brazil.

In reality, despite the strong trade links between the two countries, Brazilian-German relations had been in something of crisis of their own, due in no small part to the Brazilian government's decision to restrict foreign political activities in Brazil. Decree 383 had been signed by Vargas on April 18, 1938, and was intended to stop all foreign political activity in the country, but was mainly directed against German activity in the south of Brazil. The arrest of German nationals in the police roundup following the events of May 11 proved too much for the German ambassador, who demanded a meeting with Aranha in which he officially protested the arrests and Decree 383. The minister of foreign affairs coolly informed the ambassador, "The government will decline to modify Decree 383 of

April 18, and if Germans were arrested in connection with 'the putsch,' there was undoubtedly good reason therefore."[32] The German ambassador left Aranha's office pausing only to nod to Caffery, who was waiting, next in line, for a meeting with Aranha. "In my opinion, there was some German connection with the putsch, Aranha confidentially informed Caffery at the start of their meeting."[33] The unofficial German line was that if they had been involved, the outcome of the events of May 11 would have been very different. It is difficult to know what wounded the Germans most—the implication that they were involved in the plot, or that they were accused of involvement in such a poorly organized and inefficient operation.

Back at the Guanabara Palace, Vargas was relieved that the major fallout from the events of May 11 was essentially restricted to internal politics. His focus could now shift back to the future, and he could enjoy a bit of free time—enough for a round of golf and, at night, a cigar and whiskey. Vargas had good reason to feel contented with events. He had managed to keep his two key ministers in the cabinet. His authority within the Brazilian armed forces remained strong, and the establishment of the Estado Novo in November 1937 appeared to have solidified his support among the leading officers of the military. He had not had to use either his preexisting or new powers to crush the Integralista movement, as he had done with the communists after their moment in November 1935. The Intregralistas simply ceased to exist as a major national movement after 1938. One of the major leaders of the movement, Plínio Salgado, who was reported to have been "overcome with excitement" when he heard news of the uprising of May 11, was not even arrested.[34] Instead he went into voluntary exile, sailing to Portugal and a position at Coimbra University in 1939.

Naturally, Vargas's failure to crush the Intregralistas, combined with the disorganized nature of the rebellion, led to a great many conspiracy theories; for years, Brazilians would debate whether the president himself had been behind the attack. He had certainly gained from the attempted putsch in more ways than one, consolidating his own power even further while winning a great deal of international praise for his bravery and his handling of the aftermath of the rebellion.

Perhaps most importantly (and ironically), the failed uprising had burnished the reputation of Vargas's dictatorship. The Estado Novo, which many countries had been nervous about when Vargas declared it in November 1937, enjoyed new legitimacy in the offices of the leaders of the most powerful nations in the world following May 11. This legitimacy was due in no small part to the support of President Roosevelt, who continued to believe that Brazil's attitude toward the United States—and not its system of government—was the most important factor in developing ties with it. Later, the American diplomat George Kennan came to articulate this important American policy in a more scientific manner. As Kennan put it in his report PPS/35, written about the Cold War, "the domestic character of a government was less important than its international behavior."[35] This tenet of realpolitik, along with the fact that Brazil was an extremely important target for the Germans, Italians, and Japanese—all of whom had large immigrant colonies there—made the American stakes in Brazil very high indeed.

Brazil was about to find itself in a position of even greater power. Guided by his two eyes, Alzira and Osvaldo, Vargas would have the historic opportunity to convert his homeland from a backward, divided nation into the new economic and political powerhouse of South America. This was to be a high-stakes, diplomatic rollercoaster, which would transform Brazil in ways that even the visionary Osvaldo Aranha had not foreseen.

# PART TWO:
## BRAZILIAN NEUTRALITY

3

# DANGEROUS GAMES

O N SEPTEMBER 1, 1939, DARKNESS HAD ALREADY FALLEN in Rio as
Osvaldo Aranha's car set out from the Itamaraty Palace to make its
3.4-mile drive to the Guanabara Palace. The car sped out of the foreign
ministry and headed east along Avenida President Vargas. Going in the opposite direction was the most direct route to get to the Guanabara Palace,
but the easterly direction was the more scenic, and Aranha preferred it—
even if it often took nearly twenty minutes and kept the president waiting
for longer than necessary.[1] The evening traffic was heavy in downtown Rio,
and the pace of the traffic was further slowed by broken-down vehicles,
minor accidents, and—the real scourge to Rio's drivers—road construction.
In September 1939, Avenida President Vargas was a straight, two-lane
road, which ran from east to west and acted as one of the major link roads
across the city. The volume of traffic in Rio, however, was simply too much
for the two lanes to bear. Traffic congestion was a constant problem across
Rio, and the leaders of the Estado Novo had ambitious plans to resolve it.

Prime among Vargas's goals for Rio was a plan to widen Avenida
President Vargas to match the scale of major European boulevards. Vargas
oversaw this effort personally, including the plan for demolishing over five
hundred buildings along the avenue and incorporating this space into the
roadway as two new side lanes. The buildings that were to be knocked
down included city hall, four churches, and Praça Onze, the central square
and home to the city's Carnaval celebrations. The finished avenue, which
was scheduled to open in 1944, aimed to give the city a hugely impressive
central throughway, which was to be a symbol of the Estado Novo and its
public works program.

Aranha's car turned right off Avenida President Vargas and entered
Avenida Rio Branco. "All streets in this city start at the Avenida Rio

Branco," Stefan Zweig, the Jewish writer, would soon declare after seeking refuge in Rio, and in 1939 this was no exaggeration.[2] Driving along the Rio Branco, one of the most splendid streets in Rio, Aranha's car passed the city's beautiful opera house, the national library (with a collection of books borrowed from Portugal), as well as one of the best hotels in the city. The avenue had been transformed at the beginning of the twentieth century, and its new buildings dominated the remaining smaller, older ones. From one side of the avenue ran the roads to Rio's harbor. There, luxury passenger liners from countries around the globe were berthed next to merchant ships flying the Nazi flag. These German merchantmen had come to Rio by way of Lisbon, and their cargos—many of them secretly containing arms—were carefully unloaded under the watchful eye of the police.

Avenida Rio Branco, like much of downtown Rio, was a work in progress in 1939. Given the rapid development of the city, it was already too narrow and had become something of a parking lot, with perennial bumper-to-bumper traffic. The resulting pollution was already having an impact on the limestone buildings, many of which looked older than they actually were. The grime disappeared somewhat at night, when Avenida Rio Branco, as if to live up to its name, was lit with powerful double-headed streetlights, out of which shone a brilliant white light that turned the avenue's buildings into a shadowy backdrop. There was a constant hum as the noise of the traffic bounced off the avenue's multistory buildings, some of which rose as high as six floors, making them among the first high-rises built in the city.

As Aranha passed along it in the mid-evening, the avenue's tree-lined, mosaic-patterned sidewalks would have been filled with pedestrians, well-dressed but tired and weary, many of them waiting for taxis and buses to take them home from their workplaces in the city center. Tracks for Rio's open-sided electric trams cut across the avenue's junctions, the trams full of passengers already on their way out for the night, with others hitching a free ride by hanging precariously to the tram's back and sides. "Tram cruising," as it was known, was frowned on by the authorities, but the police turned a blind eye to it, and for each paying passenger there could be as many as twice that number hanging on to the open window frames.

After pushing through the avenue's traffic, Aranha's car headed southwest past the official presidential palace, the Catete Palace, and toward the Guanabara Palace where Vargas held his evening meetings. This night, however, was unusual: the world war that Vargas had long anticipated was now, finally, in the offing.

Neither Vargas nor Aranha was surprised by the German attack on Poland. President Roosevelt had warned Brazil of the probability of a major European war for some time, and Aranha and Vargas were also well informed by the Brazilian embassies in Berlin, Rome, Paris, London, and Lisbon about developments in Europe and Hitler's expansionist agenda. Aranha understood that these were going to be uncertain times for Brazil, as the country's longtime trading partner, Germany, found new ways to provoke its other allies, Great Britain and the United States. Aranha had outlined the dangers from the Axis countries to Brazil in a personal letter, written on November 8, 1938, which he had sent to the US undersecretary of state, Sumner Welles. Aranha deemed the contents of the letter so sensitive that he did not send it in the usual manner, by means of the Brazilian ambassador in Washington, but instead used US ambassador Jefferson Caffery—even going so far as to make clear that he did not wish for the letter's contents to be shared with the Brazilian ambassador.[3] Caffery warned Welles about the content of the letter in a covering note, explaining that tensions in Europe had only heightened Brazil's desire to arm itself. "Since the Munich Conference," Caffery explained from Rio, "the impression has gained ground here that protection is needed in case of European aggression and [Brazil] must, therefore, build up [its] own armies and navies."[4]

In his letter to Welles, Aranha succinctly outlined Axis intentions in Brazil and Latin America. Hitler, he warned, envisaged the following:

a. Fomenting disorders, revolutions, and civil wars, in order to justify an intervention similar to that in Spain.

b. Dominating, by means of an *Anschluss* (political annexation) extending across the Atlantic, regions populated by Germans.

c. If the above were impossible, obtaining at least political concessions such as would permit them to maintain their political parties, as in their own countries, developed around their colonies and interests, thus retarding but not abandoning their future domination.

Aranha's comparison of Brazil to Spain spoke mountains of his appraisal of the German threat. In Spain, Germans had armed and sent forces to help the cause of General Francisco Franco's Nationalists in their war against the Republicans.

Surely the Germans' support for the Integralistas was at the forefront of Aranha's mind as he stressed that his concerns were based on concrete proof. "The documentary evidence leaves no doubt," he assured Welles, "as to the organization, activities, and purposes of Germany in Brazil, and as to the participation of German diplomatic agents in Uruguay and the Argentine in this work against the innermost economy and sovereignty of our countries."[5]

Aranha's letter was mostly a pitch for American arms, which had not been forthcoming, and which the minister believed were essential for both Brazil's defense and the foreign policy orientation of the Brazilian regime. He went on to suggest that the Axis powers were "unsatisfied countries," which needed colonies, areas of culture, resources, and zones of expansion. It was not possible to further divide Old Europe, nor to further divide Africa to create a German colony there. He concluded, "South America is natural prey because:

1. It is where there exists good and underdeveloped land;
2. Its fabulous mineral wealth is still to be utilized;
3. It is a source of basic raw materials;
4. An invasion is already facilitated by reason of zones of racial influence, and even of economic industrial and commercial predominance;
5. It is a continent of completely unarmed nations;
6. It is the formula most acceptable to European opinion for the solution of the colonial problem, one England wishes to defend before all her own colonies."[6]

Brazil's geography, resources, and heavy concentrations of German nationals put it at risk of a Nazi invasion, Aranha suggested, but the most pointed of his critiques was aimed squarely at Brazil's relative defenselessness. Without a stronger military equipped with up-to-date weapons, Aranha hinted, his government would have very little means of defending itself against another German-backed putsch.

The plea for American arms was somewhat negated by the plentiful supply of German weaponry to Brazil. The United States was aware that

German weapons and war material were flowing into Brazil, and while Roosevelt was not as concerned as his British allies about the prospect of this advanced military hardware being used against Vargas by the allegedly pro-Nazi elements in Brazil's armed forces, he was enough of a political realist to see that a country already receiving weapons from Germany—with which the United States already had a contentious relationship—did not need his help on this front, as well.

These German arms shipments had been negotiated by Aranha's local political enemies, war minister Eurico Gaspar Dutra and General Góes Monteiro, the mighty head of the Brazilian armed forces. Góes Monteiro's admiration for the German war machine had become all the stronger following his extended visit to the country, when he had witnessed first-hand the scale and quality of its military industrial complex. The weapons deal was proof that Góes Monteiro and Dutra's political sympathies were leaning toward the Axis powers. But while this confirmed Allied suspicions that the Brazilian military was in the pocket of the Germans, it also offered Aranha and other pro-democracy elements in the Vargas administration an opportunity to advance their own foreign policy agenda.

Aranha's letter to Welles was a call for the Americans to help him realize his dream of a stronger partnership between the two nations. Without tangible American military and economic support, he feared, Dutra and Góes Monteiro's more pro-Nazi vision for Brazil's future would prevail. For now, however, he needed to reassure President Vargas that a partnership with the United States was still possible given recent international developments, and to convince him that it was the best way to maximize Brazil's political and economic gain from the increasingly perilous situation in Europe.

By the time he had left his ministerial car and headed up the steps to the Guanabara Palace on September 1, Aranha had already decided that he would adopt a careful listen-and-watch approach with the president, rather than spelling out his own vision. It was a sound strategy, given Vargas's state. Inside the palace, Aranha found the president tired, having just finished a lengthy meeting with the minister of farming about the continued exportation of Brazilian coffee during a war.[7]

While Germany's invasion of Poland had not yet precipitated a broader conflict, Vargas and Aranha knew it was only a matter of time until the fire spread. Great Britain and France were both allies of the overrun nation, and while they had scrupulously avoided a confrontation with Germany over issues such as its unlawful rearmament following the Versailles Treaty and its annexation of Czechoslovakia and Austria, this latest act of German aggression was a step too far. The French and British simply could not ignore such a brazen attack on one of their client states, and there was a strong likelihood that, once they stepped in to defend Poland, the United States would be drawn into the fight as well.

Vargas's meeting with Aranha was primarily an opportunity for the president to catch up on information about the dramatic, late-breaking international events, as well as a chance to prepare for the full cabinet meeting that Vargas had scheduled for 2 P.M. the following day.[8] Both men understood that, at that meeting, Brazil would formally declare its neutrality in the war. Even before hostilities had broken out in Europe, Vargas and Aranha had both made up their minds that Brazil would need to stay out of any conflict involving Nazi Germany; Rio did not have the military strength to participate in heavy fighting overseas, for one thing, but it also could not afford to risk losing its valuable economic relationship with Germany over a fight that—for the time being, at least—did not directly involve Brazil.

Given the lack of any other viable choice, both Vargas and Aranha presumed, correctly, that the rest of the cabinet would go along with their decision to stay out of the onrushing conflict. The more pressing question was how best to align Brazil's foreign policy so as to maximize its returns. With huge foreign debt problems and with the United States and Germany as its two most important trading partners, Brazil stood to gain substantially from the increased tensions between them, but also had much to lose. The opportunities to continue trading openly with the Axis powers would be greatly reduced in wartime, for instance, not least because Brazil expected the British navy to blockade its ports so as to deny Germany access to Brazilian exports. Vargas and Aranha both knew that Brazil's prewar "cloak and dagger" strategy of developing closer ties with both the Americans and the Germans for the benefit of the national economy was likely to be unsustainable in the medium to long term.

The Brazilian ambassador to Washington, Mário de Pimentel Brandão, had warned Aranha the previous year, "We have to decide: the United States or Germany."[9] While Aranha clearly favored the United States (and was deeply suspicious of Nazi Germany), he did not want to completely burn his bridges with the Axis powers. Aranha understood that the importance of Brazilian-German trade was so great to Brazil that there would be major economic implications if it ceased. He wanted to avoid having to make the choice of one country over the other, as Brandão advocated, until it was absolutely necessary to do so. Until then, Brazil could effectively stall for time by playing the United States and Germany against one another—a dangerous game, to be sure, but an enormously profitable one as long as it lasted.

For the time being, Aranha advised Vargas that Brazil conduct "business as usual." Vargas agreed. He, too, wanted to avoid placing all Brazil's eggs in one basket until he had no choice but to do so.[10] Caffery would neatly sum up the rationale for Brazil's policy, noting that by taking this approach, "it could squeeze the maximum out of the United States on the one hand and the fascist powers on the other."[11] But Caffery could not know what the next stage of Brazil's strategy might be—or that it hoped to someday throw its lot in with the United States entirely.

Vargas saw that Brazil's long-term future was more contingent on its relations with the United States than with Germany, but he keenly understood the pitfalls of cozying up to Washington. A strong alliance with the United States made the most sense from a geostrategic perspective; after all, the two countries were much closer than Brazil and Germany, and President Roosevelt had made it clear that he desired a close and supportive relationship with Latin America—unlike Germany, which as far as Vargas could tell was in bed with his domestic enemies. For Vargas, the crux of the problem was how best to move toward the American camp without Brazil—and his regime—becoming vulnerable to heightened levels of US influence. On this point, there was clear blue water between Vargas and Aranha. Brazil's minister of foreign affairs did not view the issue of growing US influence with the same degree of concern as did Vargas.

The intimate meeting on the evening of September 1 ended earlier than most. Having discussed the international situation and prepared for the next day's cabinet meeting, both men wanted a relatively early night so as to be ready for the next day. Alzira walked the minister out of the building. Lost in their thoughts and fears, neither spoke much. As they parted, they exchanged the traditional farewell, "*até amanhã*" (until tomorrow).

At exactly 2 P.M. the next day, September 2, President Vargas banged on the table of the cabinet room in the Catete Palace and called the meeting to order. Being punctual was not a Brazilian trait, but all the ministers had managed to arrive on time for the crucial meeting. As usual, each minister had a pad of paper and an ashtray in front of him. Most ministers smoked both inside the room and outside in the hallway, where they had gathered before the meeting in twos and threes to discuss events. Vargas sat at the head of the table, with Aranha two seats down on his right. The cabinet room was smoky, and there was much clearing of throats and coughing as the meeting started.

There was only one item on the agenda: Brazil's response to the international crisis. Vargas spoke first, outlining in his quiet bureaucratic manner the impact of the German invasion of Poland and the likelihood of Great Britain and France joining the war. Vargas added at the end, "While the war might appear to be remote, its impact on Brazil will be felt in all sectors of the state." Aranha's remarks followed the president's and went into more detail about the challenges facing the government. "Brazil will need to position itself with care, and we must make sure we are clear in what we need, and want, from the war, which will have no doubt regional and international consequences for the country," he explained. After these opening remarks, each minister was given an opportunity to address the meeting. It soon became clear that the consensus was to go along with Vargas's proposal of Brazilian neutrality.[12] The meeting finished at 4:30 P.M., and as the ministers filed out, Vargas was already working on a public statement explaining the Brazilian position.

The key to Brazilian neutrality was the position of the United States, and Vargas remained nervous about the potential impact of heightened American political and cultural influence in Brazil. The president worked long into the evening after returning to the Guanabara Palace. Using his colored pencils, he continued to map out Brazil's future development and what he would be able to get from the war. Vargas also gave careful consideration to how the war might affect Brazil's major internal problem—the question of what to do with the large foreign immigrant groups that had settled in Brazil. One of the major rationales for the establishment of the Estado Novo in 1937 had been the desire to create a more nationalist and centralized Brazilian state. But a unified Brazil had yet to materialize.

The country's immigrant populations had not fully integrated into Brazilian society.[13] They had brought with them their own political organizations, newspapers, schools, and radio stations. Radio was an especially powerful tool in Brazil during the 1930s. Indeed, Vargas himself used it often and to great effect in getting his message across to the nation. While President Roosevelt did only a couple of radio broadcasts a year, Vargas used it on a weekly basis. But he was not the only person projecting a political message across Brazil's airwaves. People turning on a Brazilian radio before 1938 would have heard all kinds of languages broadcast on the air: Yiddish, German, Italian, Polish, and even Japanese. These foreign-language radio shows allowed immigrant groups to stay connected, and many were hugely popular among their target groups.

After 1938, the state attempted to curb the insularity of Brazil's immigrant groups by forcing their assimilation into Brazilian society. Vargas worried about what the perceived "dual loyalty" of these immigrant groups, particularly the large German and Italian communities, might mean for Brazil during wartime. A report from the US embassy in Rio in 1937 confirmed that the Italian and German governments were attempting to stoke the nationalism of their expatriate communities in Brazil. The US embassy outlined in detail the methods the Nazis used to teach fascist ideology in Brazil's German schools,[14] few of which offered lessons in Portuguese, and none of which had a Brazilian curriculum. German- and Italian-run businesses, too, were targeted by "both fascist and Nazi agents in the numerous fascist and Nazi societies" in Brazil, the embassy's report continued:

> The local Nazi as well as fascist agents, including the German and Italian consuls, are known to keep black lists of Germans and Italians who are not in sympathy with [the] political creed of Hitler and Mussolini, and that every effort is made to bring these dissenting individuals into line by inducing loyal German and Italian fascists to refrain from doing business with them.[15]

Brazil, to hear the Americans tell it, was teeming with acolytes of Hitler and Mussolini—a prospect that could not but worry Vargas, who was no doubt still smarting from the role the Germans and Italians had played in the recent Integralista putsch.

The German ambassador, Karl Ritter, who had arrived in Rio the same year as Caffery, was quick to dismiss such accusations against the German colony. In an interview with the Brazilian press in late 1937 he claimed,

"As far as the German colony is concerned, it is composed of orderly, in-
dustrious men, hard workers, who have contributed much to the prosperity
of their adapted country."[16] Despite Ritter's reassurances, however, both
Vargas and Aranha had long feared that Hitler would use the country's
large German colony to undermine Brazilian neutrality in the event of a
world war.

From 1938 onward, Vargas tried to preempt any German plot to med-
dle in Brazilian politics by banning foreign political parties and agents
from operating in Brazil, closing down radio stations, and insisting on
the use of Portuguese in schools. Decree 383 of April 18, 1938, seemingly
spelled this out clearly by stipulating the following: "Foreigners domiciled
in the national territory and those temporary established therein shall
not be allowed to exercise any activity of a political nature nor intervene
directly or indirectly in the public affairs of the country." Article two, part
three, of the decree was aimed primarily at Nazi activities. It stated, "They
are specifically forbidden to raise flags, pennants, standards, uniforms,
badges, insignia, or any symbols of a foreign political party."[17]

The United States was acutely aware of the threat that fascism posed
to its international interests, and in a report to the State Department in
1938, Jefferson Caffery had credited Vargas for this tough stance against
Axis elements in Brazil. "The vigorous anti-Nazi campaign now being
conducted by the Brazilian authorities, a campaign which is in direct con-
tradiction to the previous historical attitude of the government of Brazil to
the German minority in this country, is due largely to the changed point
of view of President Vargas," Caffery noted. Whereas previous Brazilian
administrations had been accommodating toward Germany, the Estado
Novo took a position that was much more amendable to the United States.
As Caffery put it, "President Vargas has now become convinced that it is
not conducive to the welfare of Brazil to permit Nazi activities here."[18]

Even as Caffery applauded Brazilian efforts to tackle the problem,
however, Germany, Italy, and Japan had all been increasing their efforts
to develop ties with their respective communities in Brazil.[19] At the start
of 1939, the German community in Rio Grande do Sul still held Nazi
parades, complete with uniforms, flags, and military drills. Such activities took place openly and were often watched by large and enthusiastic
crowds. Alert to the evolving threat, Washington was constantly demanding more information from Caffery about fascist activities in Brazil and

about the country's immigrant communities in general, information that Caffery was not always able to provide.

Following one such request from the State Department, Caffery summoned American consular officials around Brazil for a conference in Rio to discuss German and Italian activity in Brazil. These foreign servicemen were asked for detailed analysis of activities in their respective areas. The meeting revealed a number of black holes in American intelligence gathering in Brazil. Following a request from Washington for statistical information of the numbers and breakdown of the various immigrant communities in Brazil, Caffery wrote, "there is a complete dearth of this type of information," admitting that "accurate information will only be available after the next census, which is to be held in 1940."[20] The Americans were not alone in their inability to properly assess the size of Brazil's immigrant communities. The British foreign office had no accurate information either, apart from data from the previous census in 1920. The political department of the British foreign office made an approximate calculation and estimated that Brazil contained 220,000 Germans, 800,000 Italians, and 280,000 Japanese, out of a national population of roughly forty million.[21] These were simply guesses, however. Nobody, including the Brazilian authorities, had any reliable information on just how many foreign immigrants were living in Brazil—a fact that greatly concerned the Americans, the British, and, not least, President Vargas himself.

Great Britain, like the United States, welcomed Vargas's efforts to tackle the problem of potentially destabilizing immigrant populations after 1938. British embassy officials dispatched to check on the German community in Rio Grande do Sul discovered that Brazilian political police were having some success in stopping the overtly pro-Nazi activities of German expatriates in the region.[22] The success rate was no more than 50 percent, however, "owing," the British claimed, "to the inefficiency of the police machinery."[23] British officials also noted that because German immigrants were by and large well educated, in contrast to much of the local Brazilian population (British estimates at the time suggested that 80 percent of Brazilians were illiterate), Germans occupied the leading positions in society.[24] A great proportion of Brazil's industry and agriculture was controlled by Axis-born citizens and their descendants, and the government was reluctant to take effective action against them for fear of damaging the state's economy.[25] Ironically, Germans' high positions in Brazil had the effect of making many of them more conservative than they might otherwise have been. Despite Nazi regimentation, German immigrants were somewhat held back by the fear of the repercussion any unsuccessful actions would have on their economic position in society.[26]

Events in Europe had only made Brazil's German question more dire. As German troops continued their advance into Poland, Vargas understood that he would need to keep an even closer eye on the Axis groups in Brazil. His commitment to tracking pro-Nazi elements in the country would become even more crucial—for both Brazil's internal politics and its international relations—in the days ahead.

September 3, 1939, was a beautiful winter morning in Rio. The weather forecast had warned of showers during the day, but the deep blue sky and bright sunshine indicated otherwise. It was a holiday in Brazil, part of a weeklong festival known as *Semana da Pátria*, a celebration of the government's achievements and a chance for the population to say "thank you" to the regime. Later in the day, some twenty thousand youths marched through Rio in a demonstration of Brazil's sporting prowess.[27] Vargas, who always watched the annual parade from a specially constructed podium, called it "a magnificent show."[28]

As Vargas enjoyed lunch in the Guanabara Palace following the parade, Cariocas, residents of Rio, were heading out to the city's beaches for a day of relaxation. Flamengo Beach, the beach closest to the palace, provided tourists and Cariocas alike with a stunning view of the mouth of Guanabara Bay, one of the largest and most famous bays in the world. Traveling through Rio in the 1930s, Waldo Frank described it as "a pause, deep blue, where sun and hill and sea have come together. . . . A conch of mountain melting into sea, a sea compressed by hills into a single sapphire, model the bay into a vision that touches the sense like a loved woman's breast; that overwhelms as the touch of a breast may be overwhelming."[29]

Viewed through the prism of Rio's natural splendor, the trouble across the ocean in Europe must have seemed a world away—even to a man as fixated on the turmoil as President Vargas, who after signing the decree on Brazilian neutrality still found time to go for a scenic ride through Rio.[30] Yet the international pressure that had been building over the past decade was about to reach its point of rupture—and its neutrality aside, Brazil would be swept up in the coming explosion just as surely as the rest of the planet.

Rio's newspapers had been full of developments from Europe, but the biggest news of all had yet to arrive. On September 3, Cariocas expected to learn at any moment that Great Britain and France had declared war on Germany, the only logical result of their alliance with Poland and Hitler's long campaign of aggression toward the Western democracies. And sure enough, the airwaves erupted with the news that the long-feared world war—the second in just three decades—had finally broken out.

Cariocas took the news of the war with their usual mixture of excitement and mild indifference. Europe appeared remote, but the older generation of men chatting in beachside cafes understood that navy ships of the warring powers were likely to come close to the shores of Brazil. Vargas's policy of Brazilian neutrality was warmly welcomed in Rio as a mature and sensible strategy. There was no appetite for war and little anti-Axis—let alone pro-Allied—sentiment could be detected among the masses heading out to the beaches. Cariocas were, in truth, more concerned about getting the first few days' worth of tanning on their skin before the start of the oppressive summer months from December.

On September 4, 1939, Vargas recorded in his diary without further comment, "the entrance of Britain and France into the war."[31] For the Brazilian president, the moment of truth had arrived. Vargas had long entertained grandiose plans for Brazil, but now events outside of his control had set those dreams within his reach. If he could maintain his trading relationships with both the United States and Germany, Brazil would be able to continue to grow and modernize even in the midst of a global war. Vargas saw no need to follow the advice of his ambassador in Washington by choosing between Brazil's two largest trading partners; the United States, he knew, could help transform the Brazilian economy, while German arms could make the Brazilian armed forces the strongest military on the continent, and cutting off either party would only set back Brazil's progress. By keeping both parties guessing as to his allegiances, Vargas could continue to reap benefits from both. If he played his cards wrong, of course, he might lose one—or even both—of his lucrative alliances, and watch his hopes for Brazil die with them.

Osvaldo Aranha spent the day after the declaration of war in his office in the Itamaraty Palace, where he could gaze out his window at the palace's beautiful garden and swimming pool. He still had much work to do before Brazil's position of neutrality was official. At the last minute, minor changes had been made to the Brazilian decree outlining the government's position. The changes were legalistic in nature, but a tired Aranha had an argument with Vargas's secretary at the Catete Palace over the exact wording of the decree. Once the decree had been finally agreed, Aranha started the process of officially informing the warring parties and the Americans of Brazil's position.

None of the ambassadors with whom Aranha spoke raised any formal objection to the position of the Brazilian government. On the contrary, they all welcomed Brazil's statement of neutrality in the hope that they would be able to continue to develop their influence within the country. Great Britain and Germany, along with the United States, hoped that the onset of war would not prevent them from developing further trade links with Brazil. In private, all three countries received assurances by members of the Brazilian government that this was very much the hope of Brazil as well.

## 4

# A SHOT ACROSS THE BOW

THE WAR IN EUROPE BEGAN WITH A SERIES of impressive and rapid German victories. The German army swiftly overran Poland, and on September 27, 1939, Warsaw surrendered. On April 9, 1940, the Germans attacked the Scandinavian countries of Denmark and Norway. The Danes surrendered the same day, but the Norwegians bravely held out for two months before surrendering on June 9. After the invasion of northern Europe, Germany turned its attention to the west, launching attacks on Belgium, the Netherlands, and Luxembourg on May 10, 1940; the German Wehrmacht occupied Luxembourg that same day, and Holland surrendered on May 14. Two weeks later, on May 28, Belgium followed suit. The Germans—now backed by Italy, which had entered the war on June 10—then moved toward France.[1]

The Brazilians watched the war in Europe with increasing concern. Germany's stunning advances in Europe had deprived Brazil of hugely valuable trading markets. The loss of the markets for Brazilian exports was problematic enough, but there was also a growing feeling that the Axis powers would prevail in the European war: Germany and Italy were poised to overrun France, and there was a chance Spain would throw in its lot with the Axis as well. The evacuation of the defeated British forces from the Dunkirk beaches in France in late May and early June, meanwhile, was covered heavily in the Brazilian press, further dampening any optimism about the Allies' prospects. Unless the United States entered the war, the consensus in Brazil was that once the Germans were finished with France, they would overrun Great Britain as well.

With the Allied position in Europe collapsing, President Vargas decided it was time to remind Washington not to take Brazil for granted, nor to forget its trading partner's needs. Benito Mussolini's decision for

Italy to join the Axis had amplified Brazilian fears about unruly immigrant populations—Brazil's Italian population, in one estimation, being second in number only to the Portuguese population—and this development, as well as Germany's spate of recent military victories, put more pressure on Brazil to abandon its relations with the United States and side with the Axis. Vargas needed to make clear to President Roosevelt that any further trade with Brazil would come at a steep price. Vargas chose a high-profile event in Rio, at which several US officials would be in attendance, to make his move. The timing of his address, coming the day after Italy joined the war, was no coincidence.

June 11, 1940, was a perfect late-autumnal morning in Rio. Tradition-ally, the autumn and winter months brought the city much less rainfall than the more tropical summer season, which ran from December through the new year to Carnaval in late February. There were only a few scattered wispy clouds in an otherwise clear sky, the temperature was a pleasant eighteen degrees Celsius, and the sea was almost totally calm, with a slight swell at the water's edge. Conditions could not have been better for Brazil's annual Navy Day.

In Rio's harbor, anchored offshore at the entry to Guanabara Bay, sat most of Brazil's naval fleet. Its flagship, the *Minas Gerais,* glistened impres-sively in the sunlight, its deeply tanned officers turned out in immaculately pressed white dress uniforms complete with colorful medal ribbons. Senior officers from other ships in the fleet had assembled on the flagship's deck for a celebratory lunch, and stood around smoking as they awaited the arrival of their commander in chief.

Vargas had worked on his speech late into the previous evening. When the text was complete, he showed it to Alzira, who was busily decoding classified diplomatic cables for her father in the presidential secretary's office. Vargas had also discussed the contents of the speech with Góes Monteiro, telling the general, "one has to shake the tree vigorously to get the dead leaves to fall." Vargas meant to shake things up a little and re-mind the Americans that he and Brazil should not be taken for granted.[2] Góes Monteiro could hardly contain his joy at the contents of the speech and its likely impact on Brazil's American friends. While he had run his message past these two confidants, however, Vargas had not discussed the speech with his minister of foreign affairs, Osvaldo Aranha, for fear that Aranha would inform the Americans of the contents of the speech, thereby reducing its impact.[3]

It wasn't that the president didn't trust Aranha, it was simply that Vargas knew his foreign minster could not help himself when it came to forwarding information to Caffery in Rio or speaking directly to the State Department in Washington. Góes Monteiro shared Vargas's wariness of Aranha; despite their considerable political differences, the general enjoyed a close personal relationship with the foreign minister, yet he too thought it best not to alert Aranha to the speech. Vargas had also not shared its contents with any other member of his cabinet. This was most unusual for the president, who liked to take the temperature of his cabinet on important matters of state—and was all the more unusual given the importance of the speech and its likely implications for US-Brazilian relations.

Vargas's normal schedule had been suspended on June 11, and he spent the morning out of the office, beginning with a visit to the naval academy to meet the new officer recruits. He was then taken by motor launch out to the *Minas Gerais,* from which he watched a simulated air attack on the assembled warships. After speaking with senior officers, Vargas settled down with them to a full lunch. When the dessert was finished, Vargas, invigorated, rose to address the gathered officers.

Following the events of May 11, 1938, and the revelation of the navy's central role in the Integralista plot, Vargas had been careful to promote "right-minded" officers—those loyal to his regime—to senior roles in the navy. In November 1939, the navy's allegiance to the president was more secure, but most of its officers still favored developing ties with Germany, not the United States. On this day, Vargas selected for his audience those military officers who were pro-German, ensuring that they would be perfect for his message. Vargas started his address on a positive note:

> There are no longer any differences on this continent. We are united by bonds of close solidarity to all of the American nations in ideals and aspirations and in the common interest of our defense. We, and all humanity, are passing through a historical moment of grave repercussions resulting from rapid and violent changes in values. We are headed for a future different from anything we have known in the line of economic, social, or political organization, and we feel that the old systems and

antiquated formulas have entered into decline. It is not, however, the end of civilization as the pessimists and staunch conservatives claim, but the tumultuous and fruitful beginning of a new era. Vigorous peoples, ready to face life, must follow the line of their aspirations instead of wasting time in the contemplation of that which is tottering and falling in ruins. It is therefore necessary to understand our times and remove the hindrances of dead ideas and dead ideals. Political order is no longer made in the shadow of the vague rhetorical humanitarianism which sought to abolish frontiers and create an international society without characteristics or friction, united and fraternal, enjoying peace as a natural right and not as a day to day conquest. Instead of this panorama of balance and of just distribution of the world's riches we are witnessing the exasperation of nationalism, strong nations imposing their will by the sentiment of nationality and being sustained by the conviction of their superiority.[4]

President Vargas's observations about the challenges facing Brazil were ones that anyone in his audience would have agreed with, although his allusion to a "new era" surely left many of them guessing what this future might look like, and how Vargas planned to lead Brazil into it. They would not have long to wait.

After these opening remarks, Vargas changed his tack and moved to the portion of his speech that he knew would cause great offense in Washington and London. He spoke slowly, to give emphasis to his words. Brazil, he said:

Was witnessing the end of the era of improvident liberalism, sterile democracy where the power, emanating directly from the people and instituted for the defense of their interests, organizes labor—the source of national greatness—and not ways for private fortune. There is no longer room for regimes founded on privilege and class distinction; only those that incorporate the nation in the same duties and offer equitable social justice and opportunities in the struggle for life can survive.

The order created by new circumstances that are guiding nations is compatible with individualism, [specifically] at least when it clashes with the collective interest. It does not recognize rights, which interfere with obligations to the nations. Happily, in Brazil we have established a regime that is adequate for our necessities without imitating or affiliating itself with any of the current ideologies. It is a Brazilian regime of order and peace in accordance with the nature and traditions of our people, capable of bringing about more rapidly our general progress and of guaranteeing the security of all.[5]

Although Vargas claimed that the political ideology he was outlining was a uniquely Brazilian one, independent of the competing systems of the Allies and Axis, his comments carried a thinly veiled warning. In his call for Brazilians to make the state's interests their own, his seeming dismissal of individual rights, and his disparaging remarks about liberalism and democracy, Vargas was beginning to sound a lot like what Washington feared most—a fascist.

The initial response to Vargas's remarks was muted. The thirty-eight senior officers who attended the luncheon on board the *Minas Gerais* received Vargas's speech politely but without much visible support for the political vision he had outlined. The one foreigner present, the American chief of the naval mission in Rio, noted, "The speech was received with no enthusiasm and was not mentioned or discussed later within the party. There had seemed to be an air of expectancy, which was not satisfied, and the effect produced seemed more that of a lecture or scolding than of flag waving."[6] Yet while the officers were the immediate recipients of Vargas's message, they were not intended as its ultimate destination.

During his visit to the *Minas Gerais,* Vargas had gone out of his way to speak to the American naval officer aboard the ship, engaging him in conversation on two occasions.[7] The president appeared extremely keen for his speech to be widely reported internationally, giving permission to the Brazilian press to publish the speech in its entirety. He need not have worried, however. News of the speech reached Washington very quickly, and it had exactly the effect Vargas intended.

This was not quite the speech that the US State Department had hoped to hear from the main benefactor of its "good neighbor" program. That policy, after all, had been intended to draw Latin America into the US sphere of influence, thereby ensuring that the European dictatorships were not able to expand their influence in the region. The secretary of state, Cordell Hull, exploded when he heard the unconfirmed reports of the contents of Vargas's speech from the undersecretary of state, Sumner Welles. Hull immediately sought clarification from Caffery in Rio.

"President Vargas of Brazil in a public speech this afternoon has alluded to the European dictatorships in a complimentary manner," he wrote to the ambassador.[8]

At first, Caffery tried to downplay the importance of Vargas's remarks to Washington:

> Italy's entrance into the war has increased the concern of the government as to the attitude of the large German and Italian populations here. This was demonstrated in the speech made today by President Vargas. While he praised Pan-American ideals and so on, in several places he made statements that are manifestly sops to those groups.[9]

Yet Vargas's address aboard the *Minas Gerais* had rattled Caffery, who was stung by the unexpected content of it and by the furious reaction it had elicited in Washington. The US ambassador struggled to piece together the motives behind Vargas's provocation. When Caffery spoke with the British embassy in Rio, he found that his counterparts there had been equally in the dark before the speech, but that they agreed with his assessment as to Vargas's motives for the speech.[10]

The ambassador's concerns increased when he phoned Aranha, who told him that he had known nothing of the speech and was pretty sure that nobody in the cabinet had been aware of its contents either.[11] To make matters worse for Caffery, the *Associated Press* ran an article suggesting that Vargas had endorsed totalitarianism, and this had been picked up by the press in Brazil's great rival, Argentina. The Argentine president instructed his foreign minister to seek clarification about the remarks from the Americans. "The sentiments expressed by President Vargas would seem to be at variance with the views held by the Argentine government," he warned the Americans.[12] The speech was no longer simply a US-Brazilian affair; it now had potentially dangerous regional implications, and particularly in terms of Argentine-Brazilian relations.

On June 12, 1940, the major newspapers in Brazil, the United States, Argentina, Germany, and Italy all led with the news of Vargas's comments. Predictably, the coverage in Italy and Germany was much more complimentary than that in the other countries. Benito Mussolini offered his congratulations in a telegram to the president. "You are a great statesman," Mussolini proclaimed, expressing his great admiration for the speech.[13] In the United States, by contrast, the *New York Times* ran the story under the ominous headline "Vargas Backs the Virile; Predicts New World Order," while the *New York Herald Tribune* began its piece under the banner "Vargas Defends Force." American reporters based in South America characterized the speech as "the first outspoken fascist speech by any South American president." In Buenos Aires, Argentina, the local paper, *Critica*, carried the headline "Vargas, with fascist language, justifies the aggression of the barbarians." Only in Brazil was there an absence of commentary. The government state censor banned all analysis of the speech, and foreign journalists operating in Brazil were prevented from wiring commentaries at the request of Aranha, who was attempting to control the international fallout from the speech.

Back in his office in the Catete Palace on the morning of June 12, Vargas feigned surprise at all the fuss. He admitted that the "Americans have expressed their dismay and that they now accuse me of being a Germanophile."[14] Under pressure from Aranha, however, he decided to prepare a note explaining his position.

At the State Department in Washington, meanwhile, a major damage control exercise was also under way, this one aimed at countering the increasingly hostile newspaper reports about Vargas's alleged fascist sympathies. The undersecretary of state, Sumner Welles, wrote to President Roosevelt expressing a viewpoint originally put forward by Caffery: the speech, he said, was simply sops to the Germans and Italians living in Brazil. He added, "There is nothing whatever in the speech except one or two ill-chosen phrases that justify the onslaught being made upon President Vargas by the American press today."[15] Welles concluded his note by suggesting that if the president could find a few words of regard for President Vargas at his next press conference, which was scheduled for later that day, it would have an "admirable effect."

Unbeknownst to Welles and Roosevelt, back in Rio, Dutra and Góes Monteiro were so incensed about the comments in the US press that they sought advice on suing the offending publications. Lawyers acting for the Brazilian government had to explain to them that the press in the United States was a free one and could say pretty much anything they liked. In Brazil, the vast majority of the press was government-controlled, with many of the newspapers in Rio taking their news and commentary directly from the statements produced by the government's propaganda office. Editors who took views that differed from the official line more often than not had their publication either temporary suspended or closed down altogether.

As the controversy over his remarks mounted, Vargas continued to coolly work through the day's large number of diplomatic cables with the help of Alzira. Unlike Aranha, who since the start of the war in Europe had been growing increasingly edgy and nervous, Vargas appeared hugely focused and in complete control. His diary records that he even continued to find time for a round of golf once a week, which took up much of the designated day.

Vargas was having a good war, and he knew it. Aranha, on the other hand, was struggling to balance the diplomatic and economic demands of the Americans, the British, the Italians, and the Germans. Inside the government, Aranha was well-liked by many; his colleagues admired his past record and his vision for Brazil's future. Within the presidential cabinet itself, however, his following was rather small. In contrast, the minister of war, Dutra, was quietly building up his own cabal. Although he would not have liked the analogy, Aranha was becoming something of a fireman putting out the conflagrations other people started—and Vargas's speech was perhaps the greatest fire he had yet confronted.

The irony of all this was not lost on the chief of the army, Góes Monteiro, who had initially mistaken Vargas's speech for a real change of course in Brazilian foreign policy toward the Axis powers. Góes Monteiro had since come to appreciate the true purpose of the speech, and in Aranha's office the general tried to explain to a clearly irritated Caffery that the speech had actually been intended to launch a Brazilian program of social and economic reforms that resembled Roosevelt's New Deal. Caffery snapped back, "United States citizens held Brazil in the highest esteem and therefore were filled with consternation."[16]

Aranha learned from Caffery that the State Department had two gripes with Vargas's speech. The first and least problematic was the content itself, which despite the dramatic newspaper headlines in New York and Buenos Aires didn't unduly alarm either Welles or Hull once they had read the complete translation of it. Curiously, both US officials took the speech at face value, rather than waiting for a deeper analysis of the motivations that lay behind it.

The major issue that the US State Department had with Vargas's speech was its timing: Vargas had cut into Roosevelt's news cycle. On June 10, the day before Vargas's speech aboard the *Minas Gerais,* the American president had given a dramatic speech at the University of Virginia, during which he had expressed in his strongest terms to date his deep sympathy for the enemies of the Axis powers. The president's speech had gone down well in London and in Rio, but President Vargas did not hear it, as he was too busy working on his own speech for the following day. And as the clamor over Vargas's address grew in the days that followed, Roosevelt's speech became lost in the noise.

Aranha decided to send the Brazilian ambassador, Carlos Martins, to Washington to meet with Cordell Hull. Martins apologized to Hull for the timing of the speech, explaining, "When President Vargas went to deliver his speech, he did not know that President Roosevelt had delivered his Charlottesville speech the night before."[17] The ambassador added a line fed to him by Aranha, telling the secretary of state that the speech had been intended only for internal consumption, and that Vargas would soon issue an explanatory statement. The following day, Martins met with the undersecretary of state, Sumner Welles, to deliver the promised explanation.

Vargas's apology was aimed at President Roosevelt, who had pointedly not uttered a "few kind words" about Vargas at his press conference, as Welles had requested. The Brazilian president's message appeared to be a simple attempt to clear up any misunderstandings Roosevelt might have had about the speech, as well as an attempt to massage the American's ego:

> Speech delivered June 11 can in no sense be regarded as contradictory to that of President Roosevelt, whose speech I had not read at that time. My speech is a warning, a call to reality, addressed to Brazilians and which might cause surprise only to persons devoted to routine, not to a far-seeing mind like that of Roosevelt, who is liberal minded, progressive, and forward looking, crying out as the voice of the whole continent regarding perils which threaten America and who knows that Brazil will not fail him in loyalty.[18]

In other words, Vargas's message implied that Brazil was very much still on the side of the Americans and was a strong supporter of President

Roosevelt. As a finishing touch, Aranha had the appropriately named department of press and propaganda issue a statement in Brazil expressing the same sentiments.

The crisis caused by Vargas's speech appeared to be over. The British noted the impression—widely held among the international diplomatic corps—that Vargas had been given a mild, but firm, rebuke by the United States.[19] From start to finish, the whole crisis appeared to have been caused by simple bad timing and a few sops by President Vargas to the Axis powers—a diplomatic maneuver the Allies were prepared to tolerate, given that Germany looked likely to prevail in the European war. Alzira, however, understood the real motivation behind the speech, which had little to do with internal Brazilian works and everything to do with US-Brazilian economic relations.

In January 1940, Vargas had unveiled a hugely ambitious five-year plan for Brazil. The core of the plan called for the development of a Brazilian industrial sector, at the heart of which was a major steel plant. Other parts of the plan called for the construction of a modern transportation infrastructure across the country, including railways and roads linking the different regions of Brazil. Alzira noted, however, that the construction of a steel mill was the project that most interested her father, due to its importance to the future industrial development of Brazil.

Vargas's five-year plan had the potential to secure a place in Brazilian history for the Estado Novo and assure its legacy as a transformational, progressive regime. The problem was that with the onset of World War II and the closing of Brazilian trading markets overseas, it looked highly improbable that Brazil would be able to contribute much in the way of funding for this project. So the Vargas administration sought outside funding, and the Americans and British became alarmed when the German company Krupp indicated that they were interested in building the steel mill.

Vargas would have welcomed US assistance with the five-year plan, but he had not received it; the United States Steel Corporation had decided not to participate in the plan.[20] In January 1940, Brazilian ambassador Carlos Martins told the US State Department that Brazil regarded the steel mill project as the litmus test of the Good Neighbor Program: if the United States would not assist Brazil with such a basic and unthreatening program, after all, could it really be considered a strong and well-meaning partner?[21]

The ambassador also warned the Americans: "President [Vargas] states that he would greatly prefer to have [the steel mill] carried out with the assistance of American enterprise and capital, but that if this is not forthcoming, he [will] turn in other directions."[22] The State Department heard the message loud and clear: if the United States wanted to stem the influence of Germany in Brazil, it would have to come up with some way of helping Vargas realize this key part of his agenda for modernizing the country. If the Americans failed to do so, the Germans were all too eager to fill the void and move Brazil further into Berlin's economic orbit.

President Vargas, who enjoyed a game of cards along with his habitual whiskey and cigar, knew he was holding a strong hand. And the Americans knew this, too. On April 11, 1940, Welles formally asked the United States Steel Corporation to reconsider its decision not to proceed with its development of a steel mill in Brazil.[23] President Vargas's patience with the US corporation snapped, however, and he decided to move ahead with the project with a Brazilian cooperation—although, in reality, he would still need loans from the Americans in order to construct the plant.[24] Finally, on May 31, after hearing of the efforts of Krupp to secure the contract to build a German steel mill in Brazil, the US secretary of state approached Vargas with some good news: the US federal loan administrator had agreed to loan Brazil the money to build the mill.[25] Initially, $10 million was offered; to sweeten the deal, the federal loan administrator promised more funds if the costs exceeded the original amount, up to $20 million. Caffery was very pleased to inform Hull: "President Vargas is delighted with the news. He tells me that he will send a commission to the United States very soon to proceed with the business."[26]

Vargas appeared happy, but on a deeper level he understood that there was still much to negotiate before the project could commence. The president was not an impatient man, but he had little understanding of the workings of US diplomacy and feared that the wrangling over the construction and running of the mill would delay the project. Vargas did understand, however, that the process would not be as easy as Hull had indicated. In order to guarantee its success, Vargas would have to remind the Americans of his importance to them—and of the fact that he had an alternative partner in the Germans, whom many in his own cabinet and in the Brazilian military preferred for the project. And what better opportunity to remind the Americans of his own importance, and that of Brazil, than in a speech

to an audience that had little time for the United States or its Good
Neighbor Program?

Alzira, for one, understood full well what the speech of June 11 was
about. The president wanted his steel mill, and he was going to do everything in his power to make sure that he got it from the Americans on terms
that were acceptable to Brazil. As he sat in his office reminding everyone,
especially Aranha, of the pain the US press was causing him, he was also
instructing the Brazilian negotiators in Washington to press the Americans
hard and to secure a quick conclusion to the steel mill negotiations.

Caffery took the hint. The ambassador warned the US State Department that Vargas was at a turning point, and that the future of the Good
Neighbor Program depended on the United States securing the contract
for the steel mill project. Perhaps sensing that Caffery was as keen to wrap
up the negotiations as he was, Vargas had Aranha keep up the pressure
on the ambassador. When the two met on September 5, Aranha told the
ambassador of Krupp's continued interest in the project. Caffery told
Hull, "Aranha told me last night that he had received another letter from
Krupp making very attractive offers in connection with the construction
of the steel plant."[27]

Aranha's comments did the trick. The last minor issues were resolved
that month, and the steel mill deal was signed on September 26, 1940. There
was widespread jubilation in Rio over the signing, and President Vargas
received a great deal of praise from all corners of Brazil.[28] Aranha wrote to
Sumner Welles, expressing his satisfaction at the signing of the deal and
highlighting its importance for Brazil. "No factor may better reveal the decision of the United States to collaborate for the prosperity of Brazil and of
the American continent," he assured the undersecretary of state.[29] Welles's
reply was equally warm, assuring Aranha: "The exchange of letters with regard to the establishment of the iron and steel industry in your great country
is a source of the greatest pleasure to this government," and he added, "I believe unquestionably that this agreement marks the reaffirmation of a policy
of close practical and intimate cooperation between our two governments to
our reciprocal advantage and the advantage of the new world."[30]

President Vargas was delighted with the deal, not least because he
suspected President Roosevelt had taken a personal role in the business.[31]
The timing and the contents of Vargas's Navy Day speech had been instrumental in hurrying the Americans along.[32] So, too, had the Germans'

ongoing interest in the project; toward the end of the negotiations, when disputes over the small print threatened to derail the deal, Vargas merely used the letters of interest from Krupp to prod the US State Department back into line.

Vargas and Aranha, the two gaúchos, had pulled off a major coup. The final deal was hugely important for Vargas, both as a symbolic economic linkage of Brazil and the United States and as a galvanic current to jump-start his hugely ambitious five-year plan for Brazil. It would be fair to say, too, that his speech to the naval officers succeeded not only in worrying the United States, but also in boosting his popularity among a branch of the armed forces that had played an outsized role in the attempted coup in 1938. This was not President Vargas's finest hour, but it was very close to it.

On January 30, 1941, Decree 3002 approved the construction and operation of the national steel mill and the establishment of the national steel company (*Companhia Siderúrgica Nacional*). Soon after the decree was signed, work began at the mill's Volta Redonda site, only ninety miles from Rio. The initial loan from the United States through the Export-Import Bank was increased to $45 million during construction, and the total cost of construction was put at $70 million.[33] It was a huge project, but by the end of World War II the plant was operational and around 80 percent completed.[34] When it officially opened in 1946, it was the first steel mill in South America. The original plant was expanded throughout the late 1940s and 1950s and well into the 1960s.[35]

The Volta Redonda mill was not the only boon of the deal. The initial project also called for the development of new infrastructure to support the plant's operation. Brazil's central rail network was expanded, linking Rio de Janeiro with the plant at Volta Redonda; some parts of the network were also converted to electricity, a major step toward modernity for a country whose railways were still powered predominately by steam.[36] Most ambitious of all was the construction of the city of Volta Redonda, where the staff of the plant eventually lived.[37] The city had new houses, schools, hotels, and churches, along with the additional infrastructure required for a large, modern metropolis.[38] It remains one of the lasting legacies of the Estado Novo in Brazil.

The construction of the giant steel mill and the city of Volta Redonda, however, were not the only elements of Vargas's five-year plan made possible by the support of the United States. As 1940 drew to a close, his plans to develop the Brazilian military into South America's most powerful army had not progressed as smoothly as Vargas and his commanders had hoped. This plan remained crucial, however, to the military leadership's goal of effectively overtaking their old rival, Argentina, as the major military power on the South American continent. In order to do this, however, Brazil would need all the weapons it could get. And in 1940, it particularly needed weapons from Nazi Germany.

Brazil had ordered a large shipment of weapons from Germany before the outbreak of the war, and had even settled on a fee. The weapons were to be sent from Germany to neutral Lisbon via rail, and from there via ship to Brazil. In order to reach Rio, however, the ship carrying the cargo of arms would have to run the British naval blockade off the coast of Portugal—a risky prospect that Vargas hoped to avoid if at all possible. Attempts to reach a negotiated solution with the British in order to let the ship depart Lisbon produced little in the way of progress. In the end, both the Brazilians and the British were left with a difficult choice to make about how best to proceed.

Once again, this was high-stakes diplomacy for the Brazilians and the Allies. The British and their US partners could not very well allow the Germans to continue profiting off international trade if they could help it. For President Vargas and Osvaldo Aranha, on the other hand, it was crucial that the Brazilian military receive the weapons from Germany; if the Estado Novo could not deliver the arms, its failure would seriously jeopardize Vargas and Aranha's carefully constructed relationship with the United States. The Allies would have been denying Brazil armaments from Germany while failing to provide any themselves.

After the cargo ship had lain in the waters off Lisbon for weeks, Vargas and Aranha came to a decision and issued the vessel an order through the Brazilian embassy in Lisbon. As the Brazilian embassy worked to decrypt the cable containing the order, British intelligence was doing the same. This was nothing out of the ordinary—from 1940 onward, all communications in and out of the Brazilian embassy were intercepted by the British, who were keen to understand the movements of Portuguese shipping back and forth to Brazil. This message, however, would have tremendous repercussions—for Brazil, for Great Britain, and for both countries' relations with the United States.

5

# DISCORDANT ALLIES

O N NOVEMBER 19, 1940, JUST WEEKS AFTER the Brazilians and Americans had signed the steel mill agreement, the Brazilian steamer SS *Siqueira Campos* was preparing to slip anchor in Lisbon harbor and head down the Tagus River and out into the Atlantic Ocean. The Lisbon docks were the scene of frantic last-minute preparations for the voyage. The Portuguese police opened and inspected the passengers' luggage, and then tall cranes, which were used to carrying far greater weights, winched the personal belongings on board.

Much earlier in the day, the same cranes had loaded heavy unmarked wooden crates into the steamer's hold.[1] The operation had been carefully overseen by the Portuguese police, as well as officials from the German embassy in Lisbon. British agents from the Secret Intelligence Service (also known as SIS or MI6), meanwhile, were carefully noting all the movements of the German officials and the crates themselves, although these observers already knew the crates' exact contents. SIS agents had bribed Portuguese customs officials for the inventory sheets, which listed a variety of deadly military hardware: machine guns, artillery pieces, and ammunition. As the *Siqueira Campos* left the docks and slowly steamed down the Tagus River toward the fiery red winter's sunset, the SIS agents reported its exact departure time to the British naval frigates waiting just outside Portuguese national waters, where they planned to intercept the Brazilian vessel.[2] In the tower room of the German embassy, located on a hill above the docks, agents of the *Abwehr* (Army Intelligence Service) watched the ship's departure through field glasses. They hurriedly cabled Berlin, which in turn contacted the German embassy in Rio with news that the *Siqueira Campos* had left Lisbon at long last.

The ship's movements were being closely monitored in London, Rio, and Washington as well as in Berlin. Earlier in the day the Brazilian ambassador to London had informed the British foreign office: "As it was found impossible to detain for a further period of time the stay at the port of Lisbon of the *Siqueira Campos,* the Brazilian government have decided to order the departure of this vessel."[3] The message to London had been loud and clear: the ship was going to try to run the British naval blockade.

The British had been quick to blockade Portugal and Brazil, along with many other neutral maritime powers, at the start of the war, and they had effectively enforced these measures in the year since. "Our control of enemy exports has become a symbol of our naval strength," a British ministry of economic warfare official had argued just days before the *Siqueira Campos* left Lisbon, and Great Britain was keen to keep up this show of strength. By attempting to run the British blockade, the Brazilians were essentially testing its effectiveness. The British were prepared to meet this challenge with a robust response, whatever the diplomatic fallout.[4] And the British understood that there would be a lot of fallout—even with their closest allies.

Prior to the departure of the *Siqueira Campos,* the United States had appealed to the British not to intercept the ship.[5] The American warning cited three key consequences if the British attempted to stop the vessel. Firstly, the Americans feared that such an action would lead to an appeal from Brazil to other Pan-American states, including the United States, to issue a joint protest to Great Britain.[6] This would naturally be most embarrassing to the United States, which—although not yet officially engaged in the war—was overtly supporting Great Britain and was supposed to be in lockstep with London. Secondly, the Americans suggested that Brazil needed the arms for defensive purposes, and that if Brazil wasn't allowed to get them from Germany, the United States would have to supply them—an outcome that would unavoidably hurt the British war effort, since the only arms Washington could spare were ones it had intended to supply to Great Britain.[7]

The third and most important American plea was that by intercepting the *Siqueira Campos,* the British might inadvertently precipitate "the downfall of Senhor Aranha whom the United States government had found invaluable in opposing German influence in Brazil including the Brazilian army."[8] Aranha had done what he could to encourage this viewpoint, telling the Americans, "The army is most insistent and . . . if Brazil fails to overcome the British objection, I will resign and permit the designation as minister of foreign affairs of a successor who holds views different from my own."[9] If the threat of losing the Allies' chief proponent in the Vargas administration wasn't enough, the Americans ended their warning with the assurance that the interception of the ship would be a serious blow to the efforts of the United States to facilitate goodwill in Latin America, so as "to drive the Pan-American team in a direction that was favorable to ourselves."[10]

The British embassy in Washington forwarded the warning to the British foreign office at 8:40 P.M. EST on November 18. The message was received in London at 5:10 A.M. on November 19, the day the *Siqueira Campos* was set to depart. Although the ship was then still docked in Lisbon, the warning had arrived too late to be seriously considered before the ship set sail with its disputed cargo of weapons.

As soon as the *Siqueira Campos* reached international waters, it was stopped and boarded by British naval officers, who ordered it to sail to Gibraltar.[11] The ship arrived there on November 22, 1940, and was promptly impounded.[12] Prohibited from docking, it remained anchored in the bay with its 140 crewmen and 260 frightened passengers still aboard. Two bad storms and several air-raid warnings did little to improve their spirits while they were in port.[13] Bouts of seasickness among the passengers were frequent, and conditions on board deteriorated quickly. To make matters worse, it appeared they were in for a lengthy stay in Gibraltar. Initial searches by British customs officials found some of the German arms in the ship's cargo hold, but as officials noted, they needed to open and search every case.

The ministry of economic warfare, under whose remit the blockade fell, adopted a hard line, demanding that an example be made of the ship. "We are anxious not to allow these regulations to fall into disregard by letting them be flouted with impunity," the ministry asserted.[14] The British embassy in Gibraltar agreed, noting that the *Siqueira Campos* was "guilty of a flagrant attempt to break the blockade, and the seizure of both ship and cargo, and severe penalties against the whole line, would be fully justified."[15] As for the passengers, the ministry recommended either sending them back to Lisbon on another ship, or—if they could get Spanish visas—by train to Lisbon.

The British were worried about one passenger in particular: the secretary of the Brazilian embassy in Berlin, who had been aboard the *Siqueira Campos* and who remained cooped up with the other passengers. His presence made the Allied authorities skittish, and limited their options. Given the enormity of the task facing the searchers, the British ministry of economic warfare recommended that the ship be sent on to Great Britain, which had greater facilities to conduct such an operation.[16] The foreign office rejected this proposal, however, for fear that any such move would further anger the Brazilians.

Osvaldo Aranha was at his desk in the Itamaraty Palace in Rio in the early evening of November 22, 1940, working through boxes of diplomatic cables, when his secretary informed him that the British navy had seized the *Siqueira Campos*.[17] It was not the news the foreign minister had been hoping for. Aranha understood all too well that the fate of the arms on the ship had become linked to his own political future. For most of the year, the German embassy in Rio had been spreading rumors that Aranha's influence was in decline and that he would soon be replaced as minister of foreign affairs by the chief of staff of the army, General Góes Monteiro—a man whose sympathies were, of course, much more pro-German than Aranha's. The speculation was false and was seen as pure German propaganda by the Americans, but it put Aranha on the defensive and kept him constantly looking over his shoulder. And if Aranha could not provide the Brazilian army with the long-promised German weapons aboard the *Siqueira Campos,* there was a distinct possibility the rumors of his replacement by Góes Monteiro could become a reality; Góes Monteiro and Dutra, Aranha's archenemies, were adamant that Brazil needed the weapons and would surely use this failure to try to bring down their rival.

The foreign minister's initial reaction to the news about the *Siqueira Campos* was one of bewilderment. He had heard that the British ambassador in Rio and the foreign office in London had both advised against stopping the ship; little did he know that the British ministry of economic warfare, in its keenness to enforce the naval blockade, had simply ignored the advice. But what was done was done, and now Aranha had no choice but to inform Vargas.

Aranha made his way to the Guanabara Palace to bring the bad news to the president. To make matters worse, it was Alzira's birthday, so when Aranha arrived at the palace he found Vargas dressing for his daughter's party.[18] Vargas took the news coolly: "We can't do much this evening," he mumbled to Aranha before going to greet guests in the lobby. He arranged to meet with Aranha and Dutra early the next day, before he left Rio to celebrate his father's ninety-sixth birthday. Tired and worried, the president did not stay at Alzira's party late, retiring to bed at 12:30 A.M. with the excuse that he had a long trip to make in the morning.[19]

On the drive back to the ministry of foreign affairs, Aranha's mind drifted away from the beautiful, brightly lit cityscape in front of him to the spectacular vision of Brazil that Vargas had outlined in his five-year plan.[20] The president's plan hinged on strengthening Brazil's armed forces so that the nation could leverage itself into a more secure position within Latin America and establish itself as an even bigger player—militarily, economically, and politically—on the international stage. With the *Siqueira Campos* and its cargo of weapons confined to port at Gibraltar, however, this dream surely seemed further away than ever on the evening of November 22.

The roots of the German arms deal stretched back to two years before Vargas had unveiled his five-year plan in January of 1940. In 1938, Brazil had signed an £8 million deal with Krupp, on the understanding that it could supply more of the weapons Brazil needed than any Allied manufacturer. The United States had agreed to supply planes and some ships, and Great Britain had committed to sending Brazil six destroyers, but with the war in Europe straining the Allies' manufacturing capabilities, Vargas knew that any request for further armaments was highly likely to be turned down. As if to prove his point, the British eventually reneged on the deal for the six destroyers.

Brazil continued to ask for arms from the United States. In 1940, talks between US and Brazilian officials usually ended with the Brazilians outlining their need for US arms for the purpose of national defense, particularly in the event of an attack by Argentina. The standard reply from US officials turned the Brazilians' plea on its head, acknowledging that more should be done to secure northeast Brazil from a potential attack by the Axis powers, but adding that this would be best accomplished by basing American forces in the area. Such a suggestion was anathema to Brazilian leaders, who remained touchy about America's legacy of intervening in their nation's affairs. When Brazilian generals presented the Americans with a shopping list of arms, which amounted to some $180 million, the Americans turned them down. The Brazilian generals did not take this very well, and for some time argued that Brazil should refuse to talk with the Americans about mutual defense unless they first promised to deliver the weapons.

Following the September 1940 signing of the deal for the steel mill at Volta Redonda, however, both sides took advantage of the resulting political goodwill to come to an accord over the thorny issue of mutual defense in case of an attack on Brazil.[21] In late October 1940, Góes Monteiro visited Washington to take part in a meeting of the army chiefs of staff from the American republics. While there, he agreed to talk with the Americans about the defense of Brazil as well as Brazil's requests for arms. On October 29, 1940, these discussions produced what became known as the Góes Monteiro Draft. This draft in turn became the basis for an agreement between the US and Brazilian armies, which was signed on July 24 of the following year in Rio by the Brazilian minister of war, Eurico Dutra, and US brigadier general Lehman W. Miller.[22]

The agreement anticipated by the Góes Monteiro Draft was a breakthrough for US-Brazilian relations, and promised to link both nations together militarily in an unprecedented way. It stated that the United States would join Brazilian forces in the defense of Brazil only if the country were attacked before it could develop its own adequate defenses. Góes Monteiro promised to try to stop Axis subversion in the country, furthermore, while the United States promised to supply Brazil with what arms it could spare. Finally, Góes Monteiro agreed that if an American country were attacked by a non-American one, Brazil would allow the United States forces to use its naval facilities and air bases to repel the assault.[23]

The deal won Brazil access to a new source of weapons in exchange for defense concessions that the United States had long craved, but the agreement was not as straightforward as it appeared. The United States didn't have an abundance of armaments, for one thing, so Brazil would not be able to count on the same steady supply it had been promised by the Germans. And while Brazil and the United States needed each other, they both also retained suspicions and fears that would strain their relationship even as they grew closer and more codependent.

Like most armies, the Brazilian armed forces were a complex beast. Even though the United States had promised to deliver weapons of its own, the Brazilian military's officer class strongly preferred the idea of purchasing arms from Germany. Any alliance with the Americans was, in their view, a mere marriage of convenience brought on by the war and the increasing difficulty of acquiring additional German weapons.[24]

The military's preference for German arms was a reflection of its strong anti-imperialist leanings and its traditional distrust of the United States and Great Britain, both of which it perceived as exploiters who wished to keep Brazil underdeveloped and poor in order to maximize their economic gain. Senior officers argued that any alliance with either the United States or Great Britain would endanger Brazilian economic independence.[25] There was also the matter of payment: both the Americans and the British demanded that Brazil pay for weapons in an acceptable international currency or in gold, neither of which it possessed in abundance.[26] Germany, on the other hand, was willing to barter weapons for Brazilian coffee and cotton, an exchange that greatly pleased the Brazilian military because it gave Brazil access to quantities of weapons that would otherwise have been out of its reach.[27]

The minister of war and the chief of staff, Dutra and Góes Monteiro, shared the nationalistic politics of the army officer corps. The Allies were deeply suspicious of both men, and Allied intelligence fed stories to their respective political leaderships that portrayed both men as being strong supporters of the Nazis. Dutra and his family were alleged to have cheered when they were informed that Paris had fallen to the Germans.[28] In public, Dutra was more diplomatic, avowing "the army is neither pro-American nor pro-German, but pro-armament."[29]

Whatever Dutra's personal sympathies, however, the reality was that— as far as Brazilian foreign policy was concerned—neither he nor Góes Monteiro favored Berlin over Washington or London. Both men realized that the United States and Great Britain represented the best long-term option for helping Brazil. For his part, Aranha was usually quick to defend Góes Monteiro against accusations of being pro-German. "His attitude is one of professional admiration for the efficiency of the German army," Aranha told a US army officer.[30]

The US State Department was less sanguine than Aranha, accusing Góes Monteiro of profiting from the clash between the Allies and the Axis. In a 1939 note, the State Department explained:

While it is believed that it may be an exaggeration to state that General Góes Monteiro is pro-German, it is nevertheless felt that he is playing a shrewd game so far as the Brazilian army is concerned. In other words, Góes Monteiro probably figures that Brazil should play ball not only with the United States but also with Germany, with the idea of playing one country off against the other in the currying of Brazil's favor, and in this manner getting the maximum for Brazil. It should be remembered that Germany has still a great deal to offer Brazil inasmuch as practically the entire re-equipment of the Brazilian army is under contract to that country.[31]

The American assessment of Góes Monteiro succinctly captured the general's outlook, but while he may have been ambivalent about allying Brazil with Germany, his willingness to entertain the Axis in order to extract concessions from the Allies nevertheless made the Americans understandably suspicious of him, and of the Brazilian army generally.

While the chief of staff was willing to tread with the Allies, he harbored no affection for them; quite the opposite, in fact. Góes Monteiro reserved special enmity for the British in particular. In private, he criticized officers who preferred an alliance with Great Britain, arguing, "They prefer British slavery because they consider it to be more agreeable and only economic and they have already experienced it."[32] What most angered both Góes Monteiro and Dutra was the British attitude toward the supply and delivery of the German arms from Lisbon to Rio.[33] The British interception of the *Siqueira Campos* only confirmed their feeling that Great Britain not only retained an imperialist attitude toward Brazil but also failed to appreciate Brazil's legitimate right to develop its own military strength in the interest of national defense. Neither leader, as a result, did anything to defuse the growing anti-British sentiment among the officer's corps of the Brazilian army.

For their part, the Allies were also quick to try to create disunity between the two military leaders, suggesting falsely on several occasions that Góes Monteiro's star was on the wane. "Góes Monteiro was the military genius of the revolution, but it is believed that Vargas and Aranha no longer trusted him and consequently would like to see his official stature diminished," American intelligence in Brazil had speculated to Washington in September 1940. "They are building up the prestige of the minister of war, Dutra, by pushing him into the limelight wherever possible."[34] It was true that there was a historical rivalry between the two leaders, but on the issue of the supply of weapons—and especially in the case of the *Siqueira Campos*—both men were in complete agreement that Brazil must take a strong stand against the British. Both men also concurred about the usefulness of one particular tactic for doing so: getting the United States, which was fearful of pushing Brazilians further into the Nazi camp, to lean heavily on the British.

President Vargas was out of Rio at the time of the *Siqueira Campos* crisis, but he had given Aranha his full authority to find a solution that best suited Brazilian interests.[35] This represented something of a poisoned chalice for the minister, who was all too aware that any failure to resolve the crisis on terms that appeared favorable to Brazil would lead Dutra and the senior generals in the army to demand his resignation. While the *Siqueira Campos* had still been in Lisbon, Aranha had of course told the Americans that he might resign if the ship were not released, but that had been a hollow threat; he had no intention of stepping down.

When word of the seizure of the *Siqueira Campos* reached Rio, Aranha made two immediate decisions: firstly, that he would use whatever leverage he had with the United States to get it to intervene on Brazil's behalf, and secondly, that he would not publish details of the crisis in the Brazilian press for fear of creating a strong anti-British sentiment in the country and thereby upsetting his own hopes for swaying the country toward the Allies. On November 22, an angry Aranha sent a clear warning to the British through the US State Department:

> The Brazilian embassy in London states that the British authorities in-
> sinuate that they have taken this step in accord with the American gov-
> ernment. I sent a denial of this insinuation. We hope that the decision of
> the British government is only a formality. We cannot understand such
> arbitrary action. If this brutality is carried out, we will be forced into an
> attitude that may unfortunately perturb the continental policy, which with
> our help has been one of goodwill toward England.[36]

Aranha's message was clear: if the United States couldn't convince Great Britain to release the ship, it would jeopardize whatever sympathies the Allies enjoyed in Latin America.

To further complicate matters for Aranha, his trusted partner Jefferson Caffery was back in the United States on annual leave, forcing the foreign minister to deal with more junior officials, with whom he was not on familiar terms. Still, Aranha stuck with his strategy, continuing to keep the matter out of the Brazilian press. On November 23, the American embassy in Rio reported back to Washington: "No mention whatsoever has yet appeared in the Brazilian press regarding the ship."[37]

In Washington the State Department did its best to resolve what it viewed as a British mess. Both Cordell Hull and his deputy, Sumner Welles, promised to do everything possible to resolve the crisis. On November 25, Hull sent a message of support to Aranha through the embassy in Rio:

> I was deeply concerned to learn that the British had stopped and detained the *Siqueira Campos* in the face of all the efforts that have been made by our two governments. Within the last few days, Caffery and I had fully explained to the British chargé d'affaires here the circumstances surrounding the purchase of the arms and all of the reasons that counseled the desirability of permitting the ship to proceed to Brazil. We could not have been more emphatic or more precise in our views. Lord Lothian, the British Ambassador, returned yesterday. I will speak with him most vigorously today, or tomorrow at the latest, in the expectation that he will understand the importance of permitting the ship to proceed.[38]

The Americans, it was clear, were bending over backward to accommodate the Brazilians, even going so far as to undercut their British allies in the process. Indeed, in private, Hull remained furious with the "ungrateful British," whose actions he believed threatened the US Good Neighbor Program in Brazil.

If anything, Hull's deputy was even angrier about Great Britain's seeming blindness to America's carefully crafted foreign policy program. Sumner Welles, whose legendary temper tantrums were already the talk of much of the State Department, blew a fuse when he heard about the British action, fearing it had endangered the entire Good Neighbor Program throughout Latin America. Both he and Hull argued that the only winners in the *Siqueira Campos* affair were the Germans, for whom the crisis was a win-win situation; either the Brazilians would ultimately receive the weapons and Germany's influence with Brazil would remain intact, or—if Great Britain permanently confiscated the weapons—Germany would be handed a ready-made tool with which to pry the Brazilians from the Allies.

It wasn't long before the Americans learned that Aranha was equally worried about the strategic implications of the British action. The minister of foreign affairs was still clearly irritated by the whole affair when the American chargé d'affaires, Burdett, met with Aranha in his office late in the evening of November 25, three days into the crisis. Rightly or wrongly, Aranha believed that the British owed him for his overtures and hospitality. Aranha pointed out that he had recently given an anti-German speech to welcome the British economic mission to Brazil headed by the Marquess of Willingdon. The Americans had themselves noted that the Willingdon mission "was received well here, has had a good press, been extensively entertained, and the visit marked by felicitous speeches"—and much of this was due to Aranha's influence and intercessions.[39]

Such overt support for the British carried risks. Aranha had made his remarks at a formal white-tie dinner at the Itamaraty Palace in front of not just Willingdon and his entourage but also a who's who of Brazil's elites—among them many of the figures from the military who favored trading with the Germans over the British or the Americans. Much of the polite dinner table gossip that had accompanied the meal centered on whether Great Britain would be able to resist a German invasion, which was expected imminently. Aranha felt that he had gone out on a limb to make such a pro-British speech at a time when the British were refusing to let German arms into Brazil.

At the end of his meeting with Burdett, Aranha presented him with a copy of the note that the Brazilian ambassador in London would present to the British foreign office the following day. The letter was a robust defense of the Brazilian position, centering on two main issues that the Brazilians felt the British had chosen to overlook. The first concerned Brazil's choice of procuring arms from Germany: "We only bought from Germany because it was impossible at that time to buy under better terms anywhere else."[40] The second and more important point was that Brazil had ordered these arms in 1938, before the start of World War II, and that it had already paid for them. Moreover, the British had not objected to earlier deliveries of armaments from this order, and some of the consignment aboard the *Siqueira Campos* was related to previous orders from Germany for goods such as spare parts and ammunition.[41] Aranha pointed out that the Germans would merely keep the other weapons, which were contractually due to be shipped to Brazil, and use them in its war against Great Britain.[42]

The clear implication of Aranha's letter was that the British actions were not only unjust but were also strengthening rather than weakening Germany's position in Latin America.[43] As Burdett took his leave, a weary Aranha told the American, "in view of the attitude of the army here I regard the matter as highly dangerous. I believe the generals will take it badly and I'm counting on the help of the State Department to avoid an intolerable situation." Just as Burdett reached the inner door to the office, Aranha delivered his punch line, which he surely knew would form the subject line of the telegram to Washington: "The success of all my efforts to maintain Brazilian opinion favorable to the democracies is menaced by this lamentable incident."[44]

To make sure the Americans got the message, Aranha enlisted the help of Góes Monteiro. He told the general to speak with American officials at the embassy. When Góes Monteiro did so, he was characteristically to the point, warning of reprisals against British commercial interests in Brazil if the *Siqueira Campos* were not released. He went on to remind the officials that Aranha had to withhold information about the detention of the ship in Gibraltar from the Brazilian people because, "they would be so incensed that they would retaliate against British interests."[45] The general concluded by thanking the Americans, as he put it, "for the splendid help you are giving us."[46]

Initially, the British were having none of what they regarded as Brazilian brinkmanship. They remained unimpressed with the attempts of both the Brazilian and American governments to effect the release of the ship, and believed that there must have been some collusion between Washington and Rio to preemptively prepare for this campaign before the ship had set sail. "It is extremely unfortunate that the United States government should have allowed themselves to be maneuvered into supporting an attempt to break our blockade," an angry foreign office official reported. He added, "The Brazilian government would not, I think, have dared to take this action if they had not thought themselves assured of US support."[47]

But the British were pragmatic. They understood, as did the Americans and Brazilians, that "the situation that has been created must be regarded as a great success for our enemies." The British embassy in Washington warned London that if the ship was not allowed to reach Brazil, Great Britain could find itself involved in a serious dispute with the US State Department for years to come.[48]

On December 5, 1940, Lord Halifax, the outgoing Foreign Secretary, informed the Americans that the British were privately considering the possibility of a compromise over the ship.[49] Their change in course was largely due to pressure from the US State Department, but the British ministry of war was adding to the pressure, arguing, "It is highly desirable that the Brazilian army be permitted to obtain these armaments insomuch as they are vitally needed for the coastal defense of Brazil."[50] The ministry of economic warfare in London, which had caused the crisis by ordering the seizure of the ship, was becoming increasingly isolated as the British struggled to find a formula that would maintain the integrity of their naval blockade while still allowing the *Siqueira Campos* to proceed to Rio.

As negotiations continued, anti-British sentiment grew in Rio and the rest of Brazil. After initially keeping the story out of the Brazilian press, Aranha had taken the crisis public and put the full force of the government's propaganda department behind it. The Brazilian press accused the British government of acting like an imperial power and treating Brazil like one of its possessions. Both Dutra and Góes Monteiro made strong public statements against the British position and called for Brazil to consider temporarily breaking relations with Great Britain. Tensions within Brazil were further heightened when Aranha announced that a second Brazilian ship, the SS *Bagé*, was readying to sail from Lisbon the following month, January 1941, with a cargo of German exports, including weapons.

Two other, smaller maritime events elicited further protests from the Brazilians. On November 27, 1940, the British had confiscated some seventy packages of goods from a Brazilian ship at Port of Spain on suspicion of their being of Axis origin.[51] It later turned out that several of the packages had been seized in error.[52] Then, on December 1, a British navy cruiser had removed twenty-two German nationals from the Brazilian steamship SS *Itapé* only eighteen miles off the Brazilian coast. The Germans, it transpired, were traveling between two internal Brazilian ports.[53] During normal times both events would have been regarded as inconsequential, but coming, as they did, at the height of the crisis surrounding the *Siqueira Campos,* they reinforced the Brazilian impression that the British were being heavy-handed with the imposition of their navy blockade.

Yet Brazil, too, was pragmatic. While President Vargas was furious with the British, labeling them "colonial bullies," he understood that a solution needed to be found in order for the *Siqueira Campos* to be allowed to sail. Góes Monteiro continued to attack the British in public, but in private, he was aware that the crisis marked the end of Brazil's arms trade with Germany. He confessed to Aranha that the game was up and that Brazil should seek a deal with Great Britain to make sure that the arms on the *Siqueira Campos* reached their destination—with the understanding that this would almost certainly be the last such shipment Brazil received from the Nazi regime. Vargas, Aranha, and Góes Monteiro waited for the British to propose a compromise formula, a precondition of which, all three men understood, would be Brazilian guarantees and strict prohibitions against any future German exports. The Brazilians agreed that Aranha should make one more effort to get the Americans to put pressure on the British, in the hopes that any compromise they offered would be on terms favorable to Rio. Aranha found the US State Department extremely willing to do this, providing that the Brazilian government continued to praise the US role in helping to resolve the crisis.

Lord Halifax made the much-anticipated compromise offer to Brazil on December 6, 1940. Halifax, known as "the holy fox" for his astute diplomatic skills, tried to explain the British dilemma to the Brazilian ambassador to London. The British could not release the *Siqueira Campos* without undercutting its own blockade policy, he pointed out, and Great Britain would therefore need to ask Brazil "to take certain measures to make the blockade more effective."[54] In other words, the British would release the cargo only if the Brazilians would help them to save face. In truth, after discussing the question, the British cabinet was keen to drive a hard bargain with the Brazilians over the conditions of the compromise, with the intention of showing Rio and Washington that it was serious about the blockade—the enforcement of which it deemed vital for its war effort. In the hopes of enlisting support from the State Department, Lord Halifax contacted Cordell Hull to plead Great Britain's case. "The Brazilians did not have a good technical case . . . and it is hoped that you will give your support in Rio to the British request for a balancing concession on the part of Brazil," he told his American colleague.[55]

Great Britain outlined the "balancing concession" it wanted from Brazil in a rather long and wordy list of demands, which included the immobilization of all enemy ships that were in Brazilian ports and the cessation of all LATI (Italian airlines) flights in and out of Brazil.[56] Not only would such measures ensure that there would not be a repeat of the *Siqueira Campos* affair, but they would also tighten Great Britain's blockade against the Axis powers. To try to encourage a speedy conclusion to the crisis, the British embassy in Rio pleaded in its covering note: "The British government are anxious that the passengers of the *Siqueira Campos* should be spared further inconveniences owing to the detention of the ship and will therefore welcome a very early reply from the Brazilian government."[57]

The British received a quick response, but it wasn't the answer for which they had hoped. Aranha took their offer to the president and advised him that Great Britain's conditions were unacceptable—Brazil couldn't allow itself to be strong-armed into abandoning its economic ties with the Axis completely. The president concurred.[58] When Vargas convened his cabinet to discuss the British demands, the meeting focused not on whether to accept the offer, but rather on what measures Brazil might take to retaliate against the impounding of the *Siqueira Campos*, such as the seizing of British properties in Brazil. The military were calling for a break in Anglo-Brazilian relations, and Aranha was finding such pressure increasingly difficult to withstand.[59]

Keen to resolve the whole affair before it cost him his job or irreparably split Brazil from the Allies, Aranha sought American help in finally bringing the crisis to an end. "England is trying to throw Brazil into the arms of Germany," he claimed, but went on to suggest that Brazil was willing to work with the British.[60] "I thought the terms were an affront and impertinent in tone, but upon careful study they are more reasonable than they seemed at first," he acknowledged. Working with the full knowledge of the president, but not Dutra or Góes Monteiro, Aranha was desperately trying to cut a deal before his countrymen's outrage made such a compromise impossible.

The Brazilian army was looking less and less interested in coming to terms with Great Britain. On December 11, Góes Monteiro vented his anger about the British to the Americans in a manner that made Washington extremely concerned that he was looking to push Brazil into the German camp. The general fumed that:

The British do not realize the irreparable harm they are doing to their cause and interests in Brazil by their stubborn and unreasonable attitude. Whereas 90 percent of the Brazilian population was formerly pro-British,

that situation has changed. They have played right into the hands of
the Germans. There is no need for the Nazis to make propaganda here.
The British are doing it for them. Even with a satisfactory solution to the
case the harm has been done. The British forget their huge interests in
this country such as the São Paulo railway, Western Telegraph, London
Bank, packing houses, etc., which we may take over if the *Siqueira Campos*
is not released. The British forget the facilities received from our naval
and port authorities in provisioning and repairing their vessels. They have
over one hundred intelligence operatives in this country all of whom are
known to us. They have been allowed to work unmolested, but we intend
to stop this situation.[61]

Góes Monteiro may have been blustering, but his threats were enough to
rattle the Americans—who knew full well that if Brazil stopped receiving
British ships in its ports or moved to arrest Great Britain's spies, it could
cause a diplomatic firestorm that would in all likelihood lead to a break
between the Allies and Brazil.

Whether intentional or not, Góes Monteiro's threats spurred American efforts to broker a settlement, and by December 13, Rio and London
seem to have agreed to the outline of a deal to secure the release of the
*Siqueira Campos*. In a sign of a thaw in Anglo-Brazilian relations, Aranha
instructed the department de impressa propaganda, or DIP—the department of press and propaganda—to suspend any references to Great Britain in newsreels shown in Rio.[62] Yet despite Aranha's efforts, anti-British
sentiment in Brazil was proving almost impossible to control.

The *Siqueira Campos* affair had pushed Brazil to the brink. Rumors
circulated in British circles in Rio that Vargas's government was drafting
legislation to seize British assets in the country.[63] Aranha, meanwhile,
feared Germany was using the crisis to make further inroads among the
Brazilian public. "I will do my best to restrain the surge of anti-British
feeling," Aranha assured the Americans, "but . . . this is most difficult in
view of the German-inspired agitations toward vigorous retaliatory action
against the British."[64]

Ultimately, however, Aranha's efforts prevailed. On December 15, Rio
and London reached a deal to release the *Siqueira Campos*. The agreement
followed the lines proposed by the British: Brazil agreed to seize Axis
ships in Brazilian harbors. In order to help seal the deal, Aranha gave his

word that this would be the last shipment of weapons that Brazil would try to acquire from Germany. On hearing the news, President Vargas wrote in his diary, "Finally, it was a relief and a time of high emotion. I was resolved to taking a strong line to vindicate the country, but understood that losses could result and preferred a peaceful solution."[65] Such a solution seemed, at long last, to have been found—and Aranha, Vargas's foreign minister, could take the lion's share of the credit.

On December 21, 1940, the *Siqueira Campos* took on coal in Gibraltar and, with its passengers and German armaments still on board, set sail for Rio.[66] The crisis, however, was far from over. Angered over their perceived humiliation at the hands of the British, the Brazilian army was looking for a confrontation—not just with Great Britain, but also with Aranha, whom it believed had caved in to Anglo-American pressure. It was going to be a long and dangerous summer for President Vargas and his left and right eyes.

6

# ESCAPE FROM RIO

DECEMBER MARKED THE START of the sweltering summer season in
Rio de Janeiro, and it was a difficult month for people who—like
President Vargas and other fixtures of Brazil's political firmament—had
to continue working in the city. Jefferson Caffery labeled December "the
three shirts a day month" and, to be sure, the menswear of the time exacerbated the problem. Short-sleeved shirts were still frowned on in 1940,
particularly on public transportation. It was a time when men wore white
pure-linen suits and carefully pressed long-sleeved shirts with no ties. The
cost of a three-piece washable suit made by a local tailor ranged from $15
to $25, a pittance for well-to-do foreigners, but most diplomats, Caffery
included, preferred to import both their linen and light wool suits—linen
for the summer, and wool for the cooler months.[1] Wealthy Carioca ladies
wore light summer dresses in pastel shades, which were imported from
Europe or copied by local seamstresses from European designs.

To make matters worse, December marked the start of the summer
social season, when the evenings of Brazil's political leaders and foreign
diplomats were taken up with formal events that demanded either black
or white tie. At dinner parties, most men opted to wear a white dinner
jacket; they were lighter and more suitable for the climate. Ladies wore
long European-style silk dresses to such events, and the cost of a locally
tailored gown ranged from $30 to $100.[2] Both gentlemen and ladies on
the Rio social circuit were advised to have at least two of everything,
since—as the American embassy warned—"the dry cleaning in Rio is of
a very inferior and unsatisfactory quality. It is therefore well to depend
upon it as little as possible."[3]

The final clothing requirement for summertime was, of course, the
bathing suit. Men wore Brazilian trunks, which were shorter and tighter

than was traditional on the French Riviera or in the United States. Women's bathing suits revealed the thigh and shoulder, and in most cases came without any decorative frills that would have detracted from their tight lines. Cariocas were more daring than European and American bathers when it came to showing skin, but away from the beach their attire remained conservative—a reflection of the continued influence of the Catholic Church in Brazil.

In the weeks leading up to Christmas, while President Vargas was holed up in the Guanabara and Catete Palaces grumpily going through the diplomatic cables, most regular Cariocas tried to escape the oppressive, sticky heat of the city by spending as much time as possible on one of the city's beaches. It was only a ten-minute drive from the center of Rio to its most famous beach at Copacabana, where the air was cooler—even in the middle of the day—than it was in the city center. Thanks to the winds that whipped along this exposed piece of coastline, Copacabana's temperature could be four or five degrees lower than that of the city center. The cool breeze and shadows cast by the growing number of tall apartment buildings and international hotels that lined the outer edge of Copacabana's wide beachfront boulevard made the summer heat all the more tolerable. Fittingly, Copacabana was known locally as "the lung through which the city breathed."[4]

The most celebrated of all Rio's hotels was the Copacabana Palace, where the rich and famous could enjoy ocean views, fine dining, and a world-class wine collection. The hotel was to Rio what the Ritz Carlton was to Nice, a status symbol and exclusive preserve of the privileged. During the summer season it was extremely difficult to secure accommodations at the hotel, with tourists and visiting dignitaries warned to book well in advance.[5] The war in Europe had increased international interest in Brazil, given its strategic importance to the Allied side, making it all the more difficult to reserve a room at the hotel. Yet the exclusivity of the Copacabana Palace was not its only appeal. The hotel's air-conditioned restaurant made it a blissful oasis in the midst of the sweltering city—and made the hotel a favorite haunt of Osvaldo Aranha, who preferred to lunch there with foreign dignitaries rather than inviting them to the ministry of foreign affairs, which lacked such an amenity.

Cariocas could normally count on an occasional rainstorm to cool the city, but December 1940 wore on without any sign of a break in the weather. Fortunately, the period between Christmas and Carnaval in late February was classified as a holiday season, and very little happened in Rio during that time—allowing people with means to try to escape the heat by leaving the city. Some headed up into the cooler mountains, where many Cariocas kept summer homes; others went to ranches or the homes of family members far from the bustle of the city. Not everyone, however, was so lucky.

For those who had to remain in Rio, December was a time for finishing up the previous year's work and preparing for the next. President Vargas was doing exactly this as 1940 drew to a close. His wife, Darci, had already left Rio to go to the presidential retreat in Petrópolis, a mountain town favored by the city's elite, while Alzira had departed for the family ranch in Rio Grande. Vargas was left alone to finish up negotiations over the budget for 1941, and to prepare his traditional end-of-year message to the Brazilian people.

Even under normal circumstances, Alzira didn't like leaving her father— but in December 1940, she felt that he was especially exposed without her at his side. There were still rumblings in the army about Aranha's deal with the British, which was seen as a slap in the face by the generals and the minister of war, Eurico Gaspar Dutra. After all that she and her father had been through, Alzira could only wonder how long such resentments would continue to simmer—and whether they would soon boil over.

Due to Rio's excessive heat, Vargas had taken to working at night in the small pavilion on top of the hill at the back of the Guanabara Palace.[6] He preferred to take meetings on the pavilion as well, hosting guests in the main palace building only reluctantly, if his visitors were members of the foreign diplomatic corps. Even the president's weekly round of golf had become something of an ordeal; "played golf, very hot," was a regular entry in his diary for December 1940.[7]

Vargas hoped to soon leave Rio for the season. Like the rest of the city's residents, the president was winding down and preparing to move to his summer residence at the Rio Negro Palace up in the mountains in Petrópolis. The town of Petrópolis had become a virtual suburb of Rio, with diplomats, government officials, and local businessmen all relocating there for the summer months. The British ambassador spent two months a year in Petrópolis, at a summer residence the embassy owned there. The Americans, much to the displeasure of Caffery, did not have any such retreat; they claimed: "It was not practical to commute from there in order to keep up business or other daily activities in Rio."[8] On several occasions, usually during the month of December, Caffery pleaded with Washington to reconsider this policy and invest in a summer residence for the ambassador up in Petrópolis.

As Caffery no doubt knew, it was possible to commute from Petrópolis to Rio relatively quickly by 1940. The trip took only about an hour and a half, allowing many husbands and fathers to spend the workweek in Rio and join their families in Petrópolis on the weekends during the summer. Such flexibility was possible because the road to Petrópolis had been steadily improving; it was now one of the longest paved routes in Brazil, making its way through the flat hinterland of Rio before curving sharply and climbing into the mountains, eventually reaching a plateau from which the town, with its quaint red bridges and old villas, was visible.

At the height of the Brazilian summer, Petrópolis was a paradise compared to Rio. The temperature remained hot in the daytime but fell considerably at nightfall, allowing people to sleep in comfort. Whereas Rio reeked of pollution in the summer months, Petrópolis was suffused with the rich perfume of the woods that surrounded the town. One of its wartime residents, Stefan Zweig, marveled at "the charm of the place . . . The mountains have no sharp contours, but leave the town in gradual undulating hills, while flowers blaze everywhere in this town of the gardens."[9]

Located in the center of Petrópolis, set amid beautiful gardens, was the impressive Rio Negro Palace, the president's two-storied summer retreat. The palace had been constructed by the baron of Rio Negro and had been heavily modernized by the Vargas family; the president enjoyed entertaining there. Some of the most important meetings of his regime took place either over a meal inside the palace's dining room or during walks around the gardens. Vargas noted that everybody appeared more relaxed when they visited him in Petrópolis; friends and foes alike dropped their masks and even the unemotional minister of war, Dutra, would manage a smile from time to time. When not engaged with official business, Vargas himself could take walks in the palace's gardens, play golf at a nearby course, and stroll around the uncrowded streets of the town, chatting with passers-by.[10] It was in Petrópolis that Vargas felt his mind was freest, and it was there that he was at his most creative and farsighted.

Problem solving proved to be a much easier art in Petrópolis than in the stuffy palaces in Rio.

Yet in December of 1940, Vargas was most looking forward to a respite from his problems. With the *Siqueira Campos* affair seemingly resolved earlier that month, the president hoped to withdraw for a time and join his wife in the mountain air. On the whole, it had been a good year. During 1940 his authoritarian government had become more popular in Brazil, with fewer threats from either the communists or the Integralistas.[11] The high point of the year had been the signing of the agreement for the huge steel mill project, which Vargas believed would help transform the economy of Brazil—not least because it would allow the country to export steel.

Yet the crisis with Great Britain aside, the year had not been without its problems. By May 1940, the British naval blockade had cut Brazil off from around two-fifths of its prewar export markets, meaning that Brazilians were poorer in 1940 than they had been prior to the war.[12] Vargas also continued to worry about the impact of the growing American influence in the country; he viewed US involvement in Brazilian affairs as a necessary evil, but wondered how far it would go. Jefferson Caffery—with his deep southern accent and pushy manner—had become something of an irritant to the president. What was more, Vargas understood that there were still men whom he couldn't trust—most notably the chief of police—in key positions of his regime. How much of a problem this really was, however, would shortly become apparent.

Four days before Christmas, late in the morning on December 21, minister of war Dutra arrived at the Guanabara Palace demanding to see the president.[13] Vargas's immediate instinct was that something was seriously wrong, and the walk from the pavilion to the main palace building left him tired, hot, and in no mood for small talk, so Dutra stuck to his short, preplanned script. "I have come to resign from my post," he declared.[14] He did not pause at the end of the sentence to give the president an opportunity to speak. "The armaments situation is hopeless," Dutra continued. "We cannot receive German weapons because of the English opposition, and nothing is expected from the United States." Vargas did not accept either Dutra's resignation or the reason he gave for it, and tried to reassure the general, but Dutra left without giving any indication of whether he would reconsider.[15]

The following day, after playing his weekly round of golf, Vargas returned to the Guanabara Palace to find the army chief of staff, General Góes Monteiro, waiting to meet with him. It soon became clear that the arms issue and its implications for the Brazilian army had deeply frustrated Góes Monteiro, just as it had Dutra. Although Góes Monteiro didn't agree with Dutra's threat of resignation, he did make it clear that Brazil's problem with Great Britain was far from settled. The army was not willing to let Brazil's deal with Great Britain prevent it from receiving further weapons shipments from Germany. Some of the contracted weapons were already loaded on the SS *Bagé* at the docks in Lisbon; other arms due to Brazil under the same contract were still sitting in Germany awaiting transportation to Portugal.

A quiet Christmas in Petrópolis was not in the cards for Vargas after all. He tried to calm the military with a speech to army and navy commanders in the Rio de Janeiro area on December 31, but did not sleep properly in the days leading up to the event owing to the heat, and was tired and irritable as a result.[16] To make matters worse, his son, Getúlinho, had been sick for a number of days, and Vargas's wife, Darci, had returned to Rio to be at the youth's bedside day and night.[17] The boy had a close relationship with his father, and Vargas's concern for his son had only increased his stress.

The president's speech started with a glowing tribute to the military, which he acknowledged was operating under very difficult circumstances. He warned his audience that this world war's impact on Brazil would be greater than that of the previous conflict, saying, "The present has much more far reaching repercussions than that of 1914."[18] Vargas then offered his audience what it most wanted to hear—a full-throated defense of Brazil's efforts to procure German weapons, and a warning to Great Britain against trying to stop such trade in the future:

We have taken steps to improve our army personnel and material. In view of the financial difficulties, which confronted us, this material represents an extraordinary effort on the part of the nation for its own safety. Our purchases are not excessive; they are the minimum for our needs. To obtain them we have used funds produced by our labor. We therefore consider them the legitimate product of our capacity to fulfill the imperative needs of our national defense without asking for help or financial assistance from others. The war material, which we ordered, is ours and was bought with our money. To impede its arrival in our hands would be a violation of our rights, and whoever attempts to do so cannot expect from us acts of good will or a spirit of friendly cooperation.[19]

Vargas's remarks represented a bald attempt to appease the Brazilian military by taking a hard line with the country it most resented. Vargas surely anticipated that his words would have the added effect of renewing Allied fears about Brazil's political leanings and strengthening his hand for future dealings with Great Britain and the United States.

The British, however, chose to ignore the warning. In January 1941, they forced the *Bagé*, which was still anchored in Lisbon, to unload its cargo of German weapons just before it was due to sail for Brazil. Both Dutra and Góes Monteiro argued that the cargo was largely comprised of parts needed for weapons Brazil had already received in previous shipments, but their protests fell on deaf ears.

Osvaldo Aranha was not surprised by the actions of the British in Lisbon or the response of the Brazilian military. Indeed, he had argued against making a fuss over the seizure of the weapons. During the resolution of the *Siqueira Campos* crisis he had promised that there would be no additional attempts to import German weapons into Brazil, and he was not willing to go back on his word for the sake of the cargo on the *Bagé*. He had made this promise to the British after consulting with the president, Dutra, and Góes Monteiro; he had to believe that the military had fully understood the implications of the deal with the British, and that any outrage they expressed was for show.

Yet Dutra, for one, appeared not to have comprehended this aspect of the agreement at all—or at least, he did not want to. He denied giving his backing to Aranha's guarantee that the *Siqueira Campos* would be the last shipment of German arms.[20] Once more, Dutra offered his resignation to the president. Aranha, too, raised the stakes. At the start of January, he informed the president that if Vargas did not back him, he would have no alternative but to resign.[21]

In the ensuing political standoff, each of the sides looked to their internal and external allies for help securing a victory. Góes Monteiro secretly asked the US army to try to help get the arms released. Aranha approached the US State Department in the hopes that it could do the same and help him save face by not seeming to go back on his promise. Within Brazil, meanwhile, both Dutra and Góes Monteiro launched a series of bitter attacks against the British in the state-controlled Brazilian press. The attacks became vicious enough for Aranha to intervene, asking the editors and publishers to tone down their coverage of the *Bagé* crisis.[22] When news of Aranha's intervention reached Góes Monteiro, the general flew into a rage. He ranted about the presence of fifth columnists in Brazil, and fumed that the army had to know who was onside. And he demanded meetings with all the owners of the country's newspapers, so that he could ask them, point-blank, "are you pro-Brazil or pro-Britain?"[23] Luckily for them, the meetings never took place, but Góes Monteiro and Dutra continued to demand a strong anti-British line from all newspapers. In London, meanwhile, the foreign office was growing edgy about the level of anti-British rhetoric in the Brazilian press. Yet there was a sense in London that Great Britain was in the right, that a deal was a deal, and it should be adhered to at all costs.[24]

The fixation on the Brazilian press in both London and the highest offices of the Brazilian military reflected a near-universal perception that because Brazilian newspapers were controlled by Vargas's government, anything they printed was essentially the opinion of the state itself. In truth, while Vargas could exert pressure on Brazil's press and censor—even shutter—them if they disobeyed, he lacked the practical apparatus or political will to muzzle the press completely. Censorship was often self-imposed and was by no means universal—a fact that would come to haunt Vargas in the days ahead.

On January 18, 1941, Vargas was in the Guanabara Palace, overseeing the final stages of packing for his summer relocation to Petrópolis, when, with a great crack of thunder, the rain finally arrived in Rio. The irony of the weather breaking on the day of his departure, following weeks of oppressive heat, was not lost on the president. He was suffering from weeks of poor sleep due to the heat of Rio's summer nights, and had been longing for a drop in the temperature. Now cooler weather was coming just as he headed into the mountains for a respite.

As Vargas's car made its way up the winding mountain road toward Petrópolis later on January 18, the rain turned torrential, forcing the president's driver to slow down and dragging the trip out longer than the usual one and a half hours. There was one upside to the rain, however; on arriving at the Rio Negro Palace, Vargas was delighted that he had made it into Petrópolis almost unnoticed.[25] That evening, he dined with Alzira and her husband, Ernâni do Amaral Peixoto, who had served as the governor of the state of Rio de Janeiro.[26] Alzira had traveled to Petrópolis from the family ranch in Rio Grande in order to be with her father. Both Alzira and Amaral warned the president about Góes Monteiro's increasing hostility toward the press, and informed him that the press was going to mount something of a thinly veiled counteroffensive against the military in the coming days. If that happened, it could cause a political firestorm within Brazil, and create even more of a rift between the military and Vargas's government. Alzira and Amaral urged the president to intercede before the newspaper publishers could go ahead with their plan. Vargas promised, "I'll give the matter some thought." The president was keen, however, to leaven his work schedule with some leisure, and had made plans to play golf the next day.[27]

Just as Alzira had predicted, events came to a head the next day, when two newspapers appeared to step over the line the military had drawn in the sand. On January 19, the daily paper *Correio da Manhã* ran a seemingly harmless advertisement by the commission of British industries, which included a pro-British remark by Aranha. At the same time, an editorial in another daily, the *Diário Carioca*, called for Brazilians to support Vargas. The latter piece was generally seen as a warning to the army to stay out of politics.[28] Dutra and Góes Monteiro were furious about both articles, believing that—by supporting the British and undercutting the army, respectively—Aranha and Vargas had set back the army's efforts to secure the release of the German arms held in Lisbon.

The proprietor of *Correio da Manhã* was a well-known Anglophile, Paulo Bittencourt, the most interesting of Brazil's newspaper owners. Slight, olive-skinned, and handsome, Bittencourt enjoyed collecting modern art and furniture and showing them off at dinner parties at his mansion, which boasted a large patio and beautifully kept gardens. He spoke perfect English, with an accent that came straight from one of Great Britain's finest public schools, and he was extremely well connected with members of the Brazilian government and with the leading Brazilian families and industrialists.[29]

Bittencourt's newspaper was widely regarded as the most influential in Rio, and while Brazil technically had no free press, Bittencourt was keen to push his agenda within the parameters set by the government. Bittencourt was well known for his strong pro-British views, which he had defended in the pages of *Correio da Manhã* and in meetings with Brazilian officials. He respected the British Empire and attacked anybody who claimed that the empire was doomed in its current confrontation with the Axis. He did not regard the Americans as the equals of the British in any sense, arguing that the Brazilians, and not the Yankees—as he referred to them—were the natural heirs of Great Britain and its empire.[30]

Not everybody in Brazil agreed with Bittencourt's viewpoint, but it did reflect a sizeable school of thought within the country's older noble families, specifically those in Rio. These influential families preferred the calm order of the British to the noise and brashness of Americans, and were concerned that the rise of American influence in Brazil would fundamentally change Brazil's way of life. Indeed, many Brazilians were uncomfortable about the effects of US involvement in Latin America, and feared that their country would become little more than a satellite outpost of the United States.

Among those who shared Bittencourt's suspicions of American imperialism was President Vargas. Although Brazil and the United States had just completed one of the most important economic deals in Brazilian history, Vargas could not quite shake his unease at Washington's growing influence in Brazilian affairs. This surely shaped his response to the newspaper crisis—but so, too, did his basic political instincts, just as Bittencourt had anticipated they would.

Before publishing the British advertisement that contained Aranha's pro-British comment, Bittencourt had thought long and hard about the repercussions he would likely face if he ran it. Bittencourt believed that he understood one crucially important point regarding the modus operandi of President Vargas: as Waldo Frank noted, "Vargas holds Brazil intact by playing the middle against both ends. By playing coolness against all the fires; by playing centripetal delay against all the tangential dynamisms of the country . . . Vargas senses the people and obeys what he senses."[31] Knowing that the president's political strategy necessarily kept him from taking sides in political clashes, Bittencourt anticipated that Vargas would not back the army in any crisis between the military and the newspapers. Brazilians valued their press, even if it was not free in the Western liberal sense, and the president would not allow the generals to close down *Correio da Manhã*. So Bittencourt had rolled the dice.

As soon as Bittencourt ran the ad, both Dutra and Góes Monteiro demanded that *Correio da Manhã* be permanently closed down. They were less harsh with the *Diário Carioca*, which had run articles in the past that were sympathetic to the chief of staff; Dutra and Góes Monteiro asked that it be only temporarily suspended as punishment for its article.

Bittencourt's political judgment, however, proved to be spot-on. Vargas rejected the idea of closing *Correio da Manhã*. He did suspend the publication of *Diário Carioca* for a short period, noting that the newspaper's article could be viewed as an attempt to create divisions between the president and the armed forces. But he refused to punish Bittencourt for running the pro-British ad, and he also refused to sanction Dutra's protests any longer. Dutra had threatened to resign unless Vargas gave him his full backing over the crisis about the latest shipment of weapons, but Vargas now informed Dutra that he did not accept his resignation and ordered him to return to his duties. The military was enraged, but impotent. On hearing the news of the temporary suspension of *Diário Carioca,* troops protested outside its headquarters until Góes Monteiro, who denied ordering the protest, demanded that Dutra call the men off; the minister of war soon complied with the request.[32]

The outcome of the newspaper crisis was viewed as a political victory for Aranha and a defeat for the military, and this vindication of the foreign minister had important ramifications for Brazilian policy toward the Allies.[33] After the crisis, the Brazilian armed forces reduced their pressure on the British to allow further shipments of German weapons into Brazil.[34] The military accepted that the prospects of receiving the final shipment of German arms from the 1938 contract were nonexistent. Instead, they would seek replacements for the undelivered weapons from the United States.

The resolution of Brazil's latest crisis marked an important turning point in US-Brazilian relations particularly. The Brazilian military had finally come to terms with the fact that German weapons were no longer an option. The mutual suspicions that had characterized the relationship between the Brazilian military and the US government remained, but the generals in Rio needed to modernize the army above all else, and they no longer had any other option than to work with the Americans.

The United States softened its policy toward Brazil as well. The two sides had yet to formalize the mutual-defense arrangements and arms shipments that they had tentatively agreed to in the Góes Monteiro Draft conceived during the *Siqueira Campos* affair, but Vargas and Aranha's fealty to the spirit of the deal had obviously made an impression in Washington. It now took a more positive position regarding which arms it was able and willing to deliver to Brazil: for the first time, the Brazilian military could expect to receive machine guns and air defense guns along with artillery and ammunition. The United States also adopted a generous credit scheme to allow Brazil to purchase the weapons—a concession that greatly relieved Rio, which had remained anxious about its ability to pay for the weapons in legal tender or gold rather than coffee and cotton.[35]

Much to the delight of Paulo Bittencourt, the ending of the crisis with Great Britain also led to a rapid improvement in Anglo-Brazilian relations. Vargas sought a rapid rapprochement with London following the crisis, and his haste—and the popular support for his efforts—appeared to confirm that many Brazilians viewed close relations with Great Britain as a popular counterfoil against the United States's creeping influence. The British, for their part, clearly felt vindicated for having stuck to the original terms of the agreement over the *Siqueira Campos,* but were keen to mend fences with the Brazilian regime as rapidly as possible. The original instigators of the dispute, the British ministry of economic warfare, eventually adopted a more liberal interpretation of the blockade policy toward Brazil, helping ensure smoother management of the blockade through 1941.[36]

The Brazilian military, however, remained angry. Despite the promise of US weapons to make up for the ones that would no longer be flowing into Brazil from Germany, the military sensed a lack of support from the president over the issue of weapons. It was not the only such cause for conflict.

The day after he rebuked the army for its attempts to close the two newspapers, Vargas incurred the wrath of the armed forces again. This time, the issue was the appointment of the first minister of air. In the autumn of 1940, Góes Monteiro had called for all aviation, with the exception of naval aviation, to be brought under the control of the ministry of war. Vargas rejected this idea and planned to establish a new ministry to cover all aviation.[37] Both the army and the navy believed that the ministry should be headed by one of their own. But on January 20, 1941, the president announced that he had appointed a civilian, Joaquim Pedro Salgado Filho, as the new minister of air.[38] Vargas had made the decision following a round of golf that had been interrupted by his chief military aide, who had tried to convince him to appoint a military man to the job so as to appease Dutra and Góes Monteiro.

The nature of the appointment, as well as its timing, represented a calculated risk by the president. It was a clear signal that he would not allow the armed forces to undermine his authority, and it elicited a strong response from the military; Dutra accused Vargas of using the establishment of the new ministry to play the various parts of the armed forces off against one another. Yet for all the danger inherent in his decision, it augured well for US-Brazilian relations. Vargas's popularity with the Brazilian people, along with his growing confidence in his authority over the military, positioned him better than ever before to lead Brazil at a time when Washington was seeking to rapidly deepen its ties with Rio.

# DEEPENING TIES AND WIDENING DIVIDES

IN THE SPRING OF 1941, A PAN AMERICAN AIRWAYS flight arrived at the airport in Rio de Janeiro carrying two American travelers. Their trip had been unusually quick; in 1941, in a sign of deepening ties with the United States, the Brazilian authorities had granted Pan Am permission to fly overland from the northern Brazilian city of Belém to Rio, a move that—along with the introduction of the airline's faster, fully pressurized strato-clipper aircraft—had shortened the arduous trip from Miami to Rio from five to just under two days.[1] After a journey that covered more than a thousand miles of Brazilian "virgin territory," Rio appeared like "a beautiful pearl set in emerald," wrote an excited passenger who had made the same voyage.[2]

The Pan Am plane had first circled the city as if doing a lap of honor before descending rapidly onto the airport runway, built on a narrow strip of land adjacent to the bay. Most of the strato-clipper's passengers were tourists on an organized eight-day air cruise, and they rushed to get out of the Rio heat by checking into the air-conditioned sanctuaries of the Copacabana Palace Hotel and the similarly luxurious Hotel Gloria. The two American gentlemen, however, had other plans. They headed straight to downtown Rio, where they immediately went to work.[3]

The men worked for the coordinator of inter-American affairs—the charismatic American businessman and philanthropist Nelson Rockefeller. Rich, handsome, ambitious, and with a sizable ego to match his many talents, Rockefeller had recently been assigned to the post to oversee America's commercial, cultural, and public relations with the Latin American countries. He was also intent on making mischief with the

State Department and the man he most loathed in its stuffy corridors, the undersecretary of state, Sumner Welles.

Nominally, Rockefeller was working for Welles—at least, he was working on the Good Neighbor Program, whose name the undersecretary of state had coined, and which he still controlled. In reality, however, Rockefeller was following his own agenda and believed that he answered directly to President Roosevelt. Welles regarded Rockefeller as something of a loose cannon that could potentially do as much damage as good in the politically sensitive environment of Latin America. The region was central to Welles's responsibilities, and although he was not against some limited cooperation between the State Department and Rockefeller's office, he envisaged a secondary role for the coordinator of inter-American affairs. He certainly had no interest in watching as an upstart like Rockefeller wreaked havoc on US diplomatic efforts south of the equator.

In private, neither Welles nor Rockefeller missed an opportunity to put the other man down, but from President Roosevelt's perspective their enmity was an advantage. The president liked to set up competing lines of communication and responsibility so as to keep his underlings from becoming too powerful; indeed, one of the reasons the president had brought Welles to the State Department in the first place was so that he would compete with Secretary of State Cordell Hull, an enemy of Welles's and a man Roosevelt regarded as a serious political threat. Sure enough, the secretary of state clashed frequently with his deputy, and the State Department was soon full of rumors—spread, no doubt, by Hull—about Welles's sexuality and his conduct when under the influence of alcohol. Welles was a known alcoholic who was prone to committing acts of the most indiscreet nature when drunk.[4] It was alleged that, in private, Hull would refer to Welles as "my fairy."[5] What most distressed Hull about Welles was his walk-in rights to the Oval Office, which were greater than those the secretary of state was permitted by the president.

Another spider in the complex web of beltway politics was the American spymaster General William "Wild Bill" Donovan, who also came to compete for influence in Brazil and who clashed, on various occasions, with Caffery, with Welles, and—most of all—with Rockefeller.[6] Donovan headed the embryonic office of strategic services (OSS), America's wartime intelligence agency, and he was convinced that Rockefeller would mess things up in Latin America unless he was reined in.

The Donovan-Rockefeller conflict was essentially a turf war over specific areas of American policy toward Latin America. Donovan believed that the continent was crawling with Nazi agents and spies, and thought of it as America's soft rear. He maintained that it made no sense for Rockefeller, who was in charge of commercial and cultural relations with Latin America, to also be responsible for American propaganda in such a vital area. As Donovan pointed out to President Roosevelt, the OSS oversaw propaganda operations in other parts of the world; his office should handle propaganda in the Americas as well.

On this occasion, the president chose to back Rockefeller, forcing Donovan to promise to stay out of Latin America.[7] In 1941, at least, Donovan kept his promise to the president, but later—when the United States entered the war following the attack on Pearl Harbor—the spy chief sent his own agents to the region, and soon thereafter found himself embroiled in further disputes with rival Washington agencies.

Rockefeller did not always prevail in his clashes with other US officials. Once, when Sumner Welles felt that Rockefeller had overstepped his authority, he took his case to President Roosevelt; the president, feeling duty bound to back his officials at the State Department despite his personal admiration for Rockefeller, threw his support behind Welles and warned Rockefeller that he would have to do the same in future disputes.[8] The young and energetic Rockefeller was a quick learner, however, and he vowed to avoid future run-ins with Welles by simply gaining presidential approval for his ideas and policies before revealing them to his immediate superior. Rockefeller did not intend to play second fiddle to anybody—least of all Welles, whose talents he felt were limited.

Like his ego, Rockefeller's ambitions were outsized. He came from one of America's wealthiest families, and had connections that reached far beyond politics. His network extended to Hollywood's movie industry, as well as the worlds of art and music, and his family's companies—such as Chase National Bank (later Chase Manhattan) and the Creole Petroleum Corporation—were among some of the most powerful in the United States. Rockefeller wanted to grow his existing business ties with Latin America and find new opportunities in the region, yet that was not what mattered most to him. Rockefeller primarily wanted to make a difference; if America was dragged into the European war, he wished to contribute to the American war effort however he could, and preferably in a major way.

Despite their differences, Rockefeller, Donovan, Welles, and Hull agreed on one point: Brazil was the major focus of American efforts in Latin America under the guise of the Good Neighbor Program. The country was never far from the minds of these competing American officials thanks to a number of factors, prime among them the strategic importance of Brazil's northeastern coastline, which the United States wished to use as a base for its submarines; the threat of the Germans achieving a bridgehead on the American continent; and the potentially destabilizing effect of the large German immigrant population in the south of the country. Brazil also had a potentially plentiful supply of rubber, which the Americans badly needed for their war effort.

The United States clearly had much to gain from developing new ties and deepening existing ones with Brazil. But there was another reason Brazil was important to the Allies. As one American put it, "Argentina is beyond the pale and we need to devote everything to help Vargas and Brazil." By 1941, it was clear to any American observer that Argentina was unswervingly pro-Axis, and that the United States would have to look elsewhere to make potential diplomatic inroads in Latin America—and to make sure the fascist "disease" did not spread. As the other behemoth of Latin America, and as a natural competitor of Argentina, Brazil was a logical choice for an American client state.

Rockefeller and his opponents Donovan, Welles, and Hull also shared a Brazilian interlocutor in Osvaldo Aranha. In many ways, Aranha represented the side of the Brazilian Estado Novo that Washington found most acceptable. None of the Americans had any time for Dutra, whom they believed was leaning toward Germany in 1941, and whom they perceived as the biggest rival and most likely successor to Vargas, should the army force the president from power. Similar suspicions surrounded Góes Monteiro, although, as chief of staff of the army, Góes Monteiro met with American military officials more often than political policy makers in Washington.

President Vargas remained somewhat aloof to US advances, and preferred for Aranha to act as Brazil's contact point for all the various competing American agencies. The only American with whom Vargas liked to correspond directly was President Roosevelt; by early 1941 Vargas was coming to regard the US president as the best hope for achieving Brazil's strategic goals. Vargas, it is fair to say, had learned from his experience negotiating with the Americans over the steel mill: it was only Roosevelt's personal intervention that had pushed the various arms of the US government to cooperate with Brazil. As a result, Vargas was happy to leave it to Aranha to meet with lower-level US officials, and to intervene only when requested to do so by his minister of foreign affairs.

As Rockefeller's main contact in the Brazilian government, Osvaldo Aranha knew the two men whom the coordinator of inter-American affairs had dispatched in semisecrecy to Rio de Janeiro. Rockefeller had charged his employees Berent Friele and Frank Nattier with establishing the coordinator's first permanent office in Latin America. Their job was to build as many business and cultural contacts for Rockefeller in Rio as they could. Both men were fluent in Portuguese, which would help their cause. So, too, would the good offices of Aranha himself, who had been informed in advance of the men's mission, and who had promised to personally help in whatever way he could.

The State Department in Washington understood that Friele and Nattier were in Rio, but Rockefeller had not informed the department of the true nature of their mission. Rather, he devised a complex cover story, telling his superiors that his two employees were on a fact-finding mission throughout all of Latin America and would not be remaining in the Rio area for any extended period of time. Still, it did not take long for Jefferson Caffery to work out the truth. He informed Welles at the State Department, but both men chose to watch and wait in the hope that Rockefeller would make a major mistake in Rio, thereby allowing the State Department to develop a strong case against the coordinator and take it up with the president.

As it turned out, it was the development and dissemination of American propaganda—that most vexed of the commissioner's prerogatives—that almost proved to be Rockefeller's downfall. In an attempt to stem the tide of Axis propaganda in Latin America, Rockefeller's staff came up with the idea of buying up huge swaths of advertising space in local newspapers across the region. The ads would highlight the virtues of travel to the United States with catch phrases such as, "come up and see us." The real aim of the ads, however, was to take up space in the newspapers, thereby preventing the Axis powers from running their own advertisements. The scheme was also intended to channel some much needed dollars to Latin American governments that were struggling with their respective war economies.

The advertising campaign was a disaster. Leaders throughout Latin America charged that the Americans were essentially bribing them, while those who had not received any revenue from the advertisements complained that they had been ignored. Others pointed out that the subject matter of the ads—tourism to the United States—was totally inappropriate given the lack of funds that most Latin Americans had for travel and given that US entrance restrictions made it very difficult for anybody from Latin America to get into the country. The most serious accusation, however, was that Rockefeller had authorized his staff to place ads in pro-Axis newspapers, thereby giving those publications crucial financial support.

Welles and Hull took the issue to the president who, as he had previously warned Rockefeller he would do, supported his two State Department leaders. Rockefeller took the hint, and from that point onward informed the State Department in advance about all his projects and plans in Latin America. "It will slow you down, but what the hell," Rockefeller conceded to a colleague.[9]

By the spring of 1941, Rockefeller and Welles had developed a relatively cordial working relationship with a much healthier degree of cooperation. Tensions still arose from time to time, but the two men were able to resolve them without invoking the president. Wherever possible, however, Rockefeller continued to bypass the State Department and rely on his men on the ground in Rio. And in the spring of 1941, the office of the coordinator of inter-American affairs in Rio had grown significantly; whereas at first only Friele and Nattier represented Rockefeller in Brazil, by 1941 the office had amassed a staff of thousands, all working to expand their boss's network of business and cultural contacts in the country.

Rockefeller's propaganda plans had backfired in a spectacular fashion, but he was correct in arguing that something needed to be done to counter the increasingly effective German propaganda in Brazil. The Germans were targeting all parts of Brazilian society despite the fact that, following Vargas's attempts to curb Nazi activities in Brazil, much of Germany's propaganda activity had been forced underground. The one exception was the press.[10] Due to Vargas's reluctance to close any newspapers, Brazil's pro-German newspapers were able to continue expressing their views (and those of their patrons in Berlin) with impunity.

German propaganda in Brazil followed three main themes, which Hitler's ministry of information outlined as follows:[11]

1. The threat of "Yankee Imperialism."
2. The menace of Communism.
3. The victory of the Allies would lead to the introduction into Brazil of a color bar similar to that operating in the southern states of the United States.[12]

Germany's propaganda campaign in Brazil hinged on the country's latent anti-American sentiment while also playing up the threat of communism, which had become a customary stalking horse for Nazi expansion throughout the world.

As with most wartime propaganda, however, the impact of Germany's efforts in Brazil was directly related to the military state of the war. By the spring of 1941, the German war machine controlled much of Europe, and while Great Britain had forestalled the immediate threat of a full-scale German invasion of the home islands, they remained vulnerable. As long as Germany's stunning success continued, the ministry of information in Berlin could be sure that the Brazilian public would be increasingly receptive to German propaganda, in all of its many forms.

The German embassy in Rio subsidized pro-German newspapers and monthly reviews. Though many of these had small circulations, their limited reach did nothing to calm the British, who were extremely concerned that the Brazilians were allowing them to circulate at all.[13] In Rio, the Germans adopted the tactic of starting false rumors about Great Britain. On March 27, 1941, the foreign office in London asked the British embassy in Rio to investigate one such rumor, which claimed that Great Britain was boycotting Brazilian beef produce.[14] The rumor proved false, but it still made its way into the local press, forcing the British embassy in Rio to carefully deny the story. As a British official in Rio explained to the foreign office, "I managed to calm feeling by favorable explanation, counter articles, and conversations. Nothing is now required except to buy from time to time from local firms, not only for publicity but also because their products are the only ones of the required standard."[15] German propaganda notwithstanding, the quality of Brazilian beef was high enough to ensure a steady British market.

While Germany cunningly manipulated public discourse in Brazil in 1941, the Brazilian press took care not to print any article that was too anti-German in tone. The Germans' continued military successes in West

Africa had brought their army closer and closer to Brazil's bulging Atlantic coastline, a development that inspired many of the country's newspaper owners to adopt a cautious, wait-and-see approach to the war. Pro-German references even cropped up in the mainstream press, camouflaged as letters to the editor or in editorials.

The German propaganda effort may not have been eclipsing that of Great Britain and the United States, but it was nonetheless causing a great deal of anxiety in Washington and London. In Washington, the State Department charged Nelson Rockefeller with countering this German threat. Rockefeller's newspaper advertisement campaign had proven disastrous, but he would soon devise propaganda projects that would have a far more positive impact on US-Brazilian relations.

Rockefeller and John Hay (Jock) Whitney, the director of the motion picture division of Rockefeller's office, made the brilliant decision to enlist Hollywood in the Latin American propaganda war. Rockefeller had personally recruited Whitney to head the motion picture division; in 1941 Whitney was one of the most powerful men in Hollywood, having recently bankrolled the hugely successful 1939 picture *Gone with the Wind*. Working closely together, Rockefeller and Whitney had recruited many of Hollywood's top names to help foster new ties between the United States and Brazil. Hollywood would quickly discover that there were huge amounts of money to be made out of the war.

In something of a masterstroke, Rockefeller and Whitney persuaded Walt Disney to come on board America's wartime efforts in Brazil by embarking on a goodwill tour of the country. In time, Disney's Brazil visit would prove something of a prototype for trips by other American filmmakers; the State Department used their status as cultural icons to spread American propaganda in South America, and specifically in Brazil. But when Whitney first proposed the tour, Disney was skeptical. To be sure, the timing could not have been better for Disney, whose employees were in the process of striking for better working conditions. Disney was deeply hurt by the strike—he believed it was unjust and the strikers' demands were unrealistic—but he was still hesitant to take on the goodwill tour. "I'm no good at that, I can't do it," Disney replied at first. "Then why not go down and make some pictures?" Whitney inquired. "Well, yes," Disney said, "I'd feel better about going to do something more than simply shaking hands."[16]

Disney was on board. Later, he reflected, "This South American expedition is a godsend. I am not so hot for it, but it gives me a chance to get away from this god-awful nightmare and to bring back some extra work into the plant. I have a case of the D.D.'s—disillusionment and discouragement."[17]

Whitney promised to accompany the party to Brazil, and the US government also agreed to underwrite the cost of the trip for Disney and his crew as well as a large chunk of the production costs of any short films that resulted from the trip. The Disney party left Los Angeles on August 17, 1941, taking the new, shorter plane route over mainland Brazil. To record the event and to maximize the publicity from it, Rockefeller arranged for staff from *Life* magazine to travel with the Disney party. The resulting photographs taken by one of the magazine's leading photographers, Hart Preston, remain one of the truly great records of Rio during World War II.

The Disney party arrived in Rio some three days after departing Los Angeles, and set up in the Copacabana Palace Hotel, from which Disney traveled around the city meeting key Brazilian filmmakers. Disney's family accompanied him, and the entertainment tycoon and his family enjoyed sketching in the city's botanical gardens and from the hotel's suite, which faced the beach. The perfect gentleman and diplomat, Disney said all the right things and was courteous to everyone he met.

On the morning of September 4, Disney, accompanied by Whitney, met with President Vargas at the Catete Palace. As was usual in meetings between her father and Americans, Alzira acted as the translator. Vargas explained to his two American guests how much he enjoyed watching movies—they were, he revealed to them, one of his best means of relaxation.[18] Indeed, prior to the meeting, the Vargas family, Disney, and Disney's daughter had attended a special premier of the Disney film *Fantasia* in Rio. All of this was carefully captured by Preston, whose images reveal two happy parties sitting together with a rather grumpy Jefferson Caffery, barely able to contain his displeasure at what amounted to a major propaganda coup for Rockefeller and his office.

Disney's visit was a great success, and not just with Brazilians. Later, Disney created a Brazilian character, Joe Carioca, who—in a short film that Disney released in 1943—took Donald Duck on an imaginary trip to discover Rio and wider Brazil. Such cartoons proved highly popular with American audiences, despite the fact that (as some critics later pointed out) they contained no black characters—a pointed omission, given Brazil's marked racial diversity. Their questionable sociocultural underpinnings aside, however, the films—like Disney's trip itself—went a long way toward repairing the damage of Rockefeller's ill-advised advertisement campaign earlier that year.

Forever restless and always looking for new ways to advance the US cause in Brazil, Rockefeller soon hit on a new propaganda scheme—this one involving the British embassy in Rio. Rockefeller realized that the British had a better-oiled propaganda machine in Rio than the Americans did at the time. He therefore was keen to develop ties with the British officials responsible for the program. As ever, Rockefeller was also looking to bypass Jefferson Caffery. At official events in Washington and Latin America, Rockefeller went out of his way to court British diplomats. He enjoyed their sense of belonging to an old boys club, and understood that Caffery had become a figure of loathing for the British officials in London and Rio.

The British, however, proved to be reluctant partners. The foreign office suggested that while cooperation with Rockefeller's office was acceptable in theory, it likely would not work in practice because they were suspicious of his mission. Instead, the British promised to inform Rockefeller of their activities and in return Rockefeller offered to provide them with US newsreels. This was to prove of some use to the British embassy in Rio; the Brazilian authorities were constantly criticizing British newsreels and BBC reports for not being pro-Brazilian enough. And, while they would not be jointly producing propaganda, both Rockefeller and the British did agree to work together to try to limit the impact of Axis propaganda in Brazil.

Lourival Fontes, the director of Brazil's department of press and propaganda (referred to in Brazil as the DIP), was central to American and British attempts to stop German propaganda; as the head of Brazil's propaganda ministry, he had the power to effectively stifle the Axis's voice in the country. The Allies regarded Fontes as a Nazi sympathizer, a charge he strongly denied. "I'm just a Brazilian and whatever should happen in the future in Brazil, I'll be the scapegoat," he allegedly claimed in private correspondence with an American journalist that was intercepted by British intelligence.[19] Fontes added, "The army has been and is still hounding me all the time to color the news releases to favor Germany, but so far

I've been able to resist."[20] Fontes went on to admit that while both Dutra and Góes Monteiro were, in his estimation, pro-German, the real leader of the Nazi element in official Brazilian circles was the chief of police in Rio de Janeiro, Major Filinto Müller. Dutra and Góes Monteiro may have been swayed by financial incentives for Brazilian cooperation—for example, German economic and military concessions—but, Fontes suggested, "Müller does not need financial encouragement to take the attitude he does." Müller had played a part in a 1924 revolution in the city of São Paulo, and following its suppression was exiled to Buenos Aires, Argentina, where he worked as a taxi driver for six years—and where he presumably breathed a good deal of the country's noxious political atmosphere.[21] Following his return to Brazil he was appointed chief of police of Rio in 1933, and since then had been active in dealing with both the communist and Integralista threats. His service aside, Müller was not really trusted by anybody in the Vargas administration, and he had his share of enemies outside of it, too; the British regarded him as "the principal instrument of Axis intrigue in Brazil."[22]

Fontes's intercepted letter suggested that he believed it was in Brazil's economic and military self-interest to throw its lot in with the United States. "Should the United States shut down on Brazil (cease to buy, for instance) Brazil would be ruined," he observed. "And it is apparent that the United States from a military point of view is able to take care of itself and South America as well."[23] His comments indicated that the DIP was keen to climb on the American bandwagon as soon as possible, and that the Brazilian propaganda ministry was trying to shed its pro-Nazi image.

While it appeared to signal progress for the Allied propaganda effort in Brazil, however, the letter—and a separate, alleged meeting between Fontes and the same American journalist—may actually have been fabricated by the US or (more likely) British intelligence services. Fabricating so-called "intercepted" letters and using them for propaganda purposes was a specialty of the British intelligence services. Naturally, Fontes denied ever making the comments that were attributed to him in the letter.

Whatever the legitimacy of the letter and Fontes's comments, in public the DIP continued to play both the Allies and Axis off against one another during the spring and summer of 1941. President Vargas sent a message of good health to Adolf Hitler on May Day, conveying to him the "felicitations of the Brazilian government and people for your personal happiness and the continued prosperity of the German nation."[24] The British would soon observe that Vargas's policy "is entirely determined by his judgment as to who is likely to win the war," and his overture to Germany was a case in point.[25] With the Germans making good progress on the Greek island of Crete and with the rumors of continued disquiet in the military, Vargas had issued what Alzira would later refer to as "a reminder to the Americans not to take him too much for granted. *Papai* always got their attention," she reflected, "when his continued support appeared a non-certainty."

On the occasion of July 4, Vargas broadcast a message to President Roosevelt, reinforcing his warning to the president and the American people.[26] This was an unusual move for Vargas, who previously had not publicly acknowledged Independence Day celebrations in the United States.[27] Yet international events had made his timing appropriate. With the entry of the Soviet Union into the war following the launch of Operation Barbarossa—the German invasion of the USSR—on June 22, 1941, President Vargas felt that war was coming ever-nearer to Brazil and he understood that the Americans shared this view. Germany's perfidious attack on her former ally had essentially pushed the Soviet Union into the arms of the Allies, swelling their ranks and splitting the German war effort between two fronts. If Hitler's early successes had seemed incredible, his defeat now seemed more likely than ever. And if Germany was defeated, Vargas would have no choice but to throw in Brazil's lot with the Allies—effectively eliminating the leverage he had been enjoying with the United States, and imperiling his grand vision for Brazil's future.

For Vargas, and for Brazil, this was the optimum time to try to extract as much out of the United States as possible. The British understood that Vargas's broadcast on July 4 was the start of a major Brazilian offensive to maximize its gains from the United States before the latter became too distracted by the deepening European war.[28] Whether the Americans saw through this latest Brazilian ploy, on the other hand, is anybody's guess.

Luckily for Vargas, he had the perfect bargaining chip. For some time, the United States had been trying and failing to get permission from the Brazilian administration for the stationing of American troops in the north of Brazil. During the previous year, fearing a German invasion in the area, Roosevelt had wanted to send one hundred thousand US military personnel to Brazil in what became known as Operation Pot of Gold. Vargas had resisted then, and in the middle of 1941 he still rejected the idea. Yet he knew the Americans remained keen to get their troops into Brazil.

The United States was indeed still concerned about the threat facing Brazil. On June 17, five days before the German invasion of the Soviet Union, US army chief of staff George Marshall had outlined the dangers in a letter to Undersecretary of State Welles, in which he also reflected the widespread American suspicion of the Brazilian president:

> The real hazard . . . which should probably not be mentioned to President Vargas, lies in the danger of an unsupported attack by German forces. The greatest peril in this situation lies in the possibility of a sudden seizure of airfields and ports in northeast Brazil by forces already in the country and acting in collusion with small German forces. The latter, arriving by air and perhaps by sea, would so time their movement as to arrive at these points immediately after the seizure. They would at once take over and organize these points for defense.[29]

The threat of a German invasion of the Americas was extraordinary, but it could not be ignored. The historical precedents were all too real: around the turn of the century, German emperor Wilhelm II had tried to frighten the United States by ordering plans drawn up for a transatlantic invasion; during World War I, moreover, the Germans had attempted to coax Mexico into entering the fight on the side of the Central Powers. Germany's military ambitions in the Americas were well proven, if not especially credible—but the possibility was there.

All of this placed Osvaldo Aranha in a difficult situation. He appeared more isolated than usual. When Jefferson Caffery visited him on June 27, 1941, to gauge his reaction to the latest US request for a troop deployment to northern Brazil, he found the foreign minister irritated and unusually abrupt in his responses. After outlining the proposal for the stationing of US troops in Brazil and the dangers Brazil was facing, Caffery came straight to the point: "Will you take this proposal to the president?" Aranha responded: "It would be a mistake to ask President Vargas to permit the sending of United States troops to northern Brazil, especially in view of the failure of the United States to supply arms to the Brazilian military."[30]

Aranha then turned to the question of the timing of any such request to Vargas. "President Vargas has been leaning more and more in your direction during the past months," he told Caffery. "He is definitely on your side, but certainly the moment has not yet arrived when he could agree to this proposal and get away with it. He would think that I should know better than to put it up to him in this way at this juncture."[31] Aranha's response illustrated the increasing fear in the Brazilian government that any stationing of US troops in Brazil would lead to a violent reaction from the Brazilian military and some Integralistas.

In the weeks preceding the meeting, both the British and the Americans had noted a subtle change in the after-dinner speeches that Aranha had been giving at official functions at the Itamaraty Palace. Unlike Aranha's normal after-dinner remarks, which often focused on trade and political links with the United States, these speeches contained troubling references to increasing admiration for the German war machine. "Does Aranha now really believe the Germans are going to win the war?" wrote a worried embassy official. In reality, he was, as were Vargas, Dutra, and Góes Monteiro watching newsreel footage of spectacular German advances with the prospect of a quick German victory looking likely. General Góes Monteiro, for one, thought the US request to station troops in Brazil was hypocritical. Later in the summer, over lunch with Aranha, he argued, "the United States seems anxious to get troops into northeastern Brazil, but does not seem anxious to help Brazil defend that region."[32]

Aranha's troubling change in attitude resonated at the highest reaches of the US government and sparked a rare intervention by President Roosevelt. On July 10, Roosevelt attempted to bypass Aranha by asking Vargas directly to allow for the stationing of US troops in the north of Brazil. Roosevelt composed a long personal message for Vargas, which Caffery delivered in person to the Brazilian president at the Guanabara Palace during the evening of July 12.

Caffery enjoyed delivering such messages, because he was not usually allowed to disturb the president while he was in his residence. When the American entered the downstairs dining room of the Guanabara Palace, he found Vargas seated at the table, with Aranha and Alzira standing next to him, as if acting as his bodyguards. Without ado, Caffery presented Vargas with the message.

The letter was to the point. After outlining the new developments in the war following the German attack on the Soviet Union, Roosevelt tried to convince Vargas of the need to act swiftly and to allow the United States to send troops to Brazil. The American president was particularly worried about Natal, the capital of the Brazilian state of Rio Grande do Norte and a major hub on Brazilian's northeastern coastline. Roosevelt warned:

> A careful survey of typical German action makes it probable that their *blitzkrieg* tactics would give to us in the Americas no breathing spell to prepare defenses in any given spot after the Germans had suddenly occupied West Africa and the Cape Verde islands. For in such an event Germany might well launch an air and sea attack against Natal almost immediately.[33]

Having observed Germany's spectacular early victories in Europe, the Americans had a wary appreciation for Hitler's ability to strike quickly and without warning when given the opportunity. And his advances in the African theater made such an opportunity seem increasingly likely, for it would put German troopships and warplanes within the closest proximity yet to the Americas, north and south alike.

Roosevelt's letter also contained a second and more intriguing request. The American asked if Brazil was willing to take part in the potential defense of the Portuguese Atlantic islands, better known as the Azores. The small group of islands were deemed to be absolutely vital to maintaining the southern Atlantic shipping corridor between the United States and Great Britain. Roosevelt believed that Portugal, while technically neutral, might be invaded at any moment by the Germans, and that—if it fell—their next move would be to occupy the Azores. Roosevelt argued:

> In the interest of the defense of the western hemisphere such occupation would have to be prevented by the United States. In such an event I hope that the government of Portugal would request the United States or Brazil, or both, to assist Portugal in defending both the Azores and the Cape Verde islands.[34]

Roosevelt was essentially suggesting a military collaboration between Brazil and the United States—but the subtext of his message was, in Vargas's mind, an invitation for Brazil to join the war against the Germans.[35]

Years later, Cordell Hull summed up the thinking behind Roosevelt's invitation, which was aimed as much at the Portuguese as the Brazilians.

In his memoirs, Hull wrote, "We felt that a Brazilian force alongside ours would have a beneficial effect on Portuguese public opinion in such case and would offset German propaganda against us in Portugal."[36] The Portuguese, however, refused to agree to anything that might endanger their own neutrality in the war, and therefore declined to give the Americans or the British any assurance that its government would make such a request if Lisbon did indeed fall to the Germans. President Roosevelt and the British prime minister, Winston Churchill, would raise the question of the Azores with both Brazil and Portugal later in the war, as the strategic importance of the islands to the Allies became even greater. For the time being, however, American hopes—about this and the question of the defense of northern Brazil—would be dashed yet again.

Vargas replied to Roosevelt on July 28 with a short note that was warm in tone, but that stopped short of making any specific commitments to the US requests.[37] Vargas simply argued that these issues should be discussed by the mixed Brazilian-American commission of general staff officers, which was due to meet in Rio.[38] He had, in effect, passed the buck—and in so doing, had delayed any sort of promise that might diminish US uncertainty about Brazil's position in the war.

After sending his reply, Vargas left Rio in order to make a rare overland trip to Paraguay. While his trip had been planned for some time, his departure so soon after sending the letter resembled that of a boy leaving town after having just stood up to the schoolyard bully.

Very little progress took place in Brazil in Vargas's absence. Two weeks later, on August 18, an increasingly alarmed Cordell Hull cabled Caffery to ask if the president's questions, which Vargas promised to put before the commission, had been decided.[39] Hull admitted that neither the State Department nor the War Department had any information as to whether the American requests had even been brought before the commission.[40] The Brazilians were clearly not in as much of a hurry as the Americans to reach agreement on the issue.

Aranha tried to smooth Caffery's ruffled feathers when the two men met three days later on August 21.[41] "Vargas is cooperating, as is the army," Aranha informed the ambassador. Caffery understood the crux of the problem and outlined it later to Hull, explaining, "I must repeat that although the Brazilians will invite us to send troops to northeastern Brazil when the German menace really seems imminent to them; in the meantime they will not do so unless we furnish them with adequate supplies of material for the defense of that region." The message was clear: Brazil wanted the economic and military means for its own defense, not just American troops.

In the months following the exchange with Roosevelt, the United States and Brazil did sign agreements for exactly the sort of support Brazil had sought from its northern neighbor. A lend-lease agreement finalized on October 1, 1941, stipulated that the United States would supply Brazil with some $100 million worth of arms over a period up until 1947.[42] Brazil was to pay $35 million for the arms between 1942 and 1947. The first shipments of arms, with a value of $16 million (comprised of $15 million of army material and $1 million of navy material), were promised to arrive in Brazil within a year from the signing of the agreement.[43]

The deal, while much heralded by Caffery and in Washington, was modest in nature, and was received with a degree of skepticism and disappointment in Brazil.[44] During the lengthy negotiations over the lend-lease deal, General Góes Monteiro had reminded the US general staff negotiators that Germany was still willing to sell arms to Brazil, and at a better rate than the United States proposed.[45] Indeed, Berlin had assured the Brazilian army it would undercut the terms of any Brazilian-US deal. While Góes Monteiro was bluffing to a degree, his response revealed the extent to which the Brazilian military remained keen on obtaining German weapons over US ones, largely because they suspected that the Americans might cancel the deal.

On October 27, 1941, a sweating Góes Monteiro arrived at the Guanabara Palace for a meeting with Vargas, having phoned ahead to warn Alzira that the meeting was extremely urgent. The head of the US staff who had conducted the negotiations with the Brazilians over the lend-lease agreement, General Lehman B. Miller, had made some worrisome public statements once he had returned home from Brazil. Góes Monteiro told Vargas, "Miller has given a talk upon his return to the United States. He alleged during the talk that our army is not to be trusted and is seen as pro-German. The arms that we are due to receive from the United States will not come soon according to Miller's comments. Furthermore, Miller talks about American troops based in northeastern Brazil and not a US-Brazilian collaboration."[46]

Somewhat taken aback by Góes Monteiro's comments, Vargas replied that only two weeks prior Miller had been an invited guest in the very room where they now spoke. "Have you spoken with Miller since we have received reports of the talk?" he asked. After a long pause, Góes Monteiro admitted, "I haven't yet had the chance."

After the general left the room, Alzira called Osvaldo Aranha and set up a meeting for him with the president. As it turned out, Aranha learned in his investigation of the case that Miller's comments were meant to have been off the record. Caffery was subsequently summoned to the foreign ministry and was forced to give an assurance of the US delivery of armaments to Brazil.

Yet this misstep was an inauspicious beginning to the closer relationship the United States had been seeking with Brazil, and it boded ill for the future. Over the autumn of 1941, relations between Brazil and the United States did not move forward at the pace the Americans had hoped for after the signing of the lend-lease agreement. Mutual, deep suspicion characterized relations between the leaders of the US and Brazilian militaries, and to some extent this distrust began to creep into the civilian sectors as well. President Vargas appeared reluctant to commit to more deals, lest he be accused of becoming an American stooge. There were rumors of an Integralista plot involving elements of the military. American and British attempts to close pro-Axis local airlines heightened tensions between the Allies and Brazil, and Vargas in particular was reluctant to move too quickly against the airlines.

In the midst of the airline dilemma, Jefferson Caffery offered Washington one of his most astute pieces of advice—a maxim that the Americans, often pushy with Brazil to formalize understandings between the two nations, were forced to remember even after the autumn of 1941.[47] "It would be a mistake to insist on signing any sort of a formal agreement at this juncture," the ambassador argued. "It is often possible to get more out of Brazilians without a signed agreement than with one."[48]

# PART THREE:
## SLIPPING TOWARD WAR

8

# RIGHT BEHIND YOU

It was late evening in Rio, and the evening temperature hadn't cooled the city's buildings enough to make working inside them tolerable. A weary President Vargas sat in his small study in the Guanabara Palace, carefully reading the diplomatic cables just as fast as Alzira could translate them from English into Portuguese. The news was not good, and he understood that it would impact the future not only of the Estado Novo, but also of Brazil as a whole.

Vargas had first learned of the Japanese attack on Pearl Harbor earlier in the day, when a presidential aide interrupted his round of golf.[1] The president had given strict instructions that he was not to be disturbed unless it was vitally important. Vargas liked to play nine holes in the morning on the links course on the outskirts of Rio and then break for lunch before completing another nine holes in the afternoon. He wasn't a particularly good golfer; his best recorded score for the eighteen holes was 122 (handicap 52, if one that high were allowed for men).[2] When footage of the president playing golf was shown in cinemas in Rio, the audience roared with laughter.

After playing golf, the president liked to nap, and he was known to have fallen asleep in the locker room at the golf club. He would get no such rest on December 7, 1941.

On hearing the news from Hawaii, Vargas had rushed back to Rio to prepare for a crucial meeting late in the evening with Osvaldo Aranha. Yet prior to the meeting, realizing that there was little he could do until he heard from Aranha, the president went out to the cinema, as he had originally planned to do. In times of crisis, as in the morning after the Integralista plot in May 1938, Vargas liked to present an air of normality by going about his usual business; it was well known that after a day of golf the president liked to unwind with a trip to the cinema followed by a cigar (usually a corona from the north of Brazil).

When the two gaúchos finally met, they fell into a deep conversation. Alzira stood by, acting as both a point of information—diplomatic cables continued to arrive at the palace even at this late hour—and an informal minute taker for the meeting.

"Do we need to convene a full meeting of the cabinet for tomorrow morning?" Vargas asked. Aranha answered in the affirmative, but Vargas's question had been rhetorical.[3] The president understood the need for the cabinet to meet at this crucial juncture, but he never liked the prospect of cabinet meetings, since every minister demanded to speak. Over the years, Vargas had developed what he considered a much more effective system, receiving two ministers each day at the Catete Palace and giving them an opportunity to discuss issues with him at length.[4] He also employed this system for officials like the chief of staff, General Góes Monteiro, who was permitted extensive access to the president. Osvaldo Aranha was one of the few people, however, who had effective walk-in rights at the Gua-nabara Palace, and at the end of 1941 the foreign minister was a frequent late-night visitor to Vargas's study.

Like the president, Aranha did not enjoy full cabinet meetings, as he knew his sworn political enemy, the minister of war, Eurico Gaspar Dutra, would use each one as an opportunity to lay political traps for him. Aranha's rule of thumb was that if a cabinet meeting was absolutely necessary, it was better to get the president fully committed to a specific foreign policy before the meeting took place, since Vargas's word was essentially law. And in the late evening of December 7, Brazil's minister of foreign affairs understood that Vargas needed to commit fully to the American cause—at least in words, if not yet in actual deeds.

Typically, Aranha had already promised Jefferson Caffery Brazilian support in the event that the United States joined the hostilities. But nobody, the Americans least of all, had foreseen the Japanese attack at Pearl Harbor, which would have the unavoidable effect of drawing the United States into the war much earlier than most of the combatants had expected. This posed a problem for Aranha: the ever-cautious Vargas appeared unprepared to make the seismic decision to throw Brazil's lot completely in with the United States, as Washington was sure to demand.

Still, Aranha did what he could. In their meeting on December 7, the foreign minister pleaded with Vargas to announce a clear and concise commitment to the Americans the following day and to offer tangible support to the Allied cause against Axis aggression. Aranha then took his leave of the president, who continued to go over the new cables from London and Washington, which Alzira had finished translating.

One question went unasked during the meeting between Vargas and Aranha, but it was at the forefront of both men's minds: If the Axis attacked Brazil, could the country defend itself? For all its negotiations with the United States, Brazil had still not received any weapons of real value, nor had it received the bulk of the German weapons for which it had contracted. Brazil was in no position to fend off a German assault.

Dutra and Góes Monteiro were widely expected to harp on this unpreparedness as a reason to keep Brazil from being dragged into the war. Sumner Welles conceded the reluctance of the Brazilian armed forces to get involved in the war when he wrote to President Roosevelt at the beginning of 1942:

> Like all armies, the Brazilian high command is not inclined to be enthusiastic about getting into a war if they have none of the basic elements for defense. If they are not promptly given the necessary assurances and if they are not able to see with their own eyes before long some concrete evidences of help coming, exactly that kind of a situation which the Nazis could use to their best advantage will be created.[5]

The undersecretary of state did not spell out what kind of "situation" the lack of American support and reassurances might create, but he did not have to. The Brazilian army's pro-German bias was by now well known in Washington, and with Brazil still uncommitted in the war, there remained a very real chance that the army could use its influence to tip Brazil into the arms of the Axis.

Yet while the Americans continued to worry about Germany's plans for Brazil, at this point, in early December 1941, the Brazilians themselves also feared another, closer threat. The Brazilian high command's concerns about its readiness for war were driven in large part by the fear that Argentina might use the uncertainty caused by the expansion of the world war to engage in an aggressive campaign against Buenos Aires's South

American rival, Rio. The truth of the matter was that, while both Vargas and Aranha had suspected that the United States would be dragged into the war, they had not foreseen this happening before Brazil was armed and able to protect itself against any escalation that might occur in Latin America as a result of US involvement in the conflict.

On the morning of December 8, 1941, the full Brazilian cabinet met in the Guanabara Palace. As it was still early, the president chose to meet the cabinet in his residence rather than in the Catete Palace, which was the usual venue for full cabinet meetings. During the meeting all members of the government were given an opportunity to speak, and many did so at great length. There was agreement on the course of action that Brazil should take and on the wording of the statement to be released to the public.

Following the meeting, it was announced that the cabinet had unanimously resolved that Brazil would declare its solidarity with the United States in accordance with its traditions and understandings. The decision marked a massive shift in Brazilian policy toward the Allies and the Axis, yet several factors tempered what might otherwise have been a clamorous reaction to the news. In Brazil itself, the statement was overshadowed by the dramatic seven-minute "Day of Infamy" speech that President Roosevelt gave to the US Congress on the same day, and that legislative body's subsequent vote to declare war on Japan. For their part, the Americans welcomed the Brazilian statement, but their enthusiasm quickly soured when it became clear that the Brazilian idea of solidarity did not mean formally entering the war alongside the United States. This news was met with disappointment in many quarters in Washington.

With America now rushing into the fray, President Roosevelt demanded more from the Brazilians. Through the remainder of December 1941, Vargas came under intense diplomatic pressure to bring Brazil toward the US position much more quickly.[6] One key US demand was that, given the onset of war between the Axis and the United States, Vargas should replace some of the officials in his government whom Washington viewed as leaning toward the Axis. On December 21, following several meetings with Jefferson Caffery, Aranha explained to Vargas his interpretation of the US position. "They do not trust elements of your government and want them replaced before they deliver arms to us," Aranha suggested. Vargas, however, was having none of it. "The truth is that they don't trust us, full stop," he retorted.[7]

The world was changing fast and Vargas, who was a cautious man, found it difficult to keep up. One thing was certain, however: he was not going to let Washington dictate who was in his government and who was not. Washington, on the other hand, had specific plans for shaping Brazilian policy to fit American needs.

A conference of the foreign ministers from all the Americas was to be held in Rio in January 1942, and the meeting would serve to showcase the Roosevelt administration's initial strategy for Latin America following the United States's entry into the war. The Americans had lofty aims for the region—the loftiest of which they had been harboring since well before Pearl Harbor. In the weeks leading up to the conference, they continued to seek permission from President Vargas to station a US military force in the northeast of Brazil. Vargas, however, continued to resist such a move until he had a better deal on the supply of US weapons.

The fundamental goal of the conference was to get as many of the Latin American countries as possible to agree to break relations with the Axis powers. On this front, however, things did not bode well for the United States. The main problem appeared to be Argentina, which in the run-up to the conference had indicated a strong reluctance to toe the American line on the issue, arguing that the attack at Pearl Harbor was not an attack on the countries of Latin America. The pro-Axis orientation of Argentina's President Ramón Castillo complicated matters further for the Allies.

Nor was the impact of the Argentine position limited to its relations with the United States. President Vargas made it clear to Washington that he wanted any deal at the conference to include all the Latin American countries, Argentina included. Vargas was concerned that if Argentina stayed neutral while the rest of Latin America sided with the United States, it would give the Germans a potential ally at Brazil's back door. Any agreement would therefore have to be worded so as to keep Argentina in line with the other Latin American countries. As the State Department soon discovered, this would be the central challenge of the conference itself.

On January 10, 1942, President Vargas convened a special meeting of the Brazilian national security council in order to discuss the forthcoming foreign ministers' conference. The president had met with Aranha the previous evening in the Guanabara Palace to prepare Vargas's statement to the council and to go over his opening speech for the conference. As ever, Aranha was keen for him and the president to coordinate their messages.[8]

The foreign minister's imprimatur was plainly visible at the council meeting, in which Vargas told the assembled cabinet members and military leaders that Brazil must fully throw its lot in with the United States.

> I have reached the decision that, both from the standpoint of the highest interests of Brazil as well as from the standpoint of the commitments which Brazil has previously made, Brazil must now stand or fall with the United States. Any member of the government who is in disagreement with this policy is at liberty to resign his position.[9]

He went on to issue a stark warning against any dissent from the armed forces, which he believed would be deeply troubled by his choice:

> The government does not have to depend upon the armed forces of the republic for the control of subversive activities, even including any attempt at a local uprising by German or Italian sympathizers. The Brazilian people are 100 percent in agreement with the policy upon which I have decided, and the people themselves will be able to take care of any attempts at Axis-inspired uprisings.[10]

Vargas's words were nothing if not an open challenge to his generals: if they didn't give him their full support, they would quickly find that their services were no longer needed.

The council voted unanimously to support Vargas's statement—although, just as he had predicted, the military voiced objections. Both Dutra and Góes Monteiro warned the meeting that Brazil's ability to defend itself was very limited, and that one of the main reasons for this was that—despite assurances from the US government—the Brazilian armed forces had not been able to secure anything more than token armaments from the United States.[11] They cited the specific example of a shipment of small tanks from the United States, which had been sent without their weaponry and were, therefore, useless. Yet despite their concern about Brazil's lack of defenses, both the minister of war and the chief of staff informed the meeting that the policy the president had announced was, in their considered opinion, "the only correct policy for Brazil to follow."[12] In private, however, both Dutra and Góes Monteiro remained unconvinced about Vargas's decision to openly back the United States without any firm guarantee of arms shipments. Both men offered their resignations, but as in the past, President Vargas refused to accept them and told Dutra and Góes Monteiro that they must remain at their respective posts at this crucial juncture in Brazilian history.[13]

The political and military leadership all agreed on one point: if Brazil broke diplomatic relations with the Axis, sooner rather than later they would be actively involved in the war. This would be quietly confirmed in letters to Vargas from the Axis ambassadors in Rio. Aranha subsequently informed US Undersecretary of State Sumner Welles of the contents of the letters, and Welles reported back to President Roosevelt:

> He [Vargas] had received during the day letters addressed to him from the German, Italian, and Japanese ambassadors. These letters, whose texts I had seen, stated—bluntly in the case of the German ambassador and in a more veiled fashion in the case of the Japanese and Italian ambassadors—that if Brazil undertook to break diplomatic relations she could anticipate a state of war with the Axis powers. The letters were regarded as personal by the Brazilian government and they are therefore anxious that no publicity should be given to their contents as yet.[14]

Brazil's options could not have been clearer: join the Allies and go to war with the Axis, or wait for an attack that, if it came, would be swifter and more devastating than anyone in Rio could imagine.

Sumner Welles had arrived in Rio on January 12 in order to participate in the foreign ministers' conference, which was scheduled to start three days later on January 15. On the afternoon of the day Welles arrived, he and Vargas met in the Guanabara Palace for a brief introductory session. During the course of the meeting, Vargas filled Welles in on the background of the policy he had announced on January 10. Alzira, who acted as the translator, noted that her father appeared deeply concerned. Writing in his diary that evening, President Vargas recorded, "I am apprehensive. It seems to me that the Americans want to drag us into war without it being useful, either for us or for them."[15]

Later that same evening, Vargas continued to work on his speech for the conference. In his eyes, he had gone out on something of a limb for the Americans, and now felt he could wait no longer for recompense; while Welles was in Rio it was vitally important that Brazil secure the arms it

needed to defend itself. Adding to Vargas's urgency was the fact that Rio
was awash with rumors of discontent within the military and of plotting between the military and some factions of the old Green Shirts of
the Integralista movement. Though many of the rumors could be traced
directly to the German embassy in Rio, they nevertheless added to the
tension. Some loose talk from an official at the US embassy in the city,
stating that it was desirable to replace Góes Monteiro, further added to
the stakes.[16] It was later suggested that the leak from the embassy made
it virtually impossible for Vargas to fire the chief of staff for fear of giving
the impression of being an American puppet.

Vargas and Aranha met on the morning of January 13 to go over
tactics for the conference and to look at the likely implications of the
Brazilian position regarding the Axis powers.[17] Aranha found the president in a pensive mood, still resolute in his decision to support the United
States, but also hoping to avoid a military confrontation with the Axis
powers. Vargas's speech was proving difficult to draft: he wanted to express
strong support for President Roosevelt but also to remind the United
States that it needed to make good on its promises to arm the Brazilian
military. Vargas agreed that, outside of the direct proceedings of the conference, he would personally lobby Welles to secure a firm commitment
from President Roosevelt on the armaments issue. Both men agreed that
this issue needed to be resolved before the end of the conference, when
Vargas planned to announce that Brazil was breaking relations with the
Axis powers.

The conference opened on January 15, 1942, in the Tiradentes Palace
in downtown Rio. Prior to the establishment of the Estado Novo in 1937,
the palace had served as the home of the chamber of deputies; after 1937
it had become the headquarters of the department of press and propaganda (DIP), which had now decorated the building with the flags of
all the participating countries at the conference. The building had been
chosen because of its size and the fact that it was cool inside, offering the
ministers some much needed respite from the oppressive January heat in
downtown Rio.

Aranha, who was hosting the conference, made himself comfortable
in the palace's large, carved wooden speaker's chair. Dressed in his favorite
white, cotton, double-breasted suit matched with a club tie, he looked
like an aging film star as he towered over the rest of the delegates. And

indeed, Aranha understood that he needed to give the performance of a lifetime if Brazil was going to avoid being dragged into the war without arms and without a similar commitment from Argentina to join the fight on the side of the Allies as well. It was left, however, to President Vargas to officially open the conference.

In his much-anticipated speech, Vargas spoke warmly about President Roosevelt and the United States. He talked of the great importance of economic cooperation both within Latin America and with the United States. And he stated in the strongest terms possible that Brazil was determined to defend its borders. He chose not to mention anything about the prime aim of the United States for the conference, which was, of course, to convince the countries of Latin America to break relations with the Axis powers.[18] It was a cautious speech, which reflected Vargas's appraisal of the difficult and unresolved internal and external struggles over Brazil's wartime role.

By pointedly not addressing what he knew was the top US priority, Vargas's speech was also intended to buy Brazil a little more time to secure an arms deal from the United States before he went and stuck his thumb in the eye of the Axis. On this issue there were mixed results. The Italian ambassador in Rio wrote to Aranha praising the speech, while the German and Japanese ambassadors reminded Brazil once more that any break in relations would lead very quickly to all-out war.

In case Sumner Welles had not picked up on the message behind the speech, Vargas took him aside at an event at the Itamaraty Palace following the conference and made his case for further arms shipments directly to the undersecretary of state. Vargas started by talking about the letters he had received from the Axis ambassadors, knowing that Welles had been informed of their contents. He then added,

The decision taken by the Brazilian government implies that we will soon actually be at war. The responsibility, which I have assumed on behalf of the Brazilian people, is very great. It is peculiarly great because of the fact that, notwithstanding all my efforts, during the past eighteen months I have not been able to obtain at least a minimum of war supplies from the United States. I feel that in view of the present circumstances I can depend upon you better than anybody else to understand my crucial difficulties.[19]

Welles, listening as best he could over the background noise of the music of the party, nodded as if to say he had understood the message. Vargas then quickly moved the conversation onto specifics.

> Brazil can not be treated as a small Central American power, which would be satisfied with the stationing of American troops upon its territory, but rather Brazil has to be regarded by the United States as a friend and ally and is entitled to be furnished under the lend-lease act with planes, tanks, and sufficient coast artillery to enable the Brazilian army to defend at least in part the regions of northeastern Brazil whose defense is as vitally necessary for the United States as for Brazil herself.[20]

Never before had the Brazilian president laid his cards on the table so openly for an American official. Now, as Vargas returned to his guests at the party, he paused, turned around, and asked that Welles come to see him, alone, two days later, on January 19 at six o'clock in the Guanabara Palace.

The undersecretary of state was experienced enough to know that the president of Brazil had just given him less than forty-eight hours to get a satisfactory response to his request for armaments from the president of the United States. Welles also understood the carrot that was being offered by Vargas—namely, that if Roosevelt came through with enough arms for the Brazilian military, Vargas would authorize the stationing of US forces in northeastern Brazil.

Later that evening, Welles sent a long cable directly to President Roosevelt in which he outlined his conversation with President Vargas at the party. Welles added that when he met with Vargas at the Guanabara Palace to relay Roosevelt's response, he would like to deliver the following message:

> I have communicated directly with you and that you [President Roosevelt] have authorized me to say to him [President Vargas] as chief executive of one great American nation to the chief executive of another great American nation, and also as a personal friend, that if the president will give me a list of the minimum requirements needed urgently by the Brazilian army for the proper protection of northeastern Brazil, you will give orders that the items contained in that list will be made available to the Brazilian government at the possible moment subject only to the exigencies of the

present defense requirements of the United States of America and to any subsequent modifications that may later be agreed upon by the United States and Brazilian general staffs.[21]

Welles's plea to President Roosevelt was an illustration of not only the importance the undersecretary of state now attached to an arms deal for Brazil, but also the disadvantage at which the United States had suddenly found itself during the conference.

The conference of foreign ministers was not progressing as smoothly as Washington had hoped. The governments of Argentina and Chile made it clear that they were not willing to formally break relations with the Axis powers. Yet in spite of these problems—or perhaps rather as a result of them—Brazil was proving to be an even more important partner than the United States could have expected. Welles noted that, in private, President Vargas and Aranha were working overtime to try to get Argentina and Chile on board while also keeping four other governments in line with the position of the United States. Vargas had sent a personal message to the president of Argentina by courier, stating, "the Brazilian government considers it indispensable that a joint declaration by all the American republics for an immediate severance of relations with the Axis powers be adopted at the conference."[22] Vargas's personal intervention had little impact, however, as the Argentine government refused to alter its position.

Relations at the conference were quickly deteriorating into regional bickering. Brazil, to be sure, was partly to blame. All the delegations at the conference had been invited to the party in the Itamaraty Palace at which Vargas had spoken to Welles—all the delegations, that is, save for Argentina's.[23] The British ambassador and his staff were invited in their place.[24]

Desperate to salvage something from the conference, Roosevelt took Welles's advice. The American president's reply to Welles the next morning, January 19, 1942, contained the words the undersecretary of state had been hoping to hear:

Tell President Vargas I wholly understand and appreciate the needs and can assure him flow of material will start at once. He will understand when I say there are shortages in a few items, which I do not trust to putting on the wire, but which are soon to come into production. I want to get away as soon as possible from token shipments and increase them to a minimum of Brazilian requirements very quickly. Tell him I am made very happy by his splendid policy and give him my very warm regards.[25]

American support for Brazil would be forthcoming, just as Vargas had requested. Carrying a copy of Roosevelt's note, Welles headed off for his meeting. Although he didn't realize it at the time, it was an encounter that would change the course of Latin American history.

The undersecretary of state arrived at the Guanabara Palace a little before six o'clock on the evening of January 19. To the American's surprise, he was not shown into one of the rooms of the palace, but instead was escorted to the small pavilion on top of the hill at the back of the Guanabara Palace where the president liked to work alone during Rio's balmy summer evenings. As he headed up the hill, Welles could hear the sounds of the staff of the palace preparing the ballroom for the evening ball for the delegations of the conference. By the time he got to the pavilion, however, there was silence save only for the murmur of distant traffic from the road in front of the palace.

"It is cooler and quieter here than in the palace," Vargas said as he greeted his guest.[26] The setting also afforded the two men the utmost privacy. There were no advisors, aides, or translators present. Instead, Vargas spoke slowly in Spanish tinged with a Brazilian Portuguese accent, while Welles—who was fluent in Spanish—made sure to respond with care in case Vargas misunderstood him. From time to time in the course of the conversation that followed, Welles threw in a phrase or two in English, especially when referring to President Roosevelt or Winston Churchill. Vargas spoke only rudimentary English, but could read it well.[27] Alzira, who was educated at an English school in Rio, was teaching her father English whenever he had a spare moment.

Welles outlined the nature of his request to President Roosevelt and then read the president's reply, translating it into Spanish as he went. After he finished reading it aloud, Welles handed it over to President Vargas, who read the text carefully by himself. The conversation then moved on to Argentina, and on this issue Welles gave Vargas his informed but personal opinion. He started, "Mr. President, I am afraid that there is little prospect of getting Argentina to agree to a formal breaking of ties with the Axis powers as our government has requested."[28] Vargas agreed with the assessment, but told Welles that he still had to try. "I need, however to find a formula for the text of the conference that the Argentine government would be able to support."[29] Vargas noted to Welles that this point was of great importance for Brazil, and Welles confirmed to Vargas that he would continue to work toward this purpose, although prospects of winning over Argentina and the other holdout, Chile, still looked slim. "Look, I do not hold out much chance of getting Chile to agree either," Welles admitted.[30] "There are cash advances being made by Japan to certain Chilean political leaders, including the minister of foreign affairs."

Welles finished by adding, "The issue of Brazil breaking relations with the Axis powers is of great importance and I have risked my own position to secure this commitment from the president for you."[31] Vargas replied, "You can count on Brazil, but I am risking my life on this as I would not survive a disaster for my motherland."[32] Vargas's life had already been in jeopardy once before, and he had no illusions about surviving a cataclysmic encounter with Argentina, Germany, or his own enemies within Brazil.

Both men's apprehensions hung over the discussion like a rain cloud, yet taken together, Roosevelt's promise of immediate arms for Brazil and Welles's agreement to try to placate Argentina constituted a breakthrough for Vargas. He and Welles had a deal.[33] Standing alone outside the pavilion as the sun dipped over the horizon, the two men shook hands and said nothing further.

As they headed back toward the palace where the first guests for the banquet were starting to arrive, Vargas and Welles were both lost in their thoughts. For Vargas this was the scenario he had long hoped to avoid: a deal with the United States that in all likelihood would not tie Argentina to a similar commitment. He understood that the military would be unhappy to have an aggressive and expansionist pro-Axis Argentine army sitting on Brazil's southern border, while most of the American weapons would have to go to the defense of northeastern Brazil to protect it from possible Axis attacks or even an invasion. The position of the Chilean government was important to Vargas, as well, but it nevertheless confirmed his impression that the foreign ministers of the Americas would never be able to agree to a meaningful regional strategy for the war.[34]

Welles, meanwhile, had to come to terms with his own failures. He had come to Rio to convince all the countries of the Americas to break ties with the Axis. Whatever he had accomplished (and he had certainly accomplished much), in that effort at least, he had not succeeded. When

Welles's boss, Secretary of State Cordell Hull, heard the details of the deal, he considered it a total surrender to Argentina.[35] On the phone with Welles following the meeting, Hull subjected him to a rant that was so full of professional and personal threats that it alarmed President Roosevelt and the State Department officials who were listening in on the conversation. "I consider this a change of policy without consulting me," Hull fumed, adding in a voice full of emotion, "The agreement contains an escape clause that will permit the Argentines to return home with a straight face and thereafter move gradually over to the camp of our Axis enemies and render the enemy aid and comfort, to our damage and even to the loss of life as the war progresses."[36] As he was winding down, Hull ordered Welles, "Repudiate the arrangement now."[37]

When Hull's outburst ended, Welles responded. Speaking slowly and without emotion he said, "I have tried hard to secure agreement to the original proposal but found this impossible, and therefore I agreed to the modified arrangement."[38] In so many words, Welles was informing his boss that in his book, this was as good an outcome as the Americans were going to get.

When Hull had calmed down, he took his case directly to Roosevelt, urging the president to support his demand to Welles. Roosevelt, however, backed Welles, swayed by "the judgment of the man in Rio."[39] Hull never forgave Welles or Buenos Aires. He was so angry at Argentina that he made it something of a crusade to pursue the country and its leaders for the rest of the war.[40] Hull came to believe that, as a country, Argentina was simply beyond the pale, and he tried to marginalize it whenever possible.[41]

For Vargas and Welles, however, all of this was in the future. Still in front of them, too, was the banquet in the Guanabara Palace, a magnificent affair with music and dancing as well as dinner. As the evening became more relaxed and some of the men adjourned to smoke cigars and remove their brilliant white dinner jackets, Welles approached the president to ask him a question that he had forgotten to put to him earlier. Vargas, however, was not in the mood. "We have talked enough already today and we will talk some more tomorrow," the president promised Welles.[42] Vargas was never one for small talk or chitchat, and often chose to leave all that in the very capable hands of Osvaldo Aranha, who reveled in such frivolity. One of the most frequent jokes made about Vargas in Rio (a joke the president quite liked) was that he could be silent in ten languages.[43] In one of the lengthiest entries in his diary Vargas recalled the events of the day, stating simply about the banquet, "I talked a little with the Argentine foreign minister."[44] President Vargas appeared preoccupied with the difficult history between Brazil and Argentina and wondered if he was not sowing the seeds of the next war between the two most important nations in South America. After returning from the banquet, Welles received a second cable, this one from the secretary of state, Cordell Hull. This cable included the list of armaments approved by the chief of staff of the US army, General George Marshall, for immediate delivery to Brazil under the lend-lease agreement. The list included thirty-one scout cars and seventy-four trucks or jeeps, as well as ten light tanks—the first batch of a total of sixty-five light tanks to be shipped to Brazil at the rate of ten per month.[45] Other supplies were to be increased on a monthly basis, as well, yet the shipments constituted just about the minimum requirements of the Brazilian army, and no more.[46] Due to shortages of ammunition, moreover, little was promised. President Roosevelt had already advised Welles that it was better to keep this point from their Brazilian friends. Welles noted that this was in effect a new lend-lease agreement, which largely replaced the old agreement of the previous year.

Welles had his agreement with Brazil, but still needed to ensure that the American timetable for the supply of armaments was acceptable to President Vargas. Given the past failings of the United States to stick to the schedule, the president would still need some further assurance that this time the United States was serious about keeping its promises. Welles also conceded that he would need to reassure Aranha over what seemed inevitably to be a collective failure to persuade Argentina to cut ties with the Axis. Brazil's minister of foreign affairs understood from past experience that the minister of war and the chief of staff would be none too pleased with the diplomatic developments. He also suspected that both men would be even more difficult to reconcile with the new arrangements if the United States attempted to deviate from the arms agreement. An early sign of the bumpy road ahead came when one of Góes Monteiro's staff officers reported to his superior that he had overheard two diplomats talking about how the United States intended to service the Brazilian army with weapons, but not ammunition.

At 3:30 P.M. on January 27, 1942, President Vargas called the Brazilian cabinet to order. As in 1939, when the cabinet met to discuss the start of the war, there was only one item on the agenda. In 1942, the debate focused solely on the question of Brazil breaking ties with the Axis powers. Vargas had already decided that Brazil would break relations with the Axis powers the following day, January 28, 1942, at the conclusion of the conference of the foreign ministers in Rio.[47]

The cabinet meeting would be the final opportunity for the Brazilian military to try to derail the process of breaking ties with the Axis. Earlier that morning, Dutra and Góes Monteiro met to discuss tactics. Vargas sent an emissary to try to persuade both men to support his decision, but they—and the rest of the military—remained unconvinced. Yet their position, when they finally outlined it at the cabinet meeting, was not appreciably different from what it had been previously. "The breaking of relations with Germany, Italy, and Japan will lead to war, and the Brazilian army is not ready for war," Dutra intoned to the assembled ministers.[48]

Vargas was having none of this. Nor was Aranha, who concluded the meeting by saying, "Tomorrow we will break relations with the Axis powers, and I take it on as my responsibility."[49] All of the meeting's participants understood the dangerous course that Brazil was about to embark on. The country's leaders expected it to be targeted for attack, although there was a difference of opinion about which would pose the biggest threat to Brazil in the coming months, the Axis powers or Argentina. As the ministers headed out into the Rio sun, they could only know that, the following day, Brazilian neutrality would come to an end.

The conference of foreign ministers drew to a close the following day. While none of the resolutions the ministers had agreed to would meaningfully change the status quo in the Americas, they would consolidate economic cooperation between the countries of the Americas and grant aid to the United States. South American countries, mainly Brazil, agreed to supply the United States with strategic raw materials for its defense industries, to create favorable conditions for the movement of capital, and to maintain internal political order.[50] The final resolution regarding relations with the Axis powers reflected the position of Argentina and Chile and merely *recommended* breaking relations with Germany, Italy, and Japan, rather than declaring such a rupture outright.[51]

Brazil, however, had arrived at a resolution of its own. Most of the nation was listening to radios either at home or in cafés as Osvaldo Aranha stood up to address the conference. His voice trembling with emotion,

Aranha briefly announced that a few hours earlier President Vargas had signed the order to break diplomatic and commercial relations with the Axis powers.[52] After Aranha finished reading the prepared statement, the conference erupted into spontaneous applause and wild cheering.

In cafés across the city of Rio de Janeiro the announcement of a break with the Axis was greeted with pride—all the more so because Argentina had not followed Brazil's lead, outing it as pro-Nazi in the eyes of many Cariocas. The announcement also represented a victory for Vargas and Aranha over the armed forces, although the sense of discontent among the senior officers did not disappear, and there remained a possibility that the military's resentment and latent pro-German feeling would resurface, presenting new problems for the Vargas regime.

For Sumner Welles, the declaration that Brazil was breaking ties with the Axis powers represented both a triumph and a failure. While Brazil had effectively joined the American camp, Argentina had refused to do so—and while not unexpected, this was nevertheless a hugely complicating factor in Washington's efforts to develop a regional policy for South America. To many Americans, including Nelson Rockefeller, Argentina's decision was utterly unacceptable, and made the nation the pariah of the Americas. This had an unanticipated consequence for Brazil, as well. As a result of Argentina's decision, Rockefeller's efforts to develop cultural ties with—and to spread propaganda in—Latin America came to focus much more on Brazil.

9

# WELLES CHECKS OUT AND WELLES CHECKS IN

THE FOREIGN MINISTERS' CONFERENCE HAD ENDED, and Sumner Welles's work in Rio was nearly complete. On January 29, Welles and Ambassador Jefferson Caffery joined President Vargas and Alzira for breakfast at the Guanabara Palace. All three men were acutely aware of the need for the United States to deliver on its promises of armaments for the Brazilian army—and to do so in a speedy fashion.[1] If the Brazilian military perceived that the United States was delaying, or suspected that it might renege on the deal entirely, all of the hard work Vargas and the Americans had done to bring Brazil into the Allied camp would be for naught.

As always, Alzira listened to the conversation intently and said very little. She understood that Brazil's relations with the United States were entering uncharted territory, and that the dangers to her father's regime from both inside and outside Brazil were all the more acute.

Characteristically, too, President Vargas was still hedging on the question of an American force being stationed in northeastern Brazil. It was the last card he had to play and he was not about to give it up easily, especially in light of the country's internal political environment. The maneuverings of the military leadership on the morning of the cabinet meeting two days earlier had unnerved the president. If the military had been so vocal about its objections to Brazil's breaking of relations with the Axis powers, could it now be relied on to back that decision—and the government behind it—completely?

Vargas used his breakfast with Welles and Caffery to shore up his position as much as possible by reminding the United States that he would not be taken for granted. The meeting also served the purpose of a handover to Caffery, with Welles informing the president that he was ready to depart for the United States as soon as the Pan Am clipper service arrived in Rio.

Sumner Welles was intent on enjoying his last few days in Rio before returning to freezing cold Washington and his equally frosty boss, Cordell Hull, who had still not come to terms with the fact that his deputy had allowed Argentina to maintain its diplomatic relations with the Axis powers. For recreation, Welles took long brisk morning walks along the wide promenade of Copacabana Beach. He could often be seen strolling, lost in thought, always wearing his trusty panama hat, which just days earlier he had waved in the air to acknowledge the crowds outside the foreign ministers' conference. Now it surely weighed heavily on his worried brow.

Rio's beachfront was in a state of transformation. As he walked along it, Welles would have been able to see old ramshackle buildings in the process of being knocked down and replaced with new modern developments, most comprised of at least six or seven stories. This was the holiday season of January and February, and so nearly all the construction work along the beachfront had stopped. Cranes stood idle, and half-completed building projects were eerily silent, without the normal din of banging metal and whistling workmen. Many of the shutters on the buildings that were already completed were closed tightly, their occupants having already decamped up to the cooler air in the mountains.

The noise on the other side of the road, however, would have more than compensated for the silence of Rio's construction sites. As Welles strolled along the beach, he would have been treated to a view of a long strip of sand packed with Europeans and Cariocas of all colors, lying next to one another as they basked in the tropical sun. Welles was broadminded, born in New York City and educated at Harvard, and he could not have helped but favorably contrast the unsegregated Rio beaches with the "white only" public spaces back in the United States. On occasion, the Louisiana-born Jefferson Caffery joined Welles on his walks, and the ambassador would comment on the integrated nature of the races in Rio and Brazil as a modern marvel of progress and hope. Welles, no doubt, agreed.

Welles liked Rio, and Rio very much liked Welles. Osvaldo Aranha organized a series of glittering diplomatic events to entertain the undersecretary of state before his return to Washington. Those who knew him well noted, however, that Welles appeared distracted in his final days in Rio. The heat, the never-ending rounds of meetings, and the high-stakes

diplomacy with President Vargas and Aranha had taken their toll. Welles
suddenly looked old. He understood all too well, too, that the war for the
United States was only just beginning, and that the battle for Brazil had
not even commenced. Perhaps it was the sea air, but Welles felt tired, and
he must have wondered how the human ball of energy that was Osvaldo
Aranha kept going without seeming to burn out.

Sumner Welles was not the only man leaving Rio for Washington
at the start of February 1942. President Vargas had decided to send his
minister of finance, Artur de Souza Costa, to the United States. Souza
Costa's main reason for going to Washington was to try to secure American arms, as well as to help conclude a series of deals for US aid for Brazil's
iron mines, rubber factories, and other natural industries that might prove
useful to the Allied war effort. In case the Roosevelt administration missed
the point, however, Souza Costa called on Caffery on January 31, the
eve of his departure for Washington, to tell him, "The principal object
of my visit to Washington is the procurement of necessary armament."[2]
Caffery promised to pass the message along to the State Department, and
duly did so the same day.[3]

Souza Costa's mission got off to a bad start. Welles and Hull had sent
a list of armaments that the United States was currently in a position
to furnish to Brazil to Caffery back in Rio. When he showed the list to
Aranha in the hope that the minister of foreign affairs would endorse it
before showing it to Vargas, Aranha had something of a moment with the
ambassador. Barely able to control his temper and the level of his voice,
Aranha barked at Caffery:

> This is just the old run around. You can't show that to President Vargas.
> Welles told him that you would give us equal treatment with England,
> Russia, China—you are doing nothing of the kind; you are dumping a lot
> of trucks on us; giving us nothing we need for the defense of the north-
> east: anti-aircraft guns, artillery, combat planes. Tell Welles that he had
> better just file this away and forget it. Our military people are going to
> raise hell with many "I told you sos." President Vargas will never believe
> the State Department again.[4]

Aranha was suggesting that this list of arms might not only damage relations between the Brazilian president and the US government, but also

turn the Brazilian military even further against Vargas. On this latter point, however, Caffery and his superiors had their doubts.

Privately, Welles suspected that Aranha's standing with the Brazilian military had been greatly damaged by the breaking of relations with the Axis powers. Caffery had heard that the armed forces held Aranha much more to account than President Vargas for what they saw as a policy disaster for Brazil. Dutra—as well as the British—had noted that after Aranha's speech breaking relations with the Axis, no other document or presidential decree was issued to officially confirm the rupture. Therefore, as the British outlined, "A change in the minister of foreign affairs would make the rupture null and void."[5] Dutra no doubt figured this out as well. Soon political, diplomatic, and military circles were all awash with rumors of plots being hatched against Aranha by his old nemesis, the minister of war Dutra, and his allies.

Welles decided to have Caffery take the list to President Vargas regardless of Aranha's opinion. Accompanied by Aranha, the US ambassador traveled by car to Petrópolis, where the president was taking his annual break from the summer heat of Rio. During the journey, Caffery looked out the window at the changing scenery as the car made its way up the winding mountain road, and silently pined, no doubt, for a summer retreat like one the British ambassador had. The usually talkative Aranha, meanwhile, was also almost completely silent for the entire journey. Caffery felt that his guest appeared distracted by the intrigues and internal plots of recent months. The burden of his office weighed heavily on Aranha's shoulders, and appeared to be pushing down on him all the harder since the foreign ministers' conference. Aranha was too much the optimist to think that he was done for, politically, but he understood that his enemies were getting more powerful and were circling, waiting for the moment to strike.

Perhaps it was the cooler mountain air or the relaxed nature of the town, but Vargas struck Caffery as being in much better fettle than the minister of foreign affairs. Dressed in casual attire and with only Alzira with him to serve as an aide, Vargas studied the document carefully before offering his verdict:

My offhand opinion is very good indeed (of course I will consult my technicians). Welles is carrying out his promises to me. This is not all we need, but the fact that he is getting it to us before the first of next month demonstrates his good faith, which I have never doubted. Thank him from me and thank also President Roosevelt for his cooperation. Tell Welles that we shall be expecting this material as fast as he can send it. I have full confidence that he appreciates our other urgent needs, especially how badly we need artillery and anti-aircraft guns at Fernando de Noronha, Natal, etc., and that without combat planes we will be hopeless in the northeast.[6]

The president had noticed the same shortcomings in the Americans' list as had Aranha, but—just as Welles and Caffery had predicted—he was not nearly as troubled by the idea of not receiving all of the supplies at once. As Caffery was taking his leave Vargas repeated to him, "Tell Welles of my high appreciation and of my full confidence in him."

Aranha was waiting outside the room for Caffery, who told him of the conversation he had just had with Vargas. Aranha harrumphed, "I hope that he keeps to that opinion."[7]

Back in Washington, Cordell Hull attempted to assuage the foreign minister's concerns, writing to Caffery, "Please tell Aranha from me that for once his uncanny intuition has been in error. This is no 'run around' and there is not going to be any 'run around.'"[8]

Yet Aranha was not so easily reassured. Vargas, Aranha, Welles, and Hull all understood perfectly well that the US list could be seen as a glass half full or half empty. Aranha, with his political troubles, needed the bulk of the armaments to arrive quickly so as to appease Dutra and the military, and chose to concentrate on what was missing. President Vargas, on the other hand, sought to please Welles and President Roosevelt at a time when Souza Costa was trying to obtain important concessions from the United States on key economic and natural resource development deals, and opted to focus on what the Americans had included, not what they had left out.

Whether or not Vargas's positive response to the list of military supplies helped to grease the wheels in Washington, Souza Costa's mission went much more smoothly thereafter. Souza Costa succeeded in accomplishing almost all of the economic objectives Vargas had assigned him. The United States offered funds of up to $100 million to help develop raw materials in Brazil, while agreeing that the price of Brazilian rubber would be increased and production would also expand in the Amazon region of Brazil. The United States also provided assurances that Brazil would still be paid for the export of its coffee and cacao, even if these commodities could not be shipped. Furthermore, the Americans would provide research and development money, as well as expertise, to help the Brazilians produce aircraft engines.[9]

These agreements, which were collectively known as the Washington Accords, were signed on March 3, 1942, and represented every bit as significant a gain for Brazil's economy as the armaments deal had been for the country's military. The accords did advance the two countries' military relationship, as well; the United States also went some way to providing Brazil with more of the armaments that it needed for the defense of northeastern Brazil. The new lend-lease agreement was also raised to $200 million, granting Brazil additional credit with which to pay for the increased shipments of armaments.[10]

In Rio the following morning, with Alzira busy transcribing Souza Costa's long and detailed encrypted telegrams, President Vargas declared himself satisfied with the final details of the accords.[11] In return for the American concessions, and after first consulting with Dutra, Vargas agreed to the stationing of US personnel in northeastern Brazil, with the understanding that their main task was to transform the region's airfields into modern, fully functioning airports in order to allow the unrestricted use of the airspace by the United States.[12] He also finished dealing with the problem of Brazil's pro-Axis aviation industry, an issue that had long concerned the Americans and British. By 1942, the Italian airline LATI no longer flew routes to Brazil, and the Brazilian airline Condor—which previously had strong German links—was being taken over by the Brazilian government.[13] The process of taking control of local airlines had been a complex one, but Vargas had been determined to succeed.[14]

The Brazilian press warmly welcomed the Washington Accords of March 3, 1942. One American in particular was singled out for his work in Latin America: Nelson Rockefeller. Central to Rockefeller's vision was the development of cultural and media ties between the two countries—ties that were aimed at countering Nazi efforts to covertly export its brand of racial culture into Brazil. The tightening of a British naval blockade in the region had already made direct German attempts to do this all the more difficult. So too, for that matter, had a recent turn of events in the Atlantic.

In February and March 1942, the German navy sank four Brazilian vessels off the coast of the United States.[15] Germany, while wishing to punish Brazil for the breaking of relations, also had geostrategic motives for attacking Brazilian shipping. The Germans believed that Brazil remained highly dependent on supplies from the United States to keep its economy going. The most vulnerable area was fuel, which was already in short supply in Brazil and for which Brazil was almost totally dependent on the United States. Fuel was brought to Brazil in large Brazilian tankers, and the Germans believed that the more Brazilian shipping its submarines sank, the more likely it was that the United States would have to organize an escort convoy, which would distract the US navy from maintaining the South Atlantic route from the United States to Great Britain. Some fifty-three Brazilian seamen were lost in one incident alone when, on March 10, 1942, seven days after the signing of the Washington Accords, a German U-boat torpedoed the SS *Cairu* between Norfolk and New York.[16]

When news of the sinking of the *Cairu* reached Brazil, serious rioting took place in Rio and the country's south. In the capital, rioters stampeded through the streets, attacking German-owned businesses. The local police were slow to restore order, and chose to intervene only as a last resort. German shopkeepers attempted to save their businesses by dropping their metal shutters and putting up signs that read "closed until further notice." The wave of anti-German feeling took many Brazilian leaders by surprise, but in the American and British embassies in Rio, it was viewed as confirmation that Brazilians were very much on the side of the Allied cause. Certainly, it would be difficult for Vargas to switch sides now that so much of the Brazilian populace had turned decisively against the Axis.

Rockefeller's main goal, however, was even more ambitious than preventing German ideology from infecting America's southerly neighbor. He aimed both to lay the groundwork in Rio for Brazilian participation in the war, and to illustrate to America that Brazil was a trusted ally. Rockefeller understood that in order to succeed in the latter effort, he would need to demystify Brazil for the American public and attempt to build Rio's credibility. He was busily waging a charm offensive in the American press; in April 1942, *Life* magazine, the periodical with the largest circulation of the era, put Rockefeller on its cover and the *New Yorker* published a detailed feature on the youthful American. Rockefeller proclaimed in the *New Yorker*, "I am optimistic about South America, but you have to qualify that by saying that I am optimistic about everything."[17] The articles in both magazines were full of praise for Rockefeller and the work of the office of the coordinator of inter-American affairs. He was seen as a man who could cut through Washington's red tape, a man who could get things done. Rockefeller's profile was growing in Rio, as well, with many Brazilians curious as to why this superwealthy, young, handsome man did not simply become a playboy.

During the first part of 1942, Rockefeller was keen to increase the pace and scale of his cultural program in Brazil. He regarded the success of Walt Disney's visit to Rio the previous year and the good reception Brazilian artists were enjoying in America as indications that the time was right for him to plan a project on a far greater scale. Naturally, such lofty aims did not come without due risk.

Without knowing it, Rockefeller would unleash a force on Rio de Janeiro that, for better or worse, would come to play a leading role in the American Good Neighbor Program. Even as Rockefeller's nominal boss, Sumner Welles, was preparing to depart Rio, thousands of miles away another Mr. Welles was getting ready to board the very same aircraft that was earmarked to bring the undersecretary of state back to the United States. The acclaimed actor-director Orson Welles was in Hollywood at the time, frantically trying to wrap up his latest film in order to catch the Pan Am clipper down to Rio. As Sumner Welles spent his last few days in Rio taking meetings in the Copacabana Palace Hotel and gently unwinding from two weeks of frantic diplomatic activity, he had no idea of the difficulties that lay ahead when this other Mr. Welles—and his film crew—arrived in Rio.

The project Rockefeller had in mind for Welles was sure to be hugely expensive. But Hollywood executives remained keen to participate in the Good Neighbor Program; they understood that there was a lot of money to be made in producing wartime propaganda movies, which drew large audiences across the United States. These executives' eagerness—and the fact that Nelson Rockefeller was a shareholder in RKO Pictures— made it relatively easy for him to find the necessary funding for a full-scale Hollywood film to be shot in Rio de Janeiro during the first part of 1942.

Rockefeller's selection of Orson Welles to make the film was not a universally popular decision. The twenty-six-year-old filmmaker was flush from the success of his landmark work *Citizen Kane,* which had been released the previous year to tremendous acclaim, having been nominated for nine Academy Awards. Welles's genius was widely acknowledged by film critics, and also by fellow filmmakers in Hollywood. The trouble was that Welles's genius was fueled by alcohol and, as Welles put it, "skirt chasing."[18] He was not, perhaps, the best man to unleash in a city where both vices were widely available. By 1942, Welles was also starting to reveal something of a persecution complex. He claimed that he was an outsider, that Hollywood didn't understand him, and that the big studio bosses were out to ruin his career. On top of all this, he was hopelessly overworked, not only making films but also acting in them.

Much was at stake, and in retrospect, Rockefeller might have been wise to take more caution in choosing a filmmaker. Certainly there were other leading directors who would have been able to make the film he had in mind. Caution, however, was not Rockefeller's style. He wanted genius, and so he dispatched Orson Welles to Rio to shoot a big-budget film that was supposed to be the icing on the newly baked cake of US-Brazilian relations.

Orson Welles had his own doubts about taking on the project. He resented being dragged out of the edit suite (where he was working on another film, *The Magnificent Ambersons,* which he felt was going to be even better than *Citizen Kane*) and dispatched without salary to Rio.[19] Welles simply could not turn the Brazil film down, however. As he put it later:

> You know why I went? I went because it was put to me in the very strongest terms by Jock Whitney and Nelson Rockefeller that this would represent a sorely needed contribution to inter-American affairs. This sounds today quite unbelievably silly, but in the first year of the war the defense of the hemisphere seemed crucially important. I was told that the value of this project would lie not in the film itself but in the fact of making it. It was put to me that my contribution as a kind of ambassador extraordinaire would be truly meaningful. Normally, I had doubts about this, but Roosevelt himself helped to persuade me that I really had no choice.[20]

With the president himself imploring Welles to use his creative genius to help shore up ties between the United States and Brazil, the filmmaker could not very well have said no. And whether or not the legendarily festive city beckoned to Welles, as well, it would soon have him in its grip.

Welles had been told that he and his crew were to be on the Pan Am clipper service to Rio at the start of February. "Rio: at the end of civilization as we know it," claimed Welles on newsreel footage as he set out for the Brazilian capital. The timing of his departure was dictated by the end of the conference of foreign ministers in Rio, since the Brazilian government did not feel it could receive Welles properly with so many other foreign dignitaries in town.[21]

During the flight down to Rio, Welles went over the initial, vague plans for the movie. The Brazilian department of press and propaganda (DIP) had decided that the film's subject was to be Carnaval in Rio. From the outset, Welles suspected that the Brazilian government wanted a film that would be of use to it both during wartime and in the postwar era:

> They were a little drunk with the potency of the motion picture medium. It is not too hard to see how their DIP would conceive luring one of the world's most creative filmmakers to make a fantastic tourist come-on (effective after hostilities ended, to be sure) centered upon their fabulous Carnaval. So they beckoned the gullible Yankees. I suggest that the record is made even clearer when it is noted that the Brazilian official put in charge of working with us on the film was the head of the department of tourism.[22]

Welles argued that the real trouble with the film, however, was that neither he nor his crew knew anything about Carnaval. Welles claimed not to even like the yearly events. "I associated them with fancy dress, which bores me silly, and the tourist banalities of the New Orleans Mardi Gras."[23]

What interested Welles much more than Carnaval itself was the samba music that accompanied the festival. In 1942, samba music was not well known outside of Brazil, and Welles wanted to bring the music to the masses back in the United States by making a film centered on the samba clubs in the poor areas of Rio known as the *favelas*.[24] This intention was not entirely realistic, given how dangerous the *favelas* were, and a cinematic tour of the city's slums was certainly not what the Brazilian government was expecting Welles and his team to produce for the war effort.

President Vargas and the Brazilian government were initially extremely flattered that a director of Welles's stature was in Rio to make a film about Brazil. Vargas was impressed by Welles's energy and his seemingly strong commitment to Brazilian culture. Osvaldo Aranha, too, was quickly won over by Welles. Aranha shepherded Welles around at official functions, making sure he was meeting the right people.

The sheer scale of Welles's movie project, moreover, staggered the Brazilians. Welles wanted to re-create the vast processions and samba parties of Carnaval, even though many of these rituals had recently been done away with. Praça Onze, the historic square in downtown Rio and traditionally the focus of Carnaval, had been knocked down in 1940 by the Vargas government as part of their attempt to exert more government control over the parade and to build a new boulevard. This was no problem for Welles, who rebuilt an exact replica of the *praça* in a movie studio, where he also re-created the dancing and music of the samba parade. It was on this film stage that photographers from *Life* captured the famous pictures of Welles dressed in a white tuxedo, brandishing a handheld camera—a filming technique that was little used at the time—and looking slightly crazed.

Early on, it was clear that Welles and his film, which he gave the working title *It's All True,* were in deep trouble. Studio executives, worried about the spiraling costs, threatened to withhold payment for Welles's expenses. One man drowned during the filming of a scene depicting Brazilian revolutionaries arriving in Rio by raft.[25] Compounding these problems was the fact that Welles was drinking too much and chasing skirts all over Rio. He was not content to remain in "white" Rio, the areas by the coastline, and instead traveled further afield. His one attempt to go to one of the city's *favelas,* however, ended when men throwing beer bottles attacked his party. Even a country as diverse as Brazil had racial strictures in the 1940s, and Rockefeller had to smooth things over with Vargas, who was increasingly worried about the "black" nature of Welles's film.

Dealing with Hollywood movie bosses proved to be a much more difficult task, even for Rockefeller, and eventually Welles was forced to abandon the film. The executives had become fed up with Welles's antics, and had taken issue with the project's producers, finally deciding to cut off Welles's funds. While a "finished"—or at least viewable—version of the film would surface in the 1980s, Rockefeller's grand ambitions for the project were never realized.

The great project had ended in failure and ruin for Welles, who would never work for a major Hollywood studio again. His usefulness to Rockefeller, however, did not end with the film. Welles, who had already gained infamy as a radio personality for his 1938 narration of H. G. Wells's *The War of the Worlds,* enjoyed something of a second career as a radio broadcaster while in Brazil, hosting joint radio programs with Brazilian broadcasters and even speaking some broken Portuguese during the shows.

Welles took part in two important radio broadcasts while in Rio, one to mark Pan-American Day on April 15, 1942, and the other one to mark Brazilian President's Day on April 19, 1942. Welles's joint radio address with Osvaldo Aranha on April 15 was an important event in helping to introduce Aranha to a wider audience in the United States. When the two men came together to conduct the broadcast, the differences between them could not have been more striking. Welles looked like a trendy but slightly mad professor, dressed in a crumpled double-breasted pin-striped suit with a white shirt and no tie. Aranha, by contrast, appeared more conservative, in a crisp suit and tie with perfectly combed hair. Prior to the broadcast the minister of foreign affairs had an attack of nerves, wondering if his heavily accented English would be understood by an American audience. Welles reassured him, suggesting that many Americans struggled to follow Welles's own lyrical style of English. Indeed, prior to, during, and after the joint broadcast, it was clear that—despite all the difficulties surrounding *It's All True*—Aranha and Welles remained on excellent terms.

During the program, which was broadcast on NBC, Aranha made the pitch that Brazil was a reliable ally and could be trusted:

I know well that the heart of Brazil is all with the United States. Our interests have been mutual always, our affections mutually profound. Today, as history itself enters upon a new epoch, our very aims are so identical that I feel justified in speaking now for the people of both our countries, for your people as well as mine, when I say that in all that family of nations of which you have made mention, we are the closest, the United States and Brazil—we are each other's favorite . . . The products of our industry, the great wealth of our natural resources, are yours—all yours, for your fight against our common enemies. Brazilian ships give first preference to your war needs. They carry little else. Our effort is more than just a supplement to yours. I need a stronger word than cooperation.[26]

True to form, the foreign minister came off as strongly pro-American, and while his assurance—"the heart of Brazil is all with the United States"—may have not been entirely grounded in reality—ignoring, for instance, the military's ongoing frustration with America's conduct toward Brazil—it did convey exactly the sort of resolute camaraderie that had become the policy of the Vargas administration, while also making clear that the war was still America's to fight, and not Brazil's.

The conversation then moved to the serious topic of the first attacks against Brazilian shipping by German U-boats, which at the time of the broadcast in April 1942 were starting to increase in frequency. Here Welles revealed his true professionalism. It would be easy to dismiss Welles simply as a drunk, perspiring party animal, whose interest in Rio was purely to stroke his own ego and pursue the thrill of sexual conquest. He had another side, however, which shone through whenever the fog of booze lifted long enough. Welles was capable of being a first-rate diplomat, and although he would have regarded the labels themselves as insulting, he was also something of a good politician and statesman who took his responsibilities seriously.

Welles had been instructed to ask about the German attacks on merchant Brazilian shipping during the course of his interview with Aranha, and the filmmaker approached the subject diplomatically:

> Another delicate subject, Mr. Aranha. The sinking of Brazilian ships, especially in North American waters. It would seem needless to say that their loss was no more avoidable than the loss of our own merchant ships, and that Brazilian ships are no easier for our navy to protect than American ships. Still, some of us here have feared that certain sections of Brazilian opinion might find in those disasters a source of resentment and perhaps even some loss of confidence in our defensive powers.[27]

Welles's comments were exceedingly careful—a fact attested to by the original script for the interview, on which he had scrawled copious notes. Welles had gone through draft after draft to craft the tone and the meaning of the segment in a way that would reflect exactly what he wished to convey to the audience—namely, that the attacks on Brazilian shipping would not alter its position on the war.

Welles's second radio appearance came on Brazilian President's Day, April 19, 1942, and was broadcast live from a glittering event during which Rio's political and social elites were treated to a musical show. Welles acted as the host, along with the very wooden and droll Jefferson Caffery, who could hardly hide his discomfort at being outshone by Welles. After the musical performance there was dancing, and everybody wanted a dance with the star attraction from America. Welles danced with Alzira under the watchful eye of her husband. Charming, cultured, and with manners perfectly tailored to the black-tie event, Welles worked the room as if he were the president and Caffery a mere junior aide.

Just as Brazil had taken to his predecessor, Sumner Welles, so it fell in love with Orson Welles. Later, he would confess that he couldn't remember a more appreciative audience than the Cariocas. Welles's part in Brazil's story may have been only a brief walk-on amid the greater drama of the first attacks on Brazilian shipping, but the warmth that much of Rio and Brazil felt for the crazy Yankee gave him a unique opportunity to play ambassador—a role he had, in reality, craved.

Despite Welles's failure to finish his film, he played a meaningful role in helping to keep Brazilian relations with the United States on an even keel in the months of February and March 1942, crucial months that saw the first Brazilian casualties of World War II. When Welles could keep himself together long enough, and keep his demons at bay, he was capable of doing the most brilliant things for his country and for Brazil. He was, however, on borrowed time; the booze, the amphetamines (which he took because he thought they made him lose weight), the heat of Rio, and the punishing work schedule were all taking their toll.

Welles didn't exactly leave Rio a broken man, but when he finally departed, his career in Hollywood was effectively over. Welles's reputation as a filmmaker would take years to recover, and even when it did, the films he directed and starred in would not win nearly the same acclaim as his earlier works.

Yet while Brazil may not have done wonders for Welles's career, he had given a great lift to his host nation. The time he spent there as an ambassador, showman, radio presenter, and lover of all things Brazilian endeared him to the country, which needed just such a distraction—indeed, just such a friend—at a time when it was having to adjust to life during the war, with all the losses and fears that such dramatic times brought. Later in the year, months after Welles had left, Osvaldo Aranha wrote warmly to his radio costar, thanking him for his work in Brazil and for the good impression he had left in the country.[28]

One man had been conspicuously absent from most of the festivities and parties for the Welles entourage: President Vargas. During February and March 1942 he continued to remain in Petrópolis and came to Rio only when the occasion demanded it. The president had much to ponder as he went for his regular morning walk around the town. As German attacks on Brazilian shipping increased, President Vargas was coming under more and more pressure to act against Axis assets in Brazil. Initially, he did so to release some steam from the boiling kettle of anti-Axis feeling in Brazil, which the local police reported to him was getting out of control. On March 12, 1942, Vargas signed a decree authorizing the seizure of 30 percent of the total funds of Axis subjects living in the country. Estimates varied as to how much this amounted to in reality, but a figure of half a billion dollars was the most widely accepted.[29]

The early days of the Axis naval campaign against Brazilian shipping proved to be very difficult for Vargas, who quickly realized that Dutra and Góes Monteiro's earlier warnings that Brazil was not ready for war were actually close to the mark. Vargas called for the support of the United States in establishing naval convoys to protect Brazilian merchant seamen and in providing arms that would help Brazil defend its shipping. But this aid had not yet arrived, despite the fact that by March 1942, nearly the entire Brazilian merchant navy was running between the United States and Brazil. Although they were carrying essential war materials to the United States, the ships remained completely vulnerable to the German U-boats prowling the Atlantic.

On March 11, the day after the sinking of the SS *Cairu,* Caffery wrote to Hull with the news that the secretary of state had feared: no more Brazilian ships would be coming to the United States. "Aranha tells me that the government has ordered all Brazilian boats to take refuge in the nearest ports," Caffery reported.[30] The day before, Vargas had written in his diary that he was determined to suspend all shipping to the United States until he got the guarantees he wanted from Washington.[31] In addition to their requests for convoy assistance, the Brazilians now also requested US help arming the Brazilian boats that were in US ports. Brazil itself would take responsibility for arming Brazilian ships in Brazilian ports.[32]

Brazilians felt the impact of the Axis campaign against their country's merchant shipping almost immediately. Shortages of some basic materials became routine. Soon, fuel was scarce, and petrol rationing commenced. Fuel shortages only became more pronounced when, on April 18, President Vargas canceled tanker sailings from the eastern coast of the United States to South America. This measure, which was introduced to protect the slow-moving tanker fleet from Axis attacks, was set to last between four to six weeks.[33]

Newsprint soon became hard to find as well.[34] This shortage threatened to stop production of several of Brazil's major daily newspapers, and caused a great deal of bad feeling toward the two principal suppliers of newsprint, the United States and Great Britain.[35] To be sure, the Allies appreciated the importance of keeping Brazilian newspapers in circulation. Not only were the state-controlled papers full of pro-Allied articles, but they also took an increasingly hostile line against the Axis powers.

The United States offered what resources it could spare and US naval officers offered advice on the routing of Brazilian shipping, but these were mere stopgap measures, and fell short of the assistance Vargas requested.[36] Meanwhile, the political situation within Brazil was growing dire. Just as Aranha suspected, the Brazilian army was full of "told you sos" about the shortages. Dutra demanded to know how the army was meant to repel any southerly Argentine attack without fuel. When Vargas reminded his minister of war that Argentina was equally short of fuel, Dutra argued that he suspected Washington would go soft on Argentina and supply it with petrol in order to try to entice it into breaking relations with the Axis powers.

In late April 1942, a worried President Vargas came down from his retreat in Petrópolis to meet with an American naval delegation in Rio.[37] Following a long discussion, President Vargas made the unprecedented decision to open all ports and airfields to the American navy and its air forces. After resisting the idea of allowing an American military presence in Brazil for so long, Vargas was finally forced to bow to this American demand in order to salvage the worsening situation in the Atlantic. Once the United States had established a military presence along the Brazilian coast, he hoped, it would drive off the wolf packs of U-boats that were hunting Brazilian shipping, and reopen the trade link between North and South America.

The man most responsible for this American coup was Vice Admiral Jonas H. Ingram. Vargas was so impressed with the US officer that he ordered Brazilian naval forces to follow Ingram's orders, whatever they may be.[38] Vargas and Ingram only grew closer during the course of the war, to the point that the US admiral would unofficially advise the Brazilian president on naval issues. Ingram eventually assumed all responsibility for the training and equipping of Brazilian naval forces and worked closely with Vargas in the battle for the South Atlantic.[39] In April 1942, however, Ingram's major contribution was to organize greater protection for Brazilian shipping against German U-boats operating out of French ports.

By the end of April 1942 it appeared that Brazil—while officially remaining a neutral country—would not retain this status for much longer. It was widely expected that the German attacks against Brazilian shipping would intensify over the summer of 1942, and would eventually draw Brazil into the war despite its best efforts to stay out of it. The Brazilian army, however, was plotting to stop this from happening.

## 10

# A QUESTION OF SUCCESSION

In the afternoon of May 1, 1942, President Vargas's limousine followed its usual path from Petrópolis down toward Rio de Janeiro and the Vasco da Gama stadium. The soccer stadium was crammed full of Cariocas who were anxious to hear their president's speech on the state of the war and the economic situation in Brazil. British and American officials were also present, equally keen to take note of Vargas's remarks. Germany was effectively at war with Brazil—at least, as far as public opinion in the country was concerned—and there was no telling what new policy announcement Vargas might make, or what his speech might dictate about Brazil's involvement in the ongoing world war.

Suddenly, as Vargas's car drove along Praia do Flamengo, a wide boulevard snaking past the mouth of Guanabara Bay, the driver lost control of the car.[1] The back of the vehicle spun violently, hitting and dislodging a large concrete post along the side of the road.[2] The back of the car was badly damaged by the post and President Vargas was injured. His jaw fractured and his hip broken, Vargas lay in pain in the backseat of the wrecked vehicle as he awaited help.

Back at the stadium, news of the accident was greeted with confusion. The audience and VIPs were initially informed that the accident was not serious, and that the president was still planning to go ahead with his speech. It soon became clear, however, that Vargas was on his way to the hospital, and he would not be able to continue with the engagement.

While Vargas's injuries were not regarded as life-threatening, they removed him from political life for three months. He would not appear in public again until the second half of August 1942. During his lengthy convalescence, the president's health became the source of much speculation and deep concern among the Allied diplomatic community in Rio. And as the autumn wore on, it was widely acknowledged that his recovery was not progressing as smoothly as had first been hoped. In June, the British ambassador, Noel Charles, sent a bulletin to his superiors in the foreign office in London, offering an update on the president's health:

> President is in bed with weights on his leg to stretch it. Leg was badly set at first and will necessitate his remaining in bed another six weeks or so. Jaw injury is healing, original contraption in mouth having been changed for something more comfortable. President transacts business though he does not see ministers frequently or give audiences. At one moment rumor had it that his mouth had become septic but United States ambassador and myself could obtain no reliable confirmation of any kind sufficient to justify my telephoning you.[3]

Luckily, Vargas's condition was not quite as severe as the British feared. Still, they were correct about one thing: there was indeed a veil of secrecy surrounding the president's injuries and his recovery.

Vargas's two eyes ran the government in his absence. Aranha and Alzira worked together to keep the country running smoothly, though they were increasingly subject to attacks from the military, which naturally viewed Vargas's ill fortune as an opportunity to shift the orientation of the government away from its increasingly overt support of the Allied cause. And with the president indisposed, these military attacks were exposing a critical weakness in the Vargas regime. Rio was awash with rumors and political intrigue, but one point was abundantly clear to all: Vargas had left no plan in place for succession.

When asked the question of who could potentially succeed the president, Aranha joked, "it will all depend on who has sufficient petrol to enable him to arrive first at the Catete Palace."[4] Indeed, if Vargas died of his injuries—an eventuality for which the British, at least, seemed to be preparing—then the leadership of the country would essentially be up for grabs. The Americans and the British feared that a revolution of sorts would be the most likely outcome should Vargas perish. And, as Charles pointed out to the foreign office back in London, if that happened, the Axis powers would no doubt seize the occasion to make a case for their preferred candidate.[5]

The timing of Vargas's accident could not have been worse for the Allies, let alone for his own supporters. He was not a young man, and his road to recovery was far from straightforward. The few people who saw him over the winter months of June and July noticed how much weight he had put on. The injury to his jaw made him reluctant to see visitors, and his broken hip all but ended his golf career. And in the absence of its authoritarian leader, Brazil seemed to be going to pieces.

The perception in Rio throughout this time was that the government was rudderless at a moment when Brazil most needed strong leadership. The country appeared to be being dragged into the war against the will of its own army. The accident also served to deepen internal divisions within the Estado Novo. In the past, most of these internecine disputes had been kept away from the public through careful management of the press, but with Vargas indisposed the regime's ability to hide the cracks in its façade diminished, and the number of leaks by senior members of the regime increased dramatically.[6] To make matters worse, the Axis attacks against Brazilian shipping did not abate during this period but rather intensified as Hitler ordered his U-boats into all-out action against Brazil, which he no longer viewed as a neutral power. In May, June, and July eight Brazilian ships were sunk off the northern coast of South America, killing some twenty-six Brazilian merchant seamen.[7] The German attacks were only worsening, despite the fact that Vice Admiral Ingram had effectively taken control of the effort to protect shipping between Brazil and the eastern coast of the United States.

By increasing pressure on the Brazilians, Hitler aimed to shift popular opinion in the country away from the Allied cause—but the attacks had a different, if still insidious, effect. While Brazilians appeared to swing in the opposite direction following attacks, Hitler's message was not lost on Dutra and much of the senior officer staff corps of the military, which continued to resist the idea of joining the Allied war effort, much to the displeasure of the United States. During his traditional July 4 speech to the American society at the Gavea golf club, Jefferson Caffery went out of his way to praise Vargas and Aranha for their "wholehearted cooperation and enlightened leadership," but pointedly made no mention of the Brazilian military despite the fact that the navy was effectively taking orders directly from the United States, per Vargas's command.[8]

The Germans did not resort to military pressure alone. Daily broadcasts from Berlin sought to drive a wedge between Germans living in
Brazil and their adopted government. The Germans had broadcast a list of
grievances ranging from the financial to the alleged mistreatment of German spies held in Brazil. Each broadcast finished with an overt threat to
Brazil. The broadcast on June 29, 1942, concluded: "Unless the Brazilian
government takes steps without delay to end these grievances, the Reich
government will take counter measures."[9]

The broadcasts also attacked Aranha, and in this they formed part of
a concerted German attempt to turn Brazilian opinion against the pro-
American foreign minister. Berlin believed Aranha was the single source
of the anti-German policy in Brazil, and the Germans later dubbed these
broadcasts their "Dear Osvaldo" messages. But in this, unlike in their war
against Brazilian shipping, Germany attempted to maintain a veneer of
plausible deniability. In private, Aranha said to Caffery, "I spoke to the German ambassador about the radio broadcasts. He assured me that all the
nasty stuff, which is being put out by German radio, comes from Argentina."

Bedridden after his accident, President Vargas struggled to deal with
these mounting challenges. Besides the German attacks, he had to manage
Brazil's deepening relationship with the United States, which continued
to needle the military and which perpetually threatened to turn his commanders against him. To make matters even more difficult, Vargas was also
facing one of the most divisive internal battles of his regime.

The internal dispute had originated with a pro-American July 4
parade organized by students in Rio. The rally was titled "The Anti-
Totalitarian Student Rally" and was the first demonstration of its type
since the establishment of the authoritarian Estado Novo in 1937.[10] Osvaldo Aranha warmly supported the march, as did the president's son-
in-law, Alzira's husband Ernâni do Amaral Peixoto, the governor of the
state of Rio. But the chief of police Filinto Müller opposed the idea of
the march, and refused to give authorization for it. Prior to the parade,
undersecretary to the minister of justice, Leitão de Cunha, placed Müller
under a forty-eight-hour house arrest for opposing the rally. The march
went forward as planned, and although it took place in the pouring rain, it
was well-attended and received widespread coverage in the local media.[11]
The students sang in support of President Vargas, President Roosevelt,
Osvaldo Aranha, and Leitão de Cunha.[12]

Müller's arrest, however, became a bone of contention between Aranha and Dutra and their respective camps. Aranha supported Cunha, while Dutra strongly backed Müller. With the president still recovering and rumors of his ill health continuing to circulate in Rio, both camps saw the dispute as part of a potential succession struggle, and pressed their cases even more vigorously as a result. Eventually Vargas had to intervene from his sickbed, acting as both referee and judge. Afraid of alienating either side of the dispute, he took the middle ground, accepting the resignations of both Filinto Müller and Leitão de Cunha, along with those of the minister of justice, Francisco Campos, and the head of the DIP, Lourival Fontes.[13] Vargas's choice of replacements for two of the officials placated both Aranha and Dutra; an old friend of Aranha's became chief of police, and an army officer was appointed head of the DIP. Neither of these appointees shone in their new roles, however. Later, when the new chief of police tried to break up a German spy ring, he discovered that police officers loyal to Muller had burned all the relevant papers and had wrecked police headquarters.[14]

The local press took its lead from all the internal strife during the winter months of 1942, and made an attempt to assert its independence. The potential of a succession struggle presented publishers with an opportunity to throw their support behind one faction or another, in the hope of gaining greater freedom and access to the Brazilian leadership should their candidate triumph. Much of the press remembered the army's recent attempt to shut down two Brazilian newspapers, and they did not think highly of Dutra, and so many of the publishers backed Aranha instead.

José Eduardo de Machedo, the publisher of the *Diário Carioca*, tried another tactic in his attempt to win more freedom for the press: he began lobbying both the British and US embassies for support. The results were mixed. Jefferson Caffery suggested that the proprietor was more interested in seeing Vargas's son-in-law replaced as governor of the state of Rio than in winning additional freedom for the press. While the British were more receptive to the press's entreaties than the Americans, they made it clear that they were not interested in undercutting Vargas at this crucial juncture by backing the rebellious newspaper publishers. Caffery took a snide swipe at the British for toying with Machedo, suggesting that any good relationship between the local press and the British was based on the generous subsidies that London offered to much of the local press.[15]

In subsidizing the Brazilian press, Great Britain conveniently ignored the growing number of anti-Semitic articles and cartoons in Brazilian newspapers. *Gazetta* was one of the country's most notorious Jew-hating publications. As an official at the British consulate noted, "The newspaper is turning very chauvinistic. The other day it brought an article calling for the immediate dismissal of not only German and Italian professors, but also of all Frenchmen similarly employed. I gather that the Germans employed at this university are Jewish refugees."[16]

Like the Brazilian press, the Estado Novo had not been kind to the country's Jewish population—though this was less an indication of institutionalized anti-Semitism than of a xenophobic streak within the Vargas regime. The ideology at the heart of the Estado Novo envisioned a more unified Brazil, and Jews were not the only group that didn't fit into this vision. To be sure, many Brazilians strongly associated Judaism with communism, a common conception in the 1940s—and one that undoubtedly fueled the persecution of the country's Jewish residents. But Japanese immigrants were also viewed with suspicion by the regime, as indeed were the large number of German immigrants living in the south of the country. Vargas mandated that all immigrants learn Portuguese, and declared that all official institutions were to operate in Portuguese only; Yiddish, Hebrew, Japanese, and German were to be stamped out in favor of a single, Brazilian tongue.

Deep divisions, more often than not based on simple personality clashes or turf wars between key families, also weakened Rio's Jewish community. There were major splits, too, between Rio's Jews and those in Brazil's second city, São Paulo.

But the biggest challenge to Jews wishing to settle in Brazil came from travel and residency restrictions imposed by the Brazilian government. Official Brazilian policy was that no Jewish refugee qualified for the documents required to secure permanent residence in Brazil, and nobody was allowed to work unless they had permanent visas. This catch-22 situation made it almost impossible for Jews to legally enter or remain in Brazil. As the US embassy in Rio succinctly explained when Washington asked whether Brazil would open its doors to Jewish refugees fleeing Nazism, "With reference to the department's airgram regarding the rescue and relief of Jews from Europe, it is apparent from Brazilian regulations that the Brazilian government does not want any more Jews."[17]

When Jewish refugees were prevented from entering Brazil, as many were, little mention was made of their religion. Brazil was closing its doors to all new immigration. The major piece of legislation that restricted Jewish immigration to Brazil was Decree-Law 3175 of April 7, 1941, which made it practically impossible for a European Jew to obtain a visa for Brazil. There were only two legal exceptions. For a temporary visa a person needed to show means of subsistence and ability to return to his or her country of origin within two years. For a permanent visa a person had to either be able to transfer from abroad the equivalent of 400 contos in foreign exchange, be an experienced technician whose services were clearly needed in Brazil, or be a famous person—that is, an internationally known figure rather than merely an icon in their country of origin.[18] More specifically, Decree-Law 3175 gave responsibility for the application of immigration regulations to the ministry of justice, which at the time was headed by the legal architect of the Estado Novo, Francisco Campos. The Americans suspected, however, that Ernâni Reis, the secretary to the minister of justice, had the final word on all immigration issues—and that Reis was anti-Semitic. Yet the US consular section in Rio could find no specific case of discrimination authorized by the secretary.[19] This, despite the fact that almost all applications to evoke the exemption clauses were turned down by the ministry.

Yet many Jewish refugees did find a way to get into the country. Jews could secure visas by bribing a government official in Rio. Brazil also occasionally allowed Jewish converts to Catholicism to enter the country—most notably in 1940, when some three thousand German Jews who had tacitly converted were allowed to settle in the south of Brazil.[20] The foreign ministry also quietly issued paperwork to "celebrity Jews," such as the writer Stefan Zweig, as well as to Jews who had managed to escape Europe specifically through Lisbon—a reflection of the historic relationship between Brazil and Portugal. Albert Einstein also requested a number of visas for refugees, which Aranha eventually approved.[21]

These refugees joined an already sizeable population of Brazilian Jews. Under orders from Washington, the US consulate in Rio tried to ascertain the exact number of Jews in the country. Given the lack of reliable statistics, this was no easy task. Jewish groups put the number at around 112,000, of which around fifty thousand had entered Brazil since 1925.[22] During World War II, there were seventy thousand foreign-born Jews living in Brazil and thirty-two thousand of their children, as well as ten thousand Sephardic Jews (who had lived in Brazil for generations).[23]

Many newly arrived Jews were living in the Copacabana Palace Hotel and in other luxury hotels across the city. Their presence became something of an irritant for the locals, who accused them of pushing up the prices of hotel rooms in the city. Many Cariocas regarded these and other first-generation Jewish immigrants as something of a security threat. As the country slid toward war with the Axis powers, it was not wise to speak German or Eastern European languages in public places in Rio. Very few of the refugees spoke any Portuguese at all, relying on the language of their respective country of origin or English.

Brazil could not have been characterized as welcoming to Jews, yet those who were able to enter the country found a respite of sorts from the terrors of Europe. While overtly Jewish activities and institutions were banned—Jewish newspapers closed, Zionist groups prevented from meeting, and symbols of Jewish culture often defaced by graffiti—there was no deep Brazilian appetite for the pursuit of physical violence against Jews. Any abuse or violence that was directed against the refugees came from German nationals based in Rio, rather than from Brazilians. Brazil's police force, however, largely ignored the verbal and physical assaults on the refugees, a fact that did not exactly cover the Estado Novo in glory.

Though perhaps not representative of the Jewish experience in Brazil during World War II, Stefan Zweig left a telling remembrance of his time in the country. Zweig chose to commit suicide in Brazil, though not because of any anti-Semitic persecution he suffered there; rather, he had made a pact with his wife. The visa that the Brazilian authorities had granted Zweig had saved his life, and in his carefully written suicide note he paid tribute to the Brazilian people for the hospitality they had shown him during his period of exile in the country. Indeed, it has been suggested that Zweig chose to write his pro-Brazil book, *Brazil: Land of the Future*, to highlight his gratitude to the Brazilian authorities.

While the US embassy highlighted the difficulty Jews faced in immigrating to Brazil as a result of Decree-Law 3175, it was also keen to mention other policies of legislation that were more favorable toward them. Central to this was a piece of legislation titled *Portaria* 4941. Issued on July 24, 1941, it granted anyone who had entered Brazil on a temporary visa permanent status for the duration of World War II.[24] While the law was only for people who had left their respective country of origin before January 1, 1941, it did help some refugees gain employment in Brazil or to start up their own businesses.[25] In other cases, Jews who had entered the country illegally were allowed to work, and on occasion they even set up their own small businesses using covers or fronts to help evade the law.

Other members of the regime held seemingly contradictory views of Jews, claiming not to be against them but still refusing Jewish refugees entry into Brazil on nationalistic grounds that were often disguised as economic rationale. Even the pro-American Aranha was not immune to criticism from the Americans that he could have done more to help alleviate anti-Jewish sentiment in Brazil, or that he could have allowed more refugees to enter the country as the situation for European Jewry deteriorated. While Aranha did quietly authorize refugees to enter the country on certain occasions, without proper documentation it is difficult to know just how many Jews were allowed into Brazil unofficially. And Aranha's ministry of foreign affairs was also hugely divided over the question of whether to allow Jewish refugees into Brazil. The Americans noted that the ministry had also had difficulty interesting President Vargas in the question of Jewish refugees.[26] Vargas simply did not seem particularly interested in the matter. Many local Jewish leaders shared the appraisal of Marc Leitchic, one of the directors of the Jewish Colonization Organization in Brazil: "The high policy of the present regime here is not anti-Jewish, but that there are anti-Jewish influences at work in it in certain critical spots."[27]

One Brazilian official was notable for helping Jewish refugees escape from Europe: Brazil's ambassador to France, Luis Martins de Souza Dantas.[28] Within the diplomatic community, the ambassador was seen as something of a Parisian playboy. A lover of champagne, fine wine, and women of all nationalities, he did not seem exactly like the heroic type. Indeed, the ambassador was well liked by many officials from the Axis powers based in Paris. As a result, he learned of the mistreatment of Jews in German-occupied Europe very early in the war.

Souza Dantas did what he could to aid European Jews. He tried to bring to Aranha's attention the plight of European Jewry, specifically those Jews in occupied France, but his messages accomplished little.[29] So Souza Dantas took matters into his own hands. He believed it was his duty to try to help any Jew who approached the embassy seeking to escape across the Atlantic. From the fall of France in the summer of 1940 until August 1942, Souza Dantas issued transit visas to Jews, helping them to get to Lisbon and, from there, to Brazil, the United States, or Palestine. He continued to issue visas despite warnings from Aranha that he would face disciplinary action if he continued to do so.[30] In fact, Souza Dantas had been warned about the issuing of visas before the outbreak of World War II, which led the ministry of foreign affairs to strip him of any power related to issuing visas. Ignoring this, Souza Dantas continued to issue them and requested that other Brazilian delegations do the same if the visas he had issued expired due to the refugees' travel being delayed.

The case of the SS *Cabo de Hornos,* which carried some one hundred Jewish refugees from Lisbon to Brazil, came to symbolize the work of Souza Dantas. The passengers had been delayed in Europe while officials acting under orders from Souza Dantas hastily updated their paperwork so that they could leave. The ship arrived in Rio de Janeiro on October 16, 1941, but the Brazilian government denied the refugees entry into the country. Several of the passengers threatened to commit suicide rather than return to Europe. As the ship sailed south to Argentina, the Catholic Church in Brazil, Jewish rescue groups, the American embassy in Rio, and individual affluent Americans frantically lobbied President Vargas to reverse the decision and allow the refugees into Brazil. Alzira herself asked her father whether something couldn't be done for the people aboard the ship. Vargas simply replied that the ministry of foreign affairs was not responsible for visas that were issued against their orders.[31] Eventually, the Dutch colony of Curaçao took in the refugees, saving their lives.

This was not an isolated incident. Later in 1941, the SS *Alsina* had left Marseilles with over five hundred passengers, around one hundred of whom were Jewish refugees with Brazilian entry visas issued in Paris by Souza Dantas. These passengers, however, were not allowed to disembark when the *Alsina* arrived in Rio. After other countries, including several British territories, also refused to let the refugees disembark, the United States took them in.[32]

The cases of the *Cabo de Hornos* and *Alsina* did not cast Vargas or the Estado Novo in a positive light, and they reinforced the widely held perception that many of the regime's senior members were anti-Jewish or at least—like Vargas—indifferent to the plight of the refugees. The regime's reaction to Souza Dantas's activism didn't help its public image. He was eventually found guilty of issuing a number of visas against the orders of the ministry of foreign affairs.[33] The number of illegal visas was never fully determined, but estimates suggest that Souza Dantas helped save the lives of between five hundred and eight hundred refugees.

The ambassador managed to escape punishment because of his age—he was technically in retirement—but with his ouster, Brazil's doors appeared to be firmly shut to European Jewry. The numbers make this painfully clear. In 1939 some four thousand Jews entered Brazil. By 1942 this number was only 108.[34] In 1943 this figure fell to eleven, and in 1944 only six Jews were granted visas. The total number of Jews who entered Brazil between 1939 and 1947 was only 12,884. This figure represented only 1,159 more for the same period than Argentina, a country where there was much more systematic anti-Jewish sentiment than there was in Brazil. The United States during this time accepted 168,053 Jews into the country.[35] Indeed, without the efforts of the United States, Brazil's numbers would have been quite different; a large number of the Jews who were allowed to enter Brazil at the start of the war did so only after the United States applied strong diplomatic pressure to convince Brazil to take in more Jews.

Ironically, the anti-Jewish sentiment of many Brazilian authorities markedly declined as Brazil shifted toward the Allied camp in 1942. This change was widely highlighted in the Brazilian press, which had previously been characterized by a distinctly anti-Semitic bent. As an editorial in the *Diário de Notícias* proclaimed: "The Jews who are today our guests prove to be determined to work with us: let us therefore accept them in our work. . . . The Jews who the tragedy of the war brought to the shores of Brazil merit praise only for the way they are helping us. Intelligent, determined, hard working, and grateful for our hospitality, they can be most useful to the country."[36]

The reasons for Brazil's growing tolerance for Jews were varied. This period coincided with a marked increase in British and American propaganda efforts in Brazil. The authorities started to clamp down on German propaganda activities as well, which had been full of overtly anti-Semitic messages. The entry of the Soviet Union into the war the previous year also removed some of the Bolshevik stigma that some Brazilians had previously attached to Jews of Eastern European origin living in the country.

One other factor was especially significant: the resignation of the three men regarded as more pro-Nazi than anyone in the regime—the minister of justice, Campos, the man most responsible for the drafting of the anti-Jewish legislation; the chief of police, Muller; and the director of the DIP, Fontes. Their resignations had nothing to do with their alleged anti-Jewish sentiments, but the impact of their departures was nevertheless felt immediately in this regard. In a marked change, Jews came to be viewed in a more positive light, as an asset rather than a threat to the country. Sadly, however, Brazil still did not open its doors to Jewish refugees struggling to escape the horrors of Nazi-occupied Europe.

President Vargas, meanwhile, remained a slightly disinterested spectator to the plight of European Jewry. Even when prompted by the United States to do more, he merely indicated a willingness to help, but never actually did so by ordering the country's doors flung open to Jewish refugees.

Brazil's president had much to distract him. During the winter months of 1942 in Brazil, not only was Vargas coping with heightened squabbling within his regime, but he was also attempting to prepare himself, the government, and the Brazilian people for war against the Axis powers. While convalescing, he met frequently with Aranha and Alzira to weigh the perils that Brazil would face if it joined the Allied cause against the development opportunities that Brazil might encounter if it became involved in the war, specifically in regard to the country's infrastructure and economy. It was clear that Brazil could expect even more in the way of military shipments and trade concessions if it joined the hostilities, and the prospect was significant enough to outweigh many of the risks of declaring war on the Axis.

But Vargas was also starting to realize that if Brazil joined the war, popular pressure for democracy would be hard to resist, and the authoritarian Estado Novo was unlikely to survive the conflict. This point was not lost on the two other men who had been instrumental in the creation of the Estado Novo, the minister of war and the chief of the army, Dutra and Góes Monteiro. Both men understood that the Estado Novo would need to be replaced by a new political system, one that gave the Brazilian population a greater say in the running of the state.

And then there was the matter of the ongoing German attacks on Brazilian shipping. Although Germany had been targeting Brazilian merchantmen since early 1942, the U-boat war in the Atlantic was about to escalate dramatically. As Vargas slowly recovered his health, this dimension of the conflict was about to present him with the biggest challenge of his reign. In the winter of 1942 the president, who had relied on Alzira and Osvaldo Aranha to keep the government functioning during his convalescence, would need his two trusted eyes more than ever.

# PART FOUR:
## BRAZIL GOES TO WAR

11

# THE DECISION

THE ATTACKS CAME SUDDENLY, ON THREE CLEAR spring days and
nights in August 1942. They were brutal, and they were much closer
to home than most Brazilians had ever anticipated.

Between August 15 and 17, five Brazilian ships—totaling some four-
teen thousand tons—were torpedoed and sank while operating inside the
country's territorial waters. Approximately six hundred men, women, and
children died; among them were 169 soldiers. These were by far the most
devastating losses Brazil had experienced thus far in the war, and unlike
previous German attacks—which had targeted merchant shipping—these
had struck ships carrying passengers and troops.

A single U-boat, *U-507*, carried out all five separate attacks. At
7:12 P.M. on August 15, the U-boat torpedoed the *Baependy* passenger
liner as it traveled from Salvador to Recife. All of its 215 passengers and
55 crewmembers were lost. Less than two hours later, at 9:03 P.M. on
August 15, *U-507* torpedoed another Brazilian ship, the *Araraquara*, also
traveling toward northern Brazil from Salvador. Out of a total of 142 people on board, 131 died. Some seven hours after the second attack, *U-507*
struck again, torpedoing the *Aníbal Benévolo*. All 83 passengers traveling
on the ship died, and out of a crew of 71, only four survived. Then, on
August 17, close to the city of Vitória, the *U-507* attacked and sank the
*Itagiba* at 10:45 A.M., killing 36. Another Brazilian ship, the *Arará*, traveling from Salvador to Santos, stopped to help the crippled *Itagiba*, only
to become the fifth Brazilian victim of the German submarine, with a
death toll of 20. The total number of dead from the attacks reached 607.

Following the attacks, the Brazilian leadership went into a collective
state of shock. The government ordered all Brazilian ships back to the
nearest ports; postponed coastal sailings; canceled all leave for Brazilian

soldiers, who were ordered to return to barracks; and cut short all shore leave for naval personnel, ordering sailors to rejoin their respective ships.[1]

When news of the losses reached the Brazilian population, the reaction was even more extreme. Riots erupted across the country as mobs attacked German and Italian businesses and personal property, smashing windows, ransacking offices, and even burning buildings. In Rio, the local police were initially reluctant to intervene and allowed the mobs to move with minimal interference. Brazilians called for reprisals against the Axis powers, in particular Germany and Italy, both of which were blamed for the attacks.[2] "Death to Hitler" and "Death to Mussolini" were frequently heard chants, although the majority of the crowd chanted pro-Brazilian and pro-Vargas slogans. In Rio, a crowd of over five thousand people passionately sang the Brazilian national anthem and cheered as two German and two Italian flags were burned in front of the Municipal Theater.[3] There were also attacks against official Spanish buildings in Rio after false rumors circulated that Spanish agents had provided Germany with details of the movements of the doomed vessels. The local press urged Brazilians to pledge funds to help the families of the victims. In the days that followed, the front pages of many of Brazil's newspapers announced the total money raised in big, bold headlines.

The Americans described the losses as Brazil's Pearl Harbor, and this comparison was spot-on.[4] The attacks on Brazilian shipping represented a tremendous setback for those Brazilians who supported an isolationist approach to the war.[5] President Vargas, who was still convalescing in the Guanabara Palace and had not been seen in public for over three months, was left to ponder Brazil's response; Osvaldo Aranha, meanwhile, called for an immediate declaration of war on the Axis powers. This was the president's moment of truth, and he could sense this fact despite his isolation since his car accident on May 1.

Vargas was also experienced enough to immediately comprehend that the attacks on the Brazilian ships changed the dynamics of his government. Whereas merchant ships were understood to be running a risk given their role in the Allied war effort, vessels carrying civilians and troops were widely considered innocent—and the attacks on them were an unmistakable display of German aggression toward Brazil itself, not the Allied powers generally. The country had been challenged, and it was clear what response the Brazilian people demanded from their leaders. The US intelligence service dramatically argued:

> The apparently deliberate attack by Germany on Brazil has forced the hand of the Góes Monteiro-Dutra clique who have always proclaimed their readiness to defend their country in the event of attack. From now on, any failure on their part to cooperate with the defense effort can be called treachery and dealt with openly. Now it will also be possible to deal with the Fifth Column without open opposition from people who have hitherto advocated a neutral course with regard to the Axis powers.[6]

Yet while both Dutra and Góes Monteiro were furious with the Germans, their position was not as clear-cut as the United States suggested; they still wanted to stop short of dragging Brazil into the war, and quickly thwarted America's hope that the attacks would lead to a political consensus among the senior figures in the regime.

Dutra and Góes Monteiro tried to counter Aranha's call for a declaration of war by strongly condemning the sinkings, while also arguing that Aranha himself had effectively caused them with his initiative to break diplomatic relations with the Axis powers at the start of the year. Dutra also blamed the sinkings on the United States and Great Britain, which he argued had neglected "the defense of Brazil as regards the supply of war material and the protection of shipping."[7] In a spectacular bit of political gamesmanship, Dutra and Góes Monteiro essentially succeeded in shifting the blame from Germany to their internal enemies and their foreign patrons. Or so, at least, they must have thought.

On the morning of August 18, 1942, President Vargas was working in his small study in the Guanabara Palace. He was still very much recuperating from his accident. Earlier that morning, he had practiced walking around the palace and its secluded grounds with a cane. His hip was still in the process of healing and he walked with a slight, but pronounced, limp. Although the president's jaw had healed sufficiently for him to be able to speak without difficulty, he was still apprehensive about speaking in public for any extended period of time. Today, however, circumstances would compel him to put aside that fear.

During the morning, angry Cariocas started to gather outside the gates of the palace, chanting anti-Axis slogans and singing in praise of Vargas and Roosevelt. The crowd wanted war and revenge. As it grew from hundreds into thousands, Vargas ordered that the gates of the palace be opened to allow the people into the grounds of the palace. He hurriedly dressed and appeared on the balcony to address the cheering throngs below. With tears in his eyes, the president told the crowd, "Brazil will act with maximum vigor to punish the Axis criminals for the torpedoing and sinking of five Brazilian ships."[8] He went on to promise that seized assets of Axis nationals would be used for the good of the country, and "those that had informed about the movements of the ships that were sunk, or who worked against Brazil, will be sent with picks and shovels to open roads in the interior." The president did not promise war, but he told the crowd to go back to their homes with their heads held high. He concluded with the emotional statement, "The flag of Brazil will not be humiliated, for Brazil is immortal."[9]

It was by no means Vargas's best speech, but as an act of political theater it was pure genius. And theater it may well have been; following Vargas's appearance on the balcony of the Guanabara Palace, the United States still speculated that he did not want to be drawn into declaring war on Germany if that could still be avoided.[10] But more than anything else, the balcony speech was a reaffirmation of Vargas's commitment to the country, and it gave the Brazilian people an opportunity to show their love for their leader. Jefferson Caffery had been proven right when he assured Brazilians following Vargas's accident, "You must not worry. President Vargas will very soon be on his feet again."[11] He added later in the month, "Today President Vargas is on his feet and Brazil is on her feet."[12] As if to prove his point, later the same day, a large crowd gathered outside the US embassy on Avenida President Wilson, where it cheered President Roosevelt and sang the Brazilian national anthem with gusto.

As the attacks at sea continued—a sixth ship was sunk on August 19—President Vargas ordered the detention of all German nationals, save diplomats, who were scheduled to sail from Brazil to Europe on two passenger ships, the SS *Bagé* and the SS *Cuyaba*.[13] The police also banned public demonstrations, out of fear that the attacks on Axis houses, businesses, and individuals were getting out of hand; the authorities were still struggling to restore order to the country.

Inside the Guanabara Palace, away from the public, Vargas listened to the arguments for and against Brazil formally declaring war on the Axis powers. But it seemed he had already made up his mind. On August 21, Vargas told a group of soldiers who were protesting outside the Guanabara Palace that Brazil would defend its territorial waters.[14] Meanwhile, he prepared to formally announce his decision at a cabinet meeting the following day.

President Vargas brought the meeting to order at 3:00 P.M. on August 22. The tone of the gathering was extremely sober, and—in a sign of the momentousness of the decision at hand—all the ministers were given an opportunity to speak at length. But it was clear from the beginning of the meeting that war was a forgone conclusion.

Vargas brought with him a draft of the proposed declaration of war, and the main topic of discussion at the cabinet meeting concerned the declaration's ninth paragraph. Aranha and his supporters were still in favor of a declaration of war, while Dutra and the armed forces still opposed it, and the disputed paragraph only intensified their disagreement. The first draft of the paragraph read as follows:

> There is no use in confusing the situation, nor can we fail to recognize the state of war which, in an inhuman and brutal manner, has been forced upon us by the German Reich.[15]

The second draft was wordier:

> There is no use in confusing the truth nor can we fail to recognize that the German Reich forces Brazil, through belligerent, inhuman, and brutal acts, into a situation that demands prompt and immediate reaction in equal degree, not only against the aggression, but also against the methods and procedures used by it against us, in a manner unprecedented in the history of civilization.[16]

Aranha was strongly in favor of adopting the first draft, which, as he told the United States, "would place Brazil in the position of saying the truth instead of merely acting without saying it." Needless to say, Dutra and the military favored the second draft, which was pointedly vague about what Brazil's "prompt and immediate reaction" to Germany's aggression would be.[17]

As was usual in such disputes, Vargas initially sat on the fence, telling the parties on both sides to consider the implications of each version of the paragraph. But, predictably, he soon came out in support of Aranha. Eventually, the cabinet agreed that—for the sake of clarity—they would adopt the first draft of paragraph nine.[18] Soon, Brazil would be at war with Germany.

The cabinet concluded that, as Japan had yet to participate in any hostile attack on Brazil, the declaration of war would be addressed to only the governments of Germany and Italy. But even this more limited war carried extreme risks for Brazil. During the meeting, the military continued to warn Vargas of the perils of declaring war when Brazil's armed forces were so poorly equipped. The possibility that Argentina might attack Brazil's south while the majority of Brazilian forces were concentrated in the north was also discussed. In the end, and after frantic diplomatic correspondence with the United States, Vargas was fully convinced that Brazil had little choice but to go to war.

At the end of the meeting, the government announced that Brazil was at war with Germany and Italy.[19] The formal announcement was broadcast across the country on the radio and repeated in hourly news bulletins. The full statement of the cabinet was printed in the daily newspapers, along with articles outlining why and how the historic decision had been taken.

After the declaration, the angry, retributive mood that had gripped Brazil gave way to a more sober outlook, as Brazilians wondered about the uncertainties and challenges that lay ahead for the nation. The Brazilian national sentiment was perhaps best summed up in an editorial in *Diário de Notícias*:

> This is an exceedingly grave moment in our history; maybe the most serious. Brazil, forced by Italy and Germany, again enters into a world war and hopes that none of her children will hesitate in fulfilling the duty circumstances have imposed upon them. We are a great nation and we are decided to resist and survive. The cause for which we fight is worthy of the ambitions and sacrifices of free people who do not provoke, but do not fear, who do not defy, but do not step back.[20]

Despite—or perhaps because of—the significance of its announcement, Brazil did not rush to get word of its decision to the Axis. When it did, however, it was clear about where the blame for its decision lay. On August 24, two days after the cabinet meeting, Aranha handed a note to the representatives of the governments of Germany and Italy in Rio. The note concluded: "There is no doubt that Germany and Italy practiced acts of war against Brazil, creating a situation of belligerency which we have been forced to recognize in defense of our dignity, our sovereignty, and our safety, as well as the safety of America, and to fight with all our strength."[21]

By the time Aranha delivered the note to the Axis representatives in Rio, Berlin had already learned of Brazil's declaration of war, and had begun to react. Up until the start of 1942, the Germans had hoped that the promise of armaments for the Brazilian army would be enough to tempt the Brazilians into sitting out the war; now it was clearer than ever that this strategy had failed. A radio broadcast from Berlin, which was transmitted from Argentina in Portuguese on August 22, the same day as the cabinet meeting, refuted the accusation that Germany had forced Brazil into its current position and also sent out a clear warning to the Brazilians:

> The declaration of war by Brazil did not surprise the Reich nor cause any impression whatsoever. From the military viewpoint it has no significance, principally because Brazil has already demonstrated that she has no will of her own, to put herself at the disposition of the Americans. . . . By violence and brute force the Brazilian people lose their neutrality to take part in a struggle in which they have nothing to gain and everything to lose. Between the Axis powers and Brazil there was no opposition of interests; on the contrary, only the interest of conserving the peace and, after the war, increasing their profitable commercial relations. In addition, insofar as the future interests of the war are concerned Brazil is threatened in the highest degree as to her sovereignty. And all of this—independence, integrity, sovereignty, and the welfare of Brazil—is now sacrificed by her government, partly suborned by the North Americans. The responsibility for this decision is solely that of the government concerned.[22]

The gist of the message was clear: Brazil had backed the wrong side in the war and would suffer the consequences.

Yet in reality, the German radio broadcasts on Brazil gave the appearance of indifference. The US broadcast monitors noted that the message appeared very similar to the one issued to Mexico earlier that year after

that Latin American country, too, had declared war on Germany. The
monitors suggested:

> The broadcast gives the impression of having come out of the file-drawer
> where they stored the discussion of Mexico's belligerency three months
> ago. The arguments are so similar to those used with Mexico as to be
> almost indistinguishable:
>
> 1 The declaration makes no difference.
> 2. The move was engineered by Washington.
> 3. The sinkings were a mere pretext.
> 4. The people of Brazil aren't really hostile to Germany.[23]

Yet even while they appeared to brush off Brazil's involvement in the war,
the Germans were racing to estimate the effects of Brazil's declaration of
war. And they were not the only ones.

On September 22, 1942, precisely a month after the Brazilian announcement, US planners circulated a secret memorandum within the war
department.[24] In detail, the document predicted the demands that Brazil
would make on the United States over the months and years ahead. The
Americans anticipated that Brazil would move to shore up its defenses
in northeastern Brazil and would also take steps to further strengthen the
power of the president. Closer military and economic cooperation between
Brazil and the United States would follow, yet there would also be an
intensification of Axis intelligence and propaganda activities in Brazil, as
well as Axis efforts to enlist the country's large German and Italian communities in anti-Allied activities. The report summed up its predictions:

> Brazil's economic and military dependence upon the United States, al-
> ready great, will be considerably increased. The United States must face
> the future possibility of diverting large stores of equipment and large con-
> tingents of troops to ensure the defense of the western hemisphere. The
> problem of supplying sufficient ships to transport Brazil's requirements of
> fuel, machinery, and manufactured goods also becomes increasingly vital.[25]

While the United States had long urged Brazil to join the war, the United
States thought the decision might have the effect of pushing Rio and

Washington into even greater codependence. This prediction would prove extremely accurate in the months ahead.

The report also illustrated that the United States understood the wartime goals of Vargas and Aranha much more clearly than the Brazilians realized. The Americans apprehended that Brazil's split from Argentina at the conference of foreign ministers in January 1942 would allow Rio to use the war as a springboard to regional supremacy—with the full assistance of the United States, which was still more concerned about potential German attacks on the Americas than about any possible flare-up in intra-American tensions. The report stated:

> Brazil, a long rival with Argentina for leadership in South America, will look forward to strengthening its military power as an ally of the United Nations. Strategically located as it is, the country should move forward greatly with United States aid. Increase in air power should be a prime objective to safeguard Axis attack from Africa. As to design on Argentine territory, it is believed that Brazil will be content to leave existing borders alone. Unless an incident develops, no action is to be expected between the two rivals.[26]

This assessment, too, would prove prescient. Yet while a war between Brazil and Argentina did not strike Washington as a likely consequence of Rio's declaration of war, there were other risks that could be every bit as serious—and which indeed were much more likely—than a transatlantic German attack.

The United States remained sensitive to the possibility that Brazil's entry into the war might well suit Axis plans.[27] Brazil's increased demands on the United States for assistance in troops and material would effectively divert forces from other theaters of the conflict, and would therefore help the Axis powers—a gain they would enjoy at little risk to themselves.[28]

As the United States looked to the medium- and long-term strategic implications of Brazil's entry into the war, President Vargas concentrated on preparing the country for the trial that lay ahead. As he did so, meeting extensively with the Brazilian military and with Jefferson Caffery, another American arrived in Rio as part of a whirlwind tour of Latin America. Nelson Rockefeller was already a bona fide star in Brazil, but his appearance in person, and so soon after the declaration of war, always created an electric atmosphere in Rio. The only person who appeared slightly miffed by Rockefeller's arrival was Jefferson Caffery, who maintained that Rockefeller's visit had no official purpose. In reality, Caffery's vanity made it difficult for him to accept his eclipse by Rockefeller or the show of love and respect that Cariocas gave the visiting coordinator of inter-American affairs.

Osvaldo Aranha laid out the Brazilian version of the red carpet treatment for Rockefeller. Large crowds greeted the American's arrival at the Rio airport, and he was paraded at public events such as at the horse racing at the Jockey Club. In private, both Aranha and Vargas hosted lunch or dinner parties in honor of their American guest. Alzira, meanwhile, took an instant shine to the handsome, energetic, and articulate American. Both she and Aranha moved Rockefeller around the room, making sure he was introduced to the right people. Despite the onset of war and the uncertainties that lay ahead for Brazil, an upbeat and positive atmosphere seemed to follow Rockefeller wherever he went. To many Brazilians, he represented everything that was good about the United States, and—much to the annoyance of Caffery—they bestowed prizes and honors on Rockefeller, making him an honorary member of some of the city's major clubs, such as the Jockey Club.

But Rockefeller had not come to Brazil just to shake hands, smile, and reassure Brazilians about the struggles that lay ahead. He had come to tie up a whole series of economic and cultural deals with the Brazilian government—huge agreements dealing with everything from rubber to banking, agreements that would soon transform Brazil's wartime economy beyond recognition.

By his very nature, Rockefeller was a doer. While in the country, he was constantly firing off quick notes to his staff on the ground in Rio and back in the United States, trying to understand how to make things work better, and not taking "no" for an answer. "What's the biggest problem here?" he asked Vargas. "Infrastructure," the president replied. So Rockefeller promised to help develop new transport systems in the huge interior of the country.

Rockefeller also saw great potential for using his Brazilian adventure as a means for solidifying his powerbase back in Washington, which was still under threat from General Donavan and his "spook agency." For all his good work and ambitions, however, Rockefeller's trip almost ended in disaster when the plane carrying him and his team crash-landed in a ditch at the end of the runway at Porto Alegre in southern Brazil.[29] Luckily, all were able to walk away from the crash with only cuts and bruises. Rockefeller, no doubt, made a note to build better and longer runways in Brazil.

While in Brazil, furthermore, Rockefeller was gathering information about the newest addition to the Allies. Shortly after his return to the United States, Rockefeller's office produced a confidential report on Brazil and its potential impact on World War II. The report represented a detailed effort on the part of his office to assess Brazil's needs and determine the immediate tasks confronting the Vargas regime. It outlined these tasks in terms of the threats facing Vargas both from within his regime and from the Axis powers. Vargas, the office of the coordinator of inter-American affairs declared, needed the following:

> The consolidation of a unitary front within the government itself; the completion of steps safeguarding against the threat of Axis invasion in the northeast; and measures to ensure internal security against the potential danger from Axis minority groups and the organized fifth column. Should it be necessary to rid the government of powerful figures hitherto in sympathy with the Axis, the president is in an excellent position to do so by seeking support from the middle and left.[30]

Vargas, no doubt, would have agreed with the Americans' assessment of the three-pronged threat he faced, although it's much less clear whether he would have been so sanguine about the possibility of removing from his government the "powerful figures" to whom the report referred—no doubt meaning Dutra and Góes Monteiro.

Rockefeller's office excelled at organizing trade links between the United States and Brazil, but the report revealed the agency's limited understanding of internal Brazilian politics, particularly as they concerned the military. The future of two key men in the armed forces, Dutra and Góes Monteiro, continued to give the United States a great deal of concern; the Americans viewed both men as relics of a past era, and felt they should be replaced as soon as possible. The United States also understood that while both men were making public and private noises to the effect that Brazil must wage an effective war against the Axis, they continued to concentrate their efforts on protecting Brazil's southern borders from what they envisaged to be the major threat of an Argentine invasion—thereby detracting from the strength of Brazil's defenses against a possible German attack.

The United States was doing what it could to counterbalance the military's fixation on Brazil's southern border. In November 1942, after protracted and complicated negotiations, Brazil and the United States concluded the administrative arrangements for a joint force to defend the northeast of the country. The deal essentially left the defense of Brazilian territory and military bases to the Brazilian armed forces, with coastal defenses being run by a joint US-Brazilian force. Admiral Jonas Ingram was formally put in charge of all aspects of security, including the protection of shipping, and for his troubles received the title chief of allied forces in the South Atlantic.[31] He was based in Recife, along the northeastern coast of Brazil, in the region where a German attack was most anticipated.

Another US senior officer, General Robert L. Walsh, commanded the US army forces in the South Atlantic and was also based in Recife. The roughly two thousand men under his command were not based in Brazil, however, but rather on the British Ascension Island, halfway across the Atlantic.[32] General Walsh himself was in Brazil to establish the air base at Natal, which would become an important staging point for planes flying to Africa and from there to the European theater. Indeed, the base would prove vital to US operations in Africa—which were part of a broader US-British invasion code-named Operation Torch—as well as in the pivotal antisubmarine war in the South Atlantic. With U-boats continuing to attack shipping convoys en route to Great Britain from the Americas, the Allies' victory would hinge on what would come to be called the Battle of the Atlantic. Short of critical military materials as well as basic necessities like food and fuel, Great Britain would not be able to continue fighting if this lifeline were cut off. For a short period during the war, Natal air base was one of the busiest in the world, with an American plane landing there every two to three minutes for eighteen hours a day, seven days a week.[33]

These security arrangements boded well for the future of US-Brazilian cooperation, yet they were also a source of ongoing tension in Rio. While Dutra remained far from happy about his relative loss of control over the Brazilian armed forces, he grudgingly understood that Brazil was in no position to defend itself on its own. As the year drew to a close, however,

PHOTO 1. This view shows the palm tree–lined avenue that leads to the presidential residence, the Guanabara Palace. The crucial decision as to whether to participate in World War II was made in the long majestic ballroom of the palace.

PHOTO 2. The façade of the Copacabana Palace Hotel is shown here as it looked during its inaugural year. The Copacabana Palace, the most famous of all the hotels in Rio de Janeiro, was where the rich and famous checked in to enjoy the sea views and fine dining and its famed wine collection.

PHOTO 3. President Getúlio Vargas laughs together with his daughter Alzira during the president's road to recovery following an automobile accident in May 1942. The injuries the president sustained in the accident could not be regarded as life-threatening, though they removed him from political life for several months.

PHOTO 4. United States ambassador Jefferson Caffery (left) works together with Osvaldo Aranha (right). Caffery regarded his posting as the most important in South America and did not take kindly to anyone who tried to undermine his authority.

PHOTO 5. This personal postcard, written by Osvaldo Aranha, shows the vista over Botafogo Beach toward Rio de Janeiro.

PHOTO 6. Brazil was the major focus of US efforts in Latin America under the guise of the Good Neighbor Program during World War II. The young and energetic Nelson Rockefeller (left), meeting in Rio de Janeiro, is shown here with Undersecretary of State Sumner Welles (center) and General Góes Monteiro (right).

PHOTO 7. Following the success of *Citizen Kane,* Orson Welles arrived in Rio in February 1942 to start work on the major Hollywood picture *It's All True.* Welles took long brisk morning walks along the wide promenade of Copacabana Beach.

PHOTO 8. Pictured here is the German community in Rio Grande do Sul holding a Nazi parade, complete with uniforms, flags, and military drills. Such events took place openly and were often watched by large crowds voicing their support.

PHOTO 9. This is a hotel registration card of the writer and Jewish refugee Stefan Zweig, who found himself in Rio during World War II.

PHOTO 10. Walt Disney's visit to Rio during August and September 1941 was part of the Good Neighbor Program. Disney enjoyed sketching in the city's botanical gardens and from the beach-facing terrace of his hotel suite. Disney (left) is pictured here meeting with Osvaldo Aranha at the Catete Palace.

PHOTO 11. President Roosevelt (seated front center) and President Vargas (seated rear) are pictured here visiting a Brazilian naval base in 1943, after a luncheon hosted by President Roosevelt in honor of his Brazilian counterpart aboard the USS *Humboldt*. Statesmanship had added years to the two leaders and had transformed their dark hair to gray and to white.

PHOTO 12. In June 1944, during the same month as the D-Day landings in Normandy, the first squadron of the Força Expedicionária Brasileira was ready to disembark for Italy. President Vargas (center), on board the USS *General Mann,* was accompanied by Osvaldo Aranha (on right) and Admiral Ingram (on left).

PHOTO 13. US film producer and actor Orson Welles (right) was be-friended by Osvaldo Aranha (left) during his time shooting a film in Brazil. Here they are seen together on August 22, 1942, the day Brazil declared war on Germany and Italy.

PHOTO 14. The Força Expedicionária Brasileira (FEB) went through basic training with US military instructors in 1943. The FEB would embark for Europe toward the later part of 1944 and would see action in Italy in some of the most bitter and intense battles of the entire war.

PHOTO 15. The Força Expedicionária Brasileira was to take part in several key battles, including Monte Castello, the outcome of which was crucial to securing a German surrender in Italy. In April 1945, a Brazilian commander, General Masarenham de Morais, received the first unconditional surrender of a German division in Italy.

PHOTO 16. Hundreds of thousands of people lined the route of the funeral procession for President Getúlio Vargas in Rio.

Góes Monteiro was becoming increasingly critical of the Brazilian military, arguing that it was doing little and was far too passive.

In choosing not to replace his two top military officials following the declaration of war, Vargas had taken somewhat of a gamble. Later, Jefferson Caffery would admit that the president had been right to hold on to both men, but during the war itself it was a significant risk to allow two outspoken critics of the war effort to remain in power. Yet while Dutra and Góes Monteiro stayed at their respective posts, at least for the time being, Vargas did clip their wings. The president made it clear to both men that he alone would guide Brazilian policy toward the war. Vargas was riding on a wave of personal popularity following the decision to go to war with the Axis, and with his authority—and Aranha's—at its peak, he obviously felt comfortable reining in his recalcitrant commanders. Dutra, however, was far from admitting defeat, and while he had put his rivalry with Aranha on hold, it was far from resolved. Dutra was biding his time, ready to put a dagger in Aranha's back the moment the minister of foreign affairs made a mistake.

It was also becoming clear that the alliance between Dutra and Góes Monteiro was starting to fray at the edges. Góes Monteiro was becoming increasingly angry about Dutra's ability to effectively transform himself politically to reflect the new realities of wartime Brazil. Yet Góes Monteiro seemed to have resigned himself to those same realities. The US military and political figures who had dealings with Góes Monteiro at this time noted that he appeared to have fully embraced the closer ties with the United States and did not have any major problems with the fact that the US military was playing a far greater role in Brazil. The dissonance between his public expressions and his private sentiment may have taken a toll. Caffery, who had known Góes Monteiro since 1937, noted that the chief of staff's health was worsening.

Within military and political circles in Brazil, the major issue remained the supply of arms from the United States. President Vargas worked away in his small office in the Guanabara Palace, trying to make sure that the United States made good on its promises to supply weapons to Brazil. The US arsenal was already overstretched, and when the Allies launched Operation Torch in North Africa on November 8, 1942, it further limited the quantity of weapons the United States was able to send to Brazil. Yet the offensive also had a positive effect in Brazil. It quickly became clear that Operation Torch would be an enormous success, and this news was widely welcomed in Brazil, where it helped to undercut the military's deeply held admiration for Germany's fighting prowess. On hearing of the landings in Africa, Osvaldo Aranha said, "With God's help and with the tenacity and fighting spirit of the defenders of freedom, we will soon emerge into a better world."[34] The Brazilian press, meanwhile, marked the landings with headlines that highlighted the Allies' military successes and the failings of the Germans. *Jornal do Brasil* commented: "The sensational event marks the beginning of the decline of the Nazi military machine. The Axis will be destroyed, Fascism will be swept away from the face of the earth, and peace will be dictated in Berlin by the representatives of England, the United States, China, Russia, Brazil, etc."[35]

The Allied victories in North Africa also convinced many Brazilians that the days of the Axis were numbered—and left them wondering how the world would look once it collapsed. Brazil's middle and upper classes understood that the African campaign would lead inexorably to the liberation of Europe, along with all of the art, culture, and civilization that Brazilians identified with that continent. There was, however, some anxiety as to what would happen at the end of the war. The two most likely outcomes of the conflict were a negotiated German defeat or a total Allied victory, yet there was no way of knowing what would replace the existing structures in Europe. Quietly, many educated, propertied, and conservative Brazilians started to wonder whether, if democracy spread in the aftermath of World War II, the Estado Novo would be compatible with the postwar order.[36]

While comfortable Brazilians experienced pangs of anxiety about the changes that lay ahead, working-class Brazilians were generally positive about the prospect of a US victory in the war. On the other hand, many Brazilians were becoming increasingly suspicious and afraid of the power of the United States.[37] Many Brazilians were concerned that the same US strength that was assisting them during the war might be used to oppress them in a US-dominated postwar world.

By the end of 1942, the likelihood of an Axis attack on northeastern Brazil had decreased due to both Admiral Ingram's organization of the joint US-Brazilian defenses in that region and also the Allies' successes in North Africa. The air base in Natal remained a vital bridge for the United States as its commitments in the European theater increased. Naturally,

Vargas welcomed developments in North Africa and was happy about the enhancement of Brazil's national security, but he needed to make the shipment of weapons to Brazil something of a priority for the United States. He also understood that the economic and political gains that Brazil stood to make in the war would require the country to make a clear military investment in the conflict.

Brazil, Vargas knew, was in danger of becoming a bit player in the war unless it could find new ways to help the war effort. Both Vargas and Aranha were aware that the postwar era would be governed by a simple equation of "what you put in = what you get out" of the war. Both men wanted to use the war to help transform Brazil, yet they now found themselves in the position of having arrived late to the party. If Vargas and Aranha were to realize their dreams for Brazil, they would need to raise the stakes and make a more dramatic contribution to the Allies than they had thus far. With Vargas and Aranha's authority at its peak, the time was ripe for just such a change.

12

# LIGHTS OUT OVER RIO

O N SEPTEMBER 6, 1942, WHILE PRESIDENT VARGAS was working alone in his small, dimly lit study in the Guanabara Palace, lights began winking out along the boulevards of some of the most beautiful beaches in the world. That night, the beaches of Leme, Copacabana, and Leblon, as well as the adjacent streets in the federal district of Rio, were experiencing their first total blackout.

Witnessing the event from the bar at the Copacabana Palace Hotel, Jefferson Caffery pronounced the blackout "very successful."[1] As the shadows grew longer and the sky turned first a deep purple, then black, the only visible light emanated from the stars in the clear night sky that hung over the ocean panorama. The unusual darkness over the city skyline was matched by a strange silence, interrupted by the gentle sounds of the waves breaking onto the soft sandy shore. In the distance, occasional shouts were heard echoing down the avenues that ran from the heart of the city to its beaches as tired, grumpy policemen reminded blackout breakers of the fines that awaited them if they didn't immediately comply with the order. Along Rio's coastline, which moments before had been brightly lit, it was as if all of the city's inhabitants had suddenly gone to sleep, or had hidden themselves behind closed doors and drawn curtains.

Wartime in Rio resembled nothing the city had known before. Hotels all along the Rio coastline hosted "blackout parties," which provided a popular amusement for their wealthy foreign guests and local customers. There was even a blackout cocktail, which was supposed to be jet black but more often than not resembled an unappealing, sooty gray. Revelers must have cared more about forgetting the war than about the color of their drinks, however, as they downed the cocktails in large quantities. Jazz quintets played mid-tempo, slightly off-key dance music to add to the atmosphere at these parties, although guests seemed to be unwilling to be seen enjoying it. Rio was finding it hard to dance to the new tune of war.

Everybody in the city was trying desperately hard to take the war seriously, but it took some time for the local authorities to get the city onto any kind of a war footing. Cariocas had long thought of the war as being far away, in Europe and Africa, but—as Caffery was fond of reminding people—parts of Brazil were within range of German bombers operating out of West Africa. And the entire Brazilian coast, Rio included, was in range of German submarines. Rumors circulated in the city that Axis submarines were lurking just over the horizon, and, at night, they came close enough to check out the nightlife in Rio through raised periscopes.

The blackout's apparent success on September 6 had come after several false starts and half-hearted attempts by the government to impose it. Initially, regulations issued by the government had called for elimination of only half the lights facing the sea, and only those streetlights that were at right angles to the coast.[2] The remaining lights were required to be dimmed along the coastal strip to a distance of one kilometer (six-tenths of a mile) from the coast. Cariocas, however, had not responded well to the dimming of the lights, and many people simply left their lights on full with their curtains wide open. When the local police announced that anybody showing light would be accused of being an Axis sympathizer, several local residents responded by claiming that if they couldn't see the coastline at night with its lit boulevards, they would start to suffer from depression and other mental ailments. Yet eventually, the local authorities cracked down hard enough that people gave in to the demands of the blackout, and plunged nighttime Rio into a darkness that was nearly complete.

Each night following the successful imposition of the blackout, Rio was transformed from a vibrant, colorful, and noisy city into a ghost town where all activity, legitimate or otherwise, took place behind drawn blinds and closed curtains. In Rio's harbor, all navigation lights on ships, buoys, and piers were turned off during the hours of darkness.[3] This order was followed all along the Brazilian coast.[4] Neon lights on the mountains in Rio and on top of skyscrapers, advertising everything from radios to local beer, were also extinguished, as were the lights on churches and monuments.[5]

Yet despite the dramatic changes it wrought in Rio, the blackout—or what Cariocas were more accurately labeling "the dim-out"—was not to last. Over the Christmas and New Year festive season in Rio several of the city's bars and luxury hotels requested that city authorities lift the ban. These requests were refused, but within a year the beach areas in Rio would slowly return to near normal lighting, as local officials and police officers effectively gave up on trying to enforce the city's blackout policy.[6]

The failure to fully impose the blackout reflected a feeling held by many Brazilians throughout the final quarter of 1942. The joint American-British landings in North Africa had changed the dynamic of the conflict, and—Caffery's warning notwithstanding—many Brazilians seemed to have adopted the view that with the threat of a German attack or invasion receding, the nation would be able to quietly sit out the war. Needless to say, however, President Vargas was not one of these people.

On December 31, 1942, Vargas observed his annual New Year's Eve tradition of lunching with senior officers in the Brazilian military. His message to the armed forces at this year's lunch was both upbeat and, for many of the officers who were present, very surprising. The president first spoke of the excellent cooperation between Brazil and the Allies and talked of the efficiency of their cooperation, a clear nod to the work of Admiral Ingram. Yet in outlining Brazil's contribution to the war effort, the president was adamant that Brazil was not merely supplying the Allies with strategically important materials, such as rubber. Rather, he argued, the Allied use of the bases on Brazil's coastline had allowed them to transport arms and men across the Atlantic and had made possible the landing in North Africa, which Vargas characterized as the first step on the road to victory in Europe. He also praised the work of the Brazilian navy, merchant navy, the air force, and the army in doing their part to defend the country.

Yet Vargas finished his remarks by suggesting that the Brazilian military had an even larger role to play in the war. At the end of the talk, in a casual manner—as if the thought had just entered his head, which it most certainly had not—he said, "We must consider the responsibilities of action outside the continent and this action should not be restricted to a simple expedition of symbolic contingents."[7] The Brazilian armed forces were intrigued by the president's closing comment; could Vargas mean that the Brazilian military would soon be given a chance to join the war, with all of the attendant power, equipment, and prestige? For officers who had spent most of their careers scrounging for the means to defend a single border, the idea of joining the winning side in a world war was enormously appealing. They would not have long to wait before they discovered exactly what he meant.

Two days later, after meeting with Góes Monteiro, Dutra dispatched the general to go to Petrópolis to seek Vargas's clarification about his comments at the luncheon. Given the heat of the January sun in Rio, the trip offered Góes Monteiro a pleasant escape. His driver picked him up early so as to avoid the post-holiday traffic, and in Petrópolis the general could look forward to cool air that was said to relax even the most agitated of minds.

But when Góes Monteiro arrived in Petrópolis, the general found Vargas distracted and distant. When Góes Monteiro got to the point of his visit and asked Vargas, "What did you mean about an overseas force?," the president began enumerating the difficulties the country would face in recruiting, training, arming, and deploying such a force. For a moment, Góes Monteiro thought that Vargas's comments on December 31 had simply reflected an aspiration or hope rather than a viable policy option. But Vargas went on. "Washington has made it clear that those nations that are involved in the fighting have priority in receiving arms from the United States," the president told Góes Monteiro. "In view of Dutra's insistence on arms, I have authorized our military delegation in Washington to tell the United States that Brazil is prepared to send soldiers overseas."

The chief of staff was taken aback by Vargas's reply. The president had informed the United States of his willingness to commit Brazilian forces to the war effort without first discussing it with either the minister of war or the chief of staff. Nonetheless, Góes Monteiro thought that joining the war was a great idea, and one that—if it occurred—would ensure that the Brazilian army would grow in size, strength, and capability to become the most powerful armed force on the South American continent.

The chief of staff hurried back to Rio to inform Dutra of this development. Vargas, Góes Monteiro noted, had looked tired and drawn, and the chief of staff wondered if the stories circulating in Rio that the president's youngest son, Getúlio (nicknamed Getúlinho), was deathly ill were really true. The boy was only in his early twenties, and—although not as close to the president as Alzira—he was handsome, talented, and one of the lights of Vargas's life; if he were to die, it would tear Vargas apart. Yet the president had seemed more hawkish than ever, a contrast that must have unsettled Góes Monteiro even as Vargas's message excited him.

Dutra was most intrigued by the news. He gave his officials seventy-two hours in which to draft a plan for mobilizing Brazil's armed forces for war. On January 5, 1943, Dutra presented this detailed memorandum to Vargas. At its center was an argument that any expeditionary force needed to be large, and that the army would have to recruit more soldiers in order to create it. Brazil's army had been primarily defensive up until this point, and it certainly was not prepared to join the offensive in a globalized conflict. Yet while pragmatic, Dutra's recommendation also coincided with an underlying goal: to seize this opportunity to expand the Brazilian military as never before.

The president did not give an immediate response to Dutra's memorandum, but he promised to study it in detail. His only comment was that he would not approve any expeditionary force unless it was properly armed by the United States, and that the soldiers who remained in Brazil to defend the country would likewise need to be adequately equipped. Put simply, Brazil would not agree to stick its neck out for the United States unless the Brazilian military first received the weapons that Washington had promised to supply to Allied combatants.

Unbeknownst to Dutra, at the same time he was baiting the Brazilian military, Vargas was also preparing for a secret meeting that would have ramifications of the highest order for Brazil and the war it had recently joined. In a note to Cordell Hull on Tuesday, January 26, 1943, Jefferson Caffery wrote in a cryptic fashion, "I leave in the morning with Osvaldo's boss [Vargas] to meet you know whom. I should be back on Friday."[8] The next day, Caffery, Admiral Ingram, and a naval attaché boarded a plane along with President Vargas and two of his aides. As soon as all six passengers were on board, the plane took off and headed to Natal. Soon after arriving, the party was transferred to a destroyer, the *Jouett*, where they dined and spent the night preparing for the next day's meetings.

Vargas was in a state of extreme anxiety. He had recently attended the celebrations in São Paulo in connection with the anniversary of the founding of the city. His son, Getúlinho, had come down with infantile paralysis during this time, and it was widely presumed in Rio's political circles that the president was still in São Paulo with his son.[9] President Vargas, however, had decided that duty called, and effectively left the bedside of his dying son to attend the meeting in Natal. Yet his anxiety notwithstanding, Vargas was well prepared for the meetings that lay ahead.

Aranha had put together a ten-page advice paper for his boss, outlining the Brazilian priorities. In a sign of the strong spirit of trust between Aranha and Caffery, the Brazilian minister of foreign affairs showed the same paper to the American.

At 8:00 A.M. on January 28, 1942, a plane carrying President Roosevelt landed in Natal. Roosevelt had just been at the Casablanca Conference in Morocco, where he had met with British prime minister Winston Churchill, and Free French generals Charles de Gaulle and Henri Giraud to discuss tactics and strategy for the remainder of the war. At the conference, these leaders had also formalized their commitment to ending the war through the total defeat of the Axis powers. This policy, which would come to be known as the doctrine of "unconditional surrender," would mark the Casablanca Conference as one of the most important summits of the war.

On his arrival in Natal, Roosevelt was immediately transferred to the destroyer USS *Humboldt*, where he would remain that day and night. Later on the morning of Roosevelt's arrival, Caffery met with the president and his special assistant, Harry Hopkins. The three men agreed that Roosevelt would "tactfully" bring up the question of Brazil joining the United Nations, which was one of the major American aims of the meeting.[10] The United Nations was to be established by the Allies as the central international feature of the postwar order and would replace the League of Nations. Caffery noted that Vargas would in all likelihood agree to such a request—Aranha's ten-page advice paper had confirmed this point.[11]

Roosevelt, Caffery, and Hopkins went on to discuss Brazil's offer to commit troops overseas. The president explained that American military leaders "are not especially interested in having Brazilian troops sent to North Africa." Yet the president hoped to convince Vargas that Brazilian troops were needed elsewhere across the Atlantic, specifically in a handful of strategically vital territories with which Brazil shared a colonial ancestry.

The day after he arrived, President Roosevelt hosted a luncheon in honor of his Brazilian counterpart in the captain's dining room of the *Humboldt*. The two presidents conversed in French, just as they had done during their first meeting in Rio de Janeiro in 1936. Vargas was dressed in a white linen suit and cotton shirt with his favorite striped club tie, while Roosevelt wore a slightly shabby, off-white cotton suit and white shirt. Yet the American president's black tie and black armband, more than any other aspect of his attire, spoke to his inner state. Roosevelt's son had died in the war and he was in mourning—a fact that no doubt resonated deeply with the Brazilian president, whose own son was at death's door.

Roosevelt and Vargas had both aged considerably since their meeting in 1936. While they both looked relaxed in the single published photo of the Rio meeting, in 1943 the two appeared tired. The black circles under Roosevelt's eyes were all too visible when he took off his glasses; Vargas still walked with a noticeable limp after his accident, and he brought his cane on the trip to Natal. Only Jefferson Caffery—still tan from his leave in the United States the previous year, and from sunbathing on Rio's summertime beaches earlier in the month—looked remotely healthy.

The atmosphere of the lunch was workmanlike and slightly subdued. Both presidents regarded this as a one-on-one meeting. Sitting at the head of the table with Vargas on his right, Roosevelt addressed the Brazilian president directly. For the entire duration of the lunch, Roosevelt barely took his eyes off his Brazilian guest, barely acknowledging the presence of anybody else in the room. He spoke quietly, but while his soft tone added to the intimacy of the meeting it was, in reality, the result of a chill he had caught due to the dramatic changes in temperature he'd been exposed to over the previous days' travel. Vargas listened to the American president intently, and interceded from time to time but only briefly—when Roosevelt asked for a response, for instance, or when he paused to let the Brazilian speak. Caffery, who sat on Roosevelt's left, said very little. He listened carefully, sometimes leaning forward to make sure he could hear his president's increasingly hoarse voice.

Roosevelt started the conversation by filling in for Vargas much of what had happened in Casablanca with Churchill and the French leaders. He went on to outline the progress of the war from an American perspective, telling Vargas how American production was getting along, how Anglo-American relations were faring, what the situation was in the Soviet Union, and what his hopes and plans were for the postwar period.

Roosevelt then moved on to the subject of Brazil, and talked in a general way about the country's economic development and its struggles with immigration. He left his first question until the end of his general opening remarks, yet then, as was his wont, Roosevelt came straight to the point. "In light of the developing situation in the war," he asked Vargas, "is Brazil willing to become a member of the United Nations?"[12]

Vargas, who had carefully studied Aranha's ten-page memorandum on the plane, wasn't surprised by the question. Looking straight into Roosevelt's eyes, he replied that—as Caffery later put it in a message to Cordell Hull—"he would take steps to become a member of the United Nations." Vargas then paused for what seemed like an eternity, but which was only a second or two, before qualifying his answer. "However," he told Roosevelt, "this might be an opportune moment to say again that we need equipment from you for our military—naval and air force."[13] Vargas left Roosevelt in little doubt that in order to bring Brazil fully into the Allied camp, the United States would need to increase its supply of weapons to Brazil.

Setting aside the question of additional US weapons shipments to Brazil, Roosevelt turned next to the Portuguese issue. He gave Vargas a brief summary of the importance of the island of Madeira to the Allied cause in the Atlantic, but specifically focused on the Azores, which were vital to Allied operations in the South Atlantic. Roosevelt confessed that he was taking something of a personal interest in the Azores and could remember them from World War I when in 1918, as assistant secretary of the navy, he came to the islands to inspect the American mid-Atlantic naval base that had recently been set up there. Now he confided to Vargas about a recent conversation with Winston Churchill, in which both men had agreed to make the establishment of air bases on the Azores a strategic priority for 1943.[14] The security of the South Atlantic trade route to Europe depended on winning the battle against the German U-boats, and a base in the Azores would allow Allied antisubmarine aircraft to operate from the islands. The air base would also be a vital staging point for the Allied invasion of Europe that was expected to take place the following year.

The one complicating factor was that Portugal controlled the archipelago. In order to gain access to the bases, the British were planning on opening negotiations with António de Oliveira Salazar, Portugal's dictator, in the springtime of 1943, with the Americans to start talks with Salazar soon after. "Salazar is something of a tricky customer," Roosevelt suggested to Vargas. The American president had already started trying to reassure Salazar that an Allied presence on the islands would last only for the duration of the war, as it had in World War I. Salazar, however, suspected both the British and the United States of plotting to establish a permanent presence on the islands. As it turned out, the wily Portuguese leader foresaw the coming of the Cold War and the ideological clash between democracy and communism, and understood that the islands would be of great use to a power—such as the United States—that wished to establish its dominance over Western Europe. Salazar feared that once the United States gained a foothold on the Azores, they would be loath to let the islands go.

Yet Roosevelt also knew—or at least suspected—that Salazar was as concerned about German ambitions for his territories as he was about America's. In his meeting with Vargas, Roosevelt suggested that Salazar feared a German invasion of mainland Portugal and the Azores, or simply an invasion of the islands by themselves. This was something of a smoke-screen, however, as the real danger of a German invasion of Portugal had already passed. With Hitler's forces tied down in the heavy fighting in the Soviet Union and with Allied forces in North Africa, a German attack against Portugal or its Atlantic possessions appeared remote.

In truth, Hitler had missed his opportunity to take the Azores. At the start of the war, his naval commanders had urged him to invade the Azores before the British did, but Hitler chose to ignore their advice. What worried Roosevelt more than a German invasion of the Azores was the prospect that Salazar might refuse to allow the Allies access to the islands. In private meetings with Sir Ronald Campbell, the British ambassador to Lisbon, Salazar indicated that when the time came, he would do the right thing for the British. Yet he stopped short of promising the Americans a presence on the islands. Both Churchill and the British foreign secretary, Anthony Eden, had promised to try to change Salazar's mind when Great Britain opened negotiations with the Portuguese leader. Roosevelt and the United States, however, remained unconvinced, and had begun preparations to potentially take the islands by force if the negotiations failed.

Roosevelt hoped his Brazilian friends would lend a hand with the Azores issue. Yet when he broached the subject with Vargas, he framed his request as one intended to aid the Portuguese, with whom he knew Brazil still had close ties. "Can you help us here and send troops to replace the Portuguese ones, who are more needed on the mainland?" Roosevelt asked Vargas.[15]

Vargas was taken by surprise by the directness of Roosevelt's approach, and concerned about its implications. The United States was asking Brazil, a former colony of Portugal, to effectively occupy sovereign Portuguese land. After a few seconds of silence, Vargas replied slowly, almost mechanically, "I am willing to take this matter up with Salazar. However, we cannot send troops to the Portuguese islands [Azores] unless you furnish adequate equipment for them."[16] It was the Brazilian party line, and Vargas was sticking to it.

Vargas and Roosevelt spent the rest of their lunch hammering out the details of how the United States could send these much-needed spare parts and machinery to the Brazilian navy. Roosevelt promised to try to send as much of the military supplies as quickly as possible to Brazil. That marked the end of the serious talks, and Roosevelt and Vargas shared a private joke with Admiral Ingram, who then told the presidents that the air base was ready for inspection.

Their meal finished, the two heads of state set off in a jeep to see the Natal base. Only at the start of the lunch had news of the meeting been released, so as the two presidents toured the base, they surprised many servicemen, who had had no idea that the two leaders were even visiting the facility. Roosevelt sat in the front of the jeep, Vargas in the backseat with Admiral Ingram. Their tour was captured in one of the most iconic photographs of this period of US-Brazilian cooperation. Showing the three men in mid-laugh, the photograph gives the impression of two carefree political leaders taking a ride together. A photograph taken a few moments after the initial shot, however, reveals a very different picture. Both Vargas and Roosevelt look almost melancholic and tired, like two old men who have too much on their plates, yet whose days are numbered. In truth, this second photograph is more representative of the day's events than the first, happier shot.

That evening, Roosevelt and Vargas dined with their staffs on the USS *Humboldt*. In contrast to the day's lunch, the dinner was a less formal affair, the talk less stilted and certainly less committal. Roosevelt promised to make good on his promises to speed up the flow of arms to Brazil, but warned Vargas that—as the Brazilian president was surely tired of hearing—they were in short supply. Both men talked of the possibility of sending a Brazilian force overseas, but only in unspecific terms. Vargas had still not got around to fully studying and discussing Dutra's memorandum for a large Brazilian force, yet Roosevelt's comments and insinuations made it clear that the US armed forces were far from keen to have Brazilian forces in North Africa. Training and arming the Brazilian forces would simply take too long and would be too expensive, because the new troops would have to be heavily armed and equipped to participate in such an operation. But what alternative purpose Brazilian troops might serve in the war, besides potentially occupying the Azores, Vargas could not yet know.

Vargas left the meeting in an upbeat mood, in marked contrast to his brooding appearance in the jeep a few hours earlier. That same night, he flew back to Rio with Caffery. Aranha met with Vargas on his return, and later marveled to Caffery, "I have rarely seen him so pleased with everything." Surely some of the joy the president felt was personal; Caffery had mentioned in the morning meeting with Roosevelt that Vargas's son was ill, and during the dinner Roosevelt had offered to help get young Getúlinho whatever medical assistance the United States could provide. But the meeting had also marked an important victory for Brazil, and Vargas knew it.

On the evening of January 30, 1943, directly after he returned from Natal, Vargas gave a press conference at the Guanabara Palace in which he outlined how and when his secret meeting with President Roosevelt had been set up. Brazil was electrified by the news that the leader of the United States had decided to stop in Brazil—on his way back from one of the most important conferences of the war, no less—to show his support for the country and demonstrate its importance to the United States. At the time of the press conference, Roosevelt had not yet arrived back in Washington, so the international press relied on Vargas's account for information about the meeting.

Vargas was still in extremely good spirits for a man whose son remained critically ill. He was particularly laudatory of Roosevelt, assuring Brazilians that the American president was "still demonstrating the firm decision to carry forward this crusade in which we are all pledged."[17] When questioned about Brazil's military cooperation with the United States, Vargas gave an upbeat response: "As we are in the war our cooperation with the United States must be complete. Everything the United States judges necessary and useful as cooperation from Brazil we shall continue to give."[18] The answer, however, masked the reality of the situation: Vargas had yet to commit to Dutra's memorandum on sending a Brazilian force overseas, and anyway the United States was reluctant to use such a force in North Africa.

At the press conference, a journalist asked Vargas, "How long does Roosevelt think that the war will last?" Over the next several hours, with Roosevelt still en route back to Washington, Vargas found himself acting as the US president's unofficial spokesman. This was surely due in part to the fact that the question of the war's duration was becoming ever more important for Brazil. A protracted war in Europe would offer Brazil great potential for economic and military gains; but if the war ended soon, Brazil would not be able to reap the sorts of benefits that the Vargas regime deemed necessary for fully modernizing the economy. Apparently still riding his optimistic streak, he told the press conference, "The Allied nations are prepared for a long war."[19] And, Vargas added soon thereafter, he was too. "We must prepare for a long war. There is no doubt, however, that we are all entirely certain of victory."[20]

The meeting received huge coverage in the Brazilian press. *Jornal do Brasil* devoted two front-page columns to it, calling Roosevelt's presence in Natal "a sincere demonstration of applause for Brazil's war effort." International coverage of the meeting was widespread, too. The *Associated Press* wired the headline, "President Roosevelt and President Vargas in a joint statement have affirmed their intention to make the Atlantic safe for the shipping of all nations." The headline on the front page of the *New York Times* on January 29, 1943, proclaimed simply, "Roosevelt stops off in Brazil."[21]

On the same page as its announcement of Roosevelt's visit to Natal, the *New York Times* carried a large photograph of a US aircrew standing in front of a US air force bomber with the caption, "Back from first American bombing of Germany."[22] As the caption suggested, the war—while far from over—was entering a new and potentially decisive phase. Vargas continued to work feverishly to maximize Brazilian returns from the conflict, but the clock was ticking, and Brazil would need to move quickly to secure the gains it had already made.

Vargas's meeting with Roosevelt, and the deals that were to result from it, would be perhaps the pinnacle of Vargas's political career and the period of the Estado Novo. Though it is simplistic to suggest that everything went downhill for Vargas from this point onward, he would never scale these dizzy heights again. And the first sign of his changing fortunes came in a devastating personal loss.

A few days after Vargas's meeting with President Roosevelt, Getúlinho died. The loss of his handsome and talented son changed Vargas forever.

His wife, Darci, withdrew from political society and concentrated only on her charity work. Vargas himself appeared to lose confidence and focus; he looked older and moved more slowly after Getúlinho's death, and came to rely increasingly on Alzira and Aranha for political guidance. As the president's political judgment deserted him, his moods became darker, and his isolation from the political elite grew more pronounced.

These changes did not have an immediate or obvious impact on Vargas's ability to govern, but the death of his son certainly clouded his political and personal judgment. For years after Getúlinho's death, Vargas was in a state of very private mourning—yet he tried as hard as he could to cover up this fact as he worked to steer Brazil through the widening war.

13

# THE DINNER PARTY

T HE WAR WAS DRAWING AMERICANS and Brazilians together—and
not just the heads of state. On January 30, 1943, while President
Vargas was holding a press conference following his return from his
meeting with President Roosevelt in Natal, Osvaldo Aranha dined at
the private residence of Jefferson Caffery along with Admiral Ingram and
General Walsh and several other US military officers.[1] It was a dinner
that proved to have important implications for the future of US-Brazilian
relations.

Caffery's residence was very much in keeping with the ambassador's
style: grand, imposing, furnished with taste, and completed with a large,
secluded outdoor swimming pool. This was the US ambassador's only
residence, unlike the British ambassador who had a summer retreat near
President Vargas in Petrópolis—yet perhaps because he had only one residence to show off, Caffery immensely enjoyed hosting guests. On this
evening, as Aranha and the American officers enjoyed a predinner drink,
Caffery made small talk by discussing the increased cost of living in Rio.
Money was very much on the ambassador's mind; in his annual reports to
Washington, Caffery argued that the expense of putting on dinners and
other official social functions expected of a US ambassador was far higher
than the State Department's allowance for such purposes.

Caffery's complaints reflected an important problem in wartime Brazil:
inflation. The ambassador reported that the cost of living index in January
1943 was forty-two points above that for 1939.[2] Living costs in Rio had
increased even more sharply than in the rest of Brazil, and in 1943 they
were 83 percent higher than in 1939.[3] In response to this increase, the
Brazilian government raised the minimum wage in the capital city by 25
percent.[4] One of the most substantial increases was in the cost of food,

which had gone up by 40 percent since 1939, and sharp rises were forecast for the rest of 1943.[5] While increases in food prices were not unique to Brazil, they did make it harder for Cariocas to maintain their standard of living. Caffery attributed this particular problem to a host of factors: "The curtailment of coastwise shipping because of the shortage of vessels and the submarine menace; a reduction in rail and motor transportation for the lack of equipment and fuel; a shortage of farm labor due to the increase in the Brazilian armed forces and higher wages in industry and the production of strategic war material; and drought affecting agricultural production."[6]

Another issue about which Caffery often complained was the huge increase in the cost of housing in wartime Brazil. The local newspaper *Diário Carioca* attributed the problem—in Rio, at least—to a new phenomenon in the capital: foreign refugees. The paper observed:

> The increase in rentals has been most accentuated in the Copacabana district. As a result of the war a multitude of refugees, the majority of them being persons of substance, invaded our most beautiful beach district, taking apartments by storm. They did not discuss price. They paid what was asked of them, making deals behind the scenes because of the law that prohibits an increase in rentals. . . . Landlords today will accept only cash as a deposit and instead of two or three months, they exact an advance deposit of rental for four months, which is never returned.[7]

The presence of such refugees in the capital, and the effect they had on Rio's economy, contributed to an already xenophobic atmosphere in Brazil. First were the concerns that immigrants were subverting the country's politics; now, it was Brazil's finances that were threatened.

As Caffery reflected on these issues over drinks at his residence, Aranha weighed in. The foreign minister suggested that the ambassador was correct that the increases in price were related to the war, but that by far the most serious issue was the lack of fuel for transportation. This shortage was essentially asphyxiating the country's economy, and its crippling effects would be felt for years. For all its wartime advances, the Brazilian economy continued to fall prey to high levels of inflation for the duration of the war and beyond.

When his guests sat down for dinner, Caffery received news that President Roosevelt had arrived safely back in Washington. It happened to be the president's birthday, so the party toasted to his health. Following the clinking of glasses, the conversation shifted away from the small talk and onto the subject of Roosevelt's meeting with Vargas on January 28. Aranha flattered his hosts by avowing that he had never seen Vargas as pleased by the outcome of a meeting as he was when he had returned to Rio.[8] Both Caffery and Ingram returned the compliment, suggesting that Roosevelt also regarded the meeting as having been friendly and productive, reflecting the two leaders' similar visions for the war effort.[9] This delicate social minuet, however, concealed pressing diplomatic objectives for both Aranha and the Americans.

Caffery and Ingram were keen to discuss the ten-page memorandum that Aranha had written for Vargas to help the president prepare for his meeting with Roosevelt.[10] The importance of the memorandum had been clear to Caffery as soon as he had glimpsed the document, for it contained details of exactly what Brazil expected to get in return for its support of the Allied war effort.[11] What Caffery didn't understand, however, was that the document represented the first attempt by Aranha to try to formally set out a series of detailed strategic goals for Brazil during World War II. The fact that he had felt able to share the document with Caffery before Roosevelt met with Vargas would have shocked many members of the Brazilian cabinet—most notably Dutra, who surely would have felt that the foreign minister should have been more circumspect in dealing with his American "allies." Aranha's decision was a reflection of his close working relationship with Caffery—but it was also a testament to his keen diplomatic skills, which were now working on overdrive.

Over dinner Aranha explained the contents of the document in more detail. From time to time Caffery interrupted in order to seek clarification on a specific point or to ask a direct question.[12] Aranha followed the same subject order of the memorandum. "Brazil must continue to support the United States in the world in exchange for its support in South America," he told Caffery, "and this should be maintained until the American victory in the war."[13] The Brazilian went on to predict: "The United States will lead the world when peace comes, and it would be a grave error on the part of Brazil not to be at its side."

As the foreign minister spoke, it became apparent that he had a grand vision for how Brazil's partnership with the United States would reshape his country. Brazil was still a weak country, Aranha knew, but in the future it would have the chance to play a much larger role in both continental and global politics.[14] Economically the country would benefit from rapid postwar growth and a major increase in the size of its population, which might very well make Brazil one of the most important economies in the world. In order to cement its position on the international stage, however, Aranha felt that Brazil should seek to attract American and British capital and should not introduce nationalistic economic policies that might endanger such foreign investment in the country.[15] Rather, Brazil should accept as an inevitable but temporary nuisance the economic difficulties that Caffery had mentioned before his guests sat down for dinner. "By ceding in war, we will gain in peacetime," Aranha quipped.[16] In the postwar period, he went on, the Brazilian economy would become ever more closely linked to that of the United States, and the country would undergo a program of industrialization and liberalization that would enable the movement of capital and immigrants, further propelling its economy.[17] Its present military weakness, moreover, would soon end thanks to the supply of American weapons, which would transform the Brazilian armed forces into a modern well-equipped army.

In terms of international politics, Aranha argued that Brazil should join the notional United Nations and seek a seat in the supreme military councils of the combined Allied powers. He also had his eye on specific regions that Brazil might influence in the postwar era. The future of the Portuguese colonies in Africa and the Atlantic, Aranha knew, would be complicated. If the Portuguese empire were to collapse due to an Axis invasion, Brazil must be ready to help defend territories such as the Azores—a role that Aranha understood would guarantee Rio a strong hand in such far-flung places.[18] He concluded that as Africa's security was related to Brazil's security, Brazil should also have a say in the future of that continent.

Aranha was calling for a partnership between the United States and Brazil not only on bilateral and continental affairs, but also on global geostrategic politics.[19] And for the foreign minister, the prospect of a Brazilian expeditionary force could be a means of deepening this strategic cooperation between the United States and Brazil. By showing the United States that it could count on Brazil's support in the war, Brazil hoped to be able to count on the United States's support on South American issues in return.[20] The price of Brazil's support, in effect, was US help in making

Brazil the dominant power—politically, economically, and militarily—in South America. Aranha suggested that the break with Argentina at the conference of foreign ministers almost exactly one year prior had created the opportunity for Brazil to achieve all these aims.[21]

Caffery was intrigued and impressed by the scale of the vision that Aranha outlined over dinner and that he had described in the memorandum for President Vargas.[22] He was likely concerned, too, because the foreign minister's lofty aims appeared to go far beyond anything Washington had authorized the ambassador to offer to the Brazilians. Instead of replying to Aranha's outline of his vision, therefore, Caffery zeroed in on two important points regarding the future of Brazil: its relations with Argentina, and the fate of the Estado Novo in the postwar era.

The US ambassador was troubled by the rivalry between the two most powerful nations in South America.[23] Yet Caffery also dismissed Brazilian hand-wringing over Argentine aggression. Writing to Washington later in 1943, he would describe Brazilian fears of an Argentine invasion as "cock-eyed."[24] He admitted, however, that he had found it difficult to gather enough evidence to allay or confirm Brazilian fears of this potential threat.[25]

The Americans felt that the Brazilians had three major motives for emphasizing the danger of an Argentine attack in 1943. For one thing, the balance of power in South America had been shifting away from Argentina and toward Brazil in the years immediately prior to World War II, and if anything, this trend had continued at a faster rate during the war itself. Brazil had experienced rapid economic development in recent years, and the majority of its population had enjoyed some improvements in their living conditions (although the gains were not as great as Vargas had promised).[26] But Brazil's big advantage was its military. In 1943 alone, the size of the Brazilian army increased to about 130,000 officers and men, compared to Argentina's strength of about 68,000 men.[27] The Brazilian army had begun to reequip itself, moreover, with the large quantities of new materials it was receiving from the United States under the lend-lease agreement, and the Brazilian air force and navy were also growing.[28] (Indeed, Washington suspected that the Brazilian government was stressing the Argentine threat in order to obtain more weapons than it would have otherwise received from the United States under the lend-lease agreement.)[29] In an assessment of the Brazilian-Argentine rivalry, however, the United States concluded that:

despite these recent changes, the Brazilians are still fearful of an Argentine attack. They have not yet completely adjusted their mental processes to the new distribution of power in Latin America. While they are in command of human and material resources, which appear superior on paper, they still lack the confidence that would be acquired by a practical test of their own strength. The feeling of insecurity is reflected in at least one basic agreement between Brazil and the United States providing for United States assistance if Brazil is attacked by a pro-Nazi American state. Brazilian anxieties are stimulated by receipt of possibly exaggerated Argentine military preparations.[30]

Militarily, Brazil held a great advantage over Argentina by the beginning of 1943. The great irony was that this had not had the effect of making Brazilians feel any safer.

The United States also suspected that Brazilians' nationalistic aspirations were behind their constant and vocal preoccupation with a possible Argentine invasion. The Americans felt that there were many prideful Brazilians who would oppose the idea of enlarging the country.[31] By 1943 Argentina was effectively cut off from any foreign arms supplies, and some Brazilians might be inclined to seize this golden opportunity and deal with the Argentine threat once and for all.[32] The Americans, however, admitted that there was no evidence that such views were widely held in Brazil, and ultimately concluded it was highly improbable that the country would launch a war of conquest against Argentina in 1943.[33]

The final motive that the United States ascribed to Brazil's claims about the Argentine menace had to do with internal Brazilian politics.[34] Relations between Góes Monteiro and other senior officers were under great strain due to the general's increasingly public criticism of the army for its poor performance. While Caffery believed that Aranha's statements were intended to extract more weapons from the United States, the statements of other senior figures in the Vargas regime, particularly Góes Monteiro, were much harder for the ambassador to interpret.[35] Caffery sensed that the chief of staff's frequent comments about the Argentine threat might have been intended to disrupt the cooperation between the United States and Brazil, and to assert Góes Monteiro's authority over the Brazilian army at a time when he found himself in competition with other senior officers.

Over dinner, Caffery ran through this American interpretation of Brazil's preoccupation with the Argentine threat. Aranha listened, and said little in reply. After Caffery finished his lecture, he, Aranha, Ingram, and Walsh all moved outside to the shaded patio, where drinks were served. The heat of another summer day was receding, but all four men nevertheless removed their white cotton jackets.

Aranha lit a cigarette and sat in a deck chair, as Caffery pressed him further for the details of his memorandum to Vargas. The ambassador noted that Aranha and Vargas appeared to be laying the groundwork for the postwar era, and he asked Aranha whether he thought the Estado Novo would survive past the end of the war. Surely, with Brazil committed to the war against tyranny abroad, Brazilians would not accept anything short of full democracy at home once the war ended.

Caffery wasn't the only one who harbored doubts about the regime's future. Aranha's memorandum made it clear that the foreign minister was aware that Brazil would need to embrace free trade if it were to compete in the postwar economy, and Aranha knew too that any fiscal liberalization in Brazil would have to be accompanied by political reforms. Now, as he spoke with Caffery, the foreign minister confirmed that he was considering how Brazil might return to the democratic system it had enjoyed before the establishment of the Estado Novo.

The postwar period was also a topic of great interest to both Admiral Ingram and General Walsh, who held distinctly different ideas of what the partnership between Brazil and the United States ought to look like after the war. Ingram, who frequently met privately with President Vargas during his tenure in Brazil, argued that no US solider would remain in Brazilian territory once the war ended. General Walsh, on the other hand, was of the opinion that the United States should continue using the air bases and facilities it had built in Brazil even after the war was over, and he felt that the United States should start negotiating with the Brazilian government as soon as possible to ensure that it would have this right.[36] Walsh saw clear military and commercial value in such an arrangement, and as the war went on—and the potential for another war between the West and the Soviet Union grew—the idea of an American military outpost in South America became only more appealing.

As the group on Caffery's patio mulled over these questions about Brazil's future, the informal discussions wound down, and the dinner party broke up. It had been a cheerful affair, and the good humor and frank exchange of views had been all but guaranteed due to the warm afterglow from the recent meeting between Roosevelt and Vargas. Aranha's elaboration on his views about Brazil's developing relationship with the United States—and his vision of Brazil's role in the postwar world—had given Caffery, Ingram, and Walsh much food for thought.

Yet a critical observer of the dinner might well have concluded that Aranha's conception of his country's future relationship with the United States was not remotely close to that of the Americans. What Aranha craved most was a partnership, while the United States essentially wanted to dominate the Brazilians—though of course American officials never would have acknowledged this goal. These two divergent aims would guide the policy of both governments until the end of the war, and indeed had already laid the groundwork for future tensions between the two countries.

The United States's greatest need for Brazil had already passed with the landings in North Africa at the end of 1942. Although Brazilian support was still needed in the war in the South Atlantic—and in the provision of critical war materials, like rubber—this support wasn't nearly vital enough for Washington to accept the idea of a full partnership with Rio. Aranha's hope that the United States would help Brazil achieve its goal of regional hegemony in exchange for Brazilian support in the war also appeared to be far-fetched. Despite the anger the US State Department—especially Secretary of State Cordell Hull—felt toward Argentina, in 1943, Washington made few signals that it was willing to formally endorse the Brazilian quest for regional dominance over its longtime rival, Argentina.

While the United States and Brazil would continue to develop economic, military, and political ties throughout 1943, their relationship was becoming more and more imbalanced. The smiles, the handshakes, and the regular warm exchange of messages between Roosevelt and Vargas cannot obscure the simple reality that from 1943 on, Brazil needed the United States far more than the United States needed Brazil. It is curious, then, that Aranha was so willing to tip his hand to the United States at a time when Brazil had lost much of the strategic value it had had at the end of 1941—and when it was in far less of a position to achieve its lofty objectives than it once had been.

One American, at least, had lost none of his enthusiasm for the Brazilian-US partnership. Nelson Rockefeller and his agency, the office of the coordinator of inter-American affairs, were becoming increasingly central to the efforts of the United States to develop ties with Brazil. Yet Rockefeller was also torn between his business in Brazil and his affairs back in the United States. In 1943, Rockefeller had one eye on the development of economic and cultural links with Brazil, and the other on the expansion of his own powerbase among the key policy makers in the Roosevelt administration. It is impossible to divorce these two aims, as Rockefeller appeared willing to use all of his personal and business connections to help facilitate the projects he supported. The ostensible failure of the Orson Welles film project of the previous year didn't dissuade Rockefeller from endorsing new cultural projects. He was still in charge of the creation and dissemination of US propaganda in South America, and believed that he could best propagandize by exporting US culture to the region.

This was not a one-way cultural effort. Rockefeller introduced the Brazilian singer Carmen Miranda to a US audience, and she became a huge overnight sensation in the United States. Rockefeller, who sat on the board of the Museum of Modern Art (MOMA) in New York, encouraged the museum to exhibit Brazilian artists for the first time and to sponsor US artists' exhibitions in Rio. Rockefeller also persuaded a reluctant Solomon R. Guggenheim to help set up scholarships for Brazilians, and he tapped the Carnegie Foundation to fund similar programs and scholarships in the United States and Brazil.

There was never a better time to be a Brazilian artist, writer, or musician. The United States opened its doors to Brazilian culture during World War II in ways that it had never done for the citizens of any other country. Much of this was due to the drive and ambition of Nelson Rockefeller. Unsurprisingly given Rockefeller's propulsive nature, he made many enemies in Washington, and felt that petty jealousies and interdepartmental rivalries got in his way. But as long as Rockefeller enjoyed the strong personal support of President Roosevelt, he was able to push the vast majority of his cultural program through.

Rockefeller was not the only famous American who traveled to Brazil to deepen cultural ties or to gather information for President Roosevelt. Other early crusaders to Rio included the Hollywood actors Errol Flynn and Douglas Fairbanks Jr. In June of 1940 Flynn, then at the height of his fame, visited Rio and stayed at the Copacabana Palace Hotel. He took part in a radio address during his stay, and also met with Vargas, of whom he formed a favorable impression. In a letter to President Roosevelt dated June 15, 1940, Flynn wrote that he was convinced Vargas was very much in favor of developing a Pan-American friendship.[37]

Douglas Fairbanks Jr. was a similar advocate of closer ties between the United States and Brazil. Fairbanks had been a vocal opponent of the American policy of isolationism since 1939, and Roosevelt personally authorized Fairbanks's trip to Brazil—a reflection of the president's latent agreement with that stance. The actor's stated purpose for visiting Brazil was to research the state of US cinema there, but the real purpose of his trip was to investigate the alleged pro-Nazi tendencies of key members of the Vargas administration. Vargas granted Fairbanks a private meeting and extended him a warm welcome, but the highlight of the actor's trip may well have been learning to samba with Alzira at a private party held in his honor.[38] American intelligence carefully debriefed Fairbanks once he returned to the United States.

The US film director John Ford also traveled to Rio. In 1943, Ford made the trip to shoot a propaganda movie about Brazil's contributions to the Allied war effort. The film was a stereotypical wartime propaganda short, with glowing references to the Vargas administration and the Brazilian armed forces, and tributes to Brazil for supplying wolfram—a rare, high-density metal that was used in the production of bullets and other projectiles—to the US war effort. The film also mentioned that the Brazilians had invited the US military to the north of Brazil to create new naval bases, which were vital staging posts for the US efforts in the Atlantic; it also touched on the controversial decision to put all Brazilian forces under the direct command of the Americans. This had been meant to impress the Americans, but it had the opposite effect. US political and military leaders viewed the decision as a sign of weakness, and felt that it reduced the respect that US officers in particular had for their senior Brazilian counterparts.

Ford's film also highlighted the huge flow of Brazilian rubber to the United States, noting that Brazil had become its single largest supplier of rubber. And significantly, for all Rockefeller's work to deepen cultural ties between the United States and Brazil, he is best remembered in Brazil for his role in the rubber trade—or rather, his role in protecting the people in it. President Vargas had given the order to recruit some thirty thousand "rubber soldiers" to work in Brazil's rubber industries, with the goal of producing sixty thousand tons of rubber a year for sale to the Americans. However, the rubber industry was based in the Amazon Basin, and the plantations were rife with disease; many young men died working there. Rockefeller and his private foundation invested heavily in efforts to improve conditions in Brazil's rubber-producing regions by introducing better sanitation technology and practices, and funding the development of vaccines for some of the diseases. The history of the "rubber soldiers" remains extremely controversial in Brazil, yet the tragedy had at least one positive legacy: to this day the Rockefeller Foundation continues to invest large amounts of money combating diseases in Brazil.

The rubber industry of Brazil during World War II was a stark reminder of how different things were in the country from its portrayal in John Ford's propaganda film. On the surface, however, all appeared well with the rubber trade in 1943. Following a suggestion from Rockefeller's office, President Vargas agreed to name June "rubber month" in Brazil. The aim of this public relations drive was to highlight the importance of the rubber trade for the US war effort and to illustrate the close cooperation between the Brazilian and US governments. In the decree announcing Rubber Month, Vargas declared to his fellow Brazilians:

> Shoulder to shoulder with our Allies we shall lead our forces to final victory. However, before we obtain this objective an urgent task awaits us: we have to win the battle of production. Brazilians: with the same frankness that I have always addressed you I now ask for your loyal and determined cooperation on behalf of a campaign which commences today: the rubber campaign. You know how gigantic is the consumption of material in the present war. And among the essential and most urgently needed raw materials for the struggle we are engaged in, there are some that depend on us and to which we must dedicate all our efforts. This is the case with rubber, which is used in enormous quantities in the manufacture of nearly all war equipment.[39]

This was a carefully choreographed attempt to reassure the Americans that Brazil was doing all it could to increase rubber production, yet the plan backfired somewhat. Vargas was meant to read the proclamation in a radio broadcast on the evening of May 31, but eventually he delegated its delivery to the director of the department of press and propaganda (DIP).[40]

The use of the director of the DIP as proxy to announce Rubber Month irritated both Washington and the US embassy in Rio, and the fact that President Vargas gave no explanation for the last-minute change did not help matters. Eventually, President Vargas's office offered a vague excuse: "The president," his staff explained, "only returned late in the evening from an automobile tour in the state of Rio, which lasted a number of days and on which he was obliged to attend many inaugurations of public works."[41]

As a result of its displeasure, the United States delayed the response it had prepared to Vargas's statement. President Roosevelt finally replied in a letter to Vargas on June 19, 1943, thanking him for his efforts. Roosevelt wrote:

> Your Excellency's announcement that June will be observed as "Rubber Month" in Brazil reminds the people of the United States once again of the extraordinary contribution the Brazilian government and people are making to the cause of the United Nations in this instance through the "Battle of Rubber." The personal interest you have shown in encouraging the intensification of rubber production is received in the United States as a symbol of the energy, vision, and goodwill, which have characterized the war polices of the Brazilian government and the activities of the Brazilian people. Each ton of rubber that Brazil can provide has an immediate important use in the United Nations production for war. Brazil already has made manifest in many ways its unwavering support of inter-American unity. We in the United States welcome this added proof of Brazilian determination to carry its great share of the fight of all the United Nations.[42]

Roosevelt's letter, which was released to the press, was intended to refocus attention on the positive elements of the expansion of the rubber program—the contribution it made to the United States war effort—and away from the hideous toll it was taking on the Brazilian people who labored on the rubber plantations.

Indeed, prior to Rubber Month it was clear that not everything was going as planned in the joint US-Brazilian drive to increase rubber production. The United States reported that some twenty thousand people had been moved into the Amazon Basin during the first part of 1943 in an attempt to boost the plantations' output, but that it was difficult to assess the impact of this increased manpower on production. American officials warned that, as they put it, "war conditions have made it impossible to carry out fully the original schedule, coastline shipping having been stopped for a period, river boats ordered for the Amazon were delayed in being delivered, and other unforeseen circumstances have interfered."[43]

Rubber Month was also intended to combat popular disaffection with the Brazilian rubber industry. Posters were placed in Rio and other Brazilian cities making the case for increased rubber production.[44] Radio programs and even a short film were made. An appeal was issued in the United States for its citizens to collect and recycle scrap rubber.[45] Finally, newspaper articles in both Brazil and the United States highlighted the importance of rubber production to the Allied war effort.[46]

The United States was extremely pleased with the Brazilian press's coverage of Rubber Month.[47] The Brazilian news media, which in 1943 remained much more tightly controlled by the state than its US counterpart, did not focus on any of the negative aspects of the policy of increased rubber production in the Amazon. The response of the US press had not been so easy to control. As part of Rubber Month, *Time* magazine published an article on the subject of Brazilian rubber production, reflecting on a number of criticisms of the industry. Yet tellingly, these arguments focused less on the human costs of Brazilian rubber production than they did on the potential economic threat it represented.

The central thrust of the *Time* article—a point of view taken by several other news agencies in the United States—was that the ongoing US program to synthesize rubber would allow US rubber producers to compete with Brazilian rubber plantations.[48] The magazine claimed that the annual production per man in synthetic rubber would be sixty tons, whereas the average production of a native rubber gatherer was only one hundred and fifty pounds.[49] The article went on to suggest that even on the most efficient plantations the total production per man per year would not exceed one ton.[50]

The accuracy of these figures could not be verified, but they—and the broader argument of which they formed a part—caused a huge amount of concern at the top of the power structure in Brazil, and even threatened to undermine the cozy relationship between the United States and Brazil's rubber industry. As the rubber development corporation complained, the

*Time* magazine piece "brought out considerable unfavorable comment on the rubber program in the sense that as soon as the war was over there would be no need for Brazilian crude rubber, and that Brazil would be left high and dry again for a market."[51] The complaint suggested that there were several Brazilian high officials who were dubious about the long-term value of the rubber program, and some Brazilians felt that the United States might not be as interested as it was in carrying out the rubber agreements it had made with Brazil.[52] Yet the rubber program remained a largely hidden controversy in greater Brazil. The tightly controlled state press made it easy enough for the Vargas administration to maintain a veil of secrecy over the appalling working conditions that laborers in the Amazon experienced.

Even as Brazil tried to maximize its returns from its alliance with the United States, the country's leaders were realizing that their contributions to the Allied war effort were not as great as they had initially thought. Delivering rubber and other strategic goods to the Allies allowed Brazil to play an important part in the war effort, yet it would not, on its own, secure Brazil an equitable partnership with the United States, or convince the United States to back Brazil's bid for hegemony in South America.

Rio had only one card left to play, and it was the best in its hand: Brazil could make an active military contribution to the Allied war effort by sending it soldiers overseas to join the fight. Aranha understood that sending such a force was in all probability the only chance left for Brazil to achieve the aims that had been outlined in the document he had shown to Caffery, which he had discussed with him, Admiral Ingram, and General Walsh over dinner that humid evening in early 1943.

# PART FIVE:
## BRAZIL'S ACTIVE
## PARTICIPATION

## 14

# LATE ARRIVALS

Brazil's time was running out. The pace of the war was quickening as 1943 progressed. The North African campaign ended on May 13, 1943, when the Axis forces in Tunisia surrendered. Then, on July 10, US and British troops landed on Sicily, and by mid-August, they controlled the entire Italian island. These Allied military successes contributed to the decision of Italy's fascist grand council to depose Benito Mussolini on July 25, and on September 8, after lengthy negotiations, Italy surrendered to the Allies.

The surrender did not end the fighting in Italy, which was quickly becoming a major theater of the war—and which seemed likely to be one of the final frontiers. Following the Italian surrender, German forces immediately seized control of Rome and northern Italy, setting up a puppet fascist government there. On September 9, 1943, the day after the Italian surrender, US and British troops landed on the beaches of Salerno, near Naples, to begin a push northward to liberate all of Italy. Meanwhile, in the east, the Soviet Union launched a major offensive that led to the liberation of Kiev on November 6. The Allies now clearly had the upper hand, but they still had much further to go before Germany was forced to surrender.

In Rio, President Vargas followed events overseas in a sort of stupor. At the time of the Brazilian Rubber Month in June 1943, he was still reeling from his son's sudden death earlier that year and his own car accident the previous year, both of which had taken a massive toll on him. His workload was unrelenting, but Vargas seemed to have fallen out of his usual, energetic rhythm. He changed his long-standing routines, no longer keeping a diary and playing less golf—often due to his injured hip.

He was still found working alone in his study at night in the Guanabara Palace, but he took fewer meetings in the evening.

Vargas's "right eye" and "left eye" kept the gears of government turning during this time. Osvaldo Aranha hosted most of the meetings with foreign diplomats and American military officers, while Vargas came to rely even more on Alzira to organize and prioritize his work. Both Aranha and Alzira understood what President Vargas would feel able to handle himself and what they should keep from him. They knew, too, how to cheer him up. The days that most pleased the president were ones in which he could see the positive results of the public works programs he had initiated. Tours—such as the one through the state of Rio de Janeiro that had precluded him from making the speech launching Rubber Month—appealed to the president, perhaps because they gave him a respite from his responsibilities in Rio. Despite his best efforts to recapture his previous zeal for governing, he remained a man running on autopilot at a time when the country needed strong, dynamic leadership.

The president knew full well that these were crucial times in Brazil's history, and he remained fond of reminding Brazilians of this fact even though he seemed less capable than ever of handling the challenges before him. He tried to keep a clear head and continued working long hours, but a sense of detached melancholy seemed to hang over him like a dark cloud. His anguish over the loss of his son mixed with a toxic sense of guilt. The president had initially been kept in the dark about his son's illness, which was ultimately diagnosed as partial paralysis and polio neuritis.[1] Getúlinho's illness came on after an intense period of work mixed with partying, which doctors believed could have triggered the affliction.[2] Following Getúlinho's collapse, he was not taken to the hospital, and Alzira was told on the phone that his case was not serious; she was warned not to alarm her parents.[3] In the end, the president believed that his son had been badly let down by all concerned.

Even extremely pressing issues such as the question of whether or not to send a Brazilian force overseas took longer than usual to resolve. Vargas took over two months to respond to the detailed memorandum that Dutra put together at the start of January 1943, which the foreign minister had presumed would receive the president's immediate attention. Vargas eventually approved Dutra's memorandum on March 5, 1943, yet his consent did not mark the end of the debate about sending a Brazilian force overseas. On the contrary, it was merely the start of a long and controversial military operation, mixed with disputes and delays over training, which meant that no Brazilian force was readied for departure before the end of 1943.

Osvaldo Aranha proved to be the strongest supporter for the idea of sending Brazilian troops to Europe as quickly as possible. For Aranha, the dispatch of an expeditionary force was the most natural way of expanding the historic alliance between Brazil and the United States. He argued that Brazil had committed itself to the United States in every way except militarily, but that only such a commitment could ensure continued US help for Brazil, particularly in industrializing the country.[4] Brazil, he argued, would also need to play a role in policing the postwar order in Europe if it were to have any hope of achieving its ambitious, long-term goals, whether in terms of its own infrastructure or its position in the hierarchy of South America.[5] Aranha saw the extension of the Brazilian mission into the postwar era as Brazil's best opportunity to maximize its returns from the United States. At the center of Aranha's thinking in 1943 was the notion of exchange; the United States would support Brazil on regional issues if Brazil supported the United States on international ones.

The formation of an expeditionary force would also have the potential effect of strengthening Brazilian defenses—both in the northeast region of the country and along its southern border with Argentina. In both regions, the promised support of the United States would be vital in supplying the Brazilian army with weapons and training.

On August 9, 1943, by way of Decree 4744, Brazil formally established an expeditionary force.[6] The decree called for a smaller force than was originally planned, but nonetheless it represented a historic decision by the Brazilian government.

It was widely anticipated that the Brazilian force, known as the Força Expedicionária Brasileira (FEB), would be sent to the Mediterranean theater of conflict. Senior US commanders hoped that it would be assigned to an already pacified area and would take little or no part in the major battles that lay ahead in Italy and elsewhere in Europe. In visits to Brazil, US officers had been far from impressed by the recruits in the Brazilian army, their training, or their antiquated equipment. When President Vargas dispatched Dutra to Washington in August to make arrangements for training and equipping the force, the minister of war carried a letter from Vargas to President Roosevelt in which the Brazilian president expressed the desire of the Brazilian army to actively participate in the war. President Roosevelt was impressed by the sentiment, but his senior staff advised him that a quiet spot should be found for the Brazilians to make their contribution to the Allied war effort.

By September 1943, the Brazilian force was slowly starting to take shape—thanks in no small part to the support of the United States. In a speech on September 7 to mark Brazilian Independence Day, President Vargas proclaimed, "If our soldiers have to participate in overseas operations, they will not lack the moral and material weapons necessary to fight with efficiency and heroism. There is no lack of enthusiasm and the problem of equipment is being met with the efficient aid of our valorous ally, the great industrial American nation."[7] Brazil, as Vargas had long maintained, would supply the troops if the United States would supply the rest.

Dutra's negotiations in Washington, meanwhile, appeared to be going well. The United States was taking full responsibility for the task of equipping the Brazilian expeditionary force. It agreed to send some military equipment to Brazil for training purposes, but the majority of the equipment would be transferred to the Brazilians when they arrived in the theater of the war. There had been some initial opposition on this point from senior US officers, who argued that by supplying the Brazilian troops, the United States would deprive its own forces of much-needed equipment, but eventually US planners decided that Vargas would receive his weapons despite the potential repercussions for other Allied forces.

Yet while the Brazilians would get their equipment, all of the weapons and supplies would be useless without troops to use them. In his speech on September 7, President Vargas had dismissed this issue:

Happily the Brazilian people—brave, proud, and vigilant of their honor—have answered the call to arms in an inspiring way. Idealistic and courageous, youth knows its duty and hastens to the defense of the country. . . . The combative spirit of the young people of Brazil is of excellent temper. It is manifested in the patriotic enthusiasm and reflected in the outstanding number of volunteers. The only difficulty in connection with individual mobilization has been the selection of those most qualified and least necessary to the economic life of the country. We can frankly state that our war problems are not the problems of manpower; of men we have plenty ready to fight.[8]

Brazilians, Vargas claimed, were rushing to join the fight; indeed, Brazil's problem was not that it didn't have enough potential soldiers, but rather that it had too many.

But President Vargas's comments were not strictly accurate. To begin with, the question of how best to staff the expeditionary force had been the subject of an ongoing internal dispute in Brazil. At the heart of the issue was the structure of the Brazilian army in 1943. The members of each division were predominately drawn from the area in which the division was stationed; most of these divisions were based in large urban areas such as Rio de Janeiro. Early on, Vargas decided that it would be unfair to commit specific divisions to the expeditionary force, as this would place an unacceptable burden of sacrifice on the particular areas from which these divisions were drawn. This was more of a political decision than a humanitarian one; Vargas knew that he might stir up opposition to the war if he overrelied on certain segments of the population. He was also keen, for political reasons, that the force should be drawn from all parts of Brazil so as to illustrate the nationalist, unifying aspects of the Estado Novo.[9] And so the expeditionary force was drawn from units from across all of Brazil, its soldiers a mix of men from different regions.

The fact that the force had not worked together before was viewed as an advantage; this would help it shift to the American model of training—which, as the soldiers soon discovered, was very different from the Brazilian model. In other words, members of the expeditionary force would adapt to the new methods much quicker than if they remained embedded in their old command structures and organization.[10]

However, in addition to these structural challenges, it was also a fact that not every Brazilian was willing to participate in the war effort, as Vargas claimed. Nearly none of the enlisted men had been abroad before. When Brazilian pilots arrived in the United States for training, their American trainers noted that most of those men had never left Brazil before, either. This presented a problem for recruitment; the force was known to be heading overseas, and many Brazilians decided they had no interest in being sent into a war zone so far from home. Draft dodging was quite common in Brazil even before it entered into World War II, but the problem became much worse in 1943 as the army tried to recruit men for the expeditionary force. Of those men that did present themselves when drafted, moreover, over 40 percent were declared medically unfit to serve. This was a problem for troops who had been drafted from other parts of the Brazilian army, as well as for new recruits.[11]

The question of who would lead the Brazilian force was the subject of much debate and rumor. Dutra suggested that he should personally lead the force, and indeed had publicly expressed this point during his meetings in Washington in August 1943. President Vargas, however, turned down Dutra's offer. According to British sources, the gossip in Rio was that Vargas preferred to keep his long-serving minister of war under his watchful eye in case the Brazilian army was tempted to, as the British put it, "emulate the performance of their neighbors [Argentina] to the south."[12] Dutra's only consolation was that the candidate suggested by his longtime political rival, Osvaldo Aranha, was also rejected for the role.[13] Yet when Dutra talked to his generals about who else might lead the force, he discovered that only one of his senior officers was willing to accept the challenge. Thus it was that General João Baptista Masarenham de Morais found himself in charge of the Brazilian military excursion to Europe.[14]

The organization and training of the force was beset by problems from the start. President Vargas's stipulation that he would send troops to Europe on the condition that the United States would supply them with arms proved to be problematic for the US military, which blocked the agreed supply of arms to the troops in Brazil. The United States blamed its failure to deliver the weapons on a shipping shortage.

The lack of weapons had an immediate and severe effect on the troops' training. General Masarenham de Morais eventually agreed that his units would receive only basic training in Brazil,[15] and they would not be equipped at all until they reached the war zone. Basic training was to be completed by mid-March 1944, at which point the Brazilian authorities would notify the US joint chiefs of staff. The force would then be moved to Europe where it would receive further training and be fully equipped by the United States.[16] All of this would take time; in December 1943, the war department in Washington predicted that the Brazilian force would not be ready for deployment overseas until May or July 1944 at the earliest.[17]

While Washington was less than sanguine about the prospects for the Brazilian troops, Rio was eager to see them deployed as soon—and as widely—as possible. In the first part of 1944, Brazilian officers were sent to the United States for training, and a number of senior officers visited North Africa to see for themselves how the US army operated in combat. They were obviously anxious to enter the fray; both the United States and the British noted that the Brazilian military authorities appeared eager to get involved in the conflict as soon as possible.[18] From the Brazilians' perspective, time was running out, and there was a very real possibility that the war might end before they would be able to make a meaningful contribution to the Allied war effort. Still, it was proving difficult for the Americans to assess just when the FEB would be ready to depart Brazil.[19] And when it did, US military planners intended to effectively sideline these untrained and—in American eyes, at least—poorly disciplined troops.

One Brazilian found it almost impossible to contain his criticism of the organization and planning of the expeditionary force: the chief of staff, General Góes Monteiro.[20] And Góes Monteiro's relationship with the minister of war, Dutra, deteriorated as the two men locked horns over these issues. Góes Monteiro wanted a more effective force, one that was better armed. As Góes Monteiro's public criticisms of the organization of the expeditionary force increased, Dutra started to build up the profile of other generals as possible replacements for the chief of staff. The fact that Góes Monteiro maintained a good relationship with Aranha despite their political differences did not help the general's case with Dutra, who continued to be the archrival of the minister of foreign affairs. This slow breakdown of the working relationship between Góes Monteiro and Dutra boded ill for the Estado Novo, as the two men had arguably done the most to help create the regime.

In December 1943, a tired and increasingly marginalized Góes Monteiro resigned as chief of staff. His career, however, was far from over, and Góes Monteiro would return to the spotlight briefly as minister of war in August 1945. Yet the immediate impact of his resignation was enormous. The alliance Dutra had enjoyed with Góes Monteiro was shattered, and this development appeared to initially strengthen the hand of President Vargas over the armed forces. But Dutra remained an extremely powerful figure and the US perception of the minister of war remained unfavorable, with US officials still highlighting his alleged pro-Nazi bias and his preference for acquiring arms from Germany over the United States. His

continued presence in talks and negotiations increased the suspicion of the
US army and made it wary of equipping the Brazilian forces.

While the Brazilian military leadership was preoccupied with the formation and training of the FEB, President Vargas was equally focused on
the domestic political consequences of World War II for his regime. The
Brazilian military was growing stronger, and Vargas was cognizant of
the potential threat. In a speech commemorating the sixth anniversary of the
establishment of the Estado Novo on November 10, 1944, the president
emphasized the themes of national unity and internal stability, which he
saw as vital for the Brazilian war effort. His speech at the inauguration of
the new military arsenal in Rio de Janeiro was something of a reminder
to opponents to not make trouble. Vargas warned:

> In these difficult circumstances, when we require above all the internal
> stability to assure us our merited place among the victorious nations, it
> would be an error and a crime to agitate the country. For this very reason
> the government will not hesitate to repress any attempts at useless distur-
> bance. This is the hour for unity and to maintain it we shall not hesitate
> to use energetic means.[21]

At the end of the speech, Vargas offered hope for those Brazilians who
longed for democracy, while also challenging those who saw little future
for the Estado Novo in the postwar period. "When the war is over,"
he assured them, "in an atmosphere of peace and order and with the
maximum guarantees of liberty of opinion, we will readjust the political
structure of the nation, which will be done by ample consultation with
the Brazilian people."[22] What such "readjustments" might entail, Vargas
didn't say—but the mere mention of the potential for political change
suggested that Vargas would try to steer his government into line with
the changing tides of public opinion in Brazil, rather than attempting to
roll right over them.

Later on that same day, Vargas gave a second address, this one at the
inauguration of the new ministry of finance in Rio de Janeiro—an office
building that, the US embassy reported, was the finest in South America.[23]
President Vargas devoted much of his second speech to the theme of the
spiraling cost of living in Brazil. He announced wage increases for all
classes, including the armed forces, and concluded with an appeal for

Brazilians from all walks of life to make a contribution to the war effort. Tellingly, he again promised political reform once the war had been won.[24]

Brazilians' reaction to Vargas's two speeches was generally very positive. Even his critics appeared resigned to letting him lead the war effort free from major political disturbance. As the Americans noted, "this reflects a generalized sentiment that internal political disturbance would be disastrous for the country at this time and that, therefore, Vargas should be unmolested until the war is over."[25] Yet by mooting the possibility of political changes in the Estado Novo, Vargas was also attempting to secure his position in the aftermath of the war, when his political foes would surely not grant him such a reprieve.

Vargas was attempting to buy time. He understood that Brazil's participation in the war would lead to demands for internal political reform and a return to democratic politics. He could argue that this was not the time for such a debate, but he knew he could not avoid it indefinitely. As Brazil committed its young men to the war effort, popular pressure on Vargas grew, and his proclamations about political reform—which essentially amounted to promises for a return to democracy in the postwar era—were a sign that Vargas was willing to meet the Brazilian people halfway.

Yet time was exactly what Vargas did not have. While Vargas attempted to shore up his political position within Brazil with wage increases and promises of reform, and while he was dealing with the training and deployment of the expeditionary force, Brazil's usefulness to the United States was declining almost by the day. By the end of 1944, the United States no longer needed Brazil's help with a potential occupation of the Portuguese islands, the Azores. Following complex and, at times, difficult negotiations between the British ambassador in Lisbon and Portuguese leader António de Oliveira Salazar, the Allies reached a deal with Portugal; Salazar granted the British access to the air bases on the Azores. The agreement, which was signed on August 18, allowed the British to use the strategically important islands as a supply depot, as a base for aircraft in the ongoing battle against submarines in the Atlantic, and as a support station for a planned Allied invasion of the European mainland.[26]

During the final quarter of 1943 the US diplomat George Kennan worked out an arrangement with Salazar for the US military to use the islands, as well. Once the United States secured access to the islands, the air bases became the focus of the major US military buildup in preparation for the Allied invasion of mainland Europe. With the Allies encamped on the Azores, there was no need for Brazil to play any role in the defense of the islands. The Brazilians' hesitation to get involved in the Azores, and Salazar's reluctance to sanction any role for Portugal's old colony in the defense of the islands, had made Brazil even less strategically valuable to the United States.

The United States still had some use for Brazil on this front, however. At the end of 1943, the United States asked Brazil to influence Salazar to cease supplying wolfram to Germany. Wolfram was a vital component in the German armaments industry, and Portugal was a major source of the metal for the Germans. In a letter to the foreign minister on September 20, 1943, the Americans explained the importance of restricting exports of wolfram to Germany:

> The importance of wolfram, a ferroalloy used in the manufacture of steel, lies in its value, as a supply item to the United Nations and as a strategic material to the Axis. According to reliable figures, German wolfram requirements for 1943 have been reduced to 5,800 tons under stringent conservation methods. This includes the German need of wolfram in the manufacture of tungsten carbide cores. To meet even the greatly reduced consumption, Germany must rely upon her purchases in the Iberian Peninsula. . . . If German acquisitions in Portugal can be kept to a minimum there is little doubt that German reserves may be completely exhausted at the end of the year and that German production of armor-piercing ammunition will be very seriously impeded.[27]

Because the metal was so vital to the Nazi war effort, it was equally vital that the Allies prevent more of it from reaching Germany. Salazar, however, was refusing to comply with Allied demands to cut the sale of wolfram to Germany. In his negotiations with Ronald Campbell in Lisbon, Salazar had adopted the line that if he refused to sell the wolfram to the Germans, they might come and take it anyway.

The United States hoped that, given Brazil's long history with Portugal, Rio might succeed where Washington failed. The Americans asked Aranha if he was willing to have the Brazilian ambassador in Lisbon raise the matter with Salazar.[28] Aranha quickly agreed, and for much of the early part of 1944, Brazil pressured Salazar to stop sales of wolfram to

Germany.[29] As one Brazilian suggested, "Our soldiers could be killed in action by guns and shells made and manufactured using Portuguese wolfram." Salazar paid little attention to the Brazilian protests, however, and continued to sell wolfram to Germany right up until the eve of D-Day.[30] Yet the perception that Brazil was doing something to help the Allied cause proved to be more important than its failure to impact Salazar's decision making.[31]

Aranha's efforts to get Salazar on board with the Allied cause notwithstanding, the Americans were finding it increasingly difficult to deal with the minister of foreign affairs. Caffery noted that since Brazil had entered the war, Aranha had become "harder and harder to deal with over economic matters."[32] Aranha spent long days working in the Itamaraty Palace, ignoring its beautifully maintained gardens and swimming pool as he attempted to steer Brazil through the war while also extracting as much from the Allies as he could. At night, Aranha often hosted formal dinners for foreign diplomats and leaders. His energy levels were impressive—but perhaps due to the hectic pace of his work, he was missing important strategic trends both inside and outside of Brazil.

At the end of 1943, Aranha remained fully committed to his cherished policy of full partnership with the United States. His political antennae told him that he was still the Brazilian leader with whom the United States most preferred doing business, which surely helped to fortify his commitment to the Americans. And as far as Aranha was concerned, there were only two points of dispute between his nation and the United States. The first was the fact that the United States had tried to stop Brazil from selling rubber to Chile the previous year, which had ruffled feathers in Rio.[33] Aranha had accused the United States of treating Brazil like a colony instead of an equal partner. The moment had passed, but to some extent Aranha had once more overplayed his hand with the Americans. In retrospect, the United States's intervention in the proposed sale should have served as a wake-up call to the minister of foreign affairs, and an indication of the true nature of the relationship between Brazil and the United States. It did not. Aranha continued to hope for a full partnership with the United States once Brazil committed its armed forces to the battle in Europe.

The second bone of contention between Brazil and the United States had to do with something called "the proclaimed list"—essentially a blacklist that aimed to prevent foreign nationals from trading with the Axis powers by cutting off their economic ties with the United States if they did so. The proclaimed list was first introduced in July 1941 as part of the program of economic warfare against individuals and companies that were based outside of the combatant nations, but that were deemed to be pro-Axis.[34] US diplomats and intelligence agencies were tasked with compiling the proclaimed list, and the implications of being named on the list were huge: people and corporations on it were prohibited from doing business with firms or individuals in the United States. Brazil, with its large German, Italian, and Japanese immigrant populations, was hit hard by the proclaimed list. And given the dearth of reliable intelligence, a number of Brazilian individuals and companies that were operating legitimately nevertheless found themselves on the list.

Aranha never liked the idea of the proclaimed list, and said on more than one occasion that he stood shoulder-to-shoulder with the United States on every issue except this one. Indeed, Aranha saw the proclaimed list as a means for the United States to replace Brazilian-owned companies with British or American ones.[35] He frequently made this argument to Caffery, pointing out that most of the 265 Brazilian companies originally placed on the blacklist were either Brazilian-owned or had operated in the country for an extended period of time, so could not possibly be construed as being pro-Axis.[36] But Caffery proved unreceptive to Aranha's argument, as did the rest of the US government. The US economic warfare teams could point to evidence for their suspicions. And though this evidence was often incomplete or had been gathered from locals who had past business dealings with the companies they ratted out to the United States, and who were thus often deeply biased, the United States held firm to the blacklist.

Curiously, while Aranha was deeply suspicious of the Allies' motives for putting together the proclaimed list, these feelings did not affect his thinking about trade between Brazil and the United States and Great Britain more generally. Perhaps they should have, for the proclaimed list was a strong indication that neither country was truly interested in an equitable partnership with Brazil. Washington viewed trade with Brazil as an element of the Good Neighbor Program, but it also regarded it as a means of deepening Brazilian dependence on the United States.

While Aranha continued his attempts to develop Brazil's alliance with the United States, and while the training program for the FEB escalated,

President Vargas was upping his own performance as well. In the months prior to his departure for the summer retreat at Petrópolis in January 1944, the president had been busy signing a huge number of decrees intended to improve the Brazilian economy. He was also trying to get Brazilians to see the silver lining of their wartime hardships. While food and fuel short-ages were a direct result of the war, Vargas talked up the positive effects the conflict was having on Brazil, namely, the fact that its alliance with the United States was allowing Brazil to initiate numerous public works programs, slowly improving the country's transportation infrastructure that was beginning to link the different regions of Brazil together.

As Vargas headed up the road to his summer retreat in January, he planned to give a great deal of thought to his country's political future, as well. The vast majority of Brazilians were now demanding democratic reforms once the war was over. The major question confronting Vargas was how far he should—or indeed could—go in promising this type of political change. But given that the impending departure of many young Brazilians for the war zone was emboldening Brazilians to demand more from their government in return for their sacrifices, Vargas considered it imprudent to wait much longer to give Brazilians an answer. He would need to make a declaration of his intentions prior to the departure of the soldiers, which was still on track to fall in the middle of 1944.

## 15

# THE PROMISE

O N THE SWELTERING SUMMER EVENING OF JANUARY 28, 1944, a huge crowd gathered in front of the Municipal Theater in downtown Rio. Large posters of the leaders of the nascent United Nations hung from the theater's balconies: black and white images of President Vargas, President Roosevelt, Winston Churchill, and, for first time, Joseph Stalin. As the sun sank behind the neighboring buildings, the shadows lengthened and the temperature cooled. Powerful backlights illuminated the building, throwing into dramatic relief its impressive, European-styled façade. On Praça Floriano square below, a noisy crowd—the local press reported there were one hundred thousand people—contented itself by singing patriotic songs.[1] The event in which they were participating had been organized by the Liga de Defesa Nacional, Brazil's government-sponsored civilian-defense league, to commemorate the second anniversary of Brazil's breaking of ties with Germany and Italy. These men, women, and children had come out to show their support for the ongoing war effort and for the leaders who were directing it.

The main speaker at the event was Osvaldo Aranha, the man who had made the dramatic announcement about Brazil's new foreign policy two years earlier. Now, addressing his countrymen, Aranha recalled one of the main reasons for Brazil's decision to break relations with Germany and Italy, calling on Brazilians to continue its "battle with the fifth column." He reminded them, too, that "Brazil must strengthen even further its ties with the United Nations, and our friendship with the United States is indestructible."[2] The speech told Cariocas nothing they didn't already know, but they received it well nonetheless, and sang the national anthem as the event drew to a close.

The popular outpouring of support on the evening of January 28 boded well for Brazil's next move in the war: its commitment of troops to the ongoing struggle in Europe. On the home front, however, the Brazilian people were finding themselves under more and more stress as the war dragged on. Although Carnaval, the most important party of the year in Brazil, took place as usual at the end of February that year, it was one of the quietest on record.[3] The local authorities withheld all funding for popular festivities and the chief of police in Rio warned that "any Axis subjects found on the street or in public places of entertainment will be arrested."[4] Warnings to this effect were also posted in the local press.[5]

As Cariocas got back to work following Carnaval, many of them grappled with drastic increases in the cost of living. The situation had worsened considerably during the first part of 1944 and now threatened to destabilize the Vargas administration, as the US embassy noted in a report to the secretary of state:

The grumblings and discontent about food shortages and high prices are now so general that unless prompt and effective action is taken to alleviate the condition of the laboring classes, it may assume proportions where dissatisfaction with the government could bring on a grave political crisis for President Vargas. The endless queues, which one sees day after day in front of the butcher's shops [and] milk distribution depots, are a source of constant irritation. Housewives and servants spend hours daily standing in line, and criticism of President Vargas and the government is so widespread that it is affecting his popularity with the masses.[6]

The rising cost of living was due to a host of factors. The salary increases that President Vargas announced in November of the previous year had all but been wiped out by inflation. Profiteering and corruption among government officials, as well as structural problems such as the lack of a modern transportation system and shortages of fuel, had all been combining to drive up prices, putting the pinch on ordinary Brazilians and increasing the risk of political unrest within the country.[7]

At first, President Vargas failed to note the seriousness of the situation. Only in March 1944 did he promise to take measures to counteract the increases. More specific promises were made to root out corruption and punish anyone caught excessively profiteering. With the country at war and so many Brazilians making sacrifices, Vargas warned, such selfishness and criminality would not be tolerated.

After returning to Rio from his summer retreat, Vargas sought other ways to defuse popular discontent. He attempted to improve the civilian food supply, particularly the shortages of meat and milk. He also devised a plan to mollify Brazilians who aspired for political change.

During his summer stay in Petrópolis, after holding meetings with Aranha and other ministers at his retreat, Vargas concluded that the Estado Novo could not survive in the postwar era. Given the populist demands for changes that the war had created, it was clear that the Brazilian political system needed significant reforming. Now, after returning from the mountains to find Rio's populace seething over the worsening domestic situation, Vargas was prepared to make a far-reaching statement to the Brazilian people about the country's political future.

The administration warned international journalists and newswire organizations in Rio that the president would make a major speech on Brazil's future during April 1944. The timing of the speech was important; the first Brazilian soldiers were almost ready to embark for Europe, and President Vargas had publicly proclaimed that he would make his announcement about Brazil's future before the Força Expedicionária Brasileira left the country's shores. The FEB's training had been going smoothly, and the US joint chiefs of staff had identified Italy as the FEB's final destination, confirming that the force would receive further training and equipment once it arrived in Europe. Given the troops' progress, May looked like the most likely month for their departure, so Vargas had to hurry.

President Vargas gave his much-anticipated speech on April 15, 1944, at the opening ceremony for a new building for the Brazilian press association. Although his remarks were lengthy, he spoke with passion and authority, increasing the intensity of his rhetoric as he reached his conclusion. Only then did Vargas deliver the lines he knew the media would highlight in the following day's newspapers:

With reference to our external situation, although there is still much fighting to do, it is not to avoid defeat but to obtain a complete victory and effectively reconstruct the world on a more humane and just basis, respecting the sovereignty of all nations, large or small, militarily weak or strong. Each nation should be able to organize itself according to its own desires, adequately expressed in accordance with its historical traditions and the needs of its autonomous existence. We are now about to enter into the struggle more actively by sending to the battlefront our young and brave soldiers alongside of our glorious fighting allies. This implies added responsibilities, which means the acceptance of additional restrictions in our usual comforts and a courageous disposition to confront new sacrifices. We have maintained exemplary internal conduct, but the hour calls for even greater union among us, putting transitory differences and selfish preoccupations aside. When the future of the country and the national destiny is at stake, we must not be occupied with sterile agitations and questions of form. Any act or word that casts doubt on our major objectives is disguised fifth columism. What is of greatest importance is winning the war, and that is our prime objective. When again we enjoy the benefits of peace, we shall complete the development of our various institutions, which are not as yet functioning. The people will then by means of the most ample and free methods without intimidation of any kind manifest themselves democratically and select their own rulers and representatives in an atmosphere of law and order.[8]

Informed ahead of time of the speech's importance, the United States had expected something of a state of the union address, but what Vargas delivered was much more unusual.[9] By directly alluding to the possibility of democratic elections in postwar Brazil, he had given the growing number of pro-reform Brazilians a reason to hope, and had signaled a momentous and imminent change in the country's political structure. While Vargas had given previous indications of a return to democratic politics after the war, this speech represented the most direct commitment he made to such a political transformation.

The British ambassador said, "The speech was listened to with apathy, but the final sentences brought terrific cheering that lasted for at least two minutes."[10] The local press, like Vargas's audience, were hugely enthusiastic about the address. Front-page headlines included, "President Vargas Promises Elections After the War," "The Free Vote of the Citizen," and "Foundation of Democracy in the Thought of President Vargas."[11] The *New York Times* reported the speech as part of a detailed article on Brazil on July 13, 1944, titled "US Aid to Brazil Spurs Her Advance." The *New*

*York Times* correspondent, Foster Hailey, was a little more cautious than the local press in assessing Vargas's promise, writing, "There is no opposition party, but there is open criticism of the government in every coffee shop. President Vargas, for whose tenure the Brazilians coined the phrase *continuismo*, meaning an intent to continue in office, has made a qualified promise that after the war free elections will be held."[12]

"A qualified promise" turned out to be a relatively accurate assessment of Vargas's closing remarks in the speech. The president's local critics suggested that he had little time for democratic politics, and that his promise of free elections at the end of the war was simply a political ploy to distract the public's attention from—and defuse their dissatisfaction with—increases in the cost of living.[13] Indeed, according to the *New York Times,* the real effect Vargas's speech had was "taking out whatever wind the sails of his active political opponents may have accumulated lately."[14] As the US embassy in Rio warned, however, "the food situation is not improving to any appreciable level, and here, as elsewhere, when bellies are empty, unrest is always latent."[15]

Back in Washington, however, President Vargas's promise was widely lauded. In an article in the *Washington Post,* Sumner Welles wrote:

> Thus the solemn assurance has now been given to the people of Brazil that they will once more enjoy popular self-government. If one may venture in this uncertain world to make a prediction, I would prophesy that in the years after the end of the present war the two nations that would most swiftly forge ahead because of the capacity of their people, because of their vast natural resources, and because of their entrance upon a period of rapid industrial expansion would be Brazil and the Soviet Union.[16]

By so favorably comparing Brazil's economic and geopolitical potential with that of the Soviet Union, Welles was elevating a former tropical backwater to the ranks of the world's great superpowers. It was, by any measure, a remarkable statement—and one that, if not entirely accurate in the short term, would prove prescient in the long run.

The British were less sanguine than the Americans about the prospects for Brazilian democracy. For some time before and after Sumner Welles's tribute in the *Washington Post,* the British argued that the US press had a tendency to "laud all things Brazilian just as it decries all that comes out of Argentina."[17] Welles and the Americans, they felt, were far too easily taken in by President Vargas, whose comments—according to the British, at least—represented little more than an attempt to distract Brazilians from the food shortages and price increases still racking their country.[18] As the British embassy in Rio warned Foreign Secretary Anthony Eden, "The Brazilians, with all their love for bestowing and receiving flattery, are no fools and in the long run are more likely to be influenced by the circumstances of the day rather than by memories of expressions of praise, however highly placed their authors may be."[19]

Whatever their attitude toward Vargas's speech, however, the British were looking toward the postwar relationship with Brazil for the greater part of 1944, and anticipating the potentially lucrative trade deals they might strike with Brazil after the war. Part of this, they knew, was dependent on a loosening of US-Brazilian ties, but that was beginning to look like a distinct possibility. London sensed that, despite Welles's warm words, elements of the Vargas regime were getting cold feet about Brazil's alliance with the United States, and were looking at Great Britain as a counterbalance to US influence in their country.[20]

Whatever misgivings certain Brazilian officials might have harbored about the United States, one American, at least, continued to enjoy high standing in Rio: Sumner Welles. Although Welles had left Rio at the start of February 1942 and had been forced to resign as secretary of state in the autumn of 1943, his presence was still felt in Latin America. He was, after all, the main architect of the original Good Neighbor Program, and he continued to laud the US policy of developing closer ties with South America. As World War II progressed toward its final phases—and as Brazilian troops prepared to enter the battle—his resounding support of the Vargas administration came to be much missed in Rio.

In June 1944, the same month as the D-Day landings in Normandy, the first squadron of the FEB was ready to leave for Italy. On June 4, the Allies liberated Rome, but German forces were still well dug in across the north of Italy and were proving very difficult to dislodge. The topography of Italy, its mountains and valleys, suited the defenders, who were disciplined and well organized; many of them were battle-tested veterans of the eastern front. Prior to the departure of the first 5,075 Brazilians on board the US troop ship the *General Mann,* the entire division of twenty-five thousand men who would eventually serve in Italy marched through the streets of central Rio. The soldiers were cheered by the huge number of Cariocas who had turned out for the occasion. It was a simultaneously joyful and somber occasion. The crowd tried its best to lift the spirits of the troops, most of whom were heading overseas for the first time; some of the girls in the crowds threw rice, while the older mothers waved hankies. The sight of the first war-ready troops was slightly unnerving for many Cariocas, and brought the reality of war home in a way that blackouts and shortages of food and fuel had not.

It was, in truth, a less than convincing display of Brazilian military might—the troops were not ready for war. The soldiers appeared poorly equipped. Their uniforms were far from appropriate for the hostile Italian winter: soft hats, thin cotton clothing, and small backpacks barely large enough to carry a packed lunch. The rifles they proudly carried on their left shoulders belonged to the era of the previous world war, and as the division marched, bits of their guns fell off, littering the streets with small fragments of gun butts and even whole barrels. Few armies in World War II had been sent into a war zone so ill equipped and badly trained. The US promise to train and equip the force once it reached its destination was vital.

The choice of Italy as the destination for the FEB had been very last minute. The United States originally planned to send them to North Africa, but the Allies' rapid victories in that region meant a new front had to be found. There had been some disagreement between senior US and British officers as to where the FEB should be located. The British wanted nothing to do with the FEB, arguing that it would get in the way of combat operations. The British viewed the force as little more than an American ruse, one intended to show that the United States enjoyed widespread support in South America. Nonetheless, the United States had promised President Vargas that the FEB would be involved in combat operations and that its members would receive the best training and equipment that the United States had to offer—and this promise eventually trumped British objections to Brazil's participation.

The farewell parade through Rio climaxed with an emotional address by President Vargas, who waved two little Brazilian flags as the parade marched past his podium. The address was pure Brazilian theater, soulful and passionate, but eschewing any mention of the difficult realities confronting the nation. Vargas concluded his relatively short speech by saying:

The hour has come for vengeance against those who in 1942 used pirate ships barbarously to massacre Brazilian lives. Our army, which has covered itself with honors in memorable deeds, will demonstrate its new arms and its traditional bravery on the battlefields of Europe. Everything has been done to make sure the FEB lacks for nothing. Your wives, mothers, sweethearts, and children await your return. . . . The [Brazilian] nation is proud of your courage and dedication. May God's blessings accompany you, as our spirits and hearts accompany you until you return with victory.[21]

The troops and their families could not have asked for a more dramatic send-off, even if Vargas's claim that they had everything they might need for the task ahead surely rang hollow for the soldiers whose weapons were literally falling apart in their hands.

On the evening of June 30, 1944, Vargas went aboard the *General Mann* to address the troops one last time. Using the captain's radio, the president wished the 5,075 Brazilian troops on the ship the best of luck, while Dutra—who had accompanied Vargas on board—contented himself by shaking the hands of a few of the soldiers.

Two days later, the men finally set off for Europe. At 5:30 A.M. on Sunday, July 2, 1944, the *General Mann* raised its anchor and, under the cover of darkness, quietly slipped out of the harbor in Rio and headed toward the open ocean. The change of destination from Algiers to Naples had caused some organizational problems, and logistically the Brazilians already seemed in over their heads, as well; US observers aboard the *General Mann* noted that the first meal on board took five to six hours to serve.[22] But far more severe problems lay ahead; although not as infested as it had been during the height of the Battle of the Atlantic, the high seas were still teeming with German U-boats, any one of which would have delighted in sending the *General Mann* and everyone on board to the bottom of the ocean.

Luckily, the trip progressed smoothly—that is, until the very end. On July 6 the troop ship crossed the equator and, on July 13, 1944, its crew spotted the Strait of Gibraltar. But as the *General Mann* sailed through the strait, the ship's radio picked up a broadcast by the BBC that informed listeners of the ship's dispatch and progress. Needless to say, nobody on board was impressed by Great Britain's manifest lack of concern for their security.

At long last, on Sunday, July 16, the *General Mann* reached Naples, where the troops immediately disembarked to the sounds of a US military band. Back in Rio, there was widespread relief that the men had made it safely across the ocean, successfully avoiding the German U-boat menace.

The arrival of the first division of Brazilian troops in Italy represented a triumph for President Vargas. Not only were Brazilian troops securing their country a greater role in the war (and thus in the postwar world), but they were also receiving free training from the United States—experience that would serve Brazil well in its long standoff with its Latin American rival, Argentina. Indeed, as the division started its intensive training program, the Brazilian air force was undergoing training of its own back in Brazil. Part of the air force would shortly follow the FEB to Italy, and at least one of its pilots had the blood of the Estado Novo coursing through his veins. Among the men training with US officers was President Vargas's oldest son, Lieutenant Lutero Vargas. At the start of October 1944, around four hundred members of the Brazilian air force were scheduled to head to Italy. Around the same time, the second group of Brazilian soldiers were scheduled to land there.

Training for the Brazilian troops, however, did not go according to plan. The equipment the United States had promised was slow to arrive, so the force had to train with their inadequate Brazilian equipment. Moreover, the soldiers found the US army trainers' methods very different from what they had experienced back in Brazil. The US trainers were tough and unsparing, and intercepted letters from Brazilian soldiers back to their loved ones in Brazil were full of complaints. The US army, for its part, was finding it hard to prepare the Brazilians for battle. The Americans praised the attitudes of both the Brazilian officers and their men, but reported that their enthusiasm often got the better of them. Another problem appeared to be the Brazilians' inability to launch coordinated attacks using artillery support. Following an exercise in which the Brazilian artillery gunners opened fire late and inaccurately, General Masarenham de Morais was forced to admit to the American trainers, "Punctuality and accuracy are not natural characteristics of the Brazilians."[23]

Still, the Brazilian soldiers' spirits were high as they joined part of the US Fifth Army and prepared for their first taste of combat against the Germans. They even devised a slogan for themselves: *a cobra vai fumar,* a common Portuguese idiom meaning, literally, "smoking snakes," but whose

English analog might be "when pigs fly." It had taken so long for the Allies to agree to the participation of the FEB, and then for the men to be recruited and trained, that many Brazilians believed it would never become a reality—hence the FEB's motto. When the soldiers of the FEB went into the battle, they proudly wore their newly created divisional shoulder patch, which showed a snake smoking a pipe. The irony of the logo may have been lost on the soldiers' US commanders in Italy, but it was not lost on their countrymen back in Rio.

The Americans were, by this time, far less cheery than the Brazilians. Brazil's original plan of sending one hundred thousand men to fight in the war had proven overly optimistic; Rio had since reduced its troop commitment to twenty-five thousand. The United States was growing tired of what it viewed as Brazilian posturing and hesitation; privately, US military commanders feared that the Brazilians would prove to be more of a burden than an asset in any active theater of the war, and they became more committed than ever to finding a quiet spot for the Brazilians to wait out the war while the other Allied troops did their work.

In truth, Vargas was not reneging on his commitment as much as the United States thought. He was fully behind the expeditionary force. From the outset, he had wanted the FEB to be drawn from across Brazil. It may not have occurred to him that drawing the FEB from across Brazil would result in such diversity that the officers and soldiers had little in common with one another.

A recruitment drive had failed to dredge up additional volunteers for the FEB, and so Vargas had turned to conscription. This exposed deep divisions within the country, and belied the myth that all Brazilians were proud to participate in the conflict. Of the young men initially called up for service, many managed to avoid the draft by producing medical reports of back trouble, poor vision, and the like. While many Brazilians cheered the departing troops, the truth was that the idea of sending the force had never been wildly popular among the Brazilian people, and especially not among those who had good lives they were leaving behind; in rich downtown Rio de Janeiro, for example, few young men had any appetite for risking their lives in a war on the other side of the ocean. In a sense, Vargas got his wish; the FEB was diverse. Those Brazilians who finally did make the trip to Italy included firemen, electricians, and historians, as well as a group of nurses.

Officials in the huge ministry of war building on Avenida President Vargas carefully tracked the FEB's progress in Italy, and the early reports were not good. It was immediately clear that US attempts to send the Brazilians to a relatively quiet and pacified front had hugely misfired. The fighting in Italy in late 1944 and early 1945 was some of the most intense of the entire war. Allied attempts to uproot the Germans during the end of autumn 1944 had not fully succeeded; as a result, the FEB found itself taking part in several key battles, including the Battle of Monte Castello, the outcome of which was crucial to securing a German surrender in Italy.

The hardships experienced by the Brazilian troops were myriad. Correspondence from soldiers at the front to their families in Brazil was routinely opened, and it revealed tensions between the Brazilian and US soldiers. To some extent, this was a product of the dissonance between the intensive and rigorous training methods that were a part of the US army manual and US military habits and the Brazilian training methods and protocols; the Brazilians were used to the more laid-back methods that had characterized much of their army service in Brazil. But the experience of being in the field quickly took a toll on the men, as well. Although there was little fighting during the harsh Italian winter, FEB members reported that some soldiers suffered frostbite during patrols. They were all unfamiliar with the snow and cold, which penetrated even their new, US-sponsored winter uniforms.

The Americans, at least, found some cause to stop complaining. US accounts of the fighting involving Brazilian forces during September and October 1944 record that the Brazilians fought with bravery and cooperated well with the US army. There were instances of small advances made by the FEB, and the Brazilian forces even captured some German prisoners of war. In a typical account of the FEB's operations in September 1944, the US army said, "During the first week of the fighting the FEB showed splendid advances all along the front. The favorable reports of the combat team were in no small part due to the tremendous activity of the Brazilian artillery personnel."[24]

In these first weeks of action, the FEB did help to push the Allied lines forward, but their advances were limited due to both the tough resistance of the Germans and the arrival of autumn rains followed by the onset of winter, which brought early snowfall to the region. There were still the familiar problems, along with these new ones. Since the bulk of the Brazilians' training did not take place until they arrived in Italy, the men who entered the line during the month of September 1944 were.not fully ready for battle.

In late September, the Brazilian minister of war, General Dutra, arrived in Italy to inspect the troops and discuss their progress with senior US officers. If Dutra was still sore at President Vargas's refusal to allow him to personally command the FEB, he did his best not to show it—even though such stoicism was not always easy. On September 26, Dutra and the senior officers of the FEB were the guests of Lieutenant General Mark W. Clark, the commander of the US Fifth Army.[25] During the ceremonies, Dutra watched as General Clark presented Legion of Merit medals on behalf of President Roosevelt to the senior Brazilian commanders. Later, Dutra and his party visited the front line to tour Brazilian positions. Finally, Dutra toured those hospitals to which the Brazilian wounded had been evacuated. US officers noted that the visit of Dutra and other senior Brazilians officers had a positive impact on the morale of the FEB. The result was, as one American put it, that "patrol activities all along the FEB front increased as enthusiastic Brazilians harassed the Germans with everything they had."[26]

Dutra's trip was hailed as a great success. When newsreel footage and photos of his visit to the troops arrived back in Rio, Dutra looked to many of his countrymen like a commander in chief. He was starting to receive more publicity, and was slowly coming into his own—and emerging from the shadows behind President Vargas. The general continued to swear loyalty to the president—at least, for the time being—but he had his own reasons to be discontented. The FEB, while holding its own, was not the success anyone in the Estado Novo had hoped. During his meetings with senior US army officers in Italy, Dutra had been informed of continuing problems between the US and Brazilian armies, much of which was put down to communication problems that plagued the two forces' cooperation, despite the best efforts of their translators. The Americans also warned Dutra that Brazilian casualty figures would sharply rise when the spring offensive got under way in 1945.

For all of the problems with the FEB's dispatch to Italy, and while its deployment had occurred on a much smaller scale than originally planned, President Vargas continued to believe the force represented Brazil's best opportunity to secure its position in the postwar order. In reality, however, the army had been sent into the field too late to achieve the lofty political goals Vargas had set for it. And even if the FEB had arrived a year earlier, it might not have made much of a difference on the Italian front. While the Allies were making progress in northern Europe, the Germans were firmly rooted throughout Italy, where the topography favored defenders over attackers. The Germans occupied the high ground, and the Brazilians and their US allies were in the unenviable position of having to dislodge their enemy with frontal assaults, on foot and uphill.

The FEB was engaged in much fiercer fighting than the United States had intended for it. And during the initial stages of its deployment in Italy, the soldiers in the FEB suffered a much higher rate of casualties than their US counterparts. The United States attributed this to the bravery of the Brazilian men but also to their naiveté. Still, the Allies were making good progress in other European theaters, and it was just a matter of time until the German army was crushed—whether in the hills of Italy, or in the heart of the continent.

Back in Rio, attention was shifting to the postwar period—and President Vargas's political problems were multiplying. During the final months of 1944, he faced growing opposition to his regime from Brazilians who were tired of the economic situation in Brazil; and as news of the Brazilian casualties in Italy trickled back to the country, the pressure for political change only increased. Curiously, at this key juncture, Vargas's political judgment—usually so sound, but in scarce supply following his accident and the death of his son—deserted him altogether. The decisions he made in the months ahead would effectively open the door to enemies both within and outside his regime. And perhaps Vargas's most fatal decision of all was his choice to withdraw support for an old friend: Osvaldo Aranha, the minister of foreign affairs.

16

# A FAREWELL TO ARANHA

On August 22, 1944, Osvaldo Aranha sat hunched over his hand-crafted desk at the Itamaraty Palace, signing one personalized letter after another. All of them were addressed to foreign diplomats in Rio, and all of them reflected on the massive political upheaval that had recently shaken the Brazilian capital.

The past few days had been filled with drama, both in Brazil and overseas, but the previous day had been particularly consequential. On August 21, Allied forces had reached the outskirts of Nazi-occupied Paris, sparking the liberation of the French capital. And that same day, thousands of miles away in Rio, Aranha had resigned as foreign minister of Brazil.

Aranha was tired, angry, and hurt by the events that had led him to resign, and he wanted nothing more than to quietly depart to his farm without further delay.[1] His one last self-imposed duty was to write to the relevant Rio-based Allied ambassadors, in order to try to reassure them and their governments, that his departure from office was caused solely by internal Brazilian political intrigues and did not represent any redirection of his nation's foreign policy.[2]

Aranha regarded many of these ambassadors as personal friends, and though he was trying his best to put on a brave face, the tone of his letters was almost funereal.[3] Several aides were in the room with Aranha as he worked; he barely acknowledged their presence, and nobody spoke for fear of breaking the stony silence.

The downturn in Aranha's fortunes had been swift and, to most, unexpected. Just months earlier he had seemed to be at the height of his power. His year had started with an address to an adoring crowd of his fellow Brazilians in front of the Municipal Theater. Now he found himself ingloriously shunted from the foreign ministry, watching from the sidelines as Brazilian troops prepared to join the fighting in Europe and bring to its culmination his policy of allying Brazil with the United States.[4]

According to British sources in Rio, the catalyst for Aranha's downfall was his support of Brazil's recognition of the Soviet Union and the two countries' exchange of diplomatic representatives. Minister of War Dutra, on the other hand, strongly opposed these decisions. Dutra, after all, had started the anticommunist campaign in Brazil, and had a hard enough time stomaching Brazil's alliance with the United States; strengthening Brazil's relationship with the Soviet Union, the bastion of international socialism, was, for Dutra, simply too much to bear.[5]

In moving Brazil closer to the Soviet Union, Aranha displayed a lapse in his famously razor-sharp judgment. For much of the year, Aranha had pushed for closer ties with the Soviet Union on the grounds that it was a partner in the war against the Axis powers, and that it was likely to play an important role in the postwar order. Aranha did not foresee a potential cold war between the west and the east. Rather, he viewed the Soviet Union as a potential trading partner for Brazil—a nation to be courted, not kept at arm's length.

Yet this misstep was only the tip of the iceberg. The reasons for Aranha's ouster were, in reality, much more complex. Dutra was not the only Brazilian official with whom Aranha had bad blood—and while he had historically been able to rely on President Vargas for support, this time he discovered that nobody had his back.

Aranha's downfall was triggered by what amounted to a power struggle with the chief of police. It was a contest in which President Vargas had, ultimately, chosen not to intervene—essentially abandoning Aranha to his fate.[6] And it was a clash, moreover, in which one could detect the shadowy hand of Dutra, who at last seemed to have succeeded in planting a dagger in his archenemy's back.

Speaking with his British counterpart at a drinks reception at the US embassy on August 23, two days after Aranha's resignation, Jefferson Caffery outlined his understanding of the political undercurrents that had led to Aranha's resignation. The US ambassador spoke in hushed tones, as if he was imparting top secret information (which he was not), pausing from time to time or clearing his throat for dramatic effect. Caffery obviously still took immense pleasure in being privy to knowledge that the British ambassador lacked.

"In recent months," Caffery told the British ambassador conspiratorially, "when I have met with the minister, he has complained that he was more and more being edged out of everything, especially internal affairs, by a group who were determined to get rid of him."[7] When the British ambassador quizzed him about the names of the ministers, Caffery replied, "the minister of war, the president's brother, the minister of labor, and the new chief of police." It was a powerful list of Dutra and his allies in the government, prime among them the police chief, who enjoyed immense national power.[8] The British ambassador may well have rolled his eyes at the mention of Benjamin Vargas—the embassy had for some time characterized the president's brother as being "little more than a high class gangster." Unbeknownst to the British, Caffery had a similar assessment of Benjamin.

Caffery continued, "the matter came to a head last week when [Aranha] was asked to assume office as the vice president of the Society of Friends of America."[9] That society, Caffery explained, was under a cloud of suspicion in Rio and was being investigated, so it was rather surprising that Aranha chose to accept the invitation. On learning that he had done so, the chief of police ordered a search of the organization's premises, and then had the place locked in order to prevent Aranha from being ceremonially installed as its vice president. "The minister of foreign affairs naturally regarded this as a deliberate insult to himself," Caffery noted, "and appealed to the president. The president, however, took the matter lightly and told the minister of foreign affairs to forget about it."[10]

Aranha chose not to forget about the chief of police's slight. He demanded that the meeting at the Society of Friends of America be allowed to go ahead as planned, a demand to which President Vargas was apparently prepared to agree. But Aranha also demanded that Vargas insist on the resignation of the chief of police—and this, the president refused to do.[11]

This was the breaking point. Aranha notified the president that he could no longer continue serving as his minister of foreign affairs. He submitted his resignation on August 21. But Aranha didn't stop there. According to Caffery, Aranha also started telling his friends that "the president has been taken over by fascist elements in the government."[12] Aranha surely understood that making such claims—especially at a time of war—amounted to high treason, and that it would be difficult for anyone, even a close ally of Vargas's, to get away with such treachery. Still, his anger at the chief of police appears to have gotten the better of him, for these comments were only the beginning of a long and bitter smear campaign he began waging against his old friend.

In the days and weeks after he submitted his resignation, Aranha made ever more personal—and painful—attacks against his fellow gaúcho. Caffery later reported to Washington that during the mounting political crisis, Aranha appeared to be baiting President Vargas, who needless to say was displeased when news of his foreign minister's malicious back-biting reached his office. The comments quickly devolved into ad hominem invective; "Ever since Getúlio has been dying his hair he has been gaga" was one remark that Caffery related to his superiors in Washington. "Getúlio has become so conceited that he now believes he is tall and handsome" was another.[13] The truth, as Aranha well knew, was that the president did touch up his hair color a bit, and that he was small and rather portly—especially following his car accident in May 1942. Sniping of this sort was intended to wound Vargas, and it inexorably widened the gulf between the two men.

Aranha's comments were a sign of his deep frustration at breaking with the president and leaving the Itamaraty Palace—but they also reflected his growing anger over Vargas's response to his departure. Like most political events in Brazil at the time, this one unfolded agonizingly slowly, and the period of time between Aranha's offering of his resignation and the president's eventual acceptance of it was anything but short. What perhaps hurt Aranha the most—apart, of course, from Vargas's refusal to support him against the chief of police—was the silence from the Guanabara Palace in the weeks following his letter of resignation. This time, there was no repeat of the political crisis of 1938: Darci Vargas delivered no olive branches to the Aranha family. There were no quiet admonishments that "the two gaúchos should stick together." On the contrary, the silence from the Guanabara Palace was deafening.

While Aranha stewed, the Allies fretted over what this development could mean for the war effort. In explaining Aranha's resignation to his bosses in Washington, Caffery argued that it was a purely Brazilian political affair and had no connection with Brazil's foreign policy orientation.[14] His assessment was based on inside information he had gleaned from several sources—from the letter he had received from Aranha, of course, but also from conversations he had had with Aranha himself.

During the crisis, Aranha naturally discussed developments with Caffery, who took careful note of what the Brazilian told him while also attempting to steer him back onto a stable track—before, that is, it became clear the foreign minister had derailed himself completely. Aranha, after all, had been one of the greatest advocates for the United States within the Estado Novo, and there was no telling how his departure from the regime might affect Brazil's international alignment. Frantically, and with the help of the State Department, Caffery arranged for Aranha to visit Washington to meet with key officials in the Roosevelt administration, including the president. Caffery wagered that by the time Aranha returned to Brazil, the crisis would have blown over and Aranha would be able to continue on in his role as foreign minister.[15] Aranha rejected the offer of a state visit, however, on the grounds that he would be representing a government in which he no longer believed.[16]

Caffery was forced to concede that his efforts to prevent his friend's resignation were not going to work. Behind the closed doors of the US embassy, there was a feeling that, on this occasion, Aranha might have overplayed his hand with President Vargas. Yet as much as they were afraid of what this rupture could mean for US-Brazilian relations, the Americans also remained cautiously optimistic about Brazil's commitment to the Allied cause. Caffery assured the British ambassador, "I do not anticipate any change in [Brazilian] foreign policy as long as the war lasts, since the policy is, in effect, prosecution of the war in cooperation with the United States."[17]

Both Washington and London soon received the reassurance they craved. On September 7, to mark Brazilian Independence Day, President Vargas delivered a speech in Rio de Janeiro pertaining to Brazil's foreign policy. It was clear that the speech was intended largely to reassure the Allies. During the course of his remarks, Vargas said:

The moment is opportune to reaffirm our acts and principles in view of World War II. We engaged in and continue to be engaged in efforts of all sorts—economic, military, and political—to help our Allies with the maximum power and efficiency. And it is not too much to say that our direct intervention in the military sector does not date from the victorious days of 1944. We began with the exclusive furnishing of strategic materials, continued with the equipping and use of maritime and air bases, developed into the arduous service of escort duty and defense of the convoys, and culminated with the incorporation of the expeditionary force into the glorious armies, which are fighting for the liberation of Europe.[18]

Having thus recapped Brazil's contributions to the war effort, Vargas went on to promise Brazilian support for the United States in the transition to the postwar era. He avowed:

> We are rigorously and enthusiastically fulfilling our commitments, and, conscious of our responsibilities, we will carry on with our aid in the war and our diplomatic collaboration necessary for the adjustments of peace.[19]

Vargas's speech did the trick. The Americans were no longer worried that Aranha's resignation signaled any sort of immediate change in Brazilian policy, although they continued to feel that it might set back their relations with Brazil in the long run. Caffery sensed that Brazil was increasingly looking to the future, and that Aranha's departure represented the starting gunshot in the struggle for the nation's postwar soul.

For his part, Dutra emerged from the crisis with his authority intact and even strengthened. He was far too clever to allow himself to be seen as the political assassin; the chief villains were regarded to be the chief of police and Benjamin Vargas. With the FEB going into action in Italy, Dutra's visit to the Italian front had put him in the news on a regular basis. Usually dour and poker-faced, the minister of war now allowed himself an occasional smile. He was slowly, and in a highly calculated manner, edging toward the center of the stage.

From Dutra's perspective, Aranha's departure caused just one complication: it had brought General Góes Monteiro back to Rio de Janeiro. After the chief of staff's falling out with Dutra and subsequent resignation, Aranha had invited Góes Monteiro to become a special ambassador to the Emergency Advisory Committee for Political Defense of the Americas. Góes Monteiro had been ensconced in Montevideo, Uruguay—where the committee was headquartered—ever since. And given the favor Aranha had shown him, it was entirely possible that Góes Monteiro would throw his support behind the fallen foreign minister.

One of the letters that Aranha had signed on August 22 had been addressed to Góes Monteiro. When the letter arrived in Montevideo,

Góes Monteiro announced his intention to resign as well. President Vargas hurriedly cabled Montevideo and demanded that the former chief of staff return immediately to Rio for consultations. The prospect of Góes Monteiro joining the opposition with Aranha was something the president wished to avoid at all costs.

Góes Monteiro's allegiance to the Brazilian military, it seems, trumped his allegiance to Aranha; once he returned to Rio, he sought out Aranha's archrival Dutra in order to update him on the sentiments of the Brazilian officer corps. As Góes Monteiro had made his way by train from Montevideo to Rio, he had met with—and taken the political temperature of—senior officers in the Brazilian armed forces stationed in the country's southern states. Now back in Rio, Góes Monteiro explained to Dutra that the generals were in favor of democratic reform, and they wanted to end the Estado Novo and replace it with some form of constitutional regime. Dutra suggested that if that were truly the case, it would be prudent to find out what vision President Vargas had for Brazil's political future. Vargas's public assurances about postwar reform had failed to convince either Dutra or Góes Monteiro; Dutra pointed out that he couldn't recall the president discussing the subject in private, let alone making a formal commitment to democratic politics.

As Góes Monteiro was leaving his meeting with Dutra, the minister of war instructed him to "go and find out what are the intentions of the president."[20] So, on November 1, 1944, when Góes Monteiro headed out for his meeting with Vargas, he found himself representing not only his own interests, but also those of the entire Brazilian military.

Working away in his office at the Guanabara Palace as he awaited his former chief of staff, President Vargas understood that Góes Monteiro would, in all likelihood, not be bringing good news. Both men understood that while the war was just starting for Brazil, it would probably be over at some point the following year. The months ahead would be decisive: for the Allies, for Brazil, for the Estado Novo, and for Vargas himself.

When Góes Monteiro arrived at the Guanabara Palace, it quickly became clear to Vargas what the future likely held for the Estado Novo. Góes Monteiro started by telling the president of his trip through southern Brazil and his meetings with senior military officers there and in Rio. Then, in dramatic fashion, he proclaimed, "I am here to end the Estado Novo." President Vargas asked him if Dutra supported this position, to which Góes

Monteiro replied that he did. The two main military mainstays of the Estado Novo were firmly in the camp of the democrats.

Góes Monteiro's declaration was enough to convince President Vargas of what he already felt in his gut: the Estado Novo would not survive the war. Yet the president's own political future was far from clear. Would he accept an orderly transition to some form of democracy? If so, what particular format would he accept? Would Vargas himself try to remain in office? If not, who were his likely successors? Vargas had led Brazil for over a decade, and under his leadership the country had already been transformed from a fractious tropical hinterland to a strong and relatively unified player in global geopolitics. Without him at the helm, what would become of Brazil?

There is little evidence that Vargas had given much thought to any of these issues prior to the end of 1944. He appeared to be locked in the present tense, fixated on his effort to—as the British put it—"get as much bounty as possible out of the United States before the war ended."[21] Now his closest advisors attempted to help him think about his own salvation as well as Brazil's.

The legal architect of the Estado Novo and former minister of justice, Francisco Campos, was a regular visitor to the Guanabara Palace during the months that followed. Meeting with Vargas to advise him on the framing of a new constitution, Campos pulled no punches. "You need to adapt," he told Vargas, "and you will be lost unless you immediately embrace democracy and freedom of the press."[22]

Vargas hesitated, seeming paralyzed by the enormity of the choice confronting him. He refused to formally commit himself, but suggested that Campos write a memorandum outlining his plans for constitutional change. When Campos presented the completed memorandum to the president, its recommendations were radical. He suggested that Vargas either agree to changes to the 1937 constitution that had ushered in the Estado Novo, or that he allow a new constitution to be framed. If Vargas chose the former option, Campos suggested that a constitutional assembly approve the changes.

Vargas promised to show the memorandum to Dutra. He need not have bothered, however; Dutra already knew its contents. When the minister of war reported back to the president, he confirmed that he fully supported Campos's proposals.

Aranha's resignation and the Vargas administration's pivot from present-day planning to strategizing for Brazil's postwar order was the talk of café society in Rio. While the press was still restricted in what it could print, Cariocas were well versed at connecting the dots. Few Brazilians believed that Vargas would cede power without a fight, and fewer still took at face value the pleasant public exchange of letters by Vargas and Aranha on the departure of the foreign minister, in which Vargas thanked his old friend for his help over nearly three decades. Aranha's departure to his farm for an extended period of time added to the intrigue. Few Brazilians thought that they had heard the last of Aranha, but Góes Monteiro's return to local political life added to the sense of uncertainty and reinforced Brazilians' sense that major developments were about to take place in the Guanabara Palace.

With the holiday season approaching, Brazilians also had cause to speculate about whether Carnaval would take place in February 1945. The cost of living increases were getting out of hand. Despite the government's promises that Brazilian workers would eventually become rich from the US aid and Brazil's war-driven economy, it was clear that most Brazilians were worse off than they had been at the start of the war. And though the newspapers were full of stories about the FEB's exploits in Italy, the conflict seemed distant to most Brazilians.

The Vargas regime's popularity had slumped during 1944, and it showed no signs of recovering. The president's opponents circulated rumors that some of his entourage, including his younger brother, Benjamin, were using the wartime economy to exploit the masses and make themselves rich. Alzira did her best to keep certain unsavory people away from her father, but with Aranha gone this task proved harder than ever. The British noted that the "forces of darkness" were coming to dominate the president's circle of friends and advisors. The British ambassador put it this way:

The unscrupulous and evil band of self-enriching satellites which gather inevitably round a dictator were assuring their master that all was well and that he had never been so firmly established. Perhaps deluded by these assurances, perhaps with one eye to the now inevitable victory for the Allies, President Vargas finally made up his mind (with the obvious and necessary reservation that he must remain in power) that the time had come for at least the shadow of democratic representation to be given to the populace.[23]

The role of these internal enemies was complex, but if the British were right, they were stoppering Vargas's ears against the voices of the Brazilian people and assuring him that he would be able to hold on to power as long as he acceded to some of their demands for democratic reforms.

Vargas was indeed falling into the orbit of certain powerful political players in Brazil. He gave no indication that he was listening to the opposition (which he categorized as either communists or fascists), let alone the powerful Catholic Church (which he didn't trust) or the more liberal members of his own regime (whom he believed were still allied with Aranha). The one group he came to rely on during 1945 was the armed forces. Vargas felt that Dutra, for all his careful plotting, remained loyal, and he did not feel that the minister of war represented a potential rival for the presidency.

The British government shared President Vargas's rather limited opinion of Dutra's political abilities. In an attempt to get to know the minister of war better, Winston Churchill had invited Dutra to visit London after he toured the FEB lines in Italy in September 1944. Once in London, Dutra appeared to have given a good account of himself in meetings with British officials, who concluded that he was firmly in the Allied camp. Still, the British described Dutra rather unflatteringly as:

> Small in stature and with no personal appeal. He is a born soldier and a good administrator of limited outlook and intelligence, conservative rather than reactionary in his general political tendencies. He is little acquainted with the rough and tumble of politics and has few personal friends among the politicians. But he is a man of considerable determination and even obstinacy.[24]

While admiring of the minister of war's military abilities, it was clear that the British, at least, did not consider him a threat to Vargas.

President Vargas, in fact, thought of Dutra as the exact opposite of a rival for power. In the back of his mind, Vargas was already considering using Dutra as a sacrificial lamb in any democratic election that might take place in Brazil. Vargas would allow Dutra to run for president, with the expectation that the Brazilian public would reject his candidacy and demand that Vargas put his own name on the ballot. This way, Vargas could promise that he would not run for the presidency, thus depriving the opposition of a rallying point in advance of an election. It was pure Machiavellian politics, but a brand that Vargas was particularly apt at employing against both his political friends and foes alike.

Vargas understood that Dutra would be eager to throw his hat into the ring—especially if Vargas appeared to support his candidacy. On top of that, it was widely acknowledged in Rio's political circles that Dutra's wife, Santinha, was the most ambitious lady in Rio. The British perspective on Santinha perhaps summed her up best—"an enormous lady with a passionate hatred of communism" and "a determined and ambitious woman."[25]

But Vargas may have underestimated his minister of war. Together, Mr. and Mrs. Dutra formed one of the most important and powerful couples in Rio. Santinha was an astute networker, making sure that her rather dour and boring husband was meeting all the right people at official and private events. What the minister of war lacked in political ability, his wife more than made up for with her famed pushiness. Vargas's plans for manipulating the general discounted the influence of Santinha—and were therefore far riskier than the president appeared to understand.

17

# THE CHALLENGE

THE FINAL HOUR WAS DRAWING NEAR. At the start of 1945, the Allies' military advances in Western and Eastern Europe accelerated. In January, the Soviet Union launched a major offensive that liberated Warsaw, the capital of Poland; on March 7, US troops crossed the Rhine River at Remagan, entering Germany. Hitler's defeat seemed imminent. The final German offensive in the west had been launched on December 16 of the previous year, culminating in the agonizing Battle of the Bulge. But this desperate bid to reverse Germany's fortunes had failed, and in all probability, the war would end by the middle of the year.

This was an extremely challenging time for President Vargas. His confidence appeared rattled, and his energy and ability to work long hours appeared once again to be on the wane. Vargas retreated to the Rio Negro Palace in Petrópolis for the summer months of early 1945, but while the cooler climate at the summer retreat was more conducive to clear-headed thinking, Vargas could not escape his problems. Prime among his concerns was the question of whether to end the Estado Novo and restore some form of democracy when World War II ended.

Seeking inspiration, Vargas took long walks alone around the town, which was full of rich summer homeowners from Rio and local diplomats, among them the British ambassador. Vargas was much more eager to deal with such men than with his internal foes; he was also keen to sign as many deals with the United States as possible—for rubber, coffee, and whatever else Brazil had to sell. Yet his decision-making process appeared frozen when it came to internal issues, especially those related to his own future. Vargas, somewhat vainly, had convinced himself that he needed to lead Brazil for at least one year after the conclusion of the war. This, he argued, would allow him to ensure that the country would be able to maximize its returns from the war and would also give him a chance to shore up—with the support of the United States—Brazil's newly prominent role in regional and international affairs. In public, Vargas refused to commit himself to any course of action regarding the country's leadership, but most of his opponents expected that he would try to hang on to power for as long as possible.

No longer able to turn to his old friend Osvaldo Aranha, and with an inner circle that appeared weak and divided, President Vargas relied ever more heavily on Alzira—and increasingly on her husband, Ernâni do Amaral Peixoto—for advice. The wild card in the pack continued to be the president's younger brother, Benjamin, yet Vargas appeared completely blind to his brother's shortcomings and lack of ability. During previous times of crisis, such as in 1937 and 1938, Vargas had been able to call on far greater minds than he now had available to him in 1945. Francisco Campos and General Góes Monteiro had, to varying degrees, edged out of the president's camp, and their replacements were more concerned with pleasing the president than challenging his decisions. To make matters worse, these "yes" men appeared to be goading the president into a fight with those of their countrymen who demanded a return to democracy. By the start of 1945, it had become clear that President Vargas still had reservations about introducing full democracy in Brazil, preferring a local version that took into account the country's political culture.

Vargas received reports from Rio of challenges to his authority on an almost daily basis—and the reports were growing. The president, however, was reluctant to break from his summer routine to return to the city, fearing that any such move could be interpreted as a sign of weakness. He would soon have cause to regret his decision.

The gathering opposition found its mouthpiece during the first Brazilian writers' conference, which opened on January 22, 1945. Dominated by communists, the conference issued a list of demands, first among them the holding of free and fair elections.[1] What surprised many people were not the demands themselves, but rather the fact that the conference's participants had been confident enough to openly challenge the president by issuing them.

The writers' conference was merely the start of a campaign to effectively oust an increasingly isolated President Vargas. Much worse followed on February 22, when José Américo, who had run for the presidency as the opposition candidate in 1937, published an article in *Correio da Manhã*. This article amounted to, as the British ambassador put it, "the most savage attack on President Vargas and his regime that had appeared for many years."[2] The article articulated the policies and demands of the writers' conference from the previous month, and it—unlike the original list of demands—was not submitted to censorship. The gauntlet had been thrown down.

Brazilians waited anxiously to see how Vargas would respond—and were shocked by the outcome. Vargas had instructed the DIP not to intervene, and so, with something of a political bang, years of censorship in Brazil came to a dramatic end. What followed was a predicable free-for-all, with anti-Vargas articles appearing in many newspapers, boldly demanding that the president step down and allow for free elections to choose his successor. The articles' authors were mainly old political foes of Vargas from the pre–Estado Novo period who had been biding their time, waiting for the opportunity to strike. One article, however, was different from all the rest.

One Brazilian newspaper published an interview with Osvaldo Aranha, in which the former minister of foreign affairs explained the reasons for his resignation. Needless to say, it didn't make pleasant reading for Vargas. Aranha claimed that Brazilian internal politics had impinged on his foreign policy and that once this interference became too great, he had little choice but to quit. Aranha refused to comment on his relationship with the president, except to say that while Vargas was not his enemy, Aranha no longer liked the regime that Vargas led.[3] The message from Aranha to his old friend was clear: Vargas needed to reform or risk becoming politically irrelevant, perhaps even before the war's end.

In his office at the Rio Negro Palace, Vargas read the piece by Américo and whatever other articles his nervous aides allowed him to see, and pondered how best to proceed. He didn't feel he could submit to the opposition's demand for free and open elections, but he knew that he could wait no longer to make a decision about elections. He opted for what was, in effect, a compromise; he allowed a vote, just not from the Brazilian people.

President Vargas summoned a full cabinet meeting at the Rio Negro Palace, demanding that all his ministers travel up to Petrópolis from Rio to decide on the fate of the Estado Novo. All of this went against Vargas's

intuition; he disliked cabinet meetings and the surprises they often unleashed. Indeed, when he brought the meeting to order, Vargas was taken
aback by his ministers' recommendations. One by one, the officials warned
the president that "the manifest desire for public elections must be met."[4]

Vargas took these comments under advisement, but continued to play
for time. After the cabinet meeting, he released an official statement assuring Brazilians that the necessary measures for changing the country's
constitution would be studied immediately.[5] Soon thereafter, on March
1, 1945, the administration announced that Vargas had signed a constitutional amendment—constitutional amendment No. 9—calling for free
elections to be scheduled within ninety days. The amendment laid down
various conditions including, rather bravely, the disenfranchisement of all
enlisted men, excluding officers.[6] Constitutional amendment No. 9 also
called for federal elections for the president (who would serve for a fixed,
six-year term) and parliamentary legislators, as well as for state elections
for local governors and parliaments.

At this stage, the opposition's proposed candidate, Brigadier Eduardo
Gomes, was the only official contender for the presidency. Gomes commanded the air routes and bases in northeastern Brazil. The United States
liked Gomes immensely, and had invited him to tour the North African
front in 1943. Gomes was, however, not the obvious choice for the opposition. The British pointed out:

> He is a great patriot and a man of unshakable integrity and decency, but is
> no statesman and only accepted the nomination after great hesitation and
> because no other candidate with his moral qualifications was available.
> But he has no program, is no economist, and is probably too simple a soul
> not to be outmaneuvered by the intrigues of the president and his friends.[7]

Gomes had other strikes against him, too. His supporters were a motley
group of liberals, including a number of older, mostly discredited politicians, whose careers had been at their height in the pre-Vargas era.[8]

One man who almost immediately offered Gomes his support was
Osvaldo Aranha. His backing, however, was limited in value—not to
mention disingenuous. In private, the former minister of foreign affairs
hoped that Vargas would see the light, get rid of the "forces of darkness"
that Aranha—like the British—believed were surrounding the president,

cast off Dutra, and run for the presidency in a democratic election. For all Vargas's many failings, Aranha believed him to be capable of arousing great populist support that no other Brazilian politician—let alone Gomes—could match. For this reason, and surely also because of their long-standing friendship, Aranha never entirely cut ties with Vargas. The political divorce between them was painful for both men, but Aranha never really gave up on Vargas and was certainly not willing to put a knife in his back, as many others in Rio were by this point.

Dutra, a more willing political assassin than Aranha, agreed—a little too quickly for comfort, Vargas thought—when the president asked him to stand as the government's candidate in the presidential election. The minister of war's candidacy was unofficially announced in São Paulo on March 15, 1945, though he could not formally accept the nomination until August 9. Vargas still hoped that Dutra would be dismissed as unelectable and that in the ensuing crisis, Brazilians would demand that he put himself forward for election. The president also wanted Dutra to split the military vote, since it would severely complicate matters for Vargas if the armed forces rallied behind Gomes, who, like Dutra, was an officer. Splitting the military, Vargas concluded, would also help to weaken its influence in the postelection era.

Dutra's unhesitating acceptance of Vargas's offer was a clear sign that he was going to take the campaign seriously and did not consider himself a benchwarmer for Vargas. As Vargas had expected, however, during the first weeks of the unofficial campaign—and despite the fact that all government ministers declared their public support for him—Dutra made little progress. His poor oratory and complete lack of charisma were ill suited to the campaign trail, and he was politically out of sync with the times; opposition figures pointed out that Dutra was perhaps more responsible than anyone for the cancellation of the previous elections and the establishment of the Estado Novo. All seemed to be going to plan; Dutra was splitting the military vote, just as Vargas had intended.

While he attempted to play his domestic enemies off against each other, Vargas also continued to steer Brazil through a complex and rapidly changing moment in world history. Aranha's departure from the ministry of foreign affairs had not changed the foreign policy goals he had outlined in his memorandum for Vargas's meeting with President Roosevelt in January 1944. Vargas, however, had a new item on his agenda: winning

Brazil a permanent seat on the world council, a mission that would help strengthen Brazil's international position. Changes in the Roosevelt administration were also forcing Vargas to rethink his priorities.

During the first part of 1945, as the war in Europe moved rapidly toward its conclusion, a number of personnel changes took place at the highest levels of government in the United States. Jefferson Caffery, the ambassador to Brazil and confidante of Aranha (and, to some extent, of Vargas as well), departed Rio in January 1945, headed for France, where he was to become Washington's representative to that newly liberated country. Segments of the Brazilian press welcomed Caffery's departure, because they viewed the ambassador as having to come to represent US imperialism.

Brazilians were certainly subjecting US interests in their country to renewed scrutiny as the war wound down. For some time prior to Caffery's departure, the fate of US bases in Brazil after the war had been the subject of intense debate in both Rio and Washington. Several US officials and military officers argued that since the United States had invested so heavily in the creation of the air bases and navy facilities, it should continue to have full access to them in peacetime. President Vargas took the view that Brazil should retain control of the bases—he knew this was vital for maintaining Brazil's regional military superiority in the postwar era. The president did, however, demonstrate a willingness to accommodate US requests to use some of the bases after the war.

The timing of Caffery's departure—coinciding as it did with the increase in internal challenges to Vargas's rule—complicated matters for the Brazilian president. For one thing, the US State Department's decision to remove Caffery from Brazil effectively denied President Vargas his direct line to Washington and increased mutual suspicions in both countries about the state of relations between Brazil and the United States. But Caffery's replacement as ambassador also proved to be a problem in his own right.

Adolf Berle, the new US ambassador to Brazil, presented his credentials to President Vargas on January 30, 1945. His bosses in Washington thought of Berle as a high-class appointment, one that was meant to flatter the Brazilians. A fellow diplomat summed up Berle in hyperbolic terms:

> He has a restless, brilliant, and independent mind with a messianic complex and an utter conviction that he was born to set the world right. Ready

to defy the State Department at any moment and in any connection, but trusting ingenuously that he can control them, he must at all times hold the center of the stage.[9]

Put simply, Berle was a meddler, and his presence in Brazil would prove anything but pleasing to the embattled Brazilian president.

At first, Brazilians were indeed flattered by Berle's appointment, but the ambassador soon attracted a growing wave of criticism from various quarters in Brazil. Berle had many new ideas about US-Brazilian relations and about President Vargas's regime—central among them the conviction that Vargas must allow free elections to take place in Brazil. From his very first day in the country, the ambassador set about making this happen by any means necessary. Berle felt that a failure to hold free elections would spell "disaster for Brazil," and in his zeal he intervened so heavy-handedly in the country's internal politics that he managed to antagonize both the government and the opposition forces.[10] The State Department took note, and by the end of the year Berle would be recalled to Washington for consultations—a move the Brazilian press would speculate was a direct result of Berle's having "intervened unduly in internal Brazilian politics."[11]

Berle's recall lay relatively far in the future when Caffery departed Rio in January 1945, but Caffery's new position was not the only US personnel change at this key juncture in the war. At the end of November 1944, the longest-serving US secretary of state, Cordell Hull, had resigned from his post due to ill health. Hull's resignation, along with Sumner Welles's earlier departure from the State Department, had removed from the Roosevelt administration the principal architects of the Good Neighbor Program. Hull and Welles had been the two individuals who had done most to promise that—in return for Brazilian support in World War II—the United States would help facilitate Brazilian aspirations in the realms of economic development and the creation of modern, well-equipped armed forces. Whether Brazil could still expect such assurances from the US government was now an open question.

The departures of Hull, Welles, and Caffery were offset to a degree by another development in Washington: Nelson Rockefeller's promotion to the rank of assistant secretary of state for American regional affairs. Rockefeller continued to be an invaluable supporter of Brazil, specifically in regard to its economic ties with the United States. The trouble was that as a result of his promotion, Rockefeller's brief was much wider than it had been previously, and the time he could devote to Brazil was much reduced.

Hull's successor as secretary of state, Edward Stettinius Jr., proved to be an additional complication for Brazil. Stettinius appeared, on the surface, to favor maintaining strong ties between the United States and Brazil. He visited Rio, arriving in the city on a scorching hot day in the third week of February 1945 to meet with President Vargas. He brought a personal gift for the president—a high-powered radio receiver, which the local press caustically claimed would finally allow Vargas to find out what was really going on in the outside world.[12] Vargas requested that the meeting take place at the Rio Negro Palace in Petrópolis, rather than in Rio. He explained to Stettinius that Rio was simply intolerable for any sort of work at this time of year. The president failed to mention that he was also maintaining a healthy distance from the mounting opposition that was manifesting itself in Rio's press.

The secretary of state's motorcade made its way up the winding mountain road to Vargas's summer retreat. Vargas was pleased to have such a high-placed member of the US administration come to visit, but he and the secretary of state had differing agendas for the meeting. Stettinius wanted assurances that in the postwar era, the United States would have access to the bases it had helped to build in Brazil. Vargas, meanwhile, demanded a permanent seat on the world council. Neither man made any promises about either issue.

The two men discussed in some detail the situation in Argentina, and specifically US policy toward the regime in Buenos Aires.[13] As Stettinius explained to Vargas, the United States hoped to conclude a deal with Argentina that would have the country enter the war on the side of the Allies in exchange for restored diplomatic ties between Buenos Aires and the capitals of the Allied nations. In addition to declaring war on Germany and Japan, the Allies also demanded that Argentina hold free elections and take action against pro-Nazi elements in the country—of which, by 1945, there were more than ever. As Germany crumbled, Nazis were already beginning to trickle into Argentina, marking the beginning of an exodus that would eventually earn the country notoriety as a safe haven for Hitler's henchmen.

The Argentine minister of war, Juan Perón, sensing that the Allies were about to win a total victory in the war, feared that Argentina would be isolated in the postwar order unless it met the Allies' demands. Argentina would eventually declare war on Germany and Japan on March 27, 1945; and on April 10, the United States, Great Britain, and France, along with the Latin American countries, restored full diplomatic relations with Argentina.

During their meeting in late February, the US secretary of state impressed on Vargas America's strong desire for Argentina to hold free elections at the end of the war, and the implications for the Estado Novo were not lost on the Brazilian president. Stettinius stopped short of making a similar demand for Brazil, but the writing was on the wall: the Estado Novo would need to reform, or it would perish.

The coverage of Stettinius's visit in the Brazilian press was less than flattering. A number of articles pointed to the fact that, as the British noted, "The visit was designed to put pressure on the president and to increase the United States hold over the country, whether militarily or politically."[14] Yet while Washington appeared to be flexing its muscles in late February, flush with confidence about the direction of the war and its clout in the postwar era, that self-assurance would soon be shaken.

On April 12, 1945, Franklin Roosevelt died of a stroke. His death received enormous coverage in the Brazilian press; *Correio de Manhã*, for instance, devoted the entire front page of its April 13 edition to the news. Interestingly, the Brazilian press gave greater prominence to, and carried in greater detail, the tribute to President Roosevelt by the opposition candidate, Eduardo Gomes, than it did to the tribute by President Vargas.[15] The latter described President Roosevelt as the leader of democracy against Nazi fascism.[16]

The timing of Roosevelt's death could not have been worse for Brazil. Two weeks earlier, on March 31, the Brazilian and US militaries had signed a secret document laying out postwar military arrangements between the parties.[17] It was a detailed document, one intended to determine the mechanics of postwar military cooperation. But with Roosevelt's death there was a real risk that these accomplishments would be overturned.[18]

Despite vague assurances from the new administration in Washington that its policies toward the Americas would be in keeping with Roosevelt's, there was a feeling in Rio that Brazilians had lost their ally in the White House. Newspapers waxed nostalgic about the key moments in Roosevelt's dealings with Brazil, naturally focusing on his meetings with President

Vargas.[19] For Vargas, moreover, Roosevelt's death would likely deal a blow
not only to Brazilian relations with the United States, but also to Vargas's
tenuous hold on power. Roosevelt had been more preoccupied with Brazil's foreign policy than with its internal political system, but now—as
Stettinius's recent visit had made clear—Washington's stance seemed to
be changing. Vargas could expect internal challenges to his rule to increase
accordingly.

At least Vargas still had the FEB. Its ongoing contributions in the
Italian theater were perhaps Vargas's last, best opportunity to recover
some internal support and to maximize his military and economic returns from the United States. Fighting in Italy resumed in February 1945,
with an Allied offensive that saw the FEB taking part in the Battle of
Monte Castello—a fight in which the German forces were dug in on high
ground, and put up fierce resistance. But unlike in their previous clashes
with battle-hardened veterans of the eastern front, the Brazilians who
fought at Monte Castello in 1945 were not facing the elite of the Nazi
war machine. Many of the German soldiers based in the area were either
young, first-time combatants or older, inexperienced fighters.[20] The German officer class, meanwhile, was by this point in the war primarily made
up of survivors from the Russian front, many of whom were exhausted and
suffering from the mental scars of that brutal campaign.

The Brazilians, for perhaps the first time in the war, found themselves
on relatively equal footing with the enemy. The soldiers of the FEB had
traveled to the Italian front essentially untrained, and received proper
combat training from the US military only after they had arrived in Italy.
While still extremely green, the Brazilian troops were also handicapped
by inadequate leadership. The Brazilian officer class appeared, at times,
overeager to please, and they failed to grasp that warfare rarely went exactly to plan. They, like President Vargas, wanted quick results to illustrate
the scale of their contribution to the Allied war effort, and this sometimes
manifested itself in overly aggressive battlefield strategy—and high numbers of casualties among Brazilian forces.

Not until February 21, after several failed assaults, did Monte Castello
fall to the FEB. The taking of Monte Castello was a key Allied aim of
the spring 1945 Italian offensive, but in accomplishing it the FEB had
suffered the loss of several hundred men and many more were wounded.
In spite of—or perhaps because of—these casualties, the Battle of Monte

Castello came to represent the FEB's contribution in Italy more than any other clash. Much was made of the congratulations offered to the Brazilian forces by General Clark. Back in Rio, the coverage was equally celebratory. The special edition of the Brazilian paper *O Cruzeiro do Sul* devoted its entire front page to the "conquest of the Castello hill."[21] *Correio de Manhã* ran the headline, "Big Brazilian Victory in Italy," and recounted the difficulties that the FEB faced in securing the mountain.[22] Tributes to the FEB by US officers in the field were also given extensive coverage.

The battle represented, in a sense, the coming of age of the FEB, but the expeditionary force paid a high price for its success. Brazilian casualties outnumbered German ones at a rate of more than ten to one. During one failed attempt to secure the hill, the FEB incurred nearly 150 casualties to a total German figure of just under twenty dead or wounded.[23]

Still, it was a heady time for the Brazilian military. In April 1945, General Masarenham de Morais received the first unconditional surrender of a German division in Italy. This was a prelude to the surrender of all German forces in Italy on May 2, 1945, just two days after Adolf Hitler committed suicide in Berlin and five days before all of Germany surrendered to the western Allies, on May 7, 1945. The Germans would hold out for two more days against the Soviets, finally succumbing on May 9, 1945.

The Brazilian army, air force, and navy had collectively earned the respect of their US commanders. Likewise, the initial tension between US and Brazilian soldiers had given way to mutual respect and friendship. Back in Rio, Brazil's military commanders were quick to seize the success of the FEB as a means to increase their own political power and leverage over the politicians.

The FEB had performed much better than expected, but the importance of its role in the Italian campaign was—and still is—heavily debated. Although the fighting in which Brazilian troops took part was indeed important, it was never decisive; the campaign in Italy would have been a success with or without the FEB's contribution. Yet it was a mark of distinction for Brazil's military that whereas the United States had originally planned to essentially sideline Brazilian troops during the conflict, they had held their own on the battlefield and even scored some hits against the Germans. The major reason for these successes, aside from the bravery of the men who served in the FEB, was the extensive training they received on arriving in Italy. The Brazilians' initial resentment at the

US army's rigorous methods was eclipsed by their pride at having become a disciplined fighting force—one that had sacrificed for the Allied cause just like any other. Of the 25,300 Brazilian soldiers originally sent to Italy, the majority took part in combat. By the end of the war, 451 Brazilians had been killed and nearly two thousand wounded in the fighting or in training accidents.[24]

The first squadron of the FEB returned home on July 18, 1945. Thousands of Cariocas gathered in downtown Rio, frantically waving Brazilian flags to greet the returning heroes. President Vargas led this outsized welcoming committee, well aware that the triumphant return of the FEB served to improve his own political fortunes. The victory parade that followed the troops' debarkation contrasted markedly with the previous year's farewell parade. The men of the FEB showed off their US equipment and uniforms, which made them look like an alien army in their own country. Modernized, highly trained, and disciplined, the force barely resembled the motley crew that had departed Rio in the winter of 1944.

Yet the soldiers received disappointing news after their initial reception in Rio: the FEB was immediately broken up and its members dispersed back to their original regiments throughout Brazil. The Americans were saddened, as well, for they had hoped that the FEB would remain in Europe and help with the occupation of the liberated territories there. Indeed, President Vargas's decision to get Brazilian troops out of Europe as quickly as possible would prove to be a huge mistake; by pulling out of Europe before the United States felt the job there was finished, he effectively cut Brazil off from much of the economic spoils of the war—and the political rewards that the Americans were beginning to dole out to their allies.

In the meantime, the wolves were at President Vargas's door. While he was still looking for a way to remain in office to oversee Brazil's first steps into peacetime, an orderly transition looked to be a distant prospect.

# PART SIX:
## POSTWAR BLUES

18

# THE EXIT

PRESIDENT VARGAS SAT ALONE IN HIS SMALL, simply furnished study in the Guanabara Palace on the evening of October 29, 1945. The situation looked hopeless.[1] Tanks and small armored personnel carriers were stationed at the front gates of the Guanabara Palace, as well as at strategic junctions around Rio. Soldiers were close enough to his study for Vargas to be able to hear the crackles of their radios and the insults they routinely exchanged with the presidential guards recruited by his younger brother, Benjamin Vargas, to protect the president. There was no escape, and the will of the army was unusually united and steadfast. They aimed to remove him from power, and—having come this far—they were unlikely to back down.

Dutra had arrived earlier to try to find some compromise, but the minister of war had found the president in no mood to back down, either.[2] Finally, the chief of staff of the army was dispatched to meet with the president and to formally present him with a message from the military demanding that Vargas resign with immediate effect. In return, the military would offer him and his family safe passage out of the palace back to his farm in Rio Grande do Sul. Later, Dutra would come to rue this offer, wondering why the president was not sent into political exile abroad—but for Vargas, at this moment, the idea of being escorted out of the Guanabara Palace like a common criminal was surely painful enough.

As the president started to write a brief letter of resignation, which was part of the deal to secure his safe passage out of the palace, he could not have but reflected on the past few months and wondered where everything had gone wrong. The end of the war in Europe, and later in Japan, had been heavily celebrated in Rio and in the rest of Brazil; the masses had hoped that the end of the war would alleviate the fuel and food shortages in the country. But as the parties ended and the flags were put away, it became clear that the country was still in a state of political crisis, which would have to be resolved before things in Brazil could truly get back to normal.

The issue of presidential elections was becoming the most divisive issue between the various forces vying for control of Brazil: those loyal to President Vargas, the opposition, and the military. The key questions that remained were whether Vargas would allow presidential elections to take place by the end of the year, as he had promised, and whether he would be a candidate in such an election. In July 1945, in a speech in the São Paulo municipality of Santos, Vargas had promised to see the elections conducted fairly on the chosen date and had also declared once more that he was not interested in running.[3]

According to those close to the president, Vargas actually meant what he had said in July. He had grown tired, and he wanted to hold elections and hand over the presidency in an orderly fashion to his elected successor.[4] The opposition, however, did not take his promise at face value and argued that the regime was managing the country's internal unrest in order to prevent the elections from taking place. Many figures in the opposition wished to take revenge on Vargas, moreover, by removing him from power prior to any elections.[5]

Stoking the fears of many in the opposition was the emergence on the Brazilian political scene of the Queremista movement, so called because of its slogan "Queremos Getúlio" (We Want Getúlio). Many members of the movement were associated with the communist party or the labor party, and opposed the military candidates for the presidential election, preferring instead to retain the country's current leader and allow him to oversee more gradual and limited reforms. The Queremista movement also argued that presidential elections should be postponed and that Brazil should instead be given a constitutional assembly, which would work with President Vargas to enact any necessary changes in the country's political structure.[6] The opposition, meanwhile, charged that associates of the Vargas regime were working with the Queremistas to try to prevent presidential elections from taking place at all. The British embassy, which was closely monitoring internal political developments in Brazil at the time, seemed to share this assessment of the Queremistas:

These people were for the most part hooligans, or at their best entirely ignorant and illiterate workers recruited by Benjamin Vargas and his gang, who began to stage noisy demonstrations first in Rio de Janeiro itself and subsequently in other parts of the country. There is no doubt that the president himself actively encouraged these elements, partly from reasons of vanity and partly to prove that, though there was such a demand for him to remain, like a true democrat, he still proposed to retire and cultivate cabbages in Rio Grande do Sul.[7]

Faced with such an obvious ploy to prop up the regime, the opposition understandably distrusted the president's denial that he would run in any presidential election.

If Vargas were to run in a presidential election, moreover, it was looking more and more likely that he would win. As Vargas had expected, Dutra's campaign appeared to be in serious trouble during the winter of 1945. To make matters worse for Dutra, the president was slowly but surely withdrawing his support for the minister of war. Vargas gave no more speeches lauding Dutra's personality and political track record. When Dutra, by electoral law, had resigned as minister of war on August 3 in order to become the regime's official candidate for the presidency, he appeared unaware that Vargas had recently been trying to find an alternative candidate. At one point, the president tried to tempt General Góes Monteiro, Dutra's successor as minister of war, to accept the nomination, suggesting that he was more charismatic than Dutra and therefore stood a better chance of winning. Góes Monteiro responded by telling the president in no uncertain terms, "If you try to stop Dutra, you will have to find another minister of war." The implied threat was not only that the general who succeeded Dutra as minister would resign, but also that the military would not tolerate such backsliding.

Góes Monteiro's comments surely chagrined Vargas. At the heart of all of the president's recent political maneuvers was an intent to divide the military as much as possible. If he could split the armed forces, Vargas hoped, the military leadership would eventually come to its senses and turn to him as a last-minute candidate, knowing that the alternative would be a sound defeat at the hands of the opposition. A unified military, however, would be able to mount a strong challenge against both Vargas and the opposition—something that Vargas wanted to avoid at all costs.

As the tensions mounted, rupture began to appear inevitable. In the early evening of October 3, more than one hundred thousand Queremistas held a rally in downtown Rio before marching to the Guanabara Palace. This caused a scramble of activity at the palace, where Vargas was scheming to use the unprecedented display of support to heighten his charade. After consulting with Alzira, he decided to announce his resignation, and began working on a short speech. Góes Monteiro and others, however, convinced Vargas that resigning at this moment would lead to a constitutional and political crisis. So instead, Vargas addressed the cheering crowd, whose indiscriminate roars of approval drowned out much of his impromptu speech. One dispassionate onlooker noted, "Vargas is in such a state of excitement that he might precipitate anything."[8]

In his remarks to the throngs of Queremistas, Vargas appeared to endorse their idea of a constituent assembly, with which he would work to steer Brazil into the postwar era. The opposition and the military were appalled, if not surprised, by Vargas's comments, which amounted to a throwing down of the gauntlet. Additional Queremista rallies followed, as did a statement from the military that presidential elections would indeed go ahead as promised. The stage was set for a conflagration.

The explosion came on October 29, 1945. That morning, President Vargas took what the British ambassador, David Gainer, described as the "fatal step": he appointed his brother, Benjamin, chief of police. The president's motives for the appointment remain something of a mystery; Vargas may in fact have been trying to help Benjamin's predecessor as chief of police fulfill his political ambitions, because that man was promoted to a prefect of the federal district.[9] Whatever the rationale behind Benjamin's appointment, however, it caused uproar in military circles and within the opposition.

The outrage over Benjamin's appointment paled in comparison to the furor over his first act as chief of police. Immediately after his appointment was confirmed, Benjamin waltzed into a meeting with the new minister of war, General Góes Monteiro, and said patly, "The president has agreed to alter the electoral procedure and to summon a constituent assembly."[10]

For the weeks leading up to this moment, Góes Monteiro's frustration had been building. He was caught between a rock and a hard place; one of President Vargas's most loyal followers over the years, he was reluctant to be the one who toppled him. Góes Monteiro had felt slightly reassured when, as the political temperature in Rio climbed in the second part of 1945, Vargas promised him on several occasions that the presidential elections would go ahead, and that he himself would not be a candidate.

Benjamin's comments on the morning of October 29 amounted to a slap in the face for the minister of war. Angry, hurt, and now completely unsure of exactly what the president had in store for the country, Góes Monteiro summoned a meeting of the generals. On the agenda was only one item: Should the armed forces remove the president from office?

The debate, if any, seems to have been brief. Góes Monteiro, feeling betrayed and mistreated, was in favor of dethroning Vargas, and his fellow generals sided with him. At the conclusion of the meeting, the military took over key junctions in Rio and took up positions near the Guanabara Palace. The coup was on.

Dutra had a prearranged meeting with the president in the early evening of October 29, and he decided to keep it. He cut straight to the point and said, "The armed forces do not accept the appointment of Benjamin, and it should be withdrawn."[11] In a rare show of emotion, President Vargas raised his voice and said, "If I am not free to choose even a chief of police whom I can trust, this means I am no longer president."[12] He calmed down, however, when Dutra informed him that troops were already in the streets, and were ready to depose him. Backpedaling, Vargas offered to cancel Benjamin's appointment and select a chief of police who was satisfactory to the armed forces.[13] Dutra promised to take the president's offer back to Góes Monteiro.

But the minister of war was in no mood for compromise. Dutra—who seemed to still feel that Vargas would back his bid for the presidency—attempted to set up a meeting between Góes Monteiro and the president, believing that if the two men could speak face-to-face, like the old days, they would be able to hammer out a deal. Góes Monteiro declined the invitation, however. He clearly felt the time had come to remove Vargas from office, and that there was no point in further discussion.

Góes Monteiro instructed his newly appointed chief of staff, Osvaldo Cordeiro de Farias, to deliver an ultimatum to the president at the Guanabara Palace. At first, Cordeiro de Farias was reluctant to carry out the assignment, arguing that he still enjoyed good relations with the president, but eventually—and under considerable pressure from Góes Monteiro—he agreed.

Before Cordeiro de Farias departed for the Guanabara Palace, the two presidential candidates met to discuss the crisis. Eduardo Gomes had left his campaign trail in southern Brazil to return to Rio, and after a brief discussion, he and Dutra agreed that they would both support the coup. They also agreed on a temporary replacement for Vargas: the chief justice, José Linhares, would take over the presidency until elections took place.[14] This decision was especially important, because the plotters did not wish to create the impression that Vargas had been removed by a military coup. Although this was of course what his ouster amounted to, the appearance of a military coup would almost certainly alienate the United States from the new regime—an unacceptable outcome, as far as the plotters were concerned.

When Cordeiro de Farias arrived to deliver the ultimatum to President Vargas, the president appeared calm. Informed that he must resign immediately, Vargas "did not lose his poise," Cordeiro de Farias later noted.[15] In a soldierly manner, he summarized the situation for the president. He reminded the president that the generals held all the cards and that the palace was surrounded. "You should resign and leave," he advised him. "This is the price the generals are demanding for the safe conduct of yourself and the family."

Vargas was initially torn between accepting the offer and resisting. He told Cordeiro de Farias, "I will die fighting against an unconstitutional military coup and leave Góes Monteiro responsible for the massacre of the president and his family."[16] Cordeiro de Farias ignored the president's histrionics, however, and calmly informed him that the generals had nothing of the sort in mind. "It is a simple case of you leaving in an orderly and dignified manner or being faced with a situation of the water and electricity to the palace being cut off," he explained.

Vargas retired to his study to mull over his options. He spent just over fifteen minutes alone. When he emerged with Alzira, who had gone in to check on him, he spoke in a calm voice. "I would prefer that you all attack me and that my death remain as a protest against this violence," he said. "But as this is to be a bloodless coup, I shall not be the cause of disturbance." With this statement, and with issuance of Vargas's letter of resignation, the immediate crisis was over.

With the president preparing to leave the Guanabara Palace, members of the military headed out into Rio to find his replacement. Chief Justice

José Linhares was attending a formal dinner party, and when the officers located him and informed him that he was to become president of Brazil early the next morning, he was taken aback. He consented only after being told that the military and both presidential candidates supported him as an interim president until either Dutra or Gomes could be elected to the post.

At 10 P.M. on the evening of October 29, 1945, the news of Vargas's deposition was broadcast to the Brazilian public. At 2 A.M. the following morning, Linhares was sworn in as president. The purr of tank engines making their slow way back to barracks could soon be heard across the city. Bloodshed had been avoided, but as Cariocas discussed events over their morning coffee in the beachfront bars, there was a general consensus that while Vargas had lost this round, his influence would still be felt in the elections—and that, one day, he would return.

Back at the Guanabara Palace, Vargas was almost ready to depart. "Take care of your mother as I'm leaving alone," he informed Alzira, who was still in a state of shock. Vargas then proceeded to hand his daughter a letter and told her to open it only if something happened to him on the way back to Rio Grande do Sul. If he arrived home safely, Alzira was to burn the note.

One of Vargas's last official acts in the palace was to write a short statement to the chief of police, who had been reinstated following Benjamin's removal from the position. Vargas explained that he did not want to discuss the reasons for his surprise departure from office, and added something of a white lie: "I hold no grudges."

Later that day, Alzira drove her father to the airport, where he was to board a plane to Rio Grande do Sul. In his final public statement before take-off, Vargas repeated his desire that Brazilians remain calm, and that public order be maintained in Rio and across the country. The people who witnessed his departure noted that he appeared calm, and in no way resembled a broken man. He seemed to sense that this was not the end of the story, that he still had a role to play in Brazil's future.

While Vargas had been preparing to leave Rio, Linhares's temporary cabinet met with several ministers who made the case that Vargas should be sent into exile abroad or to the interior of the country, rather than being allowed to retreat to his home state. Yet the military, led by Góes Monteiro, refused to contemplate such plans. Vargas had kept his side of the bargain, so the military was intent on keeping its side; the president, his family, and several close advisors departed Rio without incident.

The Rio-based press welcomed these developments—ever since the effective ending of censorship earlier in the year, the papers had been full of anti-Vargas articles. *Correio de Manhã* declared simply "Vargas Deposed" on its front page, which contained several detailed accounts of the events, including an interview with Cordeiro de Farias, who suggested that the military had been left with no alternative but to act swiftly to unseat the dictator.[17] *Jornal do Brasil* ran with the headline "Resignation of Vargas," and its coverage discussed the political implications of his demise.[18]

The British described Vargas's ouster as a "bloodless revolution." In his correspondence with London the ambassador wrote, "President Vargas was deposed (for it was really a deposition) by general consent, as it was feared, with some reason, that he would prevent the elections: in other words, action was taken not against him personally so much as against his policy, or what was believed to be his policy."[19]

For many Vargas supporters, the question of Vargas's intentions was a sticking point. No one had any conclusive proof that Vargas was going to cancel the presidential elections. Vargas's enemies had taken Benjamin Vargas's comments to Góes Monteiro on the morning of October 29 as evidence of the president's intention of doing so, but there was likely a bit of confirmation bias at work here; the case against Vargas was founded largely in his enemies' expectations (based, fairly, on ample evidence of Vargas's past political intrigues) that he would cancel elections, but in the months leading up to the coup he had said nothing to this effect. In his remarks to the Queremista rally on October 3, he had appeared to support the idea of a constitutional assembly—but this is as close as he ever came to suggesting the elections would be cancelled.

Whatever questions Brazilians may have had about the coup, one thing was certain: Vargas's enemies had gotten their man. It remained to be seen whether they had been able to do so in a way that would be palatable to the United States. But on this count, the plotters had reason to be confident. Berle, the US ambassador, had essentially given the military the green light in a speech he had delivered to a group of journalists on September 29. The speech had been a thinly veiled warning to Vargas that the United States expected "impartial elections" to take place in Brazil as promised, and that any attempt to cancel the elections in favor of a constitutional assembly would be a disaster for Brazil.[20] In fact, to some extent Berle viewed Vargas's overthrow as a vindication of his comments the previous month.

Washington's reaction to the coup was more complex than that of its ambassador in Rio. Vargas had proven himself to be a strong ally of the United States in the war. For a time, there had seemed to be a chance of Latin America slipping into the Axis sphere of influence, and Vargas had stepped in to check the slide. He had also moved against German and Italian influence in his country's southlands, and he had provided the United States territory for air and naval bases—bases that, moreover, remained alluring to US military planners.

The problem was that Vargas's best friends in Washington—Roosevelt, Hull, and Welles—were no longer around to make the case that Brazil's internal politics were not as important as its foreign policy orientation. Harry Truman, Roosevelt's successor in the White House, was still well disposed toward Brazil, but his administration was preoccupied with the challenges of the postwar era—namely, the onrushing Cold War with the Soviet Union. In other words, any personal considerations that might have driven US policy toward Brazil had long since vanished.

US officials seemed more concerned with the Brazilian military's role in facilitating free elections than with the fact that a coup had taken place. The fact that it had been a bloodless coup made this all the easier. Berle did note that if Vargas had resigned from the presidency and ran for office as one of the candidates in the presidential election, he would have won.[21] There were no opinion polls to verify this claim, but it is clear that Vargas did continue to enjoy widespread support among the masses. His enemies, predominantly middle-class liberals, dominated the press and were on the ascendency, but it was by no means certain that Vargas would have been deposed had it not been for the appointment of his younger brother as chief of police, and Benjamin Vargas's subsequent face-off with Góes Monteiro on the day of his appointment. It all was a very particularly Brazilian coup.

The coup's biggest winner appeared to be the opposition candidate for president, Eduardo Gomes. Praised for his calm intervention in the crisis (and untainted by having served in the Vargas administration), he looked like a shoo-in for the presidency. Dutra, for his part, was still in a slump. His campaign style hadn't changed and his oratory was second rate; he spoke like a bureaucrat instead of a national leader.

The presidential election took place on December 2, 1945, as planned. It was characterized by a sense of calm, with no reports of political violence anywhere in the country. Gomes had reason to be confident as Brazilians lined up at the polls—but any confidence he might have felt quickly dissipated as the results came in.

Dutra was in the lead. As officials tallied the numbers, in fact, it became clear that the presidency was his—and that Gomes had not even really come close to beating him. One of the keys to Dutra's success appeared to be the support he received from the Catholic Church, which feared that Gomes and his supporters would prove to be too liberal if elected to office.[22] The church's intervention on Dutra's behalf was heavily criticized in the newspapers, but it made a difference in a country where Catholicism remained a powerful force with strong political as well as social influence. The church had been relatively weak under Vargas, who was not a religious man, and so the 1945 election marked its resumption of a prominent role in the nation's politics.[23]

The real story of the election, however, was the return of Getúlio Vargas. In truth, although he was exiled to his ranch in the south of Brazil, Vargas had never been far from the political action. Despite the military's promise to keep his influence in check and to prevent him from running for the senate (which Góes Monteiro and other officers feared he might do in order to reclaim some of his lost power), politicians had continued to fly to Rio Grande do Sul to visit the ex-president. Eventually, Vargas was persuaded by his political allies and family to run for the senate, and was duly elected to that body thanks to Brazil's complex system of proportional representation. The military seemed to be reluctant to confront Vargas, and it didn't challenge his election—so his exile proved to be extremely short-lived.

It was in the presidential election, however, that Vargas's influence was most strongly felt. When Alzira and other interlocutors pinned him down on the question of which presidential candidate he preferred, Vargas was forced to concede that it was Dutra over Gomes. In the last few weeks of the campaign, he issued a signed statement to that effect, recommending that the electorate choose Dutra. His intervention proved vital in mobilizing regional and national political forces to support Dutra, and also in rallying the electorate—particularly the nation's workers—behind him. Dutra later conceded that his victory over Gomes was due almost entirely to Vargas's endorsement.[24] A large portion of the Brazilian press took the same view, regarding Dutra's election as, in effect, a victory for

Vargas. *Diário de Notícias* opined that "Brazilian reality is still a crepuscular prolongation of the dictatorial darkness."[25]

January 31, 1946, the date of Dutra's inauguration, was a hot summer's day in Rio. And as Dutra was sworn in, becoming Brazil's first post–World War II democratically elected president, Vargas, the ex-president turned kingmaker, was orchestrating his own political comeback.[26] In agreeing to leave the Guanabara Palace quietly at the end of October 1945, Vargas had lived to fight another day—and, in a sense, had also ensured that his political exile would not be permanent. The man who appeared to have run out of energy and ideas the previous year had to some extent been rejuvenated by his spell away from Rio, and by his respite from the pressures of leadership after such an extended period in office. His road back to the palace would not be easy, short, or straight, but his sense of injustice at his treatment at the hands of the military was a strong motivation to keep him going.[27]

Vargas also knew an opportunity when he saw one. He understood that despite Dutra's comfortable victory in the recent elections, Dutra's presidency would ultimately fail; Vargas had known Dutra for decades, and was confident that his former minister of war was not up to the job. This belief was why he had originally recommended Dutra for the position, and it would prove to be an additional motivation as he attempted to claw his way back to the top of Brazilian politics.

For all the economic and military advancements that Brazil had gleaned from World War II, the country was still in rough shape in 1946. The British embassy in Rio perhaps summed up Brazil's predicament best:

> Brazil is at present in a most difficult financial and economic situation. Inflation, profiteering, and corruption are rife, the food situation and (closely connected therewith) the transport situation are most serious, as is also the housing problem . . . The present regime does not at present command a sufficient majority, or perhaps sufficient constructive talent, to initiate the drastic measures which alone could save the situation.[28]

The problems facing Brazil were the same ones that Vargas had dealt with during the war, but though he had outlined plans for solving Brazil's economic and infrastructure woes, Dutra did not share Vargas's vision.

The economic gains that Vargas had helped Brazil to reap from the war had proved insufficient to fully and instantaneously transform the country.

He had sown the seeds for growth, however. Following the war, conditions were slowly starting to improve in terms of fuel supplies and shipping. Many merchant ships that had been converted to wartime service were decommissioned and returned to the civilian economy and were able to help deliver more fuel and other urgent supplies that were vital for the economy. This growth was recognized by Brazilians across the country as the result of Vargas's strong administration, instead of being connected to the current regime.

# THE FINAL ACT

IT TOOK ANOTHER FOUR YEARS, but Getúlio Vargas eventually did re-turn to the presidency. On October 3, 1950, the ex-president defeated Eduardo Gomes and Cristiano Machado in Brazil's second postwar pres-idential election, winning more votes than the combined total of the two other candidates. Vargas's victory was proof of his continued popularity among Brazil's masses, but it was also the product of an energetic and brilliant campaign. Vargas felt he was the only man capable of extracting Brazil from the mess in which it found itself at the dawn of the 1950s, and he had vied for the presidency like a man possessed.

On January 31, 1951, Vargas took the oath of office at the Tiradentes Palace in Rio. It was the same place where, nearly a decade earlier, the president's old friend and sparring partner Osvaldo Aranha had an-nounced Brazil's break of diplomatic relations with Germany and Italy. Among the foreign dignitaries who attended the inauguration was Nelson Rockefeller, with whom Vargas met prior to taking the oath of office. A more auspicious ceremony is hard to imagine.

In his speech at the inauguration, Vargas thumbed his nose at the people who had forced him from office some five years earlier. He was still angry at the military's treatment of him in October 1945 and at the lies that had been written about him since that fateful evening when he had been ousted from power. "The people have carried me back to the presi-dency," he proclaimed to the huge crowd that had gathered in front of the Tiradentes Palace.

Following his speech, Vargas toured Rio in a large open-topped car, standing on the backseat as onlookers threw confetti from the city's sky-scrapers and soldiers saluted their new commander in chief. Cariocas turned out by the hundreds of thousands to cheer the new president, bringing the city to a virtual standstill.

When Vargas eventually reached the Catete Palace, the new seat of the presidency, he paid a less than glowing tribute to his predecessor, General Dutra, for arranging such a fair and free election. When questioned by journalists, Vargas couldn't resist also taking a swipe at Adolf Berle, who he believed had stoked the military's discontent with him in September and October 1945. Though he didn't mention the former ambassador by name, President Vargas left little to the imagination when he commented that US-Brazilian relations had been hijacked by certain officials who didn't understand their true nature.[1]

Vargas had waited a long time for this day, and he struggled to control the pent-up frustration that he had harbored since being removed from power. Yet despite his palpable anger, a sense of wild optimism was sweeping through the city and the country as a whole. It was the holiday season in Rio, and Carnaval was on its way. January 31 was a hot summer day in the city; the sun was shining, the city's hotels were filled to the rafters with rich foreign guests, and new sambas were being written in tribute to the country's new president. Vargas was back on top, and Brazilians were obviously happy to have him there.

As the light dimmed over the Atlantic Ocean and shadows lengthened across the Catete Palace, the president and his entourage, including Alzira, left Rio and—in time-honored fashion—headed up the winding road to Petrópolis to escape the city's oppressive heat. By every measure, it had been a triumphant day for the president, one that seemed to have confirmed his place in Brazilian democratic political history. And that evening, as he puffed on his large corona cigar in Petrópolis, surrounded by family and friends, Vargas went to work finalizing the composition of his new government.

On the campaign trail in 1950, Vargas had talked a great deal about World War II and what he saw as the fruits of Brazil's participation in the fighting. He reminded Brazilians of his close relationship with President Roosevelt and the US training and equipment that had made the Brazilian army, air force, and navy the strongest armed forces on the South American continent. With help from the United States, Brazil had also constructed modern airfields and naval facilities, which had since been converted into postwar airports and ports. The improvement of the air and road transportation system in the country's interior was also directly attributable to Vargas's wartime policies. Arguably the most important of all these projects, however, was the Volta Redonda steel mill, which had been built with the help of funding from the United States. The Volta Redonda mill had played a vital role in Brazil's economic transformation during and after the war, and had helped to convert the country from an underdeveloped hinterland to an industrial powerhouse.

Vargas could also point to a strengthened Brazilian nationalism as another of his achievements during the war. Key to this was his suppression of German and Italian influence in the country.[2] His efforts from 1938 onward to bring the country's German immigrant population into line with Brazilian national culture through education and language had helped to make Brazil a more unified country during World War II.[3]

What Vargas did not highlight in his 1950 campaign were the opportunities he had missed and the decisions he had mistimed during the war. For a complex set of reasons—not least, the military's reluctance to give up on the hope of continued armament supplies from Germany—Vargas hadn't committed Brazil to the Allied cause until relatively late in the war. This had had the unintended effect of limiting Brazil's returns. By the time Brazil did formally commit to the Allies, the tide of the conflict had turned in their favor. If Vargas had committed earlier, Brazil could have played a much more strategically important role in the war. His hesitation had been part of the problem, but so too had the extensive negotiations over the FEB's equipment, training, and dispatch to Europe—all of which dragged on for so long that by the time the expeditionary force reached Europe, D-Day had already taken place and the Allies were well on the way to securing a total victory over the Axis. Vargas's decision to recall the FEB as soon as the fighting in Europe ended also cost Brazil dearly in the postwar era. Had Vargas agreed to requests from the United States to leave the force in Europe to help manage the continent in the aftermath of the war, its presence there would have strengthened Brazil's claim for a permanent seat at the United Nations. Vargas's legendary caution, as well as the restraints the military imposed on his decision making, meant that Brazil had arrived at the party too late and had left too early.

In 1950, however, Brazilians either could not see the ways in which Vargas had mismanaged the war or they didn't care. They were intent on electing the architect of Brazil's wartime policy, in the hope that he could reignite Brazil's economy and return the country to the starring role on the world stage that it had played during the war. Despite the improvements brought by World War II, Brazil's economy continued to lurch from crisis to crisis. Brazilians hoped that by winning back some of the international prominence Brazil had enjoyed in the previous decade, Vargas would be able to resuscitate the country's economy as well.

Brazil certainly had changed during the war—politically, as well as economically. The Brazilian electorate had higher expectations for their leaders, and the press was more aggressive, practicing a tabloid style of journalism that had been relatively unheard of during Vargas's previous reign. To a certain extent, Vargas managed to adapt to the new Brazilian politics, although his leadership style changed in the process. He was no longer the cool politician who carefully weighed all available opinions and options before coming down on one side or the other.[4] Instead, he aggressively took on his rivals and articulated his agenda in a manner that resembled that of his old friend, President Roosevelt.

Vargas's new style reflected his understanding that he could no longer rule by decree. Brazil had morphed into a democracy practically overnight, and he had to play by a new set of rules—and cater to a new set of Brazilians. Vargas's constituency was a curious mixture of Brazil's elites and its masses. He spoke directly to the latter in frequent national radio addresses and in mass rallies at football stadiums. His speeches and broadcasts were fiery and laced with promises of reforms, but he increasingly had trouble delivering on them. His dealings with Brazil's national congress often left him frustrated. The masses appeared to stick with him nevertheless, but the elites slowly started to peel off from his camp.

World War II had made Brazil's military extremely powerful, as Vargas had found out the hard way in October 1945. In the early 1950s, his allies were forced to concede that if the military wished to stage another coup against Vargas, there was little the president would be able to do to resist. During Vargas's term in office, the danger of a coup by some segment of the military was ever-present.

An even more serious threat was Brazil's ongoing financial crisis, which was fueled by inflationary pressures and which resulted in widespread unrest among the country's working class—unrest exacerbated by anti-Vargas communist forces. The president's long-standing personal problems, too, had started to resurface by 1953, two years into his rule. He slipped on a marble palace floor, fracturing his arm and leg. Alzira, who oversaw her father's physical rehabilitation, noted that he appeared lonely and was suffering from acute insomnia—classic signs of depression. Vargas increasingly refused to have visitors to the Catete Palace, and with the exception of a few trusted friends and family he had less and less contact with other people. Many of his circle of political associates were starting to abandon him, whether because of his failed reforms or his confrontational style, or perhaps because they were positioning themselves for future elections. As his presidency wore on, Vargas came to rely on his own family more than ever, with Alzira taking on greater influence and Benjamin, whose shortcomings the president still refused to admit, remaining as much a behind-the-scenes force as ever.

Vargas had at least one friend left: his "left eye," Osvaldo Aranha. The former foreign minister returned to the fold when an increasingly desperate Vargas appointed him to serve as his minister of finance in mid-1953. Aranha was given the herculean task of trying to manage the Brazilian economy, but his influence on Vargas went well beyond his ministerial brief. The rehabilitated Aranha gave his fellow gaúcho much-needed counsel, and spent his time trying to push a tired and worn-out president toward the path of reform.

Yet to some degree, Vargas's hands were tied—many of the problems facing Brazil at mid-century were the result of US policies over which he had little control. In the years following World War II, the United States was focused on the international fight against communism and the extension of its Marshall Plan, a program intended to reconstruct Europe both physically and economically. Washington now lavished a great deal of attention on Brazil's regional rival, Argentina, and on the strong nationalist movements that were emerging in other parts of South America, worrying—as it had once worried about Brazil—that unless it pandered to these unaligned actors, they would gravitate toward its enemy.

The United States had moved on. The administration of President Dwight D. Eisenhower was far less interested in Brazil than Roosevelt had been, and Vargas missed the attention that Washington had paid to both him and Brazil during the war.[5] That attention wasn't likely to be coming back anytime soon. The United States appeared weary of aiding Brazil; some US officials were calling for the country to take better care of itself economically. Indeed, whereas Aranha had once envisioned a full partnership between Brazil and the United States, the relationship between the two countries could now be seen for what it was: a marriage of convenience. It was a fact that Vargas, lying awake in his bed at night, surely reflected on with no small amount of bitterness.

In the end, it was not the economy or any foreign policy issue that brought down Vargas a second time, but rather a largely unforeseen series of events and intrigues, the origins of which could be traced back to the fallout from the 1938 attack on the Guanabara Palace. Once more, the military's attitude toward Vargas—and its willingness to intervene against him—was of critical importance in this new crisis, which occurred within the heated political climate that characterized much of Vargas's final term in office.

Carlos Lacerda, the publisher of Rio's daily newspaper, *Tribuna da Imprensa,* was one of the most outspoken critics of President Vargas and his regime. Lacerda had previously tried to expose corruption within the Vargas administration, as well as secret deals that, Lacerda claimed, the president had struck with Argentina. Lacerda's newspaper was full of scathing attacks on Vargas and the government, and these articles helped the publisher's nascent political career; by the start of August 1954, Lacerda was well ahead of Vargas's son, Lutero, in Brazil's congressional elections.[6] By this time, Vargas had few friends among the country's civilian elite or within its armed forces, yet he retained enough power to worry Lacerda's supporters (who counted among their number many members of Brazil's military). Following unconfirmed reports that Lacerda's life was in danger, the Brazilian air force decided to guard him on the campaign trail.

Concerns about Lacerda's safety proved accurate. At around 1 A.M. on the morning of August 5, 1954, as the publisher returned to his small apartment in the Copacabana part of the city, a gunman shot at him from a passing taxi. Lacerda was only wounded in the foot, but his air force guard, Major Rubens Vaz, was killed. The attacker fled the scene, shooting at a police car as the taxi disappeared down one of Copacabana's narrow, tree-lined avenues that link the neighborhood's interior with the beach.

Writing in his newspaper the following day, Lacerda laid down the gauntlet, accusing President Vargas of protecting the people who had carried out the attack. The result electrified an already volatile situation in Rio. Demonstrators marched past the Catete Palace calling for justice for the assassins and shouting anti-Vargas slogans.[7] The president and Aranha watched from a second-floor window in the palace, twitching at the curtains like a couple of worried old men spying on their neighbors.

The unrest did not end there. Major Vaz's funeral became a major political event; hundreds of officers from all the armed services attended, among them Eduardo Gomes and Eurico Dutra, the two military candidates from the 1945 presidential election that Dutra had—surprisingly—won. Following the funeral, more than five hundred officers met at Rio's Air Force Club to voice their anger and swap theories about the event's links to the presidential palace. The air force subsequently launched its own investigation into the shooting, claiming that it did not trust the police to do the job.

Worse soon followed. Shortly after authorities apprehended the taxi driver involved in the shooting, the head of the presidential bodyguard and the only person of color in the president's inner circle, Gregório Fortunato, was linked to the plot, accused of hiring the gunman who wounded Lacerda and killed Major Vaz. Fortunato had joined the presidential guard when it was formed by Benjamin in 1938, and succeeded Benjamin as its head in 1950. Fortunato was a simple man with little education, and he had also proven himself something of an opportunist, violating the president's trust by accepting bribes and arrangement fees from eager Brazilian bankers.[8] Soon it was discovered that Vargas's other son, Manuel, had transferred to Fortunato the deed of a property owned by the president in Rio Grande do Sul. The president denied any knowledge of the transfer, but it was another piece of evidence that he had somehow been involved in the plot.

President Vargas, who even before the crisis had been deeply depressed and racked by insomnia, was starting to sink. The situation demanded leadership and quick thinking, but Vargas hesitated; in the palace, a siege mentality deepened with each passing day. The president appeared to be sleepwalking toward a precipice.

Meanwhile the military, led by the air force, was rapidly mobilizing against Vargas. Using helicopters and spotter planes, the armed forces caught the killer in a dramatic sweep of Rio, and his arrest appeared to bring the scandal closer to the palace. When investigators searched Fortunato's files, they discovered a web of corruption and deceit that linked him to both the killing and other shady dealings.

The calls for Vargas's immediate resignation grew daily. When the investigation into Fortunato's files was complete and its results disseminated by a hostile press, the country's elites—from lawyers to academics to leaders of commerce—backed these demands. Dutra joined the fray, arguing that for the good of the country and the maintenance of law and order, the president should resign with immediate effect.

Vargas, however, vowed to withstand the pressure, arguing that there was no evidence linking his son to the plot and that he had moved quickly to disband the presidential guard to ensure that there would be no repetition of the shooting. He had ordered all palace officials to cooperate fully with investigators. He had even tried leaving Rio for Belo Horizonte, in order to refocus attention on what he saw as the government's good work there in dealing with the economic crisis.

All his efforts failed. The media were interested only in the developing scandal and its implications for the president and the country's future. Opposition forces made good use of radio to make their case for Vargas's resignation, while the president—who had once mastered that medium but had since given up his regular broadcasts—looked more and more like a politician from a bygone age.

Senior air force officers met on August 22, and led by Eduardo Gomes, demanded Vargas's resignation, effectively sealing his political fate.[9] A note containing the same demand and signed by all the officers present at the meeting was delivered to Vargas that same evening by the chief of staff of the armed forces, General Masarenham de Morais.

Everybody waited for the president's reaction. It was thought unlikely that he would be willing to agree to a deal to leave Rio and enter political exile for a second time in his career. Elements within the military called for him to be exiled from Brazil and warned that the mistakes of 1945 should not be repeated; the president should not be allowed to return to Rio Grande do Sul to start building up his political power base once again. In truth, a repeat of that scenario appeared highly unlikely in 1954. Vargas was in his early seventies and not in the best of health, and he seemed more and more like a beaten man. This time, few Brazilians expected him to make a comeback.

When the chief of staff delivered the military's note to Vargas on the evening of August 22, the president responded:

I can't agree with this. They want to slip me away from here as though I were a criminal. I have committed no crime. I'll stay in power. If necessary I'll leave bathed in blood, but I can't be made to flee like this. . . . I shall fulfill my mandate until the end, with the collaboration of the armed forces. But even if I should be abandoned by the navy, army, and air force and by my own friends, I'll resist alone . . . I have lived so much. . . . Now I can die. . . . I am too old to be demoralized, and now I have no reason to fear death.[10]

Vargas appeared calm, and the atmosphere inside the palace mirrored his demeanor; to the extent possible, it was business as usual at the Catete Palace. Alzira noted that her father appeared detached and seemed to be preparing to make a stand against what he saw as the bullying tactics of the military. He continued to plan additional trips away from Rio, saying they would be good for his spirits and would take him away from the center of the political storm.

The storm, however, hit Vargas with full force—and much quicker than he had anticipated. Just before midnight on the evening of August 23, the same night he had received a visit from the chief of staff, Vargas was informed that the military's two most senior officers were waiting downstairs, urgently asking to meet with him. Just after midnight, they were shown into Vargas's small study where the president and his brother, Benjamin, were waiting for them.

The meeting was short and tense. The officers demanded, in the name of the armed forces, that Vargas resign immediately. They gave him the choice of formally resigning or taking a leave of absence; whichever method he chose, however, the result would be the same. The military would remove Vargas from power for a second time.

Vargas refused to take either option, but he agreed to discuss the military's request at an emergency cabinet meeting, which was to be held during the early morning hours. Aranha arrived for the cabinet meeting soon after Vargas had concluded his meeting with the military; when the finance minister joined Vargas, he noted that the president was signing some papers he had taken out of a drawer. Vargas appeared calm, if slightly withdrawn. It was clear that he had played for time once more, and did not intend to take either option the military had presented.

The president appeared to be preparing for a last stand. Sandbags were being stacked outside the Catete Palace, and Alzira and her husband arrived to be with the president. Vargas, dressed in a blue-gray suit, spoke with Aranha and then his son-in-law, in front of whom he signed some more papers.[11] As he made his way downstairs to the cabinet meeting just before 3 A.M., Vargas looked relaxed, smoking a Brazilian corona cigar and talking with Benjamin.

The cabinet was in a somber state as Vargas entered. The ministers seemed to know that the meeting would not end well. Aranha took a seat on Vargas's right. Breaking with tradition, Alzira was also in the room, along with other members of the Vargas clan and a few close advisors to the president.

Vargas always handled cabinet meetings in the same methodical manner, and this time was no different. He announced in a quiet voice that there was only one item on the agenda: the future of the presidency and of his administration. He then went around the table, asking each minister to express his view on what to do. Euclides Zenóbio da Costa, the minister of war, said that, while he remained loyal to the president, he felt that if Vargas did not resign, much of the army would follow the lead of the air force and navy and take a stand against him. "If you resist," the minister said, "much blood will flow and the outcome would be far from certain."[12] Most of the other ministers dodged Vargas's question, stating simply that the eventual choice would be his alone, but that they would back him come what may.

It was left to Aranha to summarize the arguments and then spell out the options, as he had done for Vargas for decades. He outlined three alternatives: the first, that Vargas and those with him in the palace could resist the military to the extent they were able; the second, that they could rally the forces loyal to the president to come to his defense; and the third, that Vargas could resign. Aranha did not indicate any personal preference for any of the three options.

At this point, Alzira did something that she had never done before at a cabinet meeting: she intervened. "Lives are at stake, including mine," she said, "so I consider myself entitled to speak."[13] She addressed the group slowly, in a voice devoid of emotion, immediately seizing the attention of everybody in the cabinet room. It was as if she were summing up the possible rebuttals to the arguments of the minister of war. "How many generals are really against the president?" she asked, adding, "Would the resignation of the president really bring peace and tranquillity to the country?" Alzira's lawyerly counterattack was too much for the minister of war, who protested, "I am only trying to point out the consequences of any resistance." Alzira shot Zenóbio da Costa a look that said everything about what she felt about him and his loyalty to her father.

Just then, a note was handed to Vargas. It stated that the generals preferred for Vargas to take a leave of absence. The president read the note's contents to the cabinet, while Alzira continued staring down the minister of war. Some discussion of the note followed, until Vargas interrupted. He said slowly: "As the cabinet has failed to reach a conclusion, I shall make the decision. I am instructing my military ministers to maintain order throughout the country. If this is maintained, I shall withdraw. I will ask for a leave of absence. If not, the rebels will find my body in here."[14]

Without further comment, Vargas brought the meeting to a close. Instructing Aranha to make an announcement to the military to this effect, and asking Zenóbio da Costa to meet with the generals to make the necessary arrangements, he then wished his ministers a good night and, not a little wearily, made his way upstairs to his study. There, he was joined by Benjamin, then by Alzira, who looked tired but who was still hoping for some miraculous solution that would leave her father in office.

Then Vargas did something that caused his daughter great alarm. Taking a key from his jacket pocket, he informed her that it opened the private safe at the palace. "If anything should happen to me," he told her, "in there are some securities and important papers . . . The securities are for Darci and the papers are for you, Alzira. Now I'm going to sleep."[15]

Alzira pleaded with her father. "Stop all this, who is going to use the key if we all go together to our end?"

"I'm only informing you," Vargas said quietly. With that, he left the room and went to bed. For the first time in a number of nights, he was able to get straight to sleep.

Downstairs, a few cabinet members hung around the palace and took note of the growing defenses outside its gates. When word reached them that the president was asleep, they slowly slipped out into the mild Rio air. Most expected to be back at the Catete Palace the following day.[16]

Aranha went upstairs, carrying the text of an announcement of the cabinet's decision. Alzira took it immediately to her father and woke him so he could review it, but she found him disinterested in the document, wanting simply to get some sleep.[17] When Alzira told Aranha of her father's reaction, his old friend took it as a cue to return home and get some sleep himself.

As Alzira escorted Aranha out of the building, he noticed that revolvers were being handed out to those in the palace who did not already carry guns. Alzira and the family were obviously preparing for the first option he had summed up at the cabinet—to resist the military. This, Aranha thought to himself, was not going to end well, and his mind was cast back to the events of May 1938, the last time he had seen Alzira armed with a revolver.

Aranha was the final minister to leave the palace, and for a time all was quiet in the building—but not for long. At exactly 6 A.M., two army officers arrived at the front door and demanded that Benjamin accompany them immediately to an air base where the air force investigators who were continuing their inquiry into the attempted assassination of Lacerda wanted to question him and take a statement. "I cannot leave my brother at this time," Benjamin informed the officers. In the back of his mind he thought it was all a ruse, and that the air force had dispatched the men to arrest him. The officers, however, were insistent that he accompany them. Benjamin tried to stall, insisting that if the investigators wished to speak with him, they should come to him at the palace. The officers simply responded that their orders were to take him to the base.

Benjamin decided that he had better wake up his older brother, and went upstairs to find President Vargas. Both men agreed that the officers' arrival at this hour of the morning signaled the military's intention to arrest Benjamin and remove him from the palace so that he was out of the way. Benjamin again told the awaiting officers that he would not leave the president's side at this crucial time.

Learning that her father was awake, Alzira tried once more to convince him that he should move against the generals who were responsible for this outrage. She suggested arresting the ring leader, Eduardo Gomes, and claimed that there were still troops loyal to Vargas who would be willing to carry out the arrest. But Vargas was tired, and he dismissed his daughter's suggestion. "Let me sleep," he said. Alzira left the room to check on the result of the meeting of the minister of war and the generals. She did not have to wait long.

At 7 A.M., news reached Benjamin that it all was final. The minister of war, Zenóbio da Costa, and the generals had reached an agreement; Vargas would take a leave of absence, with immediate effect. Benjamin broke the news to Vargas, who queried the statement. "This means that

I am deposed?" he asked his brother. Benjamin replied in the affirmative, and tried to reassure Vargas that he had received the information from a reliable source. "Go and double check," Vargas quietly asked his brother.

At 7:45 A.M., Vargas asked his valet, who was due to give him a shave, to let him rest a little bit more. Just after 8 A.M., while Vargas was still waiting for his brother to return to formally confirm the news of his deposition, he walked across the corridor from his bedroom to his study. Still dressed in his pajamas, he startled Alzira, who had thought her father was sleeping.[18] She decided not to say anything to him, and Vargas went back into to his bedroom.

At 8:41 A.M., holding his Colt .32 pistol in his right hand, President Getúlio Vargas shot himself through the heart.[19] The gunshot echoed through the palace. On hearing the noise, Alzira ran into her father's room. There she discovered his motionless body, the pistol lying nearby. She screamed, "It can't be, it can't be, you promised." Vargas's son Lutero entered the room and pronounced his father dead.

Benjamin was left with the task of breaking the news of Vargas's death to the minister of war and thereby to the military and to Osvaldo Aranha. In a state of shock, Aranha raced toward the Catete Palace in his ministerial car. On his way, Aranha learned that Vargas's death had been a suicide.[20]

The police arrived in the president's bedroom as family members were embracing. Everybody present noticed the white envelope on the bedside table. Alzira's husband opened it, and discovered that it was the two-page message to the Brazilian people—one of the very documents that the president had signed at the last cabinet meeting.

Soon after Aranha arrived at the palace, he entered Vargas's bedroom and proclaimed, "He died in order not to sacrifice us." When he saw the farewell message, Aranha asked to take it to the director of the national radio channel, which had already begun to announce the news of Vargas's death, so that the president's last words to his country could be broadcast for all Brazil to hear. Before he left, however, Aranha read the note out loud in the corridor of the palace for the president's family and members of his staff to hear.[21] His voice choking with emotion, the old gaucho related his departed friend's last message:

Once more the forces and interests, which work against the people, have organized themselves afresh and break out against me.

They do not accuse me, they insult me; they do not fight me, they vilify and do not allow me the right to defend myself. They must silence my voice and impede my actions so that I shall not continue to defend, as I have always defended, the people and especially the humble. I follow my destiny. After decades of domination and plunder on the part of international economic and financial groups, I placed myself at the head of a revolution and won. I began the work of liberation and I installed a regime of social freedom. I had to resign. I returned to the government on the arms of the people. The underground campaign of international groups joined that of the national groups, which were working against the regime of assuring employment. The excess-profits law was held up by Congress. Hatreds were unleashed against the just revision of minimum wages. I wished to bring about national freedom in the utilization of our resources by means of Petrobrás; this had hardly begun to operate when the wave of agitation swelled. Electrobrás was obstructed to the point of despair. They do not want the worker to be free. They do not want the people to be independent.

I assumed the government in the midst of an inflationary spiral, which was destroying the rewards of work. Profits of foreign companies were reaching as much as 500 percent per year. In declarations of import values, frauds of more than $100 million per year were proved. Came the coffee crisis and the value of our main product rose. We tried to defend its price and the reply was such violent pressure on our economy that we were forced to give in.

I have fought month after month, day after day, hour after hour, resisting constant, incessant pressure, suffering everything in silence, forgetting everything, giving myself in order to defend the people who now are left deserted. There is nothing more I can give you except my blood. If the birds of prey want someone's blood, if they want to go on draining the Brazilian people, I offer my life as a holocaust. I choose this means of being always with you. When they humiliate you, you will feel my soul suffering at your side. When hunger knocks at your door, you will feel in your breast the energy to struggle for yourselves and your children. When you are scorned, my memory will give you the strength to react. My sacrifice will keep you united and my name will be your battle standard.

Each drop of my blood will be an immortal flame in your conscience and will uphold the sacred will to resist. To hatred, I answer with pardon.

And to those who think they have to defend me, I reply with my victory.
I was a slave of the people, and today I am freeing myself for eternal life.
But this people whose slave I was will no longer be slave to anyone. My
sacrifice will remain forever in their souls and my blood will be the price
of their ransom.

I fought against the spoliation of Brazil. I fought against the spoliation
of the people. I have fought with my whole heart. Hatred, infamy, and
slander have not conquered my spirit. I have given you my life. Now I offer
you my death. I fear nothing. Serenely I take my first step toward eternity
and leave life to enter history.[22]

It was a fittingly grandiose closing statement by the undersized statesman
who had led Brazil into the modern age. The note became one of the most
important and controversial documents in Brazilian history.

News of the president's death spread quickly, and soon angry mobs
had taken to the streets of Rio.[23] The front pages of some newspapers'
early editions, which had gone to print hours before Vargas had died,
falsely reported that the president had resigned and that at 5:20 A.M.
the vice president had assumed power.[24] Angry Brazilians attacked vans
carrying newspapers that had recently been hostile to Vargas, setting
the vehicles alight as they tried to distribute the afternoon edition of the
paper—the one confirming his death.[25] When it came time for Brazil to
bury its fallen president, hundreds of thousands of people lined the route
of the funeral procession.[26]

It was, ironically, the Brazilian masses who most mourned Vargas's
death. Many Brazilians thought of Vargas as the "father of the poor," but in
reality he had promised them much and delivered very little. The paradox
of his life could be seen in his World War II policies. A strong Brazilian
nationalist who was suspicious of US cultural and political aims, he had
nevertheless opened up Brazil to levels of US influence hitherto unseen
in Latin America. Under Vargas's leadership, Brazil became powerful in
ways—industrially, militarily, and to some extent geopolitically—that it
had never been before. Brazil's elites—its military leaders, politicians, business moguls, and industrial tycoons—benefited tremendously from these
advancements. But for ordinary Brazilians, still struggling with high prices
and stagnating wages, the father of the poor turned out to be a cold and
distant patriarch.

A more apt legacy for Vargas, and one more commensurate with his goals, could be seen in the city where he died. World War II and Vargas changed Rio de Janeiro beyond recognition. The city's new infrastructure amplified Brazil's international appeal and drew visitors from around the world. Guanabara Bay proved to be a gateway into the entire country— if not for the travelers themselves, then at least for their money, which gradually helped to return Brazil's economy to an even keel. The guest list at the Copacabana Palace Hotel during the 1950s and 1960s reveals a host of American stars, including John Wayne and Kirk Douglas. There were new international airports and expanded port facilities. The highway connections to the rest of the country dramatically improved and the rise of domestic steel production enabled the building of skyscrapers to tower over the city.

These changes were due as much to World War II itself as they were to the man who led Brazil through it. Thanks in large part to the opportunities afforded by the conflict, Brazil and its capital city could no longer be dismissed as postcolonial outposts at the fringes of civilization. Brazil may still have been waiting for its future to arrive, but by the time Vargas was entombed, his capital was at least living in the present.

# EPILOGUE
## THE LEGACY

$A$N EXHAUSTED OSVALDO ARANHA climbed into his ministerial car after embracing Alzira and the other surviving members of the Vargas family.[1] As the sun started to burn off the morning mist that hung over Rio's coastline, the finance minister's car pushed its way through the angry, pro-Vargas crowds that had gathered outside the Catete Palace, and made its way back downtown.

As he rode along the city's long avenues, Aranha thought of his old friend's achievements and the changes that Brazil had undergone in the years since Vargas first seized power.[2] Aranha's mind may well have drifted back to the foreign policy document he had produced for Vargas's meeting with President Roosevelt. The document had become something of a yardstick for measuring Brazil's foreign policy goals during the war, and it now revealed the distance the country had come since the war.

The original document concluded by listing the eleven objectives that Brazil should aim to achieve in the war, and by the middle of the 1950s, it was clear that Vargas's wartime policies had gone a long way toward helping Brazil to achieve these goals. Perhaps most importantly, Vargas had won Brazil a much better position in world politics than it had enjoyed before the war. True, the nation had not achieved its goal of securing a permanent seat on the United Nations Security Council. At a regional level, however, Brazil emerged from the war and its immediate aftermath as the dominant force in South America. To be sure, Brazil's rivalry with Argentina would continue, but the professionalization of Brazil's military during World War II would enable it to rest easy in its national security. Argentina had developed and strengthened with US assistance during the postwar period; indeed, Brazil's military confidence may well have helped to prevent a military confrontation with Argentina. Thanks to World War II, the Brazilian army, air force, and navy collectively became the most powerful armed forces in South America.

Perhaps the most disappointing aspect of postwar Brazilian foreign policy was its failure to develop closer cooperation with the United States. Aranha's dream of a formal alliance between the two nations was never truly fulfilled. Then, too, Brazil's militarization had its dark side. Trained and armed by the United States during World War II, the Brazilian military continued to intervene in civilian politics in the post–World War II era. Much of the political instability that characterized Brazilian postwar politics was attributable to the influence of the armed forces.

Perhaps Vargas's greatest achievement during the war was his development of Brazilian industries—especially the creation of the huge steel mill at Volta Redonda with the help of US funding. President Vargas proved himself to be a clever negotiator with the United States on this project; his victory was a huge boon for Brazil and for its ability to develop a modern economy.

Overall, however, there remains a sense that Brazil could have extracted more from the United States had it made the decision to break with the Axis powers sooner than it did, and had it formally entered the war before the conflict's outcome was certain. Had the FEB been dispatched to Europe before the middle of 1944, moreover, and had it remained there in the immediate postwar era, Brazil might have won from the conflict even more than it did.

The Vargas "revolution" in Brazil continued after his death. His political style was dominated by a powerful survival instinct, and he never succeeded in fully taking on the interest groups whose influence often rivaled his own. Ironically, the war strengthened some of Vargas's strongest opponents, particularly those in the military, who were willing to challenge and ultimately remove him from power on two occasions, in 1945 and in 1954.

Vargas's closest political allies never regained the same heights they had enjoyed while he was alive. Shortly after Vargas's death, his left eye, Osvaldo Aranha, retired from politics. He died on January 27, 1960, following a heart attack.[3] His role in the development of Brazilian foreign policy had been profound, and his close relationship with the Roosevelt administration had been critical in securing US support for the modernization of Brazil's economic infrastructure and armed forces. Today, he is remembered as the man who helped develop the close ties between Brazil and the United States at a crucial time in the nation's history.

As for Vargas's right eye, following his death Alzira became the spirited guardian of her father's political legacy. She worked with great vigor to record the key events of his career and to defend his memory against attacks from his political enemies.

And what of the legacy that Vargas worked so hard to cement in his final hours, and which Alzira spent the rest of her life protecting? The Vargas era remains a divisive issue in Brazil. For all his international pretensions and grandiose visions, the domestic implications of Vargas's politics remain the most hotly contested. Today, half a century after he took his own life (and that "first step toward eternity"), there is still no definitive answer to the charge by his critics that Vargas was the father of the poor and the mother of the rich.

# ACKNOWLEDGMENTS

Over the two and a half years that it has taken to research and write this book I have been very fortunate to receive the help and support of a number of people to whom I am extremely grateful. David Lewis has helped support my position at University College London for a number of years and has been hugely supportive of all my research and books. For this book I was very fortunate to be able to spend time in archives in Rio de Janeiro, Lisbon, London, New York, and Washington, DC. I would like to thank the British Academy and University College London for helping to finance these research trips. Even in the age of digital online archives it is vitally important to spend time in the overseas archives, many of which provide unexpected treasures.

In Rio de Janeiro, a special mention must go to Duncan and Elizabeth Barker who were fantastic hosts and did so much to make my initial trip to Brazil such a success for this book and for future projects. In Brazil, a number of people very kindly helped me navigate my way through the archives. I am especially grateful to Jaime Antunes da Silva, director general of the National Archives based in Rio de Janeiro, for giving me so much of his time and explaining exactly in which archives I needed to look for material. To Sátiro Nunes for helping me specifically with the photographs from World War II and the wider documentation in the National Archives. The whole staff at the National Archives in Rio was wonderfully helpful.

Tenente Coronel José Luiz Cruz Andrade, director of the Military Archives, helped me enormously with documents about the Força Expedicionária Brasileira (FEB) in Italy. Likewise, Leo Christiano, who kindly sent me newspaper documentation of the FEB in Italy during 1944–1945. Ruth Aqunio and George Iso helped me get started in Rio, as did Elmer C. Corrêa Barbosa. I would also like to thank the staff at O Centro de Pesquisa e Documentação de História Contemporânea do Brasil (CPDOC) é a Escola de Ciências Sociais da Fundação Getúlio Vargas for their help both in Brazil and with subsequent enquiries. The staff at Copacabana Palace Hotel were extremely helpful in providing material from the hotel's archive.

In Lisbon, I would like to thank all the staff at Torre do Tombo (the Portuguese National Archive) for their assistance in handling my frequent requests for documents. At the Portuguese Foreign Ministry Archives, I am grateful to the staff for their guidance as to which files to look for and for their guidance around their first-class archive. I would also like to thank the staff at both the Lisbon and Cascais Municipality Archives—these two local archives contain important information and records for the period.

In London, the staff at the Public Records Office (National Archives) in Kew were, as ever, extremely helpful and enthusiastic in helping direct me to the huge volume of documentary material that Brazil and its role in World War II had created. Also thank you to Professor Michael Berkowitz at University College London for his amazing enthusiasm and to Professor Joachim Shloer at Southampton University for sending me much-needed material.

In the United States, the staff at the US Holocaust Memorial Museum (USHMM) were very good in helping me locate material on the Jewish refugees in both Portugal and Brazil during World War II. Judith Cohen, director of the photographic collection at USHMM, helped identify some wonderful images. At the US National Archives in Maryland, I am extremely grateful to the staff who assisted me in locating the files (both civilian and military) that I needed in order to write this book. The lack of a good centralized computer system in the archive made the help provided by the team there absolutely invaluable. In New York at the Solomon R. Guggenheim Archive, a special note of thanks to the foundation director, Richard Armstrong, and to the archive manager, Francine Snyder, for their assistance in preparing all the documents in advance of my arrival.

At Basic Books, it has been a great pleasure working with my editor, Alex Littlefield, who has enormously helped this book develop into its final form, and also a special note of thanks to Lara Heimert, publisher at Basic Books. My thanks also to Isabelle Bleecker and the international rights team at Perseus Books Group. It has been a pleasure dealing with such a professional publisher. Additional thanks must also be given to

Francisco Espadinha at Editorial Presença for his continued support on this project and other future ones.

There are a number of people to whom I owe a debt of gratitude for their help and support during my research: both Rob and Jane Wilson, as well as Simon Frederick. Matt Freeman and Helena Shaw have done a marvelous job developing and maintaining my website over the years. To José Mateus for his boundless enthusiasm for all things to do with history and banking. Antonio Costa (Mayor of Lisbon) and Catarina Vaz-Pinto for their strong support over the years. Pureza Fino is a wonderful publicist, and it has been a great pleasure to work with her on this project as well as on the Lisbon book.

Finally, and most important of all, I owe a huge debt of gratitude to my family for their continued love and support: to my mother, my wife, Emma, and most of all my children, Benjamin and Hélèna. The book is dedicated to my wife and children, with an apology for my long absences at my writing desk.

# PHOTO CREDITS

PHOTO 1:     Fundação Joaquim Nabuco - Biblioteca Digital do MEC.

PHOTO 2:     Copacabana Hotel Arquivo Histórico.

PHOTO 3:     O Centro de Pesquisa e Documentação de História Contemporânea do Brasil (CPDOC) é a Escola de Ciências Sociais da Fundação Getúlio Vargas.

PHOTO 4:     O Centro de Pesquisa e Documentação de História Contemporânea do Brasil (CPDOC) é a Escola de Ciências Sociais da Fundação Getúlio Vargas.

PHOTO 5:     O Centro de Pesquisa e Documentação de História Contemporânea do Brasil (CPDOC) é a Escola de Ciências Sociais da Fundação Getúlio Vargas.

PHOTO 6:     O Centro de Pesquisa e Documentação de História Contemporânea do Brasil (CPDOC) é a Escola de Ciências Sociais da Fundação Getúlio Vargas.

PHOTO 7:     Copacabana Hotel Arquivo Histórico.

PHOTO 8:     O Centro de Pesquisa e Documentação de História Contemporânea do Brasil (CPDOC) é a Escola de Ciências Sociais da Fundação Getúlio Vargas.

PHOTO 9:     Copacabana Hotel Arquivo Histórico.

PHOTO 10:   O Centro de Pesquisa e Documentação de História Contemporânea do Brasil (CPDOC) é a Escola de Ciências Sociais da Fundação Getúlio Vargas.

PHOTO 11:   O Centro de Pesquisa e Documentação de História Contemporânea do Brasil (CPDOC) é a Escola de Ciências Sociais da Fundação Getúlio Vargas.

PHOTO 12:   O Centro de Pesquisa e Documentação de História Contemporânea do Brasil (CPDOC) é a Escola de Ciências Sociais da Fundação Getúlio Vargas.

PHOTO 13:   O Centro de Pesquisa e Documentação de História Contemporânea do Brasil (CPDOC) é a Escola de Ciências Sociais da Fundação Getúlio Vargas.

PHOTO 14:   Fundação Biblioteca Nacional.

PHOTO 15:   Public domain.

PHOTO 16:   O Centro de Pesquisa e Documentação de História Contemporânea do Brasil (CPDOC) é a Escola de Ciências Sociais da Fundação Getúlio Vargas.

# BIBLIOGRAPHY

## Unpublished Documents and Photographs

### *National Archives (Public Records Office), Kew, London*

| | |
|---|---|
| ADM | Records of the Royal Admiralty, Royal Naval Forces, Royal Marines, Royal Coastguard, and related bodies. |
| AIR | Records created or inherited by the Air Ministry, the Royal Air Force, and related bodies. |
| BT | Records of the Board of Trade and of successor and related bodies. |
| CAB | Records of the Cabinet Office. |
| CO | Records of the Colonial Office, Commonwealth Office, Foreign and Commonwealth Offices, Empire Marketing Board, and related bodies. |
| FO | Records created and inherited by the Foreign Office. |
| GFM | Copies of captured records of the German, Italian, and Japanese governments. |
| HO | Records created or inherited by the Home Office, Ministry of Home Security, and related bodies. |
| HW | Records created and inherited by Government Communications Headquarters (GCHQ). |
| KV | Records of the Security Service. |
| T | Records created and inherited by HM Treasury. |
| WO | Records created or inherited by the War Office, Armed Forces, Judge Advocate General, and related bodies. |

### *Rio de Janeiro*

Arquivo Geral da Cidade do Rio de Janeiro.
Arquivo Histórico do Exército.
Arquivo Histórico do Itamaraty.
Arquivo Nacional.
O Centro de Pesquisa e Documentação de História Contemporânea do Brasil (CPDOC).

### *Arquivo Nacional, Torre do Tombo, Lisboa, Portugal*

AOS Arquivo Salazar.
Comissão de Livro Branco do Ministério dos Negócios Estrangeiros.
Correspondência Diplomática. 1935–1946.

Correspondência Oficial. 1928–1946.
Correspondência Oficial Especial. 1934–1946.
Diários. 1936–1946.
Papéis Pessoais. 1936–1946.

### The Wiener Library, London

| | |
|---|---|
| Mf Doc 2 | International Committee of the Red Cross: G59 Israélites. 1939–1961. |
| Mf Doc 56 | World Jewish Congress: Central Files. 1919–1976. |
| 548 | Wilfred Israel papers. 1940s. |
| 585 | Documents regarding the Nazis in Spain. 1933–1936. |
| 660 | Thomas Cook and Son: Storage Records Book. 1914–1969. |
| 683 | Jewish Refugees in Portugal: various papers. 1930s. |
| 1072 | Records and correspondence regarding Gurs and other French concentration camps. 1940s. |
| 1100 | Nsdap Auswaertigesamt: papers on Jews in Spain and Portugal. 1930s. |

### US Holocaust Memorial Museum (USHMM), Washington, DC

General correspondence between Jewish refugees in Brazil and officials and relatives.
Steven Spielberg Film and Video Archive at US Holocaust Memorial Museum.
US Holocaust Memorial Museum Photograph Archive, Washington, DC.
W/S/59581–86458: photographs of Jewish refugees in (and departing) Lisbon during World War II.

### US National Archives, College Park, Maryland

| | |
|---|---|
| RG84 | Classified records of the US Embassy in Rio. 1937–1954. |
| RG165 | Records of the War Department, Military Intelligence Division, Brazil. 1937–1946. |
| RG84 | Classified records of the US Embassy in Lisbon. 1939–1945. |
| RG84 | Classified records of the US Embassy in Madrid. 1940–1963. |
| RG84 | Classified records of the US Embassy in Paris. 1944–1963. |
| RG226 | Records of the Office of Strategic Services, relevant files to Brazil and Operation Safehaven. |

## Published Documents

"Foreign Relations of the United States, Brazil: 1939–1942."
"Foreign Relations of the United States, Brazil: 1943–1945."
*O Cruzeiro do Sul: Coleção Completa do Órgão Especial da FEB na Itália.* Rio de Janeiro: Léo Christiano Editorial, Biblioteca do Exército, 2011.

## Magazines, News Agencies, Newspapers, and Television News

| | | |
|---|---|---|
| *Associated Press* | *Correio de Manhã* | *Daily Telegraph* |
| BBC News | *Daily Express* | *Diário Carioca* |
| British Pathé News | *Daily Mail* | *Diário da Manhã* |

| | | |
|---|---|---|
| *Diário de Lisboa* | *Life* | *The Economist* |
| *Diário de Notícias* | *New York Times* | *Time* |
| Fatos e Fotos | *O Premeiro de Janeiro* | *Times* (London) |
| *Financial Times* | *Reuters* | *United Press* |
| *Harpers* | *San Francisco Chronicle* | *Washington Post* |
| *Jornal do Brasil* | *The Atlantic* | |

## Books, Journals, and Articles

Anderson, James A. *The History of Portugal.* Westport, CT: Greenwood Press, 2000.

Bachrach, Fabian. *The Memoirs of Cordell Hull; In Two Volumes.* New York: MacMillan, 1948.

Baer, Werner. *The Brazilian Economy: Growth and Development.* Westport, CT: Praeger Publishers, 2001.

Beevor, Antony. *The Second World War.* London: Weidenfeld and Nicolson, 2012.

Benamou, Catherine L. *It's All True: Orson Welles's Pan-American Odyssey.* Berkeley, Los Angeles, and London: University of California Press, 2007.

Bethencourt, Francisco, and Diogo Ramada Curto. *Portuguese Oceanic Expansion, 1400–1800.* New York: Cambridge University Press, 2007.

Birmingham, David. *A Concise History of Portugal.* Cambridge: Cambridge University Press, 2003.

Bower, Tom. *Nazi Gold: The Full Story of the Fifty-Year Swiss-Nazi Conspiracy to Steal Billions from Europe's Jews and Holocaust Survivors.* New York: HarperCollins, 1997.

Bradsher, Greg. *Holocaust-Era Assets: A Finding Aid to Records at the National Archives at College Park, Maryland.* College Park, MD: NARA, 1999.

Branco, Manoel Thomaz Castello. *O Brasil na II Grande Guerra.* Rio de Janeiro: Biblioteca do Exército, 1960.

Brandão, Fernando de Castro. *Antonio de Oliveira Salazar: Uma Cronologia.* Lisboa: Editora Prefacio, 2011.

Burleigh, Michael. *The Third Reich: A New History.* London: Pan Books, 2001.

Caetano, Marcello. *Minhas Memórias de Salazar.* Lisboa: Editorial Verbo, 2006.

Callow, Simon. *Orson Welles: Hello Americans.* London: Vintage Books, 2007.

———. *Orson Welles: The Road to Xanadu.* London: Vintage Books, 1996.

Carneiro, Maria Luiza Tucci. *O Anti-Semitismo na Era Vargas.* São Paulo: Editora Perspectiva, 2001.

Caron, Vicki. *Uneasy Asylum: France and the Jewish Refugee Crisis, 1933–1942.* Stanford, CA: Stanford University Press, 1999.

Carrazzoni, André. *Getúlio Vargas.* Rio de Janeiro: Livaria José Olympio Editora, 1939.

Carvalho, José Murilo de. "Armed Forces and Politics in Brazil, 1930–45." *Hispanic American Historical Review* 62, no. 2 (May 1982): 193–223.

Castaño, David. *Paternalismo e Cumplicidade: As Relações Luso-Britânicas de 1943 a 1949.* Lisboa: Associação dos Amigos do Arquivo Histórico-Diplomático, 2006.

Churchill, Winston. *The Second World War (Abridged Version).* London: Pimlico, 2002.

———. *The Second World War.* 6 vols. London: Folio Society, 2000.

Claret, Martin. *O Pansemento Vivo de Getúlio Vargas.* São Paulo: Martin Claret Editores, 1989.

Cruz, Natália dos Reis. "A Imigração Judaica no Brasil e o Anti-Semitismo no Discurso das Elites." *Politica and Sociedade* 8, no. 15 (October 2009): 225–250.

Davis, Darién J., and Oliver Marshall. *Stefan and Lotte Zweig's South American Letters: New York, Argentina and Brazil, 1940–42.* New York and London: Continuum Books, 2010.

Delgado, Humberto. *The Memoirs of General Delgado.* London: Cassell, 1964.

Disney, Anthony R. *A History of Portugal and the Portuguese Empire.* 2 vols. Cambridge: Cambridge University Press, 2009.

Duggan, Christopher. *A Concise History of Italy.* Cambridge: Cambridge University Press, 1997.

Dulles, John W. F. *Vargas of Brazil: A Political Biography.* Austin and London: University of Texas Press, 1967.

Eccles, David. *By Safe Hand: Letters of Sybil and David Eccles, 1939–42.* London, Sydney, and Toronto: The Bodley Head, 1983.

Eisenhower, Dwight D. *Crusade in Europe.* London and Toronto: William Heinemann, 1946.

Eizenstat, Stuart E. *Imperfect Justice: Looted Assets, Slave Labor, and the Unfinished Business of World War II.* New York: PublicAffairs, 2003.

Evans, Richard J. *The Third Reich at War: How the Nazis Led Germany from Conquest to Disaster.* London: Penguin Books, 2009.

Falbel, Nachman. "Jewish Agricultural Settlement in Brazil." *Jewish History* 21, no. 3/4 (2007): 325–340.

Fausto, Boris. *A Concise History of Brazil.* New York: Cambridge University Press, 1999.

Ferguson, Niall. *The House of Rothschild: Money's Prophets, 1798–1848.* New York: Penguin Books, 1999.

———. *The House of Rothschild: The World's Banker, 1849–1999.* New York: Penguin Books, 2000.

Ferraz, Francisco Alves. "Brazilian Participation in World War II." *Luso-Brazilian Review* 47, no. 1 (2010): 11–39.

Ferro, Antonio. *Salazar: Portugal and Her Leader.* London: Faber and Faber, 1935.

Figueiredo, Antonio de. *Portugal: Fifty Years of Dictatorship.* London: Penguin Books, 1975.

Foot, Michael R. D., and James M. Langley. *MI9: Escape and Evasion 1939–1945.* London: Biteback Publishing, 2011.

Frank, Waldo. *America Hispana: A Portrait and a Prospect.* New York and London: Charles Scribner's Sons, 1931.

———. *South American Journey.* London: Travel Book Club, 1946.

Friedman, Max Paul. *Nazis and Good Neighbors: The United States Campaign Against the Germans of Latin America in World War II.* Cambridge and New York: Cambridge University Press, 2003.

Fry, Varian. *Surrender on Demand.* Boulder, CO: Johnson Publishing/United States Holocaust Memorial Museum, 1997.

Gaddis, John L. *George F. Kennan: An American Life.* New York: Penguin Press, 2011.

García, Juan Pujol, and Nigel West. *Operation Garbo: The Personal Story of the Most Successful Spy of World War II.* London: Biteback Publishing, 2011.

Garcia, Maria M. *Arquivo Salazar: Inventário e Índices.* Lisboa: Editorial Estampa/ Biblioteca Nacional, 1992.

Garnier, Christine. *Salazar in Portugal: An Intimate Portrait.* New York: Farrar, Straus and Young, 1954.

Gellman, Irwin F. *Secret Affairs: FDR, Cordell Hull, and Sumner Welles.* New York: Enigma Books, 1995.

Ginsburg, Solomon L. *A Wandering Jew in Brazil: An Autobiography of Solomon L. Ginsburg.* Victoria, BC: Trafford Publishing, 2006.

Gunther, John. *Inside Latin America.* London: Hamish Hamilton, 1942.

Hastings, Max. *All Hell Let Loose: The World at War, 1939–1945.* London: Harper-Press, 2011.

Herz, Norman. *Operation Alacrity: The Azores and the War in the Atlantic.* Annapolis, MD: Naval Institute Press, 2004.

Hildebrand, Klaus. *The Foreign Policy of the Third Reich.* Berkeley and Los Angeles: University of California Press, 1973.

———. *The Third Reich.* London: George Allen and Unwin, 1984.

Hilton, Stanley E. "Diplomacy and the Washington–Rio de Janeiro 'Axis' During the World War II Era." *Hispanic American Historical Review* 59, no. 2 (May 1979): 201–231.

———. *Hitler's Secret War in South America, 1939–1945: German Military Espionage and Allied Counterespionage in Brazil.* New York: Ballantine Books, 1982.

———. "The Overthrow of Getúlio Vargas in 1945: Diplomatic Intervention, Defense of Democracy, or Political Retribution?" *Hispanic American Historical Review* 67, no. 1 (February 1987): 1–37.

———. "The United States, Brazil, and the Cold War, 1945–1960: End of the Special Relationship." *The Journal of American History* 68, no. 3 (December 1981): 599–624.

Hinsely, Francis H. *British Intelligence in the Second World War.* London: Her Majesty's Stationery Office, 1993.

Hoare, Samuel (Viscount Templewood). *Ambassador on Special Mission.* London: Collins, 1946.

———. *Nine Troubled Years.* London: Collins, 1954.

Holland, James. *Italy's Sorrow: A Year of War, 1944–45.* London: HarperPress, 2008.

Holt, Taddeus. *The Deceivers: Allied Military Deception in the Second World War.* London: Phoenix, 2005.

Hull, Cordell. *The Memoirs of Cordell Hull.* 2 vols. London: Hodder and Stoughton, 1948.

Justino, Ana C., ed. *O Século XX em Revista: Actas do Ciclo de Conferencias Realizado No Espaço-Memória dos Exílios, Estoril, em 2000/2001.* Cascais: Câmara Municipal de Cascais, 2002.

Kay, Hugh. *Salazar and Modern Portugal: A Biography.* New York: Hawthorn Books, 1970.

Laqueur, Walter. *Generation Exodus: The Fate of Young Jewish Refugees from Nazi Germany.* Hanover, NH, and London, UK: University Press of New England, 2001.

Lauderbaugh, George M. "Bolivarian Nations: Securing the Northern Frontier." In *Latin America During World War II,* edited by Thomas M. Leonard and John F. Bratzel, 109–125. Plymouth, UK: Rowan and Littlefield Publishers, 2007.

Lesser, Jeffrey. *Welcoming the Undesirables: Brazil and the Jewish Question.* Berkeley: University of California Press, 1995.

———. "Continuity and Change Within an Immigrant Community: The Jews of São Paulo, 1924–1945." *Luso-Brazilian Review* 25, no. 2 (Winter 1988): 45–58.

———. "How the Jews Became Japanese and Other Stories of Nation and Ethnicity." *Jewish History* 18, no. 1 (2004): 7–17.

———. "The Immigration and Integration of Polish Jews in Brazil, 1924–1934." *The Americas* 51, no. 2 (October 1994): 173–191.

———. "Immigration and Shifting Concepts of National Identity in Brazil During the Vargas Era." *Luso-Brazilian Review* 31, no. 2 (1994): 23–44.

———. *Welcoming the Undesirables: Brazil and the Jewish Question.* Berkeley and Los Angeles: University of California Press, 1995.

Levine, Robert M. *The Brazilian Photographs of Genevieve Naylor, 1940–1942.* Durham, NC: Duke University Press, 1998.

———. "Brazil's Jews During the Vargas Era and After." *Luso-Brazilian Review* 5, no. 1 (Summer 1968): 45–58.

———. *Father of the Poor? Vargas and His Era.* New York and Cambridge: Cambridge University Press, 1998.

———. *The History of Brazil.* Wesport, CT, and London: Greenwood Press, 1999.

———. *The Vargas Regime: The Critical Years, 1934–1938.* New York and London: Columbia University Press, 1970.

Livermore, Harold V. *A New History of Portugal.* Cambridge: Cambridge University Press, 1966.

Lochery, Neill. *Lisbon: War in the Shadows of the City of Light, 1939–1945.* New York: PublicAffairs, 2011.

MacDonald, Callum A. "The Politics of Intervention: The United States and Argentina, 1941–1946." *Journal of Latin American Studies* 12, no. 2 (November 1980): 365–396.

Machado, F. Zenha. *Os Últimas Dias do Govêrno de Vargas: A Crise Política de Agôsto de 1954.* Rio de Janeiro: Editora Lux, 1955.

Macintyre, Ben. *Agent ZigZag: The True Wartime Story of Eddie Chapman: Lover, Betrayer, Hero, Spy.* London: Bloomsbury, 2010.

Madeira, Lina Alves. *Correspondência de um Diplomata no III Reich: Veiga Simões, Ministro Acreditado em Berlim de 1933 a 1940.* Coimbra: Mar da Palavra Edições, 2001.

Mandrell, James. "Carmen Miranda Betwixt and Between, or, Neither Here Nor There." *Latin American Literary Review* 29, no. 57 (January–June 2001): 26–39.

Matos, Helena. *Salazar: A Construção do Mito, 1928–1933.* Lisboa: Círculode Leitores e Temas e Debates, 2010.

———. *Salazar: A Propoganda, 1934–1938.* Lisboa: Círculode Leitores e Temas e Debates, 2010.

Maxwell, Kenneth. *The Making of Portuguese Democracy.* Cambridge: Cambridge

University Press, 1995.

McCann, Bryan. *Hello, Hello Brazil: Popular Music in the Making of Modern Brazil.* Durham, NC, and London: Duke University Press, 2004.

McCann, Frank D. "Brazil and World War II: The Forgotten Ally. What Did You Do in the War, Zé Carioca?" Tel Aviv University, 1997. This article was also published in *Estudios Interdisciplinarios de America Latina y el Caribe* 6, no. 2 (July–December 1995): 35–70. http://www.tau.ac.il/eial/VI_2/mccann.htm.

———. "The Brazilian Army and the Problem of Mission, 1939–1964." *Journal of Latin American Studies* 12, no. 1 (May 1980): 107–126.

———. "Brazil, the United States, and World War II: A Commentary." *Diplomatic History* 3, no. 1 (January 1979): 59–76.

Mendes, Oswaldo. *Getúlio Vargas.* São Paulo: Editora Moderna, 1986.

Meneses, Filipe Ribeiro de. *Salazar: A Political Biography.* New York: Enigma Books, 2009.

Milgram, Avraham. *Portugal, Salazar e os Judeus.* Lisboa: Gravida Publicações, 2010.

Muggeridge, Malcolm. *Ciano's Diary: 1939–1943.* London and Toronto: William Heinemann, 1947.

Narloch, Leandro. *Guia Politicamente Incorreto da História do Brasil.* Alfragide: Dom Quixote, 2011.

Niemeyer, Oscar. *The Curves of Time: The Memoirs of Oscar Niemeyer.* London and New York: Phaidon Press, 2000.

Nunes, João Paulo Avelãs. *O Estado Novo e o Volfrâmio, 1933–1947.* Coimbra: Coimbra University Press. 2010.

Overy, Richard. *The Dictators: Hitler's Germany, Stalin's Russia.* London: Penguin Books, 2005.

Paxton, Robert O. *The Anatomy of Fascism.* London: Penguin Books, 2005.

Payne, Stanley G. *A History of Fascism, 1914–45.* Abingdon, UK: Routledge, 2005.

———. *A History of Spain and Portugal.* 2 vols. Madison and London: The University of Wisconsin Press, 1973.

Peixoto, Alzira Vargas de Amaral. *Getúlio Vargas: Meu Pai.* Rio de Janeiro: Editôra Globo, 1960.

Persico, Joseph E. *The Imperial Rockefeller: A Biography of Nelson A. Rockefeller.* New York: Simon and Schuster, 1982.

Philby, Kim. *My Silent War: The Autobiography of a Spy.* New York: Modern Library, 1968.

Philips, Harlan B. *Felix Frankfurter Reminisces: Recorded in Talks with Dr. Harlan B. Philips.* London: Secker and Warburg, 1960.

Pimental, Irene Flunser. *Judeus em Portugal Durante a II Guerra Mundial: Em Fuga de Hitlier e do Holocausto.* Lisboa: A Esfera dos Livros, 2006.

Pinheiro, Magda. *Biografia de Lisboa.* Lisboa: A Estefra dos Livros, 2011.

Rambali, Paul. *It's All True: In the Cities and Jungles of Brazil.* London: William Heinemann, 1993.

Reich, Cary. *The Life of Nelson A. Rockefeller: Worlds to Conquer, 1908–1958.* New York and London: Doubleday, 1996.

Roberts, Andrew. *The Storm of War: A New History of the Second World War.* London: Penguin Books, 2010.

Rodrigues, Luís Nuno. *Franklin Roosevelt: E Os Açores Na Duas Guerras Mundial.* Lisboa: Fundação Luso-Americana, 2008.

Roett, Riordan. *The New Brazil.* Washington, DC: Brookings Institution Press, 2011.

Rosas, Fernando, Julia Leitão de Barros, and Pedro de Oliveira. *Armindo Monteiro e Oliveira Salazar: Correspondência Política, 1926–1955.* Lisboa: Editorial Estampa, 1996.

Russell-Wood, Anthony J. R. *The Portuguese Empire, 1415–1808: A World on the Move.* Baltimore, MD, and London: Johns Hopkins University Press, 1998.

Salazar, António de Oliveira. *Pensamento e Doutrina Política.* Lisboa: Babel, 2010.

Saraiva, José Hermano. *Portugal: A Companion History.* Manchester, UK: Carcanet Press, 1997.

Schellenberg, Walter. *Walter Schellenberg: The Memoirs of Hitler's Spymaster.* London: André Deutsch (Carlton Publishing Group), 2006.

Schreiner, Claus. *Múscia Brasileira: A History of Popular Music and the People of Brazil.* New York and London: Marion Boyars Publishers, 2002.

Selby, Walford. *Diplomatic Twilight, 1930–1940.* London: John Murray Publishers, 1953.

Shepherd, Naomi. *A Refuge from Darkness: Wilfred Israel and the Rescue of the Jews.* New York: Pantheon Books, 1984.

Skidmore, Thomas E. *Brazil: Five Centuries of Change.* New York and Oxford: Oxford University Press, 1999.

———. "Brazil's American Illusion: From Dom Pedro II to the Coup of 1964." *Luso-Brazilian Review* 23, no. 2 (Winter 1986): 71–84.

———. *Politics in Brazil, 1930–1964: An Experiment in Democracy.* New York and Oxford: Oxford University Press, 2007.

Smallman, Shawn C. *Fear and Memory in the Brazilian Army and Society, 1889–1954.* Chapel Hill and London: University of North Carolina Press, 2002.

Smith, Michael. *The Secrets of Station X: How the Bletchley Park Codebreakers Helped Win the War.* London: Biteback Publishing, 2011.

Stone, Glyn. *The Oldest Ally: Britain and the Portuguese Connection, 1936–1941.* Suffolk, UK: Royal Historical Society/Boydell Press, 1994.

———. *Spain, Portugal and the Great Powers, 1931–1941.* Hampshire, UK, and New York: Palgrave MacMillan, 2005.

Taylor, Alan J. P. *The Origins of the Second World War.* London: Penguin Books, 1991.

Telo, António José. *A Neutralidade Portuguesa e o Ouro Nazi.* Lisboa: Quetzal Editores, 2000.

———. *Portugal na Segunda Guerra, 1941–1945.* 2 vols. Lisboa: Vega, 1991.

Thomas, Bob. *Walt Disney: An American Original.* New York: Disney Editions, 1994.

Tota, Antonio Pedro. *The Seduction of Brazil: The Americanization of Brazil During World War II.* Austin: University of Texas Press, 2009.

Trabulo, António. *O Diário de Salazar.* Lisboa: Parceria A. M. Pereira, 2008.

Turner, Ewart Edmund. "German Influence in South Brazil." *Public Opinion Quarterly* 6, no. 1 (Spring 1942): 57–69.

Vargas, Getúlio. *Diário: Volume II, 1937–1942.* Rio de Janeiro: Editora Siciliano/ Fundação Getúlio Vargas, 1995.

———. *Discurso de Posse na Academia Brasileira de Letras.* Rio de Janeiro: Americedit, 1944.

Vincent, Isabel. "Luis Martins de Souza Dantas: Brazil's Schindler." *Macleans,* May 15, 2005.

Vincente, Ana. *Portugal: Visto Pela Espanha, Correspondência Diplomática, 1939–1960.* Lisboa: Assírio e Alvim, 1992.

Waller, Douglas. *Wild Bill Donovan: The Spymaster Who Created the OSS and Modern American Espionage.* New York and London: Free Press, 2011.

Walters, Guy. *Hunting Evil: How the Nazi War Criminals Escaped and the Hunt to Bring Them to Justice.* London: Bantam Press, 2009.

Weis, W. Michael. "The Fundação Getúlio Vargas and the New Getúlio." *Luso-Brazilian Review* 24, no. 2 (Winter 1987): 49–60.

Welles, Orson, and Peter Bogdanovich. *This Is Orson Welles.* New York: Da Capo Press, 1998.

Wheeler, Douglas L. *Historical Dictionary of Portugal.* Metuchen, NJ, and London: Scarecrow Press, 1993.

Wilken, Patrick. *Empire Adrift: The Portuguese Court in Rio de Janeiro, 1808–1821.* London: Bloomsbury, 2004.

Williams, Daryle. *Culture Wars in Brazil: The First Vargas Regime, 1930–1945.* Durham, NC, and London: Duke University Press, 2001.

Williamson, Edwin. *The Penguin History of Latin America.* London: Penguin Books, 2009.

Woodward, Llewellyn. *History of the Second World War: British Foreign Policy in the Second World War.* London: Her Majesty's Stationery Office, 1962.

Zweig, Stefan. *Brazil: Land of the Future.* New York: Viking Press, 1941.

# NOTES

## Introduction

1. John Gunther, *Inside Latin America* (London: Hamish Hamilton, 1942), 296.

2. Ibid., 281. For United States population data, see: http://www.npg.org/facts/us_historical_pops.htm. For the current Brazilian population, see: https://www.cia.gov/library/publications/the-world-factbook/geos/br.html.

3. Stefan Zweig, *Brazil: Land of the Future* (New York: Viking Press, 1941), 128.

4. Frank D. McCann, "Brazil and World War II: The Forgotten Ally. What Did You Do in the War, Zé Carioca?" Tel Aviv University, 1997, 19. This article was published in *Estudios Interdisciplinarios de América Latina y el Caribe* 6, no. 2 (July–December 1995), 35–70, http://www.tau.ac.il/eial/VI_2/mccann.htm.

## Prologue: The Good Neighbor

1. Inaugural Address, Swearing-In Ceremony for Franklin D. Roosevelt, Joint Congressional Committee on Inaugural Ceremonies, March 4, 1933.

2. Cordell Hull, *The Memoirs of Cordell Hull*, vol. 1 (London: Hodder and Stoughton, 1948), 308.

3. Hull, *The Memoirs of Cordell Hull*, vol. 1, 310.

4. NARA/RG165/304, Records of the War Department, Military Intelligence Division, Brazil, Brazilian Statements Regarding Argentina, November 23, 1943, 1.

5. Hull, *The Memoirs of Cordell Hull*, vol. 1, 170.

6. NARA/RG84/18, General Records of the Embassy in Rio de Janeiro, Embassy in Rio to State Department, April 23, 1937, 1.

7. Ibid, 2.

8. NARA/RG84/21, General Records of the Embassy in Rio de Janeiro, Embassy in Rio to State Department, December 17, 1937, 1.

9. Ibid.

10. Ibid.

11. Antonio Pedro Tota, *The Seduction of Brazil: The Americanization of Brazil During World War II* (Austin: University of Texas Press, 2009), 112.

12. Hull, *The Memoirs of Cordell Hull*, vol. 1, 495.

13. NARA/RG84/23, General Records of the Embassy in Rio de Janeiro, Embassy in Rio to State Department, Address of President Vargas to the Nation, November 11, 1937, 1.

14. Ibid.

15. For more background on this topic, see Jeffrey Lesser, *Welcoming the Undesirables: Brazil and the Jewish Question* (Berkeley and Los Angeles: University of California Press, 1995).

## Chapter 1: The Key

1. Waldo Frank, *South American Journey* (London: Travel Book Club, 1946), 202.

2. Ibid.

3. John W. F. Dulles, *Vargas of Brazil: A Political Biography* (Austin and London: University of Texas Press, 1967), 205.

4. PRO/FO/371/30372, Personalities in Brazil in 1942, 20–21.

5. Dulles, *Vargas of Brazil*, 9.

6. Alzira Vargas do Amaral Peixoto, *Getúlio Vargas: Meu Pai* (Rio de Janeiro: Editôra Globo, 1960), 119.

7. Dulles, *Vargas of Brazil*, 168.

8. Peixoto, *Getúlio Vargas: Meu Pai*, 120.

9. Getúlio Vargas, *Diário: Volume II, 1937–1942* (Rio de Janeiro: Editora Siciliano/ Fundação Getúlio Vargas, 1995), 130.

10. Peixoto, *Getúlio Vargas: Meu Pai*, 124.

11. Vargas, *Diário*, 130.

12. Peixoto, *Getúlio Vargas: Meu Pai*, 124.

13. Dulles, *Vargas of Brazil*, 183.

14. Robert M. Levine, *The Vargas Regime: The Critical Years, 1934–1938* (New York and London: Columbia University Press, 1970), 164.

15. Peixoto, *Getúlio Vargas: Meu Pai*, 125.

16. NARA/RG84/37, General Records of the Embassy in Rio de Janeiro, Caffery to Secretary of State, May 12, 1938.

17. FGV/CPDOC, Revolta Integralista, May 11, 1938.

18. FGV/CPDOC, Belmiro Valverde/Verbete.

19. NARA/RG84/37, General Records of the Embassy in Rio de Janeiro, Caffery to Secretary of State, May 12, 1938.

20. Levine, *The Vargas Regime*, 164.

21. FGV/CPDOC, Revolta Integralista, May 11, 1938.

22. FGV/CPDOC, Belmiro Valverde/Verbete.

23. NARA/RG84/37, General Records of the Embassy in Rio de Janeiro, Caffery to Secretary of State, May 12, 1938.

24. Ibid.

25. Levine, *The Vargas Regime*, 164.

26. Ibid.

27. Thomas E. Skidmore, *Politics in Brazil, 1930–1964: An Experiment in Democracy* (Oxford and New York: Oxford University Press, 2007), 342n56.

28. Dulles, *Vargas of Brazil*, 186.

29. Peixoto, *Getúlio Vargas: Meu Pai*, 130.

30. Levine, *The Vargas Regime*, 164.

31. PRO/FO/371/30361, Letter from Noel Charles to Anthony Eden, April 27, 1942.

32. Dulles, *Vargas of Brazil,* 186.

33. Peixoto, *Getúlio Vargas: Meu Pai,* 133.

34. Vargas, *Diário,* 131.

35. Dulles, *Vargas of Brazil,* 189.

36. Frank, *South American Journey,* 202.

## Chapter 2: The Left Eye of Vargas

1. NARA/RG84/37, General Records of the Embassy in Rio de Janeiro, Ministry of Foreign Affairs in Rio de Janeiro to Foreign Diplomatic Corps, May 12, 1938.

2. Getúlio Vargas, *Diário: Volume II, 1937–1942* (Rio de Janeiro: Editora Siciliano/ Fundação Getúlio Vargas, 1995), 132.

3. Robert M. Levine, *The Vargas Regime: The Critical Years, 1934–1938* (New York and London: Columbia University Press, 1970), 164.

4. John W. F. Dulles, *Vargas of Brazil: A Political Biography* (Austin and London: University of Texas Press, 1967), 188.

5. FGV/CPDOC, Revolta Integralista, May 11, 1938.

6. FGV/CPDOC, Severo Fournier/Verbete.

7. Ibid.

8. Dulles, *Vargas of Brazil,* 189.

9. FGV/CPDOC, Severo Fournier/Verbete.

10. Dulles, *Vargas of Brazil,* 187.

11. FGV/CPDOC, Severo Fournier/Verbete.

12. Fournier, like many of the plotters of May 11, was released early from prison. During his time in jail, however, he contracted tuberculosis and died soon after his release.

13. Thomas E. Skidmore, *Politics in Brazil, 1930–1964: An Experiment in Democracy* (Oxford and New York: Oxford University Press, 2007), 342n56.

14. FGV/CPDOC/GV, Aranha to Vargas, June 26, 1938.

15. Vargas, *Diário,* 142–143.

16. Ibid., 144.

17. Ibid., 145.

18. Dulles, *Vargas of Brazil,* 188.

19. Ibid., 244.

20. Vargas kept a diary until a car accident in 1942. A round of golf would often be the only entry for a particular day.

21. Waldo Frank, *South American Journey* (London: Travel Book Club, 1946), 201.

22. Frank, *South American Journey,* 23.

23. NARA/RG84/147, General Records of the Embassy in Rio de Janeiro/Radio Script for Orson Welles and Osvaldo Aranha, National Broadcasting Company, April 16, 1942.

24. PRO/FO/371/25817, Records of Leading Personalities in Brazil for 1941, October 25, 1941, 3.

25. Alzira Vargas do Amaral Peixoto, *Getúlio Vargas: Meu Pai* (Rio de Janeiro: Editôra Globo, 1960), 235.

26. NARA/RG84/31, General Records of the Embassy in Rio de Janeiro, Caffery to State Department, January 28, 1938.

27. NARA/RG84/15, General Records of the Embassy in Rio de Janeiro, Biographical Sketch of Mr. Jefferson Caffery, June 23, 1937.

28. NARA/RG84/37, General Records of the Embassy in Rio de Janeiro, Revision of Post Report, April 7, 1938.

29. PRO/FO/371/30365, From Charles to Foreign Office, February 5, 1938.

30. PRO/FO/371/30365, Foreign Office to Charles, April 21, 1938.

31. NARA/RG84/37, General Records of the Embassy in Rio de Janeiro, Hull to Caffery, May 12, 1938.

32. NARA/RG84/37, General Records of the Embassy in Rio de Janeiro, Caffery to Secretary of State, May 13, 1938.

33. Ibid.

34. Levine, *The Vargas Regime,* 165.

35. John Lewis Landis, *George F. Kennan: An American Life* (New York and London: Penguin Books, 2011), 323.

## Chapter 3: Dangerous Games

1. FGV/CPDOC/OA, Documenos Pessoais, September 1, 1939.

2. Stefan Zweig, *Brazil: Land of the Future* (New York: Viking Press, 1941), 179.

3. NARA/RG84/37, General Records of the Embassy in Rio de Janeiro, Caffery to Sumner Welles, November 11, 1938.

4. Ibid.

5. NARA/RG84/37, General Records of the Embassy in Rio de Janeiro, Aranha to Welles, November 8, 1938.

6. Ibid., 5–6.

7. Getúlio Vargas, *Diário: Volume II, 1937–1942* (Rio de Janeiro: Editora Siciliano/ Fundação Getúlio Vargas, 1995), 252.

8. Ibid.

9. Frank D. McCann, "Brazil and World War II: The Forgotten Ally. What Did You Do in the War, Zé Carioca?" Tel Aviv University, 1997, 9.

10. Ibid.

11. Ibid.

12. Vargas, *Diário,* 252.

13. For more detail on this, see Jeffrey Lesser, "Immigration and Shifting Concepts of National Identity in Brazil During the Vargas Era," *Luso-Brazilian Review* 31, no. 2 (Winter 1994): 23–44.

14. Ibid.

15. NARA/RG84/21, General Records of the Embassy in Rio de Janeiro, Nazi-Fascist Propaganda in Brazil, December 17, 1937, 2–3.

16. Ibid., 4–5.

17. NARA/RG84/37, General Records of the Embassy in Rio de Janeiro, Decree Law No. 383, April 18, 1938.

18. NARA/RG84/37, General Records of the Embassy in Rio de Janeiro, Caffery to Secretary of State, March 28, 1938, 5–6.

19. Ibid.

20. NARA/RG84/37, General Records of the Embassy in Rio de Janeiro, Caffery to Secretary of State, September 22, 1938.

21. Ibid., 2.

22. PRO/FO/371/30361, Visit of Wilson-Young to Southern Brazil to Investigate Reports of Enemy Sabotage, April 27, 1942.

23. PRO/FO/371/30361, Charles to Anthony Eden, April 27, 1942.

24. PRO/FO/371/30361, Visit of Wilson-Young to Southern Brazil to Investigate Reports of Enemy Sabotage, April 27, 1942.

25. Ibid.

26. PRO/FO/371/30361, Foreign Office Minutes, June 2, 1942.

27. Vargas, *Diário*, 252.

28. Ibid.

29. Waldo Frank, *America Hispana: A Portrait and a Prospect* (New York and London: Charles Scribner's Sons, 1931), 198.

30. Vargas, *Diário*, 252.

31. Ibid., 253.

## Chapter 4: A Shot Across the Bow

1. United States Holocaust Memorial Museum (USMM), World War II Timeline.

2. John W. F. Dulles, *Vargas of Brazil: A Political Biography* (Austin and London: University of Texas Press, 1967), 210.

3. FRUS/740.0011/1939/3730, Caffery to Secretary of State, June 12, 1940.

4. FRUS/740.0011/1939/3721, Caffery to Secretary of State, June 11, 1940.

5. Ibid.

6. NARA/RG165/260, Records of the War Department, Military Intelligence Division, Chief of US Naval Mission to Brazil to Chief of Naval Operations, June 26, 1940.

7. Ibid.

8. FRUS/740.0011/1939/3711a, Secretary of State to Caffery, June 11, 1940.

9. FRUS/740.0022/1939/3680, Caffery to Secretary of State, June 11, 1940.

10. PRO/FO/371/25807, Annual Report on Brazil for 1940.

11. FRUS/740.001/1939/3712, Caffery to Secretary of State, June 11, 1940.

12. FRUS/740.0011/1939/3730, Armour to Secretary of State, June 12, 1940.

13. FGV/CPDOC/*Companhia Siderúrgica Nacional (CSN)*, Verbete.

14. Getúlio Vargas, *Diário: Volume II, 1937–1942* (Rio de Janeiro: Editora Siciliano/ Fundação Getúlio Vargas, 1995), 319.

15. FRUS/740.0011/1939/3721, Undersecretary of State to Roosevelt, June 12, 1940.

16. Dulles, *Vargas of Brazil*, 211.

17. FRUS/740.0011/1939/3947, Memorandum by Secretary of State, June 13, 1940.

18. FRUS/740.0011/1939/3731a, President Vargas to Brazilian Embassy in Washington, June 14, 1940.

19. PRO/FO/371/25807, Annual Report on Brazil for 1940.

20. Ibid.

21. FRUS/832/6511/63, Memorandum of Conversation by Advisor on International Economic Affairs, January 22, 1940.

22. Ibid.

23. FRUS/832.6511/100, Memorandum by the Chief of the Division of the American Republics, April 11, 1940.

24. Dulles, *Vargas of Brazil*, 207.

25. FRUS/832.6511/109, Secretary of State to Caffery, May 31, 1940.

26. FRUS/832.6511/110, Caffery to Secretary of State, June 1, 1940.

27. FRUS/832.6511/132, Caffery to Secretary of State, September 5, 1940.

28. Dulles, *Vargas of Brazil*, 207.

29. FRUS/832.6511/169, Aranha to Welles, September 30, 1940.

30. FRUS/832.6511/169, Welles to Aranha, October 1, 1940.

31. FRUS/832.6511/164, Caffery to Secretary of State, October 4, 1940.

32. FGV/CPDOC, *Companhia Siderúrgica Nacional (CSN)*, Verbete.

33. Dulles, *Vargas of Brazil*, 208.

34. FRUS/832.6511/164, Caffery to Secretary of State, October 4, 1940.

35. The steel mill was privatized in 1993 and was renamed the President Vargas Steelworks.

36. FGV/CPDOC, *Companhia Siderúrgica Nacional (CSN)*, Verbete.

37. The population of the city in 2010 was 257,686 inhabitants.

38. FGV/CPDOC, *Companhia Siderúrgica Nacional (CSN)*, Verbete.

## Chapter 5: Discordant Allies

1. PRO/FO/371/25807, Annual Report on Brazil for 1940, 6.

2. Ibid.

3. PRO/FO/371/24172, Brazilian Embassy in London to Foreign Office, November 19, 1939.

4. PRO/FO/371/24172, Foreign Office Minutes, November 12, 1940.

5. PRO/FO/371/24172, British Embassy in Washington to Foreign Office, November 18, 1939.

6. Ibid.

7. Ibid.

8. Ibid.

9. FRUS/832.24/255, Burdett to Secretary of State, November 1, 1940.

10. PRO/FO/371/24172, British Embassy in Washington to Foreign Office, November 18, 1939.

11. Ibid.

12. PRO/FO/371/24172, Telegram from Gibraltar to Foreign Office, December 4, 1940.

13. Ibid.

14. PRO/FO/371/24172, Ministry of Economic Warfare to Rab Butler, November 23, 1940.

15. PRO/FO/371/24172, Telegram from Gibraltar to Foreign Office, December 5, 1940.

16. Ibid.

17. FGV/CPDOC/OA, Documenos Pessoais, November 22, 1940.

18. Getúlio Vargas, *Diário: Volume II, 1937–1942* (Rio de Janeiro: Editora Siciliano/Fundação Getúlio Vargas, 1995), 354.

19. Ibid.

20. FGV/CPDOC/OA, Documenos Pessoais, November 22, 1940.

21. John W. F. Dulles, *Vargas of Brazil: A Political Biography* (Austin and London: University of Texas Press, 1967), 215.

22. FRUS/810.20/1262, Caffery to Secretary of State, July 25, 1941.

23. Dulles, *Vargas of Brazil,* 215.

24. Frank D. McCann, "The Brazilian Army and the Problem of Mission, 1939–1964," *Journal of Latin American Studies* 12, no. 1 (May 1980): 117.

25. Shawn C. Smallman, *Fear and Memory in the Brazilian Army and Society, 1889–1954* (Chapel Hill and London: University of North Carolina Press, 2002), 72.

26. McCann, "The Brazilian Army and the Problem of Mission," 117.

27. Ibid.

28. Smallman, *Fear and Memory in the Brazilian Army and Society,* 74.

29. FRUS/832.24/268, Burdett to Secretary of State, November 27, 1940.

30. NARA/RG165/77/262, Records of the War Department, Military Intelligence Division Brazil, Sibert to War Department, August 17, 1940.

31. NARA/RG165/260, Records of the War Department, Military Intelligence Division, State Department Report, No. 1227, Rio de Janeiro, April 3, 1939.

32. Smallman, *Fear and Memory in the Brazilian Army and Society,* 72.

33. Dulles, *Vargas of Brazil,* 215.

34. NARA/RG165/260, Records of the War Department, Military Intelligence Division Brazil, Sibert to War Office, September 20, 1940.

35. FRUS/832.24/268, Burdett to Secretary of State, November 27, 1940.

36. FRUS/832.24/258, Burdett to Secretary of State, November 22, 1940.

37. FRUS/832.24/259, Burdett to Secretary of State, November 23, 1940.

38. FRUS/832.24/258, Secretary of State to Burdett, November 23, 1940.

39. FRUS/832.24/258, Burdett to Secretary of State, November 22, 1940.

40. FRUS/832.24/264, Burdett to Secretary of State, November 26, 1940.

41. FRUS/832.24/266, Burdett to Secretary of State, November 27, 1940.

42. FRUS/832.24/264, Burdett to Secretary of State, November 26, 1940.

43. Ibid.

44. FRUS/832.24/260, Burdett to Secretary of State, November 25, 1940.

45. FRUS/832.24/267, Burdett to Secretary of State, November 27, 1940.

46. Ibid.

47. PRO/FO/371/24171, Foreign Office Minutes, November 19, 1940.

48. PRO/FO/371/24171, Butler in Washington to Sir A. Cadogan, Foreign Office, November 20, 1940.

49. PRO/FO/371/24171, Halifax to Butler, December 5, 1940.

50. PRO/FO/371/24171, Halifax to Lothian, December 5, 1940.

51. PRO/FO/371/25807, Annual Report on Brazil for 1940, 7.

52. Ibid.

53. Ibid.

54. PRO/FO/371/24172, Halifax to Knox, December 6, 1940.

55. FRUS/832.24/276, Johnson to Secretary of State, December 5, 1940.

56. Dulles, *Vargas of Brazil*, 207.

57. Ibid.

58. Vargas, *Diário*, 357.

59. Ibid.

60. FRUS/832.24/281, Burdett to Secretary of State, December 7, 1940.

61. FRUS/832.24/287, Burdett to Secretary of State, December 11, 1940.

62. FRUS/832.24/292, Burdett to Secretary of State, December 13, 1940.

63. Ibid.

64. FRUS/832.24/295, Burdett to Secretary of State, December 14, 1940.

65. Vargas, *Diário*, 359.

66. FRUS/832/304, Burdett to Secretary of State, December 21, 1940.

## Chapter 6: Escape from Rio

1. NARA/RG84/31, General Records of the Embassy in Rio de Janeiro, Basic Post Report, April 7, 1938, 19.

2. Ibid., 18.

3. Ibid., 19.

4. Stefan Zweig, *Brazil: Land of the Future* (New York: Viking Press, 1941), 186.

5. NARA/RG84/31, Basic Post Report, April 7, 1938, 10.

6. Getúlio Vargas, *Diário: Volume II, 1937–1942* (Rio de Janeiro: Editora Siciliano/ Fundação Getúlio Vargas, 1995), 358.

7. Ibid., 362.

8. NARA/RG84/31/, Basic Post Report, April 7, 1938, 5.

9. Zweig, *Brazil: Land of the Future*, 206.

10. John W. F. Dulles, *Vargas of Brazil: A Political Biography* (Austin and London: University of Texas Press, 1967), 124.

11. PRO/FO/371/25807, Annual Report on Brazil for 1940.

12. Ibid., 2.

13. Vargas, *Diário,* 360.

14. Ibid.

15. Ibid.

16. Ibid., 362.

17. Ibid.

18. NARA/RG165/260, Records of the War Department, Military Intelligence Division, Speech by President Vargas, January 31, 1940.

19. Ibid.

20. Dulles, *Vargas of Brazil,* 216.

21. Vargas, *Diário,* 367.

22. Dulles, *Vargas of Brazil,* 216.

23. Ibid.

24. PRO/FO/371/30366, Annual Report on Brazil for 1941.

25. Vargas, *Diário,* 371.

26. Ibid.

27. Ibid.

28. Dulles, *Vargas of Brazil,* 216.

29. Waldo Frank, *South American Journey* (London: Travel Book Club, 1946), 29.

30. Ibid., 30.

31. Ibid., 199.

32. Dulles, *Vargas of Brazil,* 217.

33. Ibid.

34. PRO/FO/371/30366, Annual Report on Brazil for 1941.

35. Dulles, *Vargas of Brazil,* 217.

36. PRO/FO/371/30366, Annual Report on Brazil for 1941.

37. Dulles, *Vargas of Brazil,* 217.

38. Vargas, *Diário,* 371.

## Chapter 7: Deepening Ties and Widening Divides

1. Frank D. McCann, "Brazil and World War II: The Forgotten Ally. What Did You Do in the War, Zé Carioca?" Tel Aviv University, 1997, 11.

2. NARA/RG84/183, General Records of the Embassy in Brazil, Intercepted Private Correspondence, June 25, 1943.

3. Cary Reich, *The Life of Nelson A. Rockefeller: Worlds To Conquer, 1908–1958* (New York and London: Doubleday, 1996), 204.

4. Reich, *The Life of Nelson A. Rockefeller,* 203.

5. Ibid.

6. Joseph P. Persico, *The Imperial Rockefeller: A Biography of Nelson A. Rockefeller* (New York: Simon and Schuster, 1982), 33.

7. Douglas Waller, *Wild Bill Donavan: The Spymaster Who Created the OSS and Modern American Espionage* (New York and London: Free Press, 2011), 25–26.

8. Reich, *The Life of Nelson A. Rockefeller,* 205–206.

9. Reich, *The Life of Nelson A. Rockefeller,* 205.

10. PRO/371/30368, Ministry of Information, Overseas Planning Committee, Plan for Propaganda for Brazil, June 4, 1942, 6.

11. Ibid.

12. Ibid.

13. PRO/FO/371/25800, German Activities in Brazil, Embassy in Rio, May 30, 1941.

14. PRO/FO/371/25800, Foreign Office to Embassy in Rio, March 27, 1941.

15. PRO/FO/371/25800, Embassy in Rio to Foreign Office, April 6, 1941.

16. Bob Thomas, *Walt Disney: An American Original,* New York: Disney Editions, 1994, 171.

17. Thomas, *Walt Disney,* 170.

18. Getúlio Vargas, *Diário: Volume II, 1937–1942* (Rio de Janeiro: Editora Siciliano/ Fundação Getúlio Vargas, 1995), 420.

19. PRO/FO/371/25800, Intercepted Private Correspondence, M. I. 5, May 26, 1941.

20. Ibid.

21. PRO/FO/371/30372, Personalities in Brazil in 1942, 16.

22. Ibid.

23. PRO/FO/371/25800, Intercepted Private Correspondence, M. I. 5, May 26, 1941.

24. *Jornal do Brasil,* May 3, 1941, 6.

25. PRO/FO/371/30368, Plan for Propaganda for Brazil, June 4, 1942, 6.

26. PRO/FO/371/25806, Embassy in Rio to Foreign Office, July 5, 1941.

27. Ibid.

28. Ibid.

29. FRUS/810.20/822, Memorandum by the Chief of Staff of the United States Army (Marshall) to Undersecretary of State (Welles), June 17, 1941.

30. FRUS/810.20/892, Caffery to Secretary of State, June 27, 1941.

31. Ibid.

32. FRUS/810.20/1333, Caffery to Secretary of State, August 21, 1941.

33. FRUS/810.20/1327a, Acting Secretary of State to Caffery, July 10, 1941.

34. Ibid.

35. Vargas, *Diário,* 406.

36. Cordell Hull, *The Memoirs of Cordell Hull,* vol. 2 (London: Hodder and Stoughton, 1948), 941.

37. FRUS/810.20/1331, Caffery to Secretary of State, July 28, 1941.

38. Ibid.

39. FRUS/810.20/1331, Secretary of State to Caffery, August 18, 1941.

40. Ibid.

41. FRUS/810.20/1331, Caffery to Secretary of State, August 21, 1941.

42. FRUS/810.20/1098a, Acting Secretary of State to Caffery, July 9, 1941.

43. FRUS/832.24/10–141, Lend-lease Agreement Between the United States and Brazil, October 1, 1941.

44. John W. F. Dulles, *Vargas of Brazil: A Political Biography* (Austin and London: University of Texas Press, 1967), 221.

45. FRUS/832.248/262, Caffery to Secretary of State, June 4, 1941.

46. Vargas, *Diário*, 431.

47. FRUS/810.20/699, Caffery to Secretary of State, July 2, 1941.

48. Ibid.

## Chapter 8: Right Behind You

1. Getúlio Vargas, *Diário: Volume II, 1937–1942* (Rio de Janeiro: Editora Siciliano/Fundação Getúlio Vargas, 1995), 440.

2. John Gunther, *Inside Latin America* (London: Hamish Hamilton, 1942), 287.

3. Vargas, *Diário*, 440.

4. Gunther, *Inside Latin America*, 286–287.

5. FRUS/740.0011/18611, Welles to President Roosevelt, January 18, 1942.

6. John W. F. Dulles, *Vargas of Brazil: A Political Biography* (Austin and London: University of Texas Press, 1967), 220.

7. Vargas, *Diário*, 443.

8. Ibid., 450.

9. FRUS/740.0011/18611, Welles to President Roosevelt, January 18, 1942.

10. Ibid.

11. Ibid.

12. Ibid.

13. Dulles, *Vargas of Brazil*, 223.

14. FRUS/740.0011/18611, Welles to President Roosevelt, January 18, 1942.

15. Vargas, *Diário*, 451.

16. Dulles, *Vargas of Brazil*, 223.

17. Vargas, *Diário*, 451.

18. Dulles, *Vargas of Brazil*, 223.

19. FRUS/740.0011/18611, Welles to President Roosevelt, January 18, 1942.

20. Ibid.

21. Ibid.

22. Ibid.

23. Vargas, *Diário*, 453.

24. Ibid.

25. FRUS/832.24/634, President Roosevelt to Welles, January 19, 1942.

26. Vargas, *Diário*, 454.

27. Gunther, *Inside Latin America*, 288.

28. Vargas, *Diário*, 454.

29. Dulles, *Vargas of Brazil*, 224.

30. Vargas, *Diário*, 454.

31. Ibid.

32. Ibid.

33. Dulles, *Vargas of Brazil*, 224.

34. Vargas, *Diário*, 454.

35. Cordell Hull, *The Memoirs of Cordell Hull*, vol. 2 (London: Hodder and Stoughton, 1948), 1149.

36. Ibid.

37. Dulles, *Vargas of Brazil*, 224.

38. Hull, *The Memoirs of Cordell Hull*, vol. 2, 1149.

39. Ibid.

40. Cary Reich, *The Life of Nelson A. Rockefeller: Worlds To Conquer, 1908–1958* (New York and London: Doubleday, 1996), 271.

41. Hull, *The Memoirs of Cordell Hull*, vol. 2, 1149.

42. Vargas, *Diário*, 454.

43. Gunther, *Inside Latin America*, 282.

44. Vargas, *Diário*, 454.

45. FRUS/832.24/651, Hull to Welles, January 19, 1942.

46. FRUS/832.24/634, President Roosevelt to Welles, January 19, 1942.

47. Vargas, *Diário*, 457.

48. Ibid.

49. Ibid.

50. FGV/CPDOC, Reunião dos chanceleres do Rio de Janeiro.

51. Ibid.

52. *Jornal do Brasil*, January 29, 1942.

## Chapter 9: Welles Checks Out and Welles Checks In

1. Getúlio Vargas, *Diário: Volume II, 1937–1942* (Rio de Janeiro: Editora Siciliano/ Fundação Getúlio Vargas, 1995), 458.

2. FRUS/832.24/651, Caffery to Secretary of State, January 31, 1942.

3. Ibid.

4. FRUS/832.24/673, Caffery to Secretary of State, February 7, 1942.

5. PRO/FO/128/406, Political Situation in Brazil, August 21, 1942.

6. FRUS/832.24/673, Caffery to Secretary of State, February 7, 1942.

7. Ibid.

8. FRUS/832.24/674, Secretary of State to Caffery, February 9, 1942.

9. John W. F. Dulles, *Vargas of Brazil: A Political Biography* (Austin and London: University of Texas Press, 1967), 226.

10. Vargas, *Diário*, 467.

11. Ibid.

12. FRUS/811.248/395a, Welles to Caffery, March 2, 1942.

13. Dulles, *Vargas of Brazil,* 227.

14. FRUS/832.796/767, Caffery to Secretary of State, February 3, 1942.

15. Frank D. McCann, "Brazil and World War II: The Forgotten Ally. What Did You Do in the War, Zé Carioca?" Tel Aviv University, 1997, 13.

16. Manoel Thomaz Castello Branco, *O Brasil na II Grande Guerra* (Rio de Janeiro: Biblioteca do Exército, 1960), 54–58.

17. Cary Reich, *The Life of Nelson A. Rockefeller: Worlds To Conquer, 1908–1958* (New York and London: Doubleday, 1996), 230.

18. Antonio Pedro Tota, *The Seduction of Brazil: The Americanization of Brazil During World War II* (Austin: University of Texas Press, 2009), 43.

19. Orson Welles and Peter Bogdanovich, *This Is Orson Welles* (New York: Da Capo Press, 1998), 149.

20. Ibid.

21. Catherine L. Benamou, *It's All True: Orson Welles's Pan-American Odyssey* (Berkeley, Los Angeles, and London: University of California Press, 2007), 47.

22. Welles and Bogdanovich, *This Is Orson Welles,* 154.

23. Ibid., 149.

24. Ibid., 159.

25. For a detailed account of the filming, see Benamou, *It's All True: Orson Welles's Pan-American Odyssey.*

26. NARA/RG84/187, Records of the Embassy in Rio, Radio Script of Pan-American Day Broadcast, April 16, 1942, 6.

27. Ibid., 9.

28. FGV/CPDOC/OA/CP, Aranha to Welles, August 13, 1942.

29. Dulles, *Vargas of Brazil,* 234.

30. FRUS/832.8595/1, Caffery to Secretary of State, March 11, 1942.

31. Vargas, *Diário,* 469.

32. Ibid.

33. Ibid.

34. FRUS/800.8830/1601, Caffery to Secretary of State, June 6, 1942.

35. Ibid.

36. FRUS/832.8595/4, Welles to Caffery, March 27, 1942.

37. Vargas, *Diário,* 475.

38. McCann, "Brazil and World War II," 13.

39. Ibid.

## Chapter 10: A Question of Succession

1. Robert M. Levine, *Father of the Poor? Vargas and His Era* (New York and Cambridge: Cambridge University Press, 1998), 69.

2. *Jornal do Brasil,* May 3, 1942, 6.

3. PRO/FO/128/406, Charles to Foreign Office, June 26, 1942.

4. PRO/FO/128/406, Charles to Foreign Office, June 8, 1942.

5. Ibid.

6. PRO/FO/128/406, Consul in Bahia to Charles, August 21, 1942.

7. John W. F. Dulles, *Vargas of Brazil: A Political Biography* (Austin and London: University of Texas Press, 1967), 234.

8. NARA/RG84/147, General Records of the Embassy in Brazil, Speech by Caffery, July 4, 1942.

9. NARA/RG84/153, General Records of the Embassy in Brazil, Caffery to Secretary of State, June 29, 1942.

10. FGV/CPDOC, Biography of Vargas.

11. NARA/RG84/147, General Records of the Embassy in Brazil, Dowling to Secretary of State, July 13, 1942.

12. Ibid.

13. FGV/CPDOC, Biography of Vargas.

14. Dulles, *Vargas of Brazil,* 230.

15. Ibid., 229.

16. PRO/FO/128/406, British Consulate in São Paulo to Embassy in Rio, October 12, 1942.

17. NARA/RG84/261, General Records of the Embassy in Brazil, Memorandum, American Embassy in Rio, February 4, 1944.

18. Ibid.

19. Ibid.

20. Robert M. Levine, "Brazil's Jews During the Vargas Era and After," *Luso-Brazilian Review* 5, no. 1 (Summer 1968): 54.

21. For more details on Einstein's quest for visas for Jewish refugees, see Jeffrey Lesser, *Welcoming the Undesirables: Brazil and the Jewish Question* (Berkeley: University of California Press, 1995), 130–131.

22. NARA/RG84/261, General Records of the Embassy in Brazil, Confidential Memorandum, American Consular Section in Rio, February 11, 1944.

23. NARA/RG84/261, General Records of the Embassy in Brazil, Simmons to Secretary of State, February 12, 1944.

24. Ibid.

25. Ibid.

26. NARA/RG84/261, General Records of the Embassy in Brazil, Simmons to Secretary of State, June 20, 1944.

27. NARA/RG84/261, General Records of the Embassy in Brazil, Confidential Memorandum, American Consular Section in Rio, February 11, 1944.

28. Maria Luiza Tucci Carneiro, *O Anti-Semitismo na Era Vargas* (São Paulo: Editora Perspectiva, 2001), 218.

29. Ibid.

30. Isabel Vincent, "Luis Martins de Souza Dantas: Brazil's Schindler," *Macleans,* May 15, 2005.

31. Lesser, *Welcoming the Undesirables*, 141.

32. Ibid., 139.

33. Germans in Paris arrested the ambassador after he tried to resist the German occupation of the embassy following Brazil's declaration of war in August 1942. He was imprisoned in Germany and was eventually released as part of a prisoner swap in 1944, after which he returned briefly to Rio. He spent his retirement living in Paris in a modest apartment following the death of his wife. He died on April 16, 1954. His work in helping to save Jewish refugees was never officially recognized by the Estado Novo or subsequent Brazilian governments.

34. Jeffery Lesser highlights two figures for Jews entering Brazil with permanent or temporary visas in 1939: 4,601 according to Jewish groups and 4,223 according to official Brazilian figures. In 1942, the number of Jews entering Brazil was 108 out of a total of less than 2,500 immigrants to Brazil in that year. See Lesser, *Welcoming the Undesirables*, 124, 144.

35. Lesser, *Welcoming the Undesirables*, 136.

36. NARA/RG84/137, Simmons to Secretary of State, October 27, 1942.

## Chapter 11: The Decision

1. PRO/FO/128/406, Memorandum, September 1, 1942.

2. Ibid.

3. NARA/RG165/299, Records of the War Department, Military Intelligence Division, Press Cutting, August 19, 1942.

4. NARA/RG165/299, Records of the War Department, Military Intelligence Division, Estimate of the Effects of the Declaration of War by Brazil, September 22, 1942, 1.

5. Ibid.

6. Ibid., 4.

7. PRO/FO/128/406, Memorandum, September 1, 1942.

8. NARA/RG165/299, Records of the War Department, Military Intelligence Division, Press Cutting, August 19, 1942.

9. PRO/FO/128/406, Memorandum, September 1, 1942.

10. NARA/RG165/299, Records of the War Department, Military Intelligence Division, Memorandum for the Assistant Chief of Staff, August 20, 1942.

11. NARA/RG165/264, Records of the War Department, Military Intelligence Division, Brazil at War, September 4, 1942, 6.

12. Ibid.

13. NARA/RG165/299, Records of the War Department, Military Intelligence Division, Memorandum for the Assistant Chief of Staff, August 20, 1942.

14. Ibid.

15. NARA/RG84/135, General Records of the Embassy in Rio, Simmons to Undersecretary of State, August 19, 1942.

16. Ibid.

17. Ibid.

18. NARA/RG84/177, General Records of the Embassy in Rio, Note Handed to Representatives of the Governments of Germany and Italy by the Brazilian Government, August 24, 1942, 2.

19. John W. F. Dulles, *Vargas of Brazil: A Political Biography* (Austin and London: University of Texas Press, 1967), 235.

20. NARA/RG165/264, Records of the War Department, Military Intelligence Division, Brazil at War, September 4, 1942, 5.

21. NARA/RG84/136, General Records of the Embassy in Rio, Brazilian Declaration of War, August 24, 1942.

22. NARA/RG84/136, General Records of the Embassy in Rio, Radio Broadcast from Berlin to Brazil, August 22, 1942.

23. Ibid.

24. NARA/RG165/299, Records of the War Department, Military Intelligence Division, Estimate of the Effects of the Declaration of War by Brazil, September 22, 1942.

25. Ibid., 2.

26. Ibid.

27. NARA/RG165/299, Records of the War Department, Military Intelligence Division, Memorandum for the Assistant Chief of Staff, August 20, 1942.

28. Ibid.

29. Cary Reich, *The Life of Nelson A. Rockefeller: Worlds To Conquer, 1908–1958* (New York and London: Doubleday, 1996), 241.

30. NARA/RG165/299, Records of the War Department, Coordinator of Inter-American Affairs, Brazil and the War, September 24, 1942.

31. Dulles, *Vargas of Brazil,* 235.

32. Dulles, *Vargas of Brazil,* 236.

33. Ibid.

34. *New York Times,* November 8, 1942.

35. NARA/RG165/264, Records of the War Department, Military Intelligence Division, Brazil's Reaction to the American Offensive, December 4, 1942, 3.

36. NARA/RG165/264, Records of the War Department, Military Intelligence Division, Reactions in Brazil to the Allied Victory in Tunisia, May 31, 1943, 1.

37. Ibid.

## Chapter 12: Lights Out over Rio

1. NARA/RG165/261, Records of the War Department, Military Intelligence Division, Caffery to Secretary of State, September 7, 1942.

2. Ibid.

3. NARA/RG165/261, Records of the War Department, Military Intelligence Division, Simmons to Secretary of State, September 4, 1942.

4. PRO/FO/128/406, Blackout, August 21, 1942.

5. Ibid.

6. NARA/RG165/261, Records of the War Department, Military Intelligence Division, Blackout in Rio, May 17, 1943.

7. John W. F. Dulles, *Vargas of Brazil: A Political Biography* (Austin and London: University of Texas Press, 1967), 240.

8. FRUS/740.0011/27475, Caffery to Secretary of State, January 26, 1943.

9. FRUS/740.0011/27586, Caffery to Secretary of State, January 29, 1943.

10. FRUS/740.0011/27588, Caffery to Secretary of State, January 30, 1943.

11. Ibid.

12. Ibid.

13. Ibid.

14. Ibid.

15. Ibid.

16. Ibid.

17. FRUS/740.0011/27590, Caffery to Secretary of State, January 30, 1943.

18. Ibid.

19. Ibid.

20. Ibid.

21. *New York Times*, January 29, 1943.

22. Ibid.

## Chapter 13: The Dinner Party

1. NARA/RG84/177, General Records of the Embassy in Rio, Caffery to Secretary of State and President Roosevelt, January 31, 1943.

2. NARA/RG84/247, General Records of the Embassy in Rio, Request that Rio de Janeiro Be Reclassified for the Purpose of Cost of Living Allowances, Caffery to Secretary of State, January 31, 1944.

3. Ibid.

4. Ibid.

5. Ibid.

6. NARA/RG84/247, General Records of the Embassy in Rio, Notes to Cost of Living Statement, January 31, 1944, 1.

7. Ibid., 4.

8. NARA/RG84/177, General Records of the Embassy in Rio, Caffery to Secretary of State and President Roosevelt, January 31, 1943.

9. Ibid.

10. Ibid.

11. Ibid.

12. Ibid.

13. Ibid.

14. NARA/RG165/304, Records of the War Department, Military Intelligence Division, From Embassy in Rio to War Department, November 18, 1943.

15. Frank D. McCann, "Brazil and World War II: The Forgotten Ally. What Did You Do in the War, Zé Carioca?" Tel Aviv University, 1997, 20.

16. NARA/RG84/177, General Records of the Embassy in Rio, Caffery to Secretary of State and President Roosevelt, January 31, 1943.

17. McCann, "Brazil and World War II," 20.

18. Frank D. McCann, "Brazil, the United States, and World War II: A Commentary," *Diplomatic History* 3, no. 1 (January 1979): 70.

19. NARA/RG84/177, General Records of the Embassy in Rio, Caffery to Secretary of State and President Roosevelt, January 31, 1943.

20. Ibid.

21. Ibid.

22. Ibid.

23. Ibid.

24. NARA/RG165/304, Records of the War Department, Military Intelligence Division, From Embassy in Rio to War Department, November 18, 1943.

25. Ibid.

26. NARA/RG165/304, Records of the War Department, Military Intelligence Division, Brazilian Statements Regarding Argentina, November 23, 1943, 1.

27. Ibid.

28. Ibid.

29. Ibid.

30. Ibid., 2.

31. Ibid.

32. Ibid.

33. Ibid.

34. Ibid., 3.

35. Ibid.

36. McCann, "Brazil, the United States, and World War II," 72.

37. Antonio Pedro Tota, *The Seduction of Brazil: The Americanization of Brazil During World War II* (Austin: University of Texas Press, 2009), 82.

38. Ibid., 38.

39. NARA/RG84/196, General Records of the Embassy in Rio, President Vargas Statement on National Rubber Month, June 1, 1943.

40. NARA/RG84/196, General Records of the Embassy in Rio, Rubber Development Cooperation, June 1, 1943.

41. Ibid.

42. NARA/RG84/196, General Records of the Embassy in Rio, President Roosevelt to President Vargas, June 16, 1943.

43. NARA/RG84/196, General Records of the Embassy in Rio, Record of Telephone Conversation with *Associated Press,* May 26, 1943.

44. Ibid.

45. Ibid.

46. NARA/RG84/196, General Records of the Embassy in Rio, Rubber Development Cooperation, April 14, 1943.

47. NARA/RG84/196, General Records of the Embassy in Rio, Rubber Development Cooperation, June 11, 1943.

48. NARA/RG84/196, General Records of the Embassy in Rio, Memorandum on Report on Synthetic Rubber as Published in *Time* Magazine, June 30, 1943.

49. Ibid.

50. Ibid.

51. NARA/RG84/196, General Records of the Embassy in Rio, Rubber Development Cooperation, July 10, 1943.

52. Ibid.

## Chapter 14: Late Arrivals

1. NARA/RG84/177, General Records of the Embassy in Rio, American Consul, São Paulo, January 26, 1943.

2. Ibid.

3. Ibid.

4. Frank D. McCann, "Brazil and World War II: The Forgotten Ally. What Did You Do in the War, Zé Carioca?" Tel Aviv University, 1997, 20.

5. Ibid.

6. FGV/CPDOC, Verbete, FEB.

7. NARA/RG84/177, General Records of the Embassy in Rio, Caffery to Secretary of State, September 8, 1943.

8. NARA/RG84/177, General Records of the Embassy in Rio, Speech by President Vargas, September 7, 1943.

9. John W. F. Dulles, *Vargas of Brazil: A Political Biography* (Austin and London: University of Texas Press, 1967), 242.

10. McCann, "Brazil and World War II," 23.

11. Ibid.

12. PRO/CAB/122/954, Halifax to Eden, December 23, 1943, 1.

13. FGV/CPDOC, Verbete, FEB.

14. Ibid.

15. PRO/CAB/122/954, Halifax to Eden, December 23, 1943, 2.

16. Ibid.

17. Ibid.

18. Ibid.

19. Ibid.

20. Dulles, *Vargas of Brazil*, 242.

21. NARA/RG84/177, General Records of the Embassy in Rio, Speech by President Vargas, November 10, 1943.

22. Ibid.

23. NARA/RG84/177, General Records of the Embassy in Rio, Simmons to Secretary of State, November 11, 1943.

24. Ibid.

25. Ibid.

26. Neill Lochery, *Lisbon: War in the Shadows of the City of Light, 1939–1945* (New York: PublicAffairs, 2011), 187.

27. NARA/RG84/208, General Records of the Embassy in Rio, Letter to Aranha, September 20, 1943, 1–2.

28. Cordell Hull, *The Memoirs of Cordell Hull,* vol. 2 (London: Hodder and Stoughton, 1948), 1336.

29. Ibid.

30. Ibid., 1337.

31. Ibid.

32. Dulles, *Vargas of Brazil,* 245.

33. Ibid.

34. George M. Lauderbaugh, "Bolivarian Nations: Securing the Northern Frontier," in *Latin America During World War II,* eds. Thomas M. Leonard and John F. Bratzel (Plymouth, UK: Rowan and Littlefield Publishers, 2007), 113.

35. Max Paul Friedman, *Nazis and Good Neighbors: The United States Campaign Against the Germans of Latin America in World War II* (Cambridge and New York: Cambridge University Press, 2003), 91.

36. Ibid.

## Chapter 15: The Promise

1. NARA/RG84/260, General Records of the Embassy in Rio, Simmons to Secretary of State, February 1, 1944.

2. Ibid.

3. NARA/RG84/260, General Records of the Embassy in Rio, Simmons to Secretary of State, February 19, 1944.

4. Ibid.

5. *Diário Carioca,* February 19, 1944.

6. NARA/RG84/260, General Records of the Embassy in Rio, Simmons to Secretary of State, March 3, 1944.

7. Ibid.

8. NARA/RG84/262, General Records of the Embassy in Rio, Address by President Vargas, April 15, 1944.

9. NARA/RG84/262, General Records of the Embassy in Rio, Simmons to Secretary of State, April 17, 1944.

10. PRO/FO/371/37846, Broadmead to Eden, April 18, 1944, 2.

11. NARA/RG84/262, General Records of the Embassy in Rio, Simmons to Secretary of State, April 17, 1944.

12. *New York Times,* July 13, 1944.

13. Ibid.

14. Ibid.

15. Ibid.

16. *Washington Post,* April 26, 1944.

17. PRO/FO/371/37846, Halifax to Eden, May 2, 1944.

18. Ibid.

19. PRO/FO/371/37846, Broadmead to Eden, June 12, 1944.

20. PRO/FO/371/37846, Foreign Office Minutes, June 30, 1943.

21. John W. F. Dulles, *Vargas of Brazil: A Political Biography* (Austin and London: University of Texas Press, 1967), 242–243.

22. PRO/WO/204/5588, Historical Account of the Brazilian Liaison Detachment, January 6, 1945, 3.

23. Ibid., 17.

24. Ibid., 15.

25. Ibid.

26. Ibid., 16.

## Chapter 16: A Farewell to Aranha

1. NARA/RG84/260, General Records of the Embassy in Rio, Caffery to Secretary of State, September 13, 1944.

2. Ibid.

3. PRO/FO/371/37846, Gainer to Cabinet Office, August 23, 1944.

4. Ibid.

5. PRO/FO/371/37846, Gainer to Secretary of State, August 16, 1944.

6. NARA/RG84/260, General Records of the Embassy in Rio, Caffery to Secretary of State, September 13, 1944.

7. PRO/FO/371/37846, Gainer to Secretary of State, August 16, 1944.

8. Ibid.

9. Ibid.

10. Ibid.

11. PRO/FO/371/37846, Gainer to Cabinet Office, August 23, 1944.

12. Ibid.

13. NARA/RG84/260, General Records of the Embassy in Rio, Caffery to Secretary of State, September 13, 1944.

14. NARA/RG84/260, General Records of the Embassy in Rio, Caffery to Secretary of State, September 8, 1944.

15. PRO/FO/371/37846, Gainer to Cabinet Office, August 23, 1944.

16. Ibid.

17. Ibid.

18. Ibid.

19. Ibid.

20. John W. F. Dulles, *Vargas of Brazil: A Political Biography* (Austin and London: University of Texas Press, 1967), 255.

21. PRO/FO/371/51899, Annual Report for Brazil for 1945, January 22, 1946.

22. Dulles, *Vargas of Brazil*, 256.

23. PRO/FO/371/51899, Annual Report for Brazil for 1945, January 22, 1946, 1.

24. PRO/FO/371/51938, Records of Leading Personalities in Brazil in 1946, 5.

25. Ibid.

## Chapter 17: The Challenge

1. John W. F. Dulles, *Vargas of Brazil: A Political Biography* (Austin and London: University of Texas Press, 1967), 259.

2. PRO/FO/371/51899, Annual Report for Brazil for 1945, January 22, 1946, 2.

3. Dulles, *Vargas of Brazil*, 258.

4. PRO/FO/371/51899, Annual Report for Brazil for 1945, January 22, 1946, 2.

5. Ibid.

6. Ibid.

7. PRO/FO/371/51938, Records of Leading Personalities in Brazil in 1946, 6.

8. PRO/FO/371/51899, Annual Report for Brazil for 1945, January 22, 1946, 2.

9. Ibid., 7–8.

10. Ibid.

11. Ibid.

12. Dulles, *Vargas of Brazil*, 257.

13. PRO/FO/371/51899, Annual Report for Brazil for 1945, January 22, 1946, 8.

14. Ibid.

15. *Correio de Manhã*, April 13, 1945, 1.

16. Ibid.

17. FRUS/810.20/7-2645, Berle to Secretary of State, July 26, 1945.

18. Ibid.

19. *Correio de Manhã*, April 14, 1945, 1.

20. Frank D. McCann, "Brazil and World War II: The Forgotten Ally. What Did You Do in the War, Zé Carioca?" Tel Aviv University, 1997, 25.

21. *O Cruzeiro do Sul*, February 25, 1945, 1.

22. *Correio de Manhã*, February 24, 1945, 1.

23. McCann, "Brazil and World War II," 25.

24. Dulles, *Vargas of Brazil*, 244.

## Chapter 18: The Exit

1. John W. F. Dulles, *Vargas of Brazil: A Political Biography* (Austin and London: University of Texas Press, 1967), 274.

2. Ibid., 273.

3. PRO/FO/371/51899, Annual Report for Brazil for 1945, January 22, 1946, 2.

4. Stanley E. Hilton, "The Overthrow of Getúlio Vargas in 1945: Diplomatic Intervention, Defense of Democracy, or Political Retribution?" *Hispanic American Historical Review* 67, no. 1 (February 1987): 15.

5. Ibid.

6. Dulles, *Vargas of Brazil,* 267.

7. PRO/FO/371/51899, Annual Report for Brazil for 1945, January 22, 1946, 2.

8. Ibid., 3.

9. Hilton, "The Overthrow of Getúlio Vargas in 1945," 32.

10. PRO/FO/371/51899, Annual Report for Brazil for 1945, January 22, 1946, 3.

11. Hilton, "The Overthrow of Getúlio Vargas in 1945," 33.

12. Dulles, *Vargas of Brazil,* 273.

13. Hilton, "The Overthrow of Getúlio Vargas in 1945," 33.

14. PRO/FO/371/51899, Annual Report for Brazil for 1945, January 22, 1946, 3.

15. Hilton, "The Overthrow of Getúlio Vargas in 1945," 34.

16. Dulles, *Vargas of Brazil,* 273.

17. *Correio de Manhã,* October 30, 1945, 1.

18. *Jornal do Brasil,* October 30, 1945, 1.

19. PRO/FO/371/51899, Annual Report for Brazil for 1945, January 22, 1946, 3.

20. Ibid., 8.

21. Hilton, "The Overthrow of Getúlio Vargas in 1945," 34.

22. PRO/FO/371/51900, Gainer to Bevin, February 22, 1946, 2.

23. Ibid.

24. Dulles, *Vargas of Brazil,* 281.

25. PRO/FO/371/51902, Memorandum on Brazilian Elections, August 16, 1946, 2.

26. Ibid.

27. Dulles, *Vargas of Brazil,* 280.

28. PRO/FO/371/51902, Political Situation in Brazil, August 14, 1946.

## Chapter 19: The Final Act

1. John W. F. Dulles, *Vargas of Brazil: A Political Biography* (Austin and London: University of Texas Press, 1967), 305.

2. NARA/RG84/37/General Records of the Embassy in Rio de Janeiro, Caffery to Secretary of State, March 28, 1938, 5–6. See also PRO/FO/371/30362, Charles to Foreign Office, September 8, 1942.

3. Ibid.

4. Robert M. Levine, *Father of the Poor? Vargas and His Era* (New York and Cambridge: Cambridge University Press, 1998), 82.

5. Dulles, *Vargas of Brazil,* 313.

6. Ibid., 318.

7. Levine, *Father of the Poor? Vargas and His Era,* 87.

8. Dulles, *Vargas of Brazil,* 320.

9. *Correio de Manhã,* August 24, 1954, 1.

10. F. Zenha Machado, *Os Últimas Dias do Govêrno de Vargas: A Crise Política de Agôsto de 1954* (Rio de Janeiro: Editora Lux, 1955), 81.

11. FGV/CPDOC/AVAP/VPR/EA, Alzira Vargas, Fatos e Fotos, July 5, 1963.

12. Dulles, *Vargas of Brazil,* 328.

13. Ibid.

14. FGV/CPDOC/AVAP/VPR/EA, Alzira Vargas, Fatos e Fotos.

15. Ibid.

16. *Correio de Manhã,* August 25, 1954, 1.

17. FGV/CPDOC/AVAP/VPR/EA, Alzira Vargas, Fatos e Fotos.

18. Ibid.

19. Levine, *Father of the Poor? Vargas and His Era,* 88.

20. Dulles, *Vargas of Brazil,* 333.

21. *Correio de Manhã,* August 25, 1954, 1.

22. Ibid.

23. *Correio de Manhã,* August 25, 1954, 3.

24. *Jornal do Brasil,* August 24, 1954, 1.

25. *Correio de Manhã,* August 25, 1954, 1.

26. *Correio de Manhã,* August 26, 1954, 1.

## Epilogue: The Legacy

1. FGV/CPDOC/AVAP/VPR/EA, Alzira Vargas, Fatos e Fotos, July 5, 1963.

2. Ibid.

3. FGV/CPDOC/Belmiro Aranha/Verbete.

# INDEX